D0204333

Personal Finance

Personal Finance

An Encyclopedia of Modern Money Management

Barbara Friedberg, Editor

GREENWOOD™

An Imprint of ABC-CLIO, LLC

Santa Barbara, California • Denver, Colorado

Library of Congress Cataloging-in-Publication Data

Personal finance : an encyclopedia of modern money management / Barbara Friedberg, editor.
     pages cm
  ISBN 978-1-4408-3031-0 (hardback) — ISBN 978-1-4408-3032-7 (ebook)
1. Finance, Personal.   I. Friedberg, Barbara, 1954-
  HG179.P3747 2015
  332.024003—dc23   2014042011

ISBN: 978-1-4408-3031-0
EISBN: 978-1-4408-3032-7

19 18 17 16 15   1 2 3 4 5

This book is also available on the World Wide Web as an eBook.
Visit www.abc-clio.com for details.

Greenwood
An Imprint of ABC-CLIO, LLC

ABC-CLIO, LLC
130 Cremona Drive, P.O. Box 1911
Santa Barbara, California 93116-1911

This book is printed on acid-free paper ∞
Manufactured in the United States of America

This encyclopedia is dedicated to Bob, who encouraged me to share my knowledge through writing. His unwavering support and encouragement is an underpinning to the creation of this important financial education resource.

Contents

Ideas and Concepts

Events

People

Guide to Related Topics

Banking

Banking

Bernanke, Ben S., 14th Chair of the U.S. Federal Reserve Board

Cash

Certificate of Deposit

Checking Account

Consumer Credit/Debt

Credit Card

Credit Union

Currency

Digital Currency—Bitcoin

Federal Reserve Bank

Flexible Saving Account

Geithner, Timothy F., 75th Secretary of the U.S. Treasury

Greenspan, Alan, 13th Chair of the U.S. Federal Reserve Board

Identity Theft

Interest Rates

Lagarde, Christine, Managing Director, International Monetary Fund

Liquidity

Loans

Money Market Account

Mortgage

Net Worth

Paulson Jr., Henry M., 74th U.S. Secretary of the Treasury

Risk

Risk Premium

Rubin, Robert E., 70th U.S. Secretary of the Treasury

Savings Account

Schapiro, Mary, 29th Chair of the U.S. Securities and Exchange Commission

Siebert, Muriel, First Woman to Own a Seat on the New York Stock Exchange

Social Lending or Peer-to-Peer Lending

Time Value of Money

Treasury Securities

Volcker, Paul A., 12th Chair of the U.S. Federal Reserve Board

Warren, Elizabeth, Former Special Advisor for the Consumer Financial Protection Bureau

Year 1930s: The Great Depression

Year 1944: Creation of the International Monetary Fund and the World Bank at the Bretton Woods International Conference

Year 1970s to 1980s: Economic Problems and the United States

Year 1987: Stock Market Crash

Year 1989–1991: U.S. Savings and Loan Crisis

Year 1999: Introduction of the Euro to World Financial Markets

Year 2002: Sarbanes-Oxley Act

Year 2005: Growth of China and India as World Economic Powers

Year 2007–2008: Subprime Housing Crisis and Mortgage Meltdown

Year 2007–2009: Global Recession and Breakdown of Major Wall Street Institutions

Year 2010: Dodd-Frank Wall Street Reform and Consumer Protection Act

Year 2011–2012: European Debt Crisis
Yellen, Janet, 15th Chair of the U.S.
Federal Reserve Board

Business

Accountant
Banking
Bankruptcy
Bernanke, Ben S., 14th Chair of the U.S.
Federal Reserve Board
Bloomberg, Michael R., American
Politician and Businessperson
Bonds
Budget
Buffett, Warren, Owner of Berkshire
Hathaway Inc.
Cash
Credit (or Bond) Rating Agency
Credit Report and Reporting Agencies
Debt
Debt Collection
Deficit
Deflation
Delinquency
Digital Currency—Bitcoin
Dividend Income
Flexible Saving Account
Geithner, Timothy F., 75th Secretary of the
U.S. Treasury
Greenspan, Alan, 13th Chair of the U.S.
Federal Reserve Board
Health Insurance
Hedge Funds
Identity Theft
Inflation
Interest Income and Payments
Interest Rates
Liabilities
Liquidity
Loans
Obama, Barack, President of the United
States
Pension Plans
Power of Attorney
Risk
Schapiro, Mary, 29th Chair of the U.S.
Securities and Exchange Commission

Shiller, Robert J., 2013 Nobel Laureate in
Economics
Siebert, Muriel, First Woman to Own a
Seat on the New York Stock Exchange
Social Lending or Peer-to-Peer Lending
Social Security
Stock Market
Stocks
Systematic Market Risk
Tax Return, Federal
Time Value of Money
Umbrella Insurance
Unemployment
U.S. Federal Tax System Overview
Year 1970s to 1980s: Economic Problems
and the United States
Year 1994: North American Free Trade
Agreement between Mexico, Canada,
and the United States
Year 1997–1998: Asian Financial Crisis
Year 1999: Introduction of the Euro to
World Financial Markets
Year 2000: Bursting of the Dot–Com
Technology Bubble
Year 2001: Enron, the Failure of Corporate
Finance and Governance
Year 2002: Sarbanes-Oxley Act
Year 2003–2011: Iraq War's Impact on the
U.S. Economy
Year 2005: Growth of China and India as
World Economic Powers
Year 2007–2008: Subprime Housing Crisis
and Mortgage Meltdown
Year 2007–2009: Global Recession and
Breakdown of Major Wall Street
Institutions
Year 2010: Dodd-Frank Wall Street
Reform and Consumer Protection Act
Yellen, Janet, 15th Chair of the U.S.
Federal Reserve Board

Consumers

Accountant
Alimony
Banking
Bankruptcy
Behavioral Finance

Debt and Credit

Economics

Finance

Government

Legal

Real Estate

Retirement

Preface

"Too many people spend money they haven't earned, to buy things they don't want, to impress people they don't like," according to Will Rogers, a historic American actor. Although Will Rogers lived a century ago, his words ring true today. This quote identifies common maladies present in today's society: lack of individual money sense, excess consumption, and spending for others' benefit.

Personal Finance: An Encyclopedia of Modern Money Management is a crucial resource for today's society. There is a greater divide between the rich and poor, our society is depending on debt to finance an advertiser-influenced lifestyle, and families are working twice as hard for the same inflation-adjusted pay as they earned in 1987. By increasing financial literacy and information, this declining financial trend can be reversed.

Abundant research supports the worsening financial picture of Americans today. Our financial strength is weakening. According to a September 10, 2012, article by Rich Morin and Seth Motel, "A Third of Americans Now Say They Are in the Lower Classes." In a survey of 2,508 adults by the Pew Research Center during the 2008 to 2012 time period, the percentage of Americans indicating they are in the lower-middle or lower class has risen from one fourth to one third.

The younger than age 30 poor are growing more quickly than other age groups. Thirty-nine percent of adults ages 18 to 29 consider themselves lower class. This is a 14 percent increase since 2008. The lower-class Caucasian and Hispanic percentages are also growing faster. Not only are the number of poor growing, but the lower class also see their future prospects in a bleak light.

Our financial lives have changed drastically during the last 25 years. Many of these financial changes are for the worse.

In 1987, the median home size was approximately 1,700 square feet. Today, the new median single-family home is 2,400 square feet. Americans dreams are expanding, but not their incomes. As we strive for grander homes, we stretch our stagnating resources to fulfill those expanding dreams.

In 1987, the median inflation-adjusted household income was $50,389. According to U.S. Census data, in 2011 the median household income was $50,054. Considering the impact of inflation, our earnings are stagnating.

In the past, the household norm was a two-parent family, with one parent staying at home and the other outside in the workforce. Today's family frequently includes two working adults without the proportionate increase (or doubling) of inflation-adjusted wages. In other words, today families work twice as much for the same amount of inflation-adjusted pay that a family earned 25 years ago.

Credit card usage was rare in the middle of the last century. By 2001, 76 percent of families had at least one credit card. Today, 92 percent of families with incomes over $30,000 have a card, with the average for all households up to 6.3 credit cards (Akers et al., 2005).

In 2011, the household median nonsecured debt amount (including credit card, student loan, medical, and other) was $7,000. Secured debt, such as a home mortgage, reached a median amount of $91,000 with 69 percent of U.S. households with some amount of debt in that same year. Growing debt levels is a major problem today. And out-of-control debt leads to another financial problem, bankruptcy.

Bankruptcies, a severe sign of financial difficulty, demonstrate the importance of financial education. During April 2012 through March 2013, there were a total of 1,170,324 bankruptcies in the United States. As the Bankruptcy entry in the encyclopedia explains, bankruptcies are not just an occurrence in the lower income, less educated population. Those with college degrees and higher incomes also file for bankruptcy.

America's deteriorating financial success and literacy create an urgent need for a comprehensive educational reference in personal finance and money management. The previous data underscore and highlight the importance of expanding financial knowledge in high school and college students. The broad financial information in this encyclopedia can help to curtail America's financial decline.

Personal Finance: An Encyclopedia of Modern Money Management is written to equip today's high school and college students with fundamental money principles along with a foundation for wise financial decision making. Without personal finance and money management knowledge, individuals have difficulty gaining long-term financial stability, specifically money for important life goals such as buying a home, funding a child's college expenses, and retirement.

This encyclopedia is an important resource to facilitate the individual's grasp of the basic economic and financial concepts necessary for successful adult money management. Not only will students find this a useful reference, but librarians, researchers, journalists, and educators will profit from this complete personal finance and money management resource. Combining the most important money management and personal finance topics in one easy-to-use reference furnishes the user with a one-stop source for financial information. The reader doesn't need to hunt through reams of online sites for essential financial terms, descriptions, explanations of personal finance concepts, people, and ideas. This encyclopedia addresses all of the important personal finance and money management topics.

Each entry ranges in length from 1,000 to 2,000 words and provides the reader with comprehensive coverage of the topic. The entries are peppered with examples and context to bring the topics to life. When important, historical context helps the reader gain a fuller understanding of the subject matter. Sidebars and fun facts enliven the topics and increase their relevancy.

The encyclopedia is comprehensive and includes almost 100 ideas and concepts related to personal finance and money management. From entries about banking, credit, debt, and insurance topics to modern and specific information concerning on-line personal finance and electronic currency, the reader will find in-depth discussion about personal finance topics. The reader approaching adulthood will garner an understanding of risk, rent to own, types of banking accounts, mortgages, and other crucial money management topics.

In addition to the ideas and concepts, 16 major financial events are explored. Beginning with the Great Depression of 1929, through the most recent European debt crisis, most major contemporary financial events are explained and analyzed. Corporate blunders such as the Enron financial crisis show how corporate malfeasance can destroy the finances of thousands of ordinary Americans. Readers will gain an understanding of financial crises and their impact on the public. By learning about historical financial and personal finance events, readers acquire knowledge to forestall common money management pitfalls. As the important Edmund Burke stated, "Those who don't understand history are destined to repeat it." And repeating financial missteps is costly.

Many individuals have impacted personal finance and money management today. Many of the approximately 20 individuals included in the encyclopedia made important contributions in the fields of government economic policy, including three former U.S. Treasury secretaries and several U.S. presidents. Women such as the International Monetary Fund president, Christine Lagarde, and the 29th chair of the U.S. Securities and Exchange Commission, Mary Schapiro, illustrate the breadth of personal finance influencers. This sample of important financial individuals spans the landscape from Nobel Prize winners to political figures and corporate giants. To include all important modern money management influencers is beyond the scope of this work, yet the men and women in this volume educate the public about how people impact the finances of the citizenry of the United States.

Each entry is followed with related topics and a further reading section. Both of these additions give readers a road map to further information on the topic. The further reading section also allows users access to the references for the entry. As is customary today, most of the resources are easy to access online or through a library.

The glossary expands the breadth of the encyclopedia with close to 200 additional financial entries. Topics such as yield, write-off, variable interest rate, and venture capital elaborate on current money-use topics. Beyond a typical glossary, this section includes examples and longer explanations, suitable for research and education.

The arrangement of the work is typical A to Z format, with an index for easy reference. The Guide to Related Topics offers the reader another way to understand the content with approximately 10 categorized areas including Government, Banking, Consumer Related, Investing, Insurance, Economics, Legal, and more. Whether the reader is using the eBook or the hard copy, ease of use contributes to the many benefits of this work.

Written by 19 academics, financial professionals, and notables in the personal finance and money management field, the work is well researched with up-to-date money facts, descriptions, and explanations. This encyclopedia would not have been possible without their contributions. I am grateful for their quality research, timely efforts, and thoughtful contributions to this important work. Without the contributors' expertise, this encyclopedia would not have been possible. The entries are comprehensive and integrated with modern money management.

The important contributing authors reside across the globe and work at major universities and other educational institutions, nonprofit organizations, and financial companies. I sincerely wish to thank the contributors: Jennifer Woolley, Kay Bell, Catherine Alford, Joe Krupka, Maria Nedeva, Yasmine Abdel Razek, Surya Mrunalini Pisapati, Leslie Linfield, John Linfield, Yousra Acherqui, Angelique McInnes, Lien Luu, Danny Kofke, Scott Glenn, Jonathan Citrin, Andrea Travillian, Ramya Ghosh, and Leo Chan. Without their thoughtful contributions, this work would not have been possible.

This encyclopedia is unique and a strong resource for both background reading and research. The book clarifies many important topics popular in today's society. Without an understanding of these personal finance and money management concepts, the consumer is at a financial disadvantage. Unlike many online sources, this encyclopedia is founded on research and the expertise of the accomplished authors.

Personal Finance: Encyclopedia of Modern Money Management is an invaluable guide in understanding today's financial landscape.

Barbara Friedberg

Further Reading

Akers, Douglas, Jay Golter, Brian Lamm, and Martha Solt. FDIC; Federal Deposit Insurance Corporation Web site. "FDIC Banking Review; Overview of Recent Developments in the Credit Card Industry." Updated November 1, 2005. http://www.fdic.gov/bank /analytical/banking/2005nov/article2.html

Fry, Richard. 2014. "Young Adults, Student Debt and Economic Well-Being." May 14. Pew Research; Social and Demographic Trends. http://www.pewsocialtrends.org /2014/05/14/young-adults-student-debt-and-economic-well-being/

Morin, Rich, and Seth Motel. 2012. "A Third of Americans Now Say They Are in the Lower Classes." September 10. Pew Research; Social and Demographic Trends. http://www.pewsocialtrends.org/2012/09/10/a-third-of-americans-now-say-they-are -in-the-lower-classes/

U.S. Courts.gov Web site. "U.S. Bankruptcy Courts—Business and Nonbusiness Cases Commenced, by Chapter of the Bankruptcy Code." Accessed July 13, 2014. http://www.uscourts.gov/uscourts/Statistics/BankruptcyStatistics/BankruptcyFilings /2013/0313_f2.pdf

Vornovytskyy, Marina, Alfred Gottschalck, and Adam Smith. 2011. "Household Debt in the U.S.: 2000 to 2011." http://www.census.gov/people/wealth/files/Debt%20 Highlights%202011.pdf

Introduction

Today, Americans are plagued with high debt levels and unemployment along with low savings and declining home ownership. College costs are skyrocketing, leading to excessive student loan debt, which serves as a financial weight on the students today. The lack of attention to personal finance and money management hurts consumers now and leads to declining future financial stability later.

According to "Reality Bites" (*The Economist,* June 21, 2012), today's young generation may be the first not to surpass their parents in financial security and success. Stagnant wages, high debt levels, and low savings rates contribute to the likelihood that most people will not be positioned to meet their future financial goals. Further underscoring this poor personal finance picture, not until 2012 was individual net worth predicted to rebound—*to 2007 levels.*

The urgent need for a personal finance resource is underscored by two more factors: the dearth of financial knowledge among citizens and dire economic predictions about our future. Furthermore, the lack of credible online sources demonstrates a void of reliable information in the personal finance landscape.

Personal Finance: An Encyclopedia of Modern Money Management is designed for both personal and scholarly use and offers the researcher quality definitions and explanations of the money topics of modern financial life. This comprehensive encyclopedia is an excellent research resource for any personal finance course taken by high school or college students. Journalists, writers, researchers, and consumers will also find a breadth of unbiased, useful financial information.

The glaring need for a personal finance and money management encyclopedia today is further underscored by the following statistics. Although frequently cited in the print, online, and television media, basic personal finance and money management topics are lacking in the ordinary American's knowledge. Financial missteps are a pervasive problem. The National Financial Educators Council reports that only 59 percent of Generation Y (18- to 29-year-olds) young adults pay their bills on time every month. Ten percent of Americans with mortgages have been late or missed a mortgage payment within the last year. Three out of four Americans say they aren't saving enough. Fifty-four percent of college students reported overdrawing their bank accounts. And 81 percent of these college students admitted to underestimating the amount of time it would take to pay off a credit card balance, by a large margin.

Unfortunately, most parents have not taught their children the important money management skills. The Financial Educators Council reports that only 34 percent of parents taught their children how to balance a checkbook and fewer than that explained how credit card interest and fees work. Over 90 percent of Americans with teenagers admit worrying that their children will falter financially by living beyond their means or overspending.

Personal finance is a component of the larger discipline of finance. In general, finance is used in the business world to analyze, measure, and organize the profits, losses, and accounting of a business. Personal finance takes these concepts and applies them to the individual. In the same way that a business must earn more than it spends, the individual must save more than he or she spends. In both cases, without proper money management, both businesses and individuals will face financial difficulty, low credit scores, inability to pay their bills, and at worst, financial bankruptcy.

This encyclopedia offers a solid foundation in all of the important personal financial management topics. *Personal Finance: An Encyclopedia of Modern Money Management* creates a map to the confusing world of personal money management. Throughout life, an individual and/or family must understand the concepts of budgeting, insurance, saving, investing, debt service, mortgages, retirement, and more. The text shows the relationship between personal finance and every aspect of economic life, from understanding the lease when renting an apartment to saving for retirement. The reader gains answers to personal finance questions related to the disciplines of economics, management, finance, and accounting in this reference book. This work provides quick and accurate answers to questions about financial terms, concepts, people, and events.

Additionally, by understanding personal finance and money management, readers will better comprehend the economic and financial news and how it impacts them. In sum, *Personal Finance: An Encyclopedia of Modern Money Management* is a unique resource for all aspects of financial and economic life today.

Encyclopedia Benefits and Sample Topics

Ideas and Concepts—The Heart of the Text

The A to Z Ideas and Concepts section begins with the Accountant topic and finishes with Wills and Trusts. Every important personal finance topic is addressed.

There are quite a few entries related to debt and credit. These critical money management topics include Liabilities, Debt Collection, Delinquency, Debt, Consumer Credit/Debt, Credit Score, Credit Report and Reporting Agencies, Credit Cards, and Debt/Credit Counseling entries. In these 1,000- to 2,000-word entries, the reader gains an understanding of important consumer financial tools from a trusted source.

A lack of consumer credit and debt knowledge negatively affects many young people today. In the Consumer Credit/Debt entry, the reader will discover how a $1,000 purchase can cost the consumer 33 percent more if the individual pays only a portion of the bill each month. According to the Federal Reserve Board, consumer debt continues to grow, which leaves less disposable income for today's Americans. Without a sound foundation in personal finance, it is difficult to imagine how this trend of rising debt will ever reverse.

The reader will learn the major components of a credit score and how this three-digit number can influence the consumer's financial life. A low credit score, caused by inattention to financial obligations, can cost thousands of dollars in interest payments when the consumer with a lower score receives a higher interest rate on a mortgage or vehicle loan. In the Credit Score entry, readers will learn to identify the crucial information that influences their credit score.

Insurance is another important and misunderstood personal finance topic that receives complete coverage in this encyclopedia. Not only are the confusing insurance terms and language explained, but the insurance entries include the following types of insurance: Health, Disability, Homeowner's and Renter's, Life, and Umbrella. Not only is there an entry for Health Insurance, but the recent Affordable Care Act receives clear and succinct treatment.

According to "Why Do I Need Insurance?" from the Wells Fargo Web site, "life turns on a dime." Consumers can't predict when misfortune will occur. Individuals take for granted that life will continue without interruption. Yet, by understanding that the relatively small premiums paid for insurance can yield huge returns should disaster occur, the consumer can avoid future catastrophic financial losses.

The insurance topics reach into all corners of one's life. Many bankruptcies are forced because of unpaid medical bills. Today, without health insurance, not only does one face fines due to the newly enacted Affordable Care Act (ACA), but consumers also face a ruined future financial life without adequate insurance to cover medical bills. The insurance entries explain insurance terms in simple language. Further, readers gain information on most important varieties of insurance. Renters will learn why this often overlooked insurance can be a lifesaver when a laptop and cell phone are stolen from their apartment. For prices as low as $14 per month, renters may be reimbursed for the loss of expensive electronics. Umbrella insurance, another type of coverage, is explained along with why some consumers may benefit from this inclusive policy. The reader learns all of the insurance basics for both research and practical situations.

Economics topics that pepper the news and impact individuals from all walks of life are included in this encyclopedia. Opportunity Cost, Human Capital, Gross Domestic and Gross National Product, Inflation, Deflation, Deficit, and Capitalism are explained along with their importance in personal finance. Without a working knowledge of basic economics concepts, the consumer is at a loss when listening to the news and understanding the world in which we live.

The Gross Domestic Product (GDP) is the monetary value of goods and services that a country produces in one year. Why should this matter to the ordinary consumer? The GDP can be used as a measure of the health and well-being of the U.S. economy. A healthy economy with robust GDP growth means companies are hiring new workers and employees are being paid well. In contrast, when GDP slows, unemployment may increase, and a recession might follow. Consumers who understand this economic concept are better able to manage their career and finances. When GDP slows, along with a possible recession, the savvy consumer works extra hard to secure his or her job and is thoughtful when considering taking on additional debt.

The Deficit also has an impact on the individual. For the government, a deficit means that the country is spending more than it is taking in through taxes and other sources of income. If the country is not receiving enough revenue, the government needs to borrow money by issuing debt to pay its bills. Greater debt levels impose a cost on each individual in the society. By understanding this and other economic concepts the reader becomes a smarter, more educated citizen, able to make sound financial decisions.

New and popular modern personal finance money management topics are not forgotten. From Digital Currency such as Bitcoin to Hedge Funds, Identity Theft, Online Personal Finance, and Social or Peer-to-Peer Lending, the newer developments in personal finance are covered. As new financial concepts enter our society, it is important to be able to understand their worth. For example, is Bitcoin a fad or a true contender for another legal currency? The reader learns more about the electronic currency debate in that entry. This encyclopedia gives the researcher and student the information to determine whether to jump on the electronic currency bandwagon or wait on the sidelines for more information.

Peer-to-peer or social lending sounds like a friendly way to borrow money or for the consumer to lend to others. But, what are the risks of this new form of financing? The Social Lending entry introduces readers to this popular new finance platform. As the new sharing economy explodes, this type of collaborative borrowing and lending will continue to expand.

Investing and retirement are intertwined. Young people who start to invest early gain a leg up on retirement. To further clarify and educate regarding these topics there are entries on a variety of investment and retirement accounts. Basic investing principles are examined in the Asset Allocation, Behavioral Finance, Bonds, Compound Interest/Return, Dividend Income, Inflation-Protected Investments, Stock Market, and Investing entries. Retirement topics dovetail with the investment entries as sound investing practice leads to a more financially secure retirement. The retirement topics address Annuity, Estate Planning, Pension Plans, and Wills and Trusts.

The comprehensive treatment of investment and retirement topics in this text are excellent middle-ground resources between comprehensive books and short online descriptions. Readers will learn about modern portfolio theory in easy-to-understand language. The important investing topics of diversification and asset allocation are given thorough treatment. The Compound Interest/Return entry provides an explanation about the benefit of planning for future retirement at a young age. Readers learn how a small amount of money diverted from their paycheck into a retirement account will yield a secure financial future. And the researcher has easy-to-understand explanations of empirically based investing approaches.

Although frequently maligned, the government has a stake in the financial well-being of Americans. If citizens fail financially, the U.S. government has a safety net in place. Medicare is there to help the elderly with medical expenses and Medicaid lends a hand to the underserved poor. The Social Security system provides retirement and disability benefits for millions of Americans. The tax system, without which there would be no safety net, is explained. As alluded to in the investing discussion, there is a suite of safe government-created investments available on the treasurydirect.gov Web site and explained more fully in the Inflation-Protected Investments entry.

The ideas and concepts entries are replete with scores of additional entries for every area of modern financial management. Next, we'll explore the events and people who influence our finances today and get a taste of the individuals and events that can lead to knowledge and understanding and, ultimately, a richer financial life.

Events—Historical Occurrences May Transform Your Financial Literacy

The events section is designed to inform and educate about major financial historical events. The purpose of these entries is to underscore the common themes that cause financial crises and arm the reader with financial tools and understanding to recognize future financial episodes as they happen. In fact, adults who are savviest about finances have an awareness of economic history and the cyclical nature of business and the economy.

It was difficult to narrow down the events entries to fewer than 20, and there are important financial crises and situations that may have been overlooked. With that disclaimer in mind, this sampling of major historical financial episodes gives the reader a context from which to understand our financial world today.

The earliest entry, according to its date, discusses the Great Depression of the 1930s. Initiated with the 1929 stock market crash, this Depression is the one to which future depressions and recessions are compared. The Great Depression influences governmental economic policies to this day. More current economic crises in this resource include the 1970s to 1980s Economic Problems. This was another dark period in American economic and financial history, with high inflation rates and long lines at the gas pump. Several more recent economic calamities are dissected along with the significant financial lessons for today.

Several global events are included, underscoring the continuing integration of world economies. From the Year 1944: Creation of the International Monetary Fund and the World Bank at the Bretton Woods International Conference to the more recent Year 2011–2012 European Debt Crisis, Americans are affected by financial and economic world events.

Corporate malfeasance and misfortune also affect today's consumer. In the entry Year 2001: Enron, the Failure of Corporate Finance and Governance, the author discusses how one of the most well-regarded corporations of its time duped investors and its own employees. This major corporate ruse caused thousands of employees to lose their life savings and investors to lose their financial outlays. The lessons learned from these types of events prove the long-standing truism, "If something sounds too good to be true, it usually is."

The Events section would be incomplete without touching on the impact of the Iraq War on the U.S. economy. As one of the longest military conflicts in U.S. history, this action took our country from a financial surplus to a huge deficit. The financing and economic influence of this war will directly or indirectly impact every American today and for years to come. This entry is a unique contribution to the conversation with treatment of the conflict from a purely monetary perspective.

Major legislation that changed the Wall Street investing environment is discussed in the entry Year 2010: Dodd-Frank Wall Street Reform and Consumer Protection Act. This massive legislation is given excellent treatment by the contributing author, attorney Leslie Linfield. The Dodd-Frank Wall Street Reform and Consumer Protection Act impacts almost every aspect of the U.S. financial system and is the most significant financial reform since those following the Great Depression. Frequent media mentions and references underscore the importance of these acts (Dodd-Frank actually incorporates many acts into the legislation) to both the consumer and researcher. The act's 16 titles cover the gamut of financial areas. The increase of Federal Deposit Insurance Corporation (FDIC) insurance on savers' deposits from $100,000 to $250,000 per depositor touches anyone with a bank account. The law protects consumers and improves access to financial products, among many other advances.

The remaining events entries are no less important. They discuss Year 2000: Bursting of the Dot-Com Technology Bubble, Year 2005: Growth of China and India as World Economic Powers, Year 1997–1998 Asian Financial Crisis, and Year 1994: North American Free Trade Agreement between Mexico, Canada, and the United States. These educational and historically relevant accounts give the reader a solid background in important financial historical happenings.

People—A Selection of Men and Women Who Impact Your Pocket

Similar to the Events section, the People entries were also a challenge to winnow to a manageable number. In modern money management, there are hundreds of influential men and women who impact the financial lives of Americans. The approximately 20 individuals highlighted in the People section lean toward political individuals and world-renowned academics. This section should not be considered an exhaustive list of personal finance and money management notables but more of an introduction to a sample of important influencers. The People section integrates with the Events and Concepts sections to show the interconnectedness of our financial world.

The U.S. presidents discussed are current. Their entries focus on presidential policies related to monetary issues. The presidents' entries include Barack Obama, George W. Bush, and William J. Clinton. For example, George W. Bush, the 43rd president of the United States, is well known for massive tax cuts in the Jobs and Growth Tax Relief Reconciliation Act of 2008. These tax cuts were initiated to halt the downward economic trend that followed the bursting of the technology bubble and the ensuing recession during the early 2000s. Although designed to expire at a certain date, several of the tax cuts are presently still in effect.

Without several of the Nobel Prize–winning economists, our financial and investing world would look much different than it does today. Harry Markowitz, Nobel Prize winner, is frequently considered the father of modern portfolio management and proved the importance of diversification in investing. He took an intuitive concept and backed it up with empirical research. His findings are now integrated into most varieties of modern investing advice. Another investing genius, John Bogle, founder of Vanguard Investments, is one of the earliest proponents of the index fund investing movement. His Vanguard Mutual Fund Company, many books, and low-cost mutual funds changed investing strategies by reducing costs and championing the index fund investing approach. Of course, a modern money management text would not be complete without a discussion of the famous investor Warren Buffett.

Several chairs of the U.S. Federal Reserve Board are also profiled. During their tenures, many of these individuals were considered among the most powerful individuals in the United States. Whether this is true or not is open to debate, although it is a fact that a speech by a Federal Reserve chair can move the investment markets.

Alan Greenspan was one of the most notable former chairs of the U.S. Federal Reserve Board and served through the administrations of presidents Ronald Reagan, George H. W. Bush, William Clinton, and George W. Bush. In a famous speech during a time of frothy stock valuations in the late 1990s, he coined the phrase "irrational exuberance." This phrase referred to consumers' enthusiasm for the stock market, especially technology stocks, without regard for their underlying values. As has occurred time and again, the stock market bubble of the late 1990s came crashing down with the bursting of the dot-com or technology bubble. The Alan Greenspan entry once again illustrates the integration of people, events, and concepts in the financial and economic world.

Finally, the recently deceased Muriel Siebert's life is profiled in her entry. As the first woman to own a seat on the New York Stock Exchange, first woman superintendent of banking in New York, and a pioneer in the discount brokerage industry, her contributions span the financial landscape. Born in 1928, her work paved the way for many women in the financial world.

Glossary, Related Topics, Bibliography, and Index

All of the personal finance and money management information contained in the encyclopedia is neatly arranged for ease of access. From the A to Z entries to the comprehensive glossary, the reader is able to quickly obtain necessary financial information. The glossary is more than a dictionary of quick definitions. The almost 200 entries go into depth about additional financial topics and when appropriate provide real-life examples. From an explanation of an Adjustable-Rate Mortgage (ARM) to Yield, the glossary covers most of the common financial terms in use today.

The glossary topics add value to consumers' financial toolkit. In our credit-driven society, the definitions of Annual Percentage Rate (APR) and Annual Percentage Yield (APY) inform the consumer of the true cost of both borrowing and investing. The APR includes not only the interest rate, but any additional borrowing costs and fees and incorporates those amounts into an annual percentage rate. By understanding the meaning of APR, the consumer is better equipped to borrow money and compare lending rates.

When investing or saving, the smart consumer strives for the highest return or yield. The Annual Percentage Yield (APY) standardizes the rate of return by incorporating into its calculation when the interest payments are made. That way, the saver or investor can be confident that she is making an "apples to apples" comparison of alternative investment opportunities.

The term *Assets* has several meanings, each of which are discussed in this glossary entry. And the Attorney glossary entry clearly describes the distinction between a lawyer and an attorney. It's likely that most readers incorrectly assume that they are the same.

Another section of the encyclopedia groups all of the entries according to related topics. That way, if a researcher is seeking economic information, there's a quick path to all related economic entries. There are over 10 theme-defined lists including Investing, Retirement, Debt and Credit, Legal, Economics, Real Estate, Consumer related, Business Topics, Retirement, Banking, and Insurance. And, as one would expect, one entry might logically fall into several theme classifications.

The bibliography brings together additional resources for further research. Journalists, researchers, and students will find articles, books, and Web sites to round out their study. If one is looking for a more complete treatment of a topic, the bibliography offers a selection of some of the most important resources in the personal finance and money management fields.

A work of this breadth wouldn't be complete without an index. For speedy reference to all the topics, the index is complete and professionally laid out. This section adds to the accessibility and ease of use of the encyclopedia.

For a quick view of several consumer-related entries or an exhaustive study of the disciplines of personal finance and money management, this encyclopedia is a welcome source of user-friendly information.

Barbara Friedberg

Further Reading

National Financial Educators Council Web site. "Financial Literacy Statistics, Research and Resources." Accessed July 15, 2014. http://www.financialeducatorscouncil.org/financial-literacy-statistics/

Wells Fargo Web site. "Why Do I Need Insurance?" Accessed July 18, 2014.

Ideas and Concepts

Accountant

An accountant is an individual who is integral to the functioning of U.S. (and international) businesses. This individual measures, discloses, and/or provides financial information professionally. The accountant's findings are provided to managers, investors, tax authorities, and others. This information is used to assist decision makers with financial resource allocation.

The accounting duties for companies include performing audits and creating financial statements and analyses. This information is crucial to the proper functioning of modern business. A business needs to understand how much money is coming in and going out. Financial records must be maintained and properly updated for tax reporting as well. Firms either employ their own internal accountants or contract their accounting work to specialized organizations.

Individuals frequently hire an accountant to assist with complicated personal financial decisions as well as tax preparation.

Accountant's Skills and Job Tasks

All financial transactions, record keeping, and analysis fall under the accountant's responsibilities. An accountant's duties in a company span payroll, cash collections, payments or disbursements, procurement, inventory, and property accounting. Preparing the company's budget and financial statements is another common accounting responsibility.

Payroll is the task of managing the salary and wages of every employee. This massive responsibility includes maintaining accurate work records and calculating gross and net pay. As a quick explanation, gross pay is the total amount earned before any deductions such as taxes, Medicare, or Social Security payments. The net pay is the remaining amount of pay after normal deductions. This is the money that remains for the employee to spend and save.

It's not unusual for a new worker to suffer a shock when she finds out her promised $13 per hour pay is really closer to $10 per hour after all of the deductions are factored in. The employee's $520 per week income leaves her with $400 to spend and save. Fortunately for the accountant, there are many computer programs that assist with the payroll process.

The cash collections responsibilities require the accountant to identify, record, and monitor all cash transactions. In addition to being tracked, the cash must be included

Accounting Scandals

The accounting field is fraught with malfeasance. Some of these episodes have caused global economic turmoil. Following are a few of the more infamous scandals.

In 1998, Waste Management, a publicly traded company, reported $1.7 billion in fake earnings. The company falsified the financial records but got caught when a new CEO and management team reviewed the financial records. The company ultimately settled a shareholder class-action suit for $457 million and the SEC fined the accounting firm, Arthur Andersen, $7 million.

In 2001, Enron, a Houston-based commodities, energy, and service corporation, kept huge corporate debts off the financial statements. Shareholders lost $74 billion and thousands of employees and investors lost their retirement accounts. Many employees lost their jobs. CEO Jeff Skilling and former CEO Ken Lay were exposed by whistle-blower Sherron Watkins. Skilling got 24 years in prison and Lay died before serving time. The company filed for bankruptcy and Arthur Andersen was found guilty once again.

In 2008, the Lehman Brothers scandal contributed to the mortgage meltdown and recession of 2007–2009. The company hid over $50 billion in loans and recorded them as sales. This complicated dance played out by selling toxic assets to Cayman Island banks with the underlying assumption that Lehman would ultimately buy back these low-worth assets. This action created the illusion that Lehman had $50 billion more in cash and $50 billion less in toxic assets. When the fraud was discovered, Lehman Brothers was forced into the largest bankruptcy in U.S. history.

Again in 2008, Bernie Madoff, founder of Bernard L. Madoff Investment Securities, LLC, bilked investors out of $64.8 billion through the largest Ponzi scheme ever. Investors were promised large returns on their investments with the firm, but were ultimately paid returns out of other investors' money in lieu of investment profits. Many investors lost their life savings. Madoff is serving 150 years in prison and was assessed $170 billion in restitution.

---

in the financial reports. Deciding how much to keep on hand and how much to bank and into which account(s) is another administrative accounting task.

As one would expect, after monitoring the incoming cash, the accountant needs to oversee payments or disbursements. The accounting department of a firm must prepare checks or pay bills and expenses electronically. These bill payment duties are similar to the ones required of individuals in everyday life

Large and small companies need to purchase so the company may run smoothly. Accountants track all procurement with purchase orders. The accountant implements and maintains the systems that track purchases, methods of payment, and reconciliation with inventory. Cash management is important so that credit purchases are paid for on time without accruing interest or late fee penalties.

Accounting departments integrate with sales to track which products are selling and which are languishing on the shelves. This information is used to drive business strategy decisions.

The corporate financial records and required government filings are under the accountant's umbrella as well. Accountants prepare the financial statements, which include the budget, cash flow statement, income (or profit and loss) statement, and balance sheet.

Generally Accepted Accounting Principles (GAAP)

All of these statements and tasks are driven by generally accepted accounting principles. GAAP is a set of accounting principles, standards, and procedures that include "common practice" and regulated procedures.

GAAP principles are crucial to standardize the accounting field. It would be quite confusing for companies to each maintain their own system of recording and tracking financial records. Not only would this be a problem for employees and managers within the company, but it would present problems for the tax authority and shareholders of public companies.

GAAP covers revenue recognition or when income is recorded, balance sheet items, and financial statements. Although there are standards and procedures for creating accounting documents, leeway remains within the documents. Thus investors and other stakeholders need to scrutinize, interpret, and analyze accounting statements.

Several examples of unscrupulous accountants who have massaged financial data to their own benefit are included in the accounting scandals described in the sidebar to this entry.

Professional Certifications and Types of Accountants

Accountants are a loosely regulated profession. Accounting professional certifications give companies and consumers a designation by which to assess a minimum level of competency. In general, the Certified Public Accountant (CPA) designation offers a consumer confidence and indicates a level of competency. Other designations also indicate expertise in specific accounting-related areas.

There are ethical standards and professional certifications for accountants. The Certified Public Accountant designation is a prestigious qualification earned by completing an examination and fulfilling specific work requirements. The American Institute of Certified Public Accountants oversees this qualification. In Canada, the Chartered Accountant (CA) is on par with the U.S. CPA.

Additional accounting certifications include the Certified Management Accountant (CMA), Certified Financial Manager (CFM), Certified Fraud Examiner (CFE), Certified Internal Auditor (CIA), Enrolled Agent (EA), and Certified Government Financial Manager (CGFM).

The various certifications equip the accountant for specialized accounting work. For example, enrolled agents are tax experts and are the only federally licensed tax practitioners who can also represent the taxpayer before the IRS. These tax professionals pass an examination on the tax code or have worked at the Internal Revenue Service and interpreted the tax code for at least five years.

The Certified Management Accountant (CMA) combines skill in accounting and strategic management. In order to obtain this designation, the college graduate must attend a CMA program and pass a series of tests. Upon completion, the CMA is well versed in both accounting and management skills and would be an asset to a company looking for a manager with the accounting expertise to make important business decisions.

In addition to an accountant, a bookkeeper may complete the more basic financial duties. Ultimately, the accountant oversees the bookkeeper's work and uses the inputs for more advanced financial processes.

Accounting responsibilities are performed in every business and the accounting field continues to evolve. Although the proliferation of computer programs makes routine accounting tasks more efficient, the accountant is responsible for financial analysis and interpretation.

Joseph Krupka

See also: Budget; Cash; Consumer Credit/Debt; Debt; Financial Advisor; Liabilities; Liquidity; Tax Return, Federal; Year 2001: Enron, the Failure of Corporate Finance and Governance; Year 2007–2009: Global Recession and Breakdown of Major Wall Street Institutions; Year 2010: Dodd-Frank Wall Street Reform and Consumer Protection Act

Further Reading

Accounting-Degree.org. "The 10 Worst Corporate Accounting Scandals of All Time." Accessed February 20, 2014. http://www.accounting-degree.org/scandals/

For Dummies. "What Does an Accountant Do?" Accessed February 20, 2014. http://www.dummies.com/how-to/content/what-does-an-accountant-do.html

National Association of Enrolled Agents. "What Is an Enrolled Agent?" Accessed February 20, 2014. http://www.naea.org/taxpayers/what-enrolled-agent

Affordable Care Act

The Affordable Care Act (ACA) is a law that seeks to provide U.S. citizens with better health coverage by implementing inclusive health insurance reforms in order to increase coverage, provide more choice of insurance, and provide valued care. In addition, the law states that it will ensure that insurance entities will be accountable for their actions, and that prices will be reasonable.

Background of the Affordable Care Act

In 2009, President Obama sought to extend and recreate health care in America, a feat that the Democrats had been trying to accomplish since before the turn of the century. Because of resistance from the Republican Party, a conflict ensued that caused some of the Democrats to favor a health care system that was somewhat like President Nixon's system from the 1970s.

The Affordable Care Act is the United States' resulting health care law, ratified in 2010. Obama's involvement in the creation of this act caused people to refer to the act as "Obamacare" colloquially. Despite the political turmoil and division, Obama put the law into force, but lingering questions continued between both parties. Only the future will tell if the act aided the American people.

U.S. Health Care History

Health care for U.S. citizens was once easy to get and reasonably priced. With new living standards in the 21st century, health care value is better than in earlier decades. However, this was complicated because of the system that was in place.

President Theodore Roosevelt (1858–1919) had a profound impact on what people considered as health care. This mindset stems from President Roosevelt himself who said that it is important for the United States to fortify a household's well-being against the danger of illness, and to implement a procedure of accepted societal insurance (American Presidency Project, 2011). Jane Addams, a distinguished social worker, supported President Roosevelt in these efforts (Selmi, 2006).

The 1930s saw the boom of the Blue Cross plan, which was advantageous for certain entities but not to the public in general. The Blue Cross plan covered many recipients due to their affiliation with organizations and professional groups but not other citizens. The Blue Cross entity flourished and was further promoted though advertisements.

During the Great Depression, President Franklin D. Roosevelt (1882–1945) made an effort to embrace health insurance as a portion of his Social Security law as he pronounced health care to be an essential right for citizens. Roosevelt wanted to add health care to his Social Security Act, but pressure from the American Medical Association (AMA) talked him into rethinking his decision. In addition, World War II became the new focus, which forced Roosevelt to put the health care issue on the back burner (History News Network).

Two strong advocates for President Roosevelt were veterans Harry Hopkins (1890–1946) and Frances Perkins (1880–1965). Both would go on to be key factors in Roosevelt's administration. Hopkins was key in terms of advising, and Perkins was key as a woman Social Security chair member. Later, President Roosevelt deserted the proposal for the attention to health care because of his personal anxiety that there would be obstruction from the AMA as well as others who would neglect the bill (Social Security History, 2011). After the Roosevelt administration left office, President Truman sought to create general coverage in the United States, but he then limited this approach to just elderly people. In Truman's later years, social workers and entities tied to them sought to instill health care reform (Gorin, 2011).

With the growing trend to provide workers with health insurance, the 1950s represented affluence. Most of the aged and underprivileged continued to collect their medical aid from hospitals, rural doctors, and private contributions. Simultaneously, Blue Cross expanded to connect to 20 million American citizens as new commercial insurance entities became more prolific. These new insurance entities provided separate rates centered on buyers' special health hazards, making them able to destabilize the rates provided by Blue Cross for a multitude of healthy, young citizens.

In the later part of the 1950s, President Eisenhower's administration did not want the government to interfere with health care. This situation lingered on into the 1960s with the introduction of the Kerr-Mills Act from a Democratically controlled House and Senate. The Kerr-Mills Act generated a federal program to fund states' health assistance for the aged. The money was insufficient as most states refused to partake in the idea.

In 1962, President Kennedy sought an assertive approach to health care. However, the idea of state health care died out again because of pressures during the voting year and from the American Medical Association. Although President Kennedy could not get enough votes for Medicare to go through, the health care matter continued to draw attention. Medical expenses were growing faster than the total inflation rate and the populace was getting old fast, causing American society to place emphasis on the health care question.

While Lyndon B. Johnson was the United States' president in 1964, approximately 10 percent of American citizens were over the age of 65, and more than 60 percent of electors were in favor of Medicare. Because of this, in 1965 a law was passed that extended Social Security to include health benefits as well as Medicaid. This delivered health care aid to various American citizens who were unable to pay. With the nomination of Richard Nixon as president in the 1970s, the health care focus turned from government's liberal ideas to improvements encompassing private initiatives and nonprofits. The Democrats resumed pushing for extending government involvement in health care until they regained the presidency in 1976. Again, the push for health care was evident. However, Congress could not find a happy medium.

During the 1980s, the "Reaganomics" years, President Reagan cut back on government aid involving Medicaid, but Medicare stood its ground. The employer-founded health care insurance that existed was diminishing, becoming less dependable because the unionized industries were less influential. In addition, extended retail and service entities started imposing severe limitations on health care requirements.

By the 1990s, President Clinton sought to create health care for all, but Clinton's bill encountered tough obstruction from Republicans and insurance entities. These groups felt that Clinton's health care system would allow the government, not doctors, to make the choices in the country's health care. In the 2000s, President George W. Bush made sure that funded health insurance did not happen, but he did agree with Democrats to extend Medicare's coverage for prescription drugs (History News Network).

The Affordable Care Act—A Work in Progress

In contemporary times, the Affordable Care Act, which President Obama put into place in 2010, is the law implemented to modify America's health care system. The plan covers various requirements that will eventually spread health coverage to 25 million people in America. By 2023, the Affordable Care Act seeks to improve the private and public health insurance regularities, spreading health coverage to 25 million American citizens.

In addition, the Affordable Care Act sought to bring down expenses while expanding benefits for buyers. The aim was to bring forth incentives in terms of quality while embracing innovation in the health care system (American Public Health Association, 2014). The results of these goals are still in progress.

Two Sections of the Affordable Care Act

The Affordable Care Act can be broken down into two sections. These two sections include the Patient Protection and Affordable Care Act and the Health Care and Educational Reconciliation Act.

The Patient Protection and Affordable Care Act is the first updated version of the U.S. health care system since the Medicare and Medicaid bill of 1965. This act should allow all American citizens to have access to outstanding and reasonably priced health care. It should also cause the change needed to restrain expenses within the health care system.

The Congressional Budget Office (CBO) concluded that the government would fully compensate the Patient Protection and Affordable Care Act. This will provide coverage for upwards of 94 percent of American citizens while remaining beneath the $900 billion threshold that President Obama stipulated. It is predicted that the health care expense arc will diminish the deficit over the subsequent decade and into the future.

In accordance with the Patient Protection and Affordability Act, the Health Care and Education Reconciliation Act will ensure that all American pupils have access to sound, affordable well-being coverage. The CBO provided for full compensation for these two bills collectively. This will allow more than 94 percent of U.S. pupils to access reasonably priced health care. Specifically, this will reduce the health care expense curvature and lessen the deficit by $143 billion during the 2020s while simultaneously continuing to lessen the debt.

Momentous savings in our economic expectations are projected to provide an affordable college outlook and become easier to manage by way of a change in student-finance programs (the Patient Protection and Affordable Care Act).

The present-day health care mandate is decent and creates a foundation for forthcoming operational expenses and restraint. The Affordable Care Act has deficiencies including the challenge to satisfy all stakeholders. However, this act creates a modernistic groundwork with sound prospects for enhancing care value and controlling expenses. The future of the Affordable Care Act appears to look good, depending on the eye of the beholder (politics).

Controversies

The Affordable Care Act controversies continue. As with most political issues, partisanship has played a role with Republican pushback against the Democratic Party's support of this legislation.

Another topic discussed is whether more who opposed the act would have favored the legislation if someone besides Barack Obama were president. On another note, the Affordable Care Act seems to be a political win-win situation. This is because the law not only helps many people who do not have health insurance but also allows the insurance entities a chance to profit from the regulation.

No matter the case, the Affordable Care Act persists as political parties continue to stay divided over the legislation and implementation of the act. The truth of the

Affordable Care Act's success or failure will lie in the future. The outcome and final evaluation will be measured statistically in the years after its implementation.

Scott Glenn

See also: Disability Insurance; Health Insurance; Medicaid; Medicare; Obama, Barack, President of the United States

Further Reading

American Presidency Project. 2011. *Progressive Platform of 1912.* Retrieved from http://www.presidency.ucsb.edu

American Public Health Association Web site. 2014. Accessed December 30, 2014. https://www.apha.org/

DeWitt, L. 2003. The Medicare Program as a Capstone to the Great Society—Recent Revelations in the LBJ White House Tapes. Retrieved from http://www.larrydewitt.net

George Mason University. The History News Network. History of Healthcare Reform. Accessed February 27, 2014. http://www.hnn.us/article/146911

Gorin, S. H. 2010. The Patient Protection and Affordable Care Act, Cost Control, and the Battle for Health Care Reform [editorial]. *Health & Social Work, 35,* 163–166.

The Patient Protection and Affordable Care Act. Accessed February 1, 2014. http://www.dpc.senate.gov/healthreformbill/healthbill04.pdf

Selmi, P. 2006. *Jane Addams, Social Work, and the Progressive Party of 1912.* Retrieved from http://sswr.confex.com

Social Security History—Chapter 2: The Second Round—1927 to 1940. 2011. http://www.ssa.gov/history

Alimony

Alimony (also referred to as spousal maintenance) is court-ordered payments made by one separated or divorced spouse to another as required by their separation agreement or divorce decree. Alimony is determined by state law and the amount and length of time can vary from one state to another. Alimony should not be confused with child support.

Historically, alimony required men to financially support their wives, during a time when men and women could separate but not divorce. Today, courts use alimony more to ensure fair economic outcomes when a couple divorces.

The alimony provision of the Uniform Marriage and Divorce Act (UMDA; a model act drafted by the Uniform Law Commission but adopted only by several states) stipulates that alimony should be awarded only if the spouse seeking support "lacks sufficient property to provide for his reasonable needs" and "is unable to support himself through appropriate employment" (UMDA § 308).

Alimony can be paid in one of three different ways: a lump sum payment as part of the divorce settlement, in regular monthly payments without a fixed end date (also

---

Fun Alimony Settlement Facts from the Associated Press

According to the Associated Press, former Italian prime minister Silvio Berlusconi, who divorced his second wife, Veronica Lario, in 2009, was ordered to pay his wife alimony of $4 million per month.

As part of Charlie Sheen's 2011 divorce settlement from Brooke Mueller, he was required to pay $55,000 per month for the support of their twin sons.

In 2009, a New Jersey Devils goalie was ordered to pay his ex-wife $500,000 a year in alimony until 2020 and an additional $132,000 per year in child support.

Hip-hop mogul and businessman Russell Simmons consented to pay $40,000 monthly child support to ex-wife Kimora Lee Simmons for the care and upbringing of daughters Ming and Aoki until both girls reach age 19½.

In 2008, Britney Spears agreed to pay $20,000 per month in child support to ex-husband Kevin Federline.

---

called permanent alimony), or in regular interim payments with a set end date (also called rehabilitative alimony).

History of Alimony

During the Middle Ages the Christian church exercised its authority over domestic matters, such as matrimony. Under canon law, marriage was viewed as a sacred rite and thought to be a permanent state. Divorce was rarely granted and only for certain causes, such as adultery or cruelty. When a divorce was requested it could only be granted through the ecclesiastical courts (religious courts). Alimony developed from the idea that a husband had a legal duty to maintain his wife and that such a duty did not terminate with a divorce decree.

The ecclesiastical courts would not award alimony to a woman if it was demonstrated that she was the cause for the dissolution of the marriage, such as her infidelity, or that she was not in economic need because she had property and income of her own. Eventually England passed legislation in 1857 that dissolved the ecclesiastical courts and made divorce a civil matter.

The United States never adopted the ecclesiastical court model but did incorporate the underlying ideas regarding marriage, divorce, and alimony. It is worth noting that there is no formally recognized right to marry or divorce in the U.S. Constitution or Bill of Rights. The reason for this is because both marriage and divorce are within the jurisdiction of the individual state legislatures and their courts.

Alimony and Gender

Though historically women have been awarded alimony, this began to change in 1979 when the U.S. Supreme Court struck down an Alabama law that required only men to make alimony payments to women. The basis for the Court's ruling was found in the Equal Protection Clause of the Fourteenth Amendment, and the court stated that only requiring men to pay women alimony was unequal treatment and unconstitutional.

However, according to the 2010 U.S. Census Bureau statistics, there were only 12,000 men receiving alimony payments compared to 380,000 women. Some family law attorneys believe that even though almost 40 percent of married women now earn more than their husbands, many of these husbands are ashamed to ask for alimony upon the dissolution of the marriage.

Some states have even stopped calling such support alimony. They have transitioned to terms such as "spousal support" or "spousal maintenance" to accommodate a more gender-neutral reality.

Evolving Relationships

In recent years more states have acknowledged various forms of relationships including domestic partnerships, civil unions, and same-sex marriages. With new ways to legally recognize the existence of relationships emerges the problem of dealing with their dissolutions and subsequent claims for support.

Palimony became a term for alimony for support of an unmarried cohabitant, coined after a 1977 case involving the request for financial support from the unmarried long-term live-in girlfriend of actor Lee Marvin. Though the lawsuit was unsuccessful, the concept did become popular both in legal circles and popular culture.

In 2013, the Supreme Court declared section 3 of the Defense of Marriage Act to be unconstitutional. Previously this section had prevented federal agencies from treating same-sex marriages as marriages for benefits and federal tax purposes. The ruling in the *Windsor* case changed this, and because alimony is included as taxable income to the recipient spouse and tax deductible to the payor spouse, this will impact same-sex divorces as well.

Alimony Reform

Historically, permanent alimony was customarily granted by courts, but most states today have moved toward using a rehabilitative alimony framework, which is paid for a certain period of time and allows a spouse to financially recover after the divorce. Specifically this means taking college courses, acquiring marketable job skills, and reentering the workforce.

Most states have moved away from awarding permanent alimony except in limited circumstances. In 2011, Massachusetts was the last state to award long-term or permanent alimony but discontinued the practice with the passage of reform legislation. Now, as in many other states, alimony awards are based on the number of years a couple was married. Texas and Mississippi award alimony only to marriages of 10 years or more and only for a short period of time. Utah will not grant alimony past a time period equal to the duration of the marriage, and Kansas curbs its duration at 121 months.

Today, the conduct of the parties during the marriage is no longer a factor, and courts have moved away from using alimony as a punitive device against unfaithful husbands. Alimony serves as a tool of economic equity for the recipient, but not imprisonment for the payor.

John C. Linfield

See also: Liabilities

Further Reading

The American Bar Association Web site. "Family Law in the 50 States." Accessed October 16, 2013. http://www.americanbar.org/groups/family_law/resources/family_law_in_the_50 _states.html

Fox News.com. 2012. "A Look at Celebrity Child Support Payments." Accessed February 22, 2014. http://www.foxnews.com/us/2012/05/08/look-at-celebrity-child -support-payments/

Kindregan, Charles P. 2013. "Reforming Alimony: Massachusetts Reconsiders Postdivorce Spousal Support." *Suffolk Law Review* (Vol. 46, No. 13): 13–43.

Vernier, Chester G., and John B. Hurlbut. 1939. "The Historical Background of Alimony Law and Its Present Statutory Structure." *Law and Contemporary Problems* (Vol. 6, No. 2): 197–212.

Annuity

An annuity is a type of insurance contract that pays the owner a stream of payments for a fixed term or lifetime in return for an up-front payment or payments (Ferro, 2010). Annuities originated centuries ago in ancient Rome. The present forms of annuities are sold by insurance companies to individuals desiring a monthly payment during retirement. Annuities are a combination of an investment and an insurance product.

Although retirees in the United States receive annuity payments from the government in the form of Social Security, this benefit was not designed to provide 100 percent income replacement for all retirement expenses. The Social Security annuity gives workers a monthly payment during retirement, which is calculated based on the amount they contributed to their Social Security account during their working years. Since the Social Security payment is less than the amount earned while working, many individuals save and invest for retirement in order to supplement government Social Security payments.

An annuity is an income option for an individual or couple's retirement financial management. The annuity holder receives regular payments to create a secure retirement income stream. A major drawback for the annuity purchaser is that since annuity contracts depend on one's life expectancy, if the annuitant dies sooner than expected, he or she may forfeit thousands of nonrefundable dollars paid in advance to the insurance company.

Funding an Annuity

Before a person can receive annuity payments, the annuity must be funded. The money for the annuity may be paid to the insurance or investment company in a lump sum, through regular salary transfers, or in several lump sums. The insurer structures the payments so that ultimately, the insurance company pays out less in benefits than it earns in aggregate. Some policyholders may receive more in benefits than they paid in, while others receive less. After receiving the annuity payments, depending on the stipulations of the contract, the annuity policy issuer invests the funds in either fixed or variable securities (stocks, bonds, or other financial assets) in order to compound the returns of the initial contribution.

Types of Annuities

Annuities convert current or previous funds into income for the future. There are a myriad of contract, fee, and payment structures. The annuity product is extremely complex with hundreds of varieties.

The basic types of annuities are immediate and deferred. Within each of these categories there are fixed or variable payment options. The terms and conditions vary from contract to contract, and the documents are long and complicated, thus it is important for the annuity purchaser to review them to understand the benefits (Zook, 2013).

In the case of a single life annuity, the payment continues until the annuitant's death. A joint-life with last survivor annuity makes a payment to the annuitant and upon his or her death, the payments continue to a second designated party, usually the annuitant's spouse, until that person's death. This type of annuity typically carries a lower payment to the individual than a single life annuity because it is paid out over two lives (the individual annuitant and the spouse).

Immediate or Deferred Annuity

The two broad categories of annuities are immediate or deferred. Their aptly named categories describe the relationship between payment into the annuity and withdrawal.

The immediate annuity is the simplest type of annuity. Investors pay a lump sum and receive guaranteed monthly payments for life or for a predetermined time period. According to the Standard Insurance Annuity Answer Booklet, "The U.S. Tax Code dictates that every annuity payment is a combination of return of principal (is not taxed) and payout of income (is taxed at normal-income rates)." This spreads tax obligations out over time.

A deferred annuity has two phases, accumulation and distribution. Accumulation is the time period during which the annuity is funded, frequently through salary transfers. While accumulating, the funds in the annuity grow tax free and may be invested in a variety of financial assets. Upon the withdrawal phase the annuitant can take income monthly or in a one-time lump sum payment.

Fixed, Variable, and Equity Index Annuities

Within each broad type of annuity, immediate and deferred, there are a variety of categories. Fixed, variable, and equity index annuities describe how payments are calculated and in what type of assets the annuity funds are invested.

A risk-adverse individual might choose a fixed annuity. The payout guarantees a fixed minimum payment, set at the time the annuity is purchased. The disadvantage with this type of contract is that in periods of high inflation, the payment does not increase. There are also fixed-rate annuities in which the interest rate paid on the annuity payment is set at purchase and is guaranteed not to fall below a minimum level.

Variable annuities are riskier than fixed. The annuity funds are invested in mutual funds, usually selected by the annuitant with the hope of growing the annuity funds by investing in equities, which have a history of higher growth rates than cash assets. The risk is that at withdrawal equity markets may decline, thereby reducing the funds available for payout. The annuitant may choose a minimum payment option for additional security.

Equity index annuities are a combination of fixed and variable annuities. The funds are invested in a broad stock market index such as the Standard & Poor's 500 (S&P 500), and the annuity value is tied to the growth of the index. Minimum payouts are set and may be increased based on the growth of the benchmark stock index.

Annuity Considerations

Gustavo Ferro (Ferro, 2010) cautions that purchasing an annuity entails weighing the possibility of losing one's funds due to early death against that of outliving one's retirement savings. In order to counteract the possibility of dying soon after annuity payments begin, there are contracts that guarantee a minimum number of payments.

Another consideration for an annuity purchaser is the complexity of the annuity product itself. According to Hube (Hube, 2011) in *Barron's* magazine, there are approximately 1,600 types of annuity products. In addition to the basic annuity structures listed above, there are countless variations in structure including those with tax advantages and with interest rate, inflation, and investment risk protections. The magnitude of differing annuity products makes the decision to purchase an annuity cumbersome and confusing.

The security of the annuity is of prime concern. Since the purchaser is depending on the financial strength of the issuing company to provide lifetime income, one must be certain that the issuer of the contract is in stable financial condition. Rating agencies such as A. M. Best and Standard & Poor's rate the stability of insurance companies, according to *Consumer Reports Money Advisor* (2011).

The fees and commissions can be quite high. Thus, the annuity purchaser needs to understand in what way and for how much the issuer is being compensated as well as any ongoing fees.

Recently, discount investment brokers such as Vanguard and Fidelity entered the annuity marketplace with lower cost and higher benefit annuity options. Without a direct sales force, compensated solely through commissions, a discount broker may offer more economical annuity options for a retiree.

If annuity payments are not tied to inflation, the annuitant runs the risk of a loss in purchasing power due to increases in the inflation rate. If one receives $750 per month at the outset of retirement and inflation increases at the historical rate of 3 percent per year, in 20 years, the $750 per month will only have the purchasing power of $407 per month. Retirees without an inflation increase in their annuity payment lose close to half of the value of their payment during the next 20 years, according to the inflation calculator at Vertex42.com.

As Americans live longer, there is a growing need for a product that gives lifetime monthly income. The annuity is an important option for retirees to fund their future, although, as with any financial product, when choosing an annuity care, research, and attention to fees are important to make sure the purchaser receives the greatest income payment for the annuity cost.

Barbara Friedberg

See also: Bonds; Index Mutual Funds; Investing; Mutual Funds and Exchange-Traded Funds; Risk; Social Security; Stocks

Further Reading

Annuity Answer Booklet—The Standard, accessed April 28, 2013, http://www.standard.com/annuities/eforms/11334.pdf

"Are Longevity Annuities for You?" April, 2011. *Consumer Reports Money Advisor.*

Ferro, Gustavo. 2010. "Annuities: An Overview of the Main Issues." *The IUP Journal of Risk & Insurance* (Vol. VII, No. 4): 18–37.

Hube, Karen. 2011. "Special Report—Retirement: With Their Steady Income Payments, Annuities Are Suddenly Hot." *Barron's Magazine* (June 20). http://online.barrons.com/article/SB50001424053111904472004576392401608661120.html#articleTabs_article%3D1

"Inflation Calculator." *Vertex42,* accessed April 28, 2013, http://www.vertex42.com/Calculators/inflation-calculator.html

Zook, Jack. 2013. "Annuities Offer Retirees Money Like Clockwork." *Pennsylvania CPA Journal* (January): 1.

Asset Allocation

Asset allocation is widely considered the first step in investment portfolio management. Investing is a money management strategy to increase the investor's long-term financial wealth. Investors are assumed to desire the largest financial return on their funds for the least amount of risk. Asset allocation is designed to smooth out the volatility or risk of a portfolio while maximizing investors' returns. Diversification among asset classes reduces an investment portfolio's risk. Asset allocation is a way to create a diversified investment portfolio.

An asset allocation represents the investor's choice of broad asset classes and the percentages distributed across the categories. This decision divides total investable funds by percent into specific investment categories.

An asset class refers to the categorization of financial investable assets. The most used asset classes include stocks, bonds, and cash equivalents. A stock asset class contains individual stocks, groups of stocks combined and sold as mutual funds, as well as many additional categorizations within the broad stock category. The cash asset class refers to bank savings accounts, money market mutual funds, and short-term U.S. government Treasury bills. There are many varieties of bonds for that particular asset class. Governments, municipalities, and corporations issue bonds for this class. Bond mutual funds are also included. The bond category is also considered the fixed income asset class. Fixed income refers to a financial asset such as a bond or certificate of deposit, which pays the holder a regular interest or dividend payment.

The asset allocation concept is derived from the seminal work of Harry Markowitz, founder of modern portfolio theory (Markowitz,1952). The asset allocation decision is grounded in a study of observed historical asset class returns and volatility. According to Davis et al., from January 1926 through June 2012 the rolling 10-year annualized geometric returns of the broad U.S. stock market averaged 10 percent (Davis et al., 2012). That stellar return hides shorter periods of low and even negative stock market returns. The benefit of asset allocation is that by combining several less correlated asset classes into an investment portfolio, when one component underperforms, the other asset classes serve to reduce the losses and may increase or hold steady the portfolio's total value.

How to Create an Asset Allocation

There are two parts to the asset allocation decision. Part one is an assessment of the investor's individual risk tolerance. Generally, although not always, a retiree who is older may be more conservative or risk averse. This is because if the value of a retiree's portfolio goes down, he doesn't have a long time or a long working life to earn back the loss in value. Younger individuals may be more aggressive or risk tolerant for the opposite reason. If a 30-year-old investor has a loss in her investment portfolio value, she has many years to recoup that loss. Although older individuals may be more conservative investors than younger folks, this is not always the case. Some 30-year-olds can't tolerate the volatility of an aggressive portfolio and do not want to see even a moderate decline in the value of the investments. Those individuals are both young and conservative investors. And of course, the opposite holds true as well. There are aggressive investors who are older and can tolerate the ups and downs in value of their investments.

There are many publicly available measures to help the investor ascertain his or her personal risk tolerance. A popular risk quiz was published in *The Wall Street Journal* in 1998 and reprinted in *Investments* (Bodie et al., 2011).Those with a higher risk tolerance and who are more willing to experience ups and downs in the value of their investments will allocate a greater percentage of their total investable assets to riskier investments. Stocks and stock mutual funds are widely considered riskier because although they historically offered a higher return, there is an accompanying chance of greater losses in the stock investments. The investors with less tolerance for risk will stick to less volatile asset classes such as cash equivalents and bonds. For example, older investors and less risk-tolerant investors might allocate a greater percentage of assets to bonds and cash investments and less to stock investments.

The second part of the asset allocation decision includes choosing which financial assets to include in each broad category. For example, in the stock asset class, the investor might choose individual stocks, actively managed stock mutual funds, or passively managed stock index funds. Simply, a stock is a part ownership in a company. For example, if Matthew buys 10 shares of Apple stock he owns a tiny portion of the company. A mutual fund is simply a combination of many individual stocks, bonds, or both, managed by a company. The mutual fund allows the small investor access to many stocks and/or bonds for a relatively low fee.

The bond category might include investments in individual bonds, bond mutual funds, or bond exchange-traded funds. A bond is a loan to a company or government. In exchange for the loan, the bond holder receives periodic interest payments. A bond mutual fund contains only bonds. An exchange-traded fund is similar to a mutual fund. The distinctions between a mutual fund and an exchange-traded fund are discussed fully in another entry.

An investor's asset allocation may be as simple as holding two mutual funds in an investment portfolio. An example of a two-fund asset allocation might include one all-world international stock index mutual fund for the equity (or stock) portion of the portfolio. This is simply a fund that buys a small amount of the stock of many different companies from the United States and across the globe. This gives the investor an opportunity to own lots of stock investments for a small amount of money.

The second mutual fund in this simple asset allocation might be a diversified bond fund. Similar to the stock mutual fund, this bond fund would buy a few bonds from many individual companies and may even include some government bonds as well. For example, an investor might have 60 percent of his or her investments in stock-type investments and 40 percent in fixed investments (bonds and cash).

The percentages in each portion are determined by the investor's age and risk tolerance. Other investors divide the asset allocation decision into more complicated asset classes and may include percentages in small, medium, and large company stock mutual funds or other types of categories. International securities and alternative investments such as real estate and commodities may also be included in more sophisticated asset allocation decisions.

Rebalancing

In deciding on their personal asset allocation percentages, investors review the historical asset class performance and adjust the expected future returns and volatility, based on economic projections and personal judgments. In general, after making the asset allocation decision, investors check the percentages in each category annually to ensure the changes in value of the financial assets have not deviated significantly from the original asset allocation decision.

The rebalancing decision returns asset class percentages to their original proportions. For example, a conservative investor might choose an asset allocation of 50 percent in an international stock mutual fund and 50 percent in a diversified bond mutual fund. At the end of one year, if the international stock markets outperformed the bond markets and the investor's stock holdings were 60 percent and bond investments were only 40 percent of the overall total, then the investor would need to sell enough of the stock investments and buy enough of the bond investments to return to the previously determined 50 percent amount in each of the asset classes.

Tactical Asset Allocation

Traditional asset allocation advocates maintain a consistent asset allocation for years and adjust when the investor ages and approaches retirement or the risk profile changes. Historically, the asset allocation decision was a "set it and forget it approach." Recently, changes in the research introduced the concept of "tactical asset allocation." This approach is an answer to the problem of long periods of subpar performance of certain asset classes and an attempt to boost investment returns. Tactical asset allocation adjusts the percentages allocated to specific asset classes based on market valuation or other economic factors.

Eighty-one percent of respondents to the Financial Planning Association's (FPA) "Trends in Investing" special report indicated that they regularly reevaluate the asset allocation decision (Kitces, 2012). Kitces reported that planners made tactical asset allocation decisions two times per year, on average. This is decidedly more frequent than the traditional age- and risk-based adjustments.

A new class of mutual funds, target date mutual funds, uses an asset allocation–age-based approach to adjust the asset allocation of the mutual funds based on an investor's age, with more equities for the younger investor, transitioning to more fixed investment percentages as the investor reaches retirement age. The target date funds use the asset allocation research along with the investor's age to provide a comprehensive financial planning product.

In summary, the asset allocation decision is an investment method to reduce the volatility in an investor's portfolio by investing in diverse classes of investment assets. Lower correlation between asset classes enables an opportunity for higher investment returns with less risk.

Barbara Friedberg

See also: Bonds; Index Mutual Funds; Investing; Mutual Funds and Exchange-Traded Funds; Risk; Stocks

Further Reading

Bodie, Zvi, Alex Kane, and Alan J. Marcus. 2011. *Investments*. New York: McGraw-Hill/Irwin, 166–167.

Davis, Joseph, Roger Aliaga-Diaz, and Charles J. Thomas. October, 2012. "Forecasting Stock Returns: What Signals Matter and What Do They Say Now?" *Vanguard Research.* https://personal.vanguard.com/pdf/s338.pdf

Kitces, Michael E. 2012. "The Rise of Tactical Asset Allocation." *Journal of Financial Planning* (June): 28–29.

Markowitz, Harry. 1952. "Portfolio Selection." *Journal of Finance* (March 1): 77–91.

Banking

Banking is the financial activity of protecting and storing capital for individuals and institutions. The bank lends that capital to others for a profit. Depositors earn interest on their deposits, and the banks use the depositors' funds to make loans to borrowers who use the funds to buy homes, expand businesses, or for a variety of personal uses.

Banks profit from the difference between the interest paid on deposits and the interest payments received from borrowers, called the "interest rate spread." For example, if the bank pays the depositor 1 percent interest on deposits and charges borrowers 5 percent interest, the bank's profit or spread is 4 percent. Banks also make money selling investment products and services.

Banking participants began as banks, savings and loan mutual companies, and credit unions and grew to include credit card companies, large financial conglomerates, investment brokerage companies, and some large retail institutions. Initially, banking occurred at a bricks-and-mortar location that handled all transactions. Today, Internet, mobile, electronic, home, and automatic teller machine (ATM) financial management is surpassing traditional banking methods. Banking methods, locations, services, and products are evolving at a rapid rate.

History

Banking began centuries ago in the United States with no regulation or oversight. Anyone could open a bank, take in deposits, and make loans. By 1920, the United States was home to almost 30,000 banks. At that time there were more banks in the United States than in the rest of the world combined. After the Great Depression and an onslaught of bank failures, the Federal Reserve Bank created the Federal Deposit Insurance Corporation (FDIC) in an attempt to reduce bank failures and protect consumers' deposits. Today, the Federal Deposit Insurance Corporation insures every depositor up to $250,000 per insured bank.

Historically, banks operated exclusively within a particular state and could not expand across state lines. In 1994 laws were passed to enable interstate banking. The Riegle-Neal Interstate Banking and Branching Efficiency Act of 1994 improved convenience and product availability for consumers and completely reshaped the banking industry in the United States.

Payment Services

Traditional banking services include checking or demand deposits. Designed as a method to pay bills, a checking account is usually a no-interest deposit account where funds are transferred in and out to meet financial obligations. Electronic bill payment and check deposits are replacing paper check payments in popularity. Automatic teller machines (ATM) add to the convenience of depositing funds and withdrawing cash. A debit card, issued by the bank, gives consumers ready access to their bank funds and can be used at ATM machines as well as to make purchases from merchants.

Fees are occasionally charged on checking accounts. Some checking accounts pay depositors interest if they agree to maintain a minimum level of cash in the account, such as $2,500 or more.

Savings

Savings accounts, or time deposits, pay interest on customers' deposits and are useful for protecting and growing cash for the future. Consumers deposit funds for easy access at a later date. Interest is paid on savings accounts. Banks may charge fees for these accounts if deposits fall below a prespecified amount. Banks offer certificates of deposit to consumers willing to tie up their funds for longer periods of time in exchange for higher interest payments.

Borrowing

At some point, most consumers need to borrow funds for a major purchase. Vehicle and home mortgage loans are among the most common types of loans. Consumers may also borrow personal loans to fund expenses such as home improvements. Businesses borrow to fund start-up and expansion costs.

In the past, banks were a major source of funding for mortgage, business, and personal loans. Consumers would apply for a loan, provide information about their work and credit history, and if they were deemed reliable, the bank would loan the funds. After lending the money, the bank serviced the loan (collected the payments) until it was paid off. Today, it is common for banks to immediately sell their loans to other financial market participants.

Supplementary Financial Services

The differences between banks, credit unions, savings and loan mutual companies, credit card companies, investment brokerage companies, insurance companies, and other financial management organizations are blurred as additional financial services are offered.

Over time, banks sought new ways to serve customers and increase their profits by offering investment and insurance products. The credit card, investment brokerage, insurance, and other financial companies now offer banking services as well. Banks and financial companies offer investment products, insurance services, and a variety of accounts in which to access these additional offerings.

Specialized retirement accounts such as Individual Retirement Accounts (IRAs), Roth IRAs (the newer form of the IRA, which allows the account holder to withdraw funds from the account during retirement without paying any tax), along with educational savings accounts, commonly known as 529 Savings plans, once the purview of investment brokers, are found in banking institutions as well.

Quasi-Banking Entities

PayPal and peer-to-peer or social lending are two banking-related services that fill a banking need with nontraditional quasi-banking entities. PayPal provides payment transfer services for electronic money transfers. Used to pay merchants and individuals online, this nonbank entity also links individuals' credit card and bank accounts to offer a myriad of payment transfer options.

Customers have alternative borrowing and lending options through social lending or peer-to-peer (PTP) networks. Peer-to-peer or social lending connects individuals with funds to lend with borrowers in need of small- to medium-sized loans. Lenders receive interest payments and borrowers get funded by their peers.

Banking Trends

Banking began as a location-specific service industry confined to operations during weekday business hours. As society evolved into an Internet, mobile, global, and electronic society, time-pressed consumers demanded around-the-clock access to their financial transactions. As the number of bank, savings and loan, and credit union branches shrank, their business hours expanded, frequently including weekends in addition to the traditional Monday through Friday hours.

Banking access continues to expand with the advent of Internet-only banks and banking services offered by credit card companies, investment brokers, and large retail conglomerates. Banking today is location independent with options spanning a multitude of providers. Fees range from free to fee-for-service structures. Returns and interest rates vary by institution and type of service. Banking from home has overtaken branch banking as consumers electronically pay bills and transfer funds. Check writing is rapidly being replaced by online bill payment. Mobile devices allow for remote bank deposits by simply scanning a check and sending it straight to the financial institution.

Quasi-banking further expanded along with the growth of electronic commerce (e-commerce) and nontraditional banking and borrowing options including PayPal payment systems, peer-to-peer lending, and prepaid debit cards. The banking industry is rapidly growing and changing to meet the needs of a demanding and evolving public.

Barbara Friedberg

See also: Certificate of Deposit; Checking Account; Federal Reserve Bank; Interest Income and Payments; Interest Rates; Investing; Loans; Retirement Accounts; Money Market Account; Social Lending or Peer-to-Peer Lending

Further Reading

Gordon, John Steele. 2008. "A Short Banking History of the United States." *The Wall Street Journal*. http://online.wsj.com/article/SB122360636585322023.html
Neely, Michelle Clark. 1994. "Going Interstate: A New Dawn for U.S. Banking." *The Regional Economist*. http://www.stlouisfed.org/publications/re/articles/?id=1885
Tinnila, Markku. 2012. "Impact of Future Trends on Banking Services." *Journal of Internet Banking and Commerce* Vol. 17, No. 2 (August): 1–15.

Bankruptcy

Bankruptcy is a legal process that allows both individuals and businesses that can no longer pay their bills to seek protection from their creditors. There are several types of bankruptcy with varying methods of debt settlement and repayment. Often referred to as an economic fresh start, bankruptcy is granted authority from the U.S. Constitution, Article I, Section 8, which authorizes Congress to enact "uniform Laws on the subject of Bankruptcies."

All individual consumers filing for bankruptcy must first undergo credit counseling within six months before filing their bankruptcy petition with an approved nonprofit budget and credit counseling agency. Also, before the court will grant the discharge of the debt all consumer debtors must complete a financial management instructional course from an approved provider.

History of Bankruptcy

In medieval Europe when merchants or tradespeople failed to pay their bills, they were deemed *banca rotta* or broken bench, and the moneylender they owed would literally come and destroy their means of livelihood. Treatment of debtors could often be harsh. In England this included imprisonment and in extreme cases even death (Tabb, 1995).

As the Founding Fathers were drafting the Constitution, a provision was made for bankruptcy. Yet not until 1898 was a long-term and comprehensive bankruptcy code passed. It was also the first time that bankruptcy law became more favorable to the debtor, as previous laws were more creditor focused.

The most recent update to the bankruptcy law was the passage of the Bankruptcy Abuse Prevention and Consumer Protection Act of 2005, also known as BAPCPA.

Bankruptcy Process

Bankruptcy is governed by federal law and therefore the process is administered in federal courts and cannot be filed in a state court. An individual or business that files a case in bankruptcy court is referred to as a debtor. The creditors are those to whom money is owed. The bankruptcy court assigns a trustee to administer the bankruptcy estate created by the filing of the petition. The trustee's responsibilities include reviewing the paperwork submitted to the court by the debtor and bringing actions against creditors or the debtor to recover the property of the bankruptcy estate.

In a chapter 7 bankruptcy, the trustee liquidates the property of the estate and repays what is available to creditors. In chapters 12 and 13, the trustee will oversee the debtor's repayment plan by actually receiving monthly payments from the debtor and then forwarding those payments to creditors. The judge in a bankruptcy court may hear and decide any matter related to a bankruptcy case; however, much of the bankruptcy process is administrative and a debtor's involvement with the judge is usually very limited.

Bankruptcy Chapters

The different types of bankruptcy that individuals and businesses can file take their names from the actual bankruptcy code itself, which appears in Title 11 of the United States Code.

Chapter 7 bankruptcy is also known as the liquidation bankruptcy. The reason is that the debtor's nonexempt (debtors are allowed to keep some items) assets are collected and sold by the trustee. The cash proceeds are then used to repay the creditors. Upon the completion of the case debtors receive discharge and forgiveness of their debts under chapter 7, with certain exceptions that are prohibited from discharge, such taxes, child support, and student loans. Forgiveness means that certain debts do not need to be repaid. Consumer debtors are required to complete a financial analysis, referred to as a means test, to determine based on their income if it is more appropriate for them to file a chapter 13 bankruptcy. Most bankruptcies filed in the United States are chapter 7 cases.

Chapter 11 bankruptcy is also known as the rehabilitation bankruptcy. Debtors can use this chapter to reorganize their debts while continuing to operate their business. The vast majority of chapter 11 cases are filed by businesses; however, higher income individuals may use this chapter also. Debtors, often working with their creditors who will form a creditor committee, will create a reorganization plan in which they repay either all or part of their debts. Upon completion of the case, the debtor receives discharge and forgiveness for any remaining debts, with certain exceptions that are prohibited from discharge.

Chapter 12 is the chapter in bankruptcy specifically designed for family farmers and fishermen. This chapter is similar to chapter 13, except it allows for higher debt levels and more flexibility regarding when payments can be made to the courts, thereby making allowances for harvest schedules. In chapter 12, debtors may keep their property and not be forced to liquidate it. They will repay all or part of their debts by making payments over a three- to five-year period through the court-appointed trustee. Upon the completion of the case debtors receive a discharge and forgiveness of their remaining debts, with certain exceptions that are prohibited from discharge.

Chapter 13 is also known as the wage-earners bankruptcy. Debtors can use this chapter to reorganize their debts, as long as they can demonstrate to the court that they have a regular income. Also, to be eligible for chapter 13, a debtor may not have more than a certain amount of debt, as set forth in the bankruptcy code. In a chapter 13 case, debtors may keep their property and not be forced to liquidate it. They will repay all or part of their debts by making payments over three to five years through the court-appointed trustee. Upon the completion of the case the debtor receives a discharge and forgiveness of the remaining debts, with certain exceptions that are prohibited from discharge.

Bankruptcy Considerations

The U.S. population continues to see growth in outstanding consumer credit levels while the national savings rate has declined to less than 3 percent per year. Each year over one million Americans file bankruptcy. Before filing bankruptcy, each of these consumers must weigh both the pros and cons of this important decision.

There are advantages to filing for bankruptcy protection. The most notable is the economic fresh start given to debtors after receiving their discharge. The idea is that debtors unburdened by unmanageable debt can become productive and contributing members of the economy. Also, with the filing of the bankruptcy petition all collection efforts must stop, and individuals cannot be fired from a job because they have filed for bankruptcy.

Conversely, there are disadvantages to filing a bankruptcy. Because bankruptcy filings are public record, debtors may find that they have to disclose this information when applying for professional licenses or credit for several years after they have filed. The information will also show on their credit reports for up to 10 years. This can impact consumers' future finances and the cost of credit. In spite of this disadvantage, a study by Purdue University found that about one-third of consumers who filed for bankruptcy had obtained new credit within three years of filing and by the fifth year one-half had obtained credit even with the negative information on the credit report.

John C. Linfield

See also: Consumer Credit/Debt, Credit Card; Debt Collection; Debt/Credit Counseling; Liabilities; Loans

Further Reading

American Bankruptcy Institute Web site. "ABI Consumer Center." Accessed October 15, 2013. http://consumer.abi.org/consumers.

American Bar Association Web site. "Bankruptcy." Accessed October 15, 2013. http://www.americanbar.org/groups/public_education/resources/law_issues_for_consumers/bankruptcypros.html.

Elias, Stephen, and Bayer, Leon. 2013. *The New Bankruptcy: Will It Work for You?* Berkeley, CA: Nolo Press.

Tabb, Charles Jordan. (1995). "The History of the Bankruptcy Laws in the United States." *American Bankruptcy Institute Law Review* (Vol. III, No. 5): 5–51.

United States Courts Web site. "Bankruptcy Basics." Accessed October 15, 2013. http://www.uscourts.gov/FederalCourts/Bankruptcy.aspx.

Behavioral Economics *(see Behavioral Finance)*

Behavioral Finance

An encyclopedia of personal finance and money management would be incomplete without a discussion of behavioral finance. This relatively new discipline, introduced in 1979 with the groundbreaking work of Daniel Kahneman and Amos Tversky, challenges the belief that human behavior is rational. When making financial decisions, the individual is subject to irrational and counterproductive decision making. Behavioral finance pinpoints these human irrationalities and exposes them to the light.

Since its inception, the integration of finance and psychology has illuminated multiple examples of deleterious financial decisions attributed to psychological mental errors. Prospect theory, as introduced by Kahneman and Tversky (1979), describes how individuals making economic decisions are irrational. One would expect that wins and losses would produce a similar level of emotion, with a win causing a positive emotion and a loss causing the opposite negative emotion. Actually, we hate to lose more than we like to win. In other words, we feel losses more deeply than we feel the pleasure of a win.

Further, an element of prospect theory, framing, states that an individual's decision making is impacted by how the event is presented, while ignoring rational evidence. Framing refers to the context of the event. Individuals assess gains and losses differently depending on how the choices are explained or framed. If the identical scenario is explained in two ways, one in terms of gains and the other in terms of losses, an individual would choose the former. For example, a rational individual would view receiving $50 in the same way as getting $100 and then losing $50. The net result, $50, is the same.

Yet, prospect theory shows losses are more potent than wins and we feel worse in the second scenario of receiving $100 and losing $50 than we do in the first of gaining $50. Framing makes one individual view a $100,000 per year salary as great, until she finds out her co-worker is making $125,000. After she discovers her co-worker is earning $25,000 more than she is, she is dissatisfied with her salary and feels underpaid. The salary remained the same, but how the $100,000 was framed changed.

Prospect theory is sometimes called loss-aversion theory and further explains how an investor is influenced by how a scenario is framed. Loss aversion, as its name implies, suggests that investors don't like to lose money.

Assume an investor is offered the same exact investment choice by two different advisors. Advisor one tells the person that an investment returned 6 percent over the last five years. The second advisor states that the investment generated above-average returns over the last 10 years but has been declining more recently. Research demonstrates that the investor is more likely to invest with advisor one, who expressed the return in positive terms (6 percent return), over advisor two, who expressed the return as declining. In simple terms, investors dislike losses more than they appreciate gains.

Framing goes hand in hand with prospect theory and states that individuals respond to the same information differently depending upon how it is explained or framed. Offer a participant a coin toss with a payoff of $50 for tails. Compare that with a $50 gift that comes with the chance of a $50 loss for a coin toss landing on heads. It is the exact same payoff, yet this popular experiment demonstrates that individuals are more likely to take the second option because it describes the second scenario in less risky terms.

The herd instinct is found in a variety of financial situations. Following the crowd is evidenced when investors jump into a well-performing mutual fund after a big gain, prompting these investors to buy near the top. On the other side, the herd mentality harms investors as they wait to sell after a large market decline, thereby selling at the bottom. The herd mentality was recently demonstrated in the dot-com bust at the beginning of the century when investors followed the crowd and bid up the prices of technology stocks to stratospheric levels.

Mental accounting prompts individuals to treat money from different sources in different ways. Splurge with a tax return and spend wisely with one's paycheck. Isn't the tax return simply part of the employee's paycheck being returned? When buying a $25,000 new car, mental accounting might cause the consumer to take the $300 paint coating with the idea that it's a small percentage of the total purchase price. Actually, that $300 is real money that could be allocated toward retirement savings, groceries, or rent.

The recency effect, forecasting error, or memory bias causes individuals to weight recent events more heavily than those further in the past. For example, the recent 2007–2008 subprime mortgage crisis caused lenders to become overly strict in issuing mortgages. This contrasts with the earlier lax mortgage standards that put unqualified buyers into real estate. The mortgage loan companies, overreacting to the ensuing foreclosures, developed overly stringent loan qualification standards. The lenders feared defaults and thus made it extremely difficult for even the most qualified borrowers to secure a loan. The recency effect impacts individuals as well as institutions. Consider investors scared to invest in the stock market after a decline in value or prospective homeowners afraid to buy a home after a decline in housing prices.

The overconfidence behavioral finance error states that individuals overestimate their own beliefs or forecasts. In a well-known Swedish survey by Ola Svenson (1981), 90 percent of drivers rated themselves as better than average drivers. In financial terms this bias influences consumers to make financial decisions that are not founded on facts. Consider supermarket shoppers who only purchase brand-name items in lieu of generic. These brand-loyal consumers discount research stating that generic products are usually equal in quality to brand-name goods. Overconfidence also causes investors to overtrade, thereby lowering their investment returns.

The getting even behavioral bias describes investors who hold on to losing investments. Their approach is to sell the investment when the price rises to the original purchase price. The fallacy in this thinking keeps an investor from selling at a loss and reinvesting the proceeds into another investment with greater future prospects.

There are many additional examples of behavioral finance errors. Understanding the field of behavioral finance gives the consumer information to avoid making ill-advised financial decisions. By understanding unhelpful behavioral mental processing errors, the citizen is a better consumer and investor.

Barbara Friedberg

See also: Banking; Investing; Loans; Stock Market; Year 1987: Stock Market Crash; Year 2000: Bursting of the Dot-Com Technology Bubble

Further Reading

Bodie, Zvi, Alex Kane, and Alan J. Marcus. 2011. *Investments*. New York: McGraw-Hill/ Irwin, 382–387.

Kahneman, Daniel, and Aaron Tversky. 1979. "Prospect Theory: An Analysis of Decision Under Risk." *Econometrica* (47): 263–91.

Shiller, Robert J. Web site. "Workshop in Behavioral Finance." Accessed on August 13, 2013. http://www.econ.yale.edu/~shiller/behfin/

Svenson, Ola. 1981. "Are We All Less Risky and More Skillful Than Our Fellow Drivers?" *Acta Psychologica* (47): 143–148. http://heatherlench.com/wp-content/uploads/2008/07/svenson.pdf

Bitcoin *(see Digital Currency)*

Bonds

Bonds are financial instruments issued by a company, municipality, or government in order to raise capital for their financing needs. Bonds can be seen as a loan owed by an issuing entity (bond issuer) to the lenders (bondholders) with a set payment schedule. Bonds are classified as fixed income investments in the investing community, meaning they usually pay an interest payment (coupon) that is the same, or fixed, throughout the life of the bond.

As a result, the bondholders receive periodic interest payments at predetermined intervals over the life of the bond, usually once or twice per year. The interest payments are determined by the coupon rate at issue and are paid if a bond is held to the end of its issued life. Upon maturity of the bond, the principal value is repaid along with the final interest or coupon payment. For example, a semiannual 10-year Treasury bond of $1,000 par value issued with a 3 percent coupon rate has interest payments of $15 (3% × 1000 × 1/2) paid twice per year over a period of 10 years. At maturity, that is, at the end of 10 years, the principal of $1,000 is repaid along with the final $15 coupon payment.

Bonds are secured by the assets of the bond issuer and are said to be in default if the issuer misses a payment. In case the bond issuer files for bankruptcy, bondholders as creditors have a right of lien on the bond issuer's assets.

Factors Affecting Bonds

The bond price is dependent on the coupon rate, the time to maturity, the credit quality of the issuer, and the current level of interest rates. When interest rates increase, bond prices fall and when interest rates decrease, bond prices increase. The sensitivity in the price of a bond to changes in the interest rates is called duration. For example, when interest rates rise, a bond with duration of five years will fall in price more than a bond with similar characteristics but with duration of three years.

A bond with a higher default risk or lower credit rating is forced to pay a higher interest rate in order to compensate for its additional risk. Longer-term bonds usually pay higher interest rates than shorter-term bonds, holding all other factors steady. This is because the purchaser must wait a longer time to receive the return of the principal, and with time comes uncertainty about the future.

Classification of Bonds

Bonds can be classified based on maturity, nature of interest payments, type of issuing entity, and credit characteristics. Bonds that are issued with a fixed coupon rate are called fixed-rate bonds, and bonds that have a coupon rate tied to a market-based interest rate like LIBOR (London Interbank Offered Rate) are called floating rate bonds. Fixed coupon rate bonds pay the same coupon or interest payment for the life of the bond, whereas a floating rate bond with a coupon of LIBOR + 100 basis points (bps) (1% = 100 basis points) is considered a floating rate bond, and the difference between coupon and the reference market rate (LIBOR in this example) is referred to as spread. The above bond is said to have 100 bps spread over LIBOR.

Bonds are issued by various entities including corporations, governments, municipalities, and educational institutions. Government-entity–issued bonds are classified as Treasury and municipal bonds. Corporate bonds are issued by companies and corporations.

Treasury bonds are the bonds issued by the U.S. government. They are marketable securities and are classified as Treasury bills (maturity of less than one year), Treasury notes (maturity between one and 10 years), and Treasury bonds (maturity of over 10 years). Securities issued by national governments (other than the United States) are referred to as sovereign bonds.

Municipal bonds are bonds issued by states, municipalities, and local government agencies to meet their funding needs and are secured by specified revenues coming from taxes or project-based revenues. Municipal bond interest payments are generally tax-exempt and this provides a tax advantage to the investors. Most municipal bonds have lower interest rates than corporate bonds.

One might think that a municipal bond secured by a city's revenues would be quite safe. Unfortunately, if a city has financial troubles, the bondholders can suffer with loss of principal or missed coupon payments. Recently Detroit, Michigan, has been experiencing deep financial difficulties and their bondholders are plagued with uncertain coupon payments and redemptions.

Corporate bonds are the bonds issued by corporations and are considered riskier than Treasury and municipal bonds. As a result, the yield on these bonds is greater than that of the Treasuries. The difference is referred to as spread over Treasuries. The spread is determined by the credit quality of the issuer, a measure of the ability of the issuer to meet the payment obligations.

Credit rating agencies like Standard & Poor's and Moody's rate the bond universe based on the quality of the issuer and these form the basis for the above classifications. For example, bonds that are rated between AAA and BBB are considered investment grade with AAA being the highest credit quality. These bonds generally have higher yields and lower risk of default. Bonds that are rated BB and lower are considered high-yield bonds (also known as junk bonds). Bonds that are rated C or below are considered to have very high default risk.

Although most bonds make coupon (interest) payments throughout the life of the bond, some bonds are issued without ongoing coupon payments. These bonds are called zero coupon bonds and are sold at a discount to their final maturity value. The interest rate is calculated using the difference between the discounted purchase price and the final maturity face value of the bond. Consider a five-year zero coupon bond bought for $8,000 and redeemed in five years at maturity for $10,000. The $2,000 difference between purchase and redemption values is equal to a 4.56 percent yield or interest rate.

What Is the Size of the U.S. Fixed Income Universe?

Other classifications of bonds include mortgage-related debt, money market funds, and asset-backed securities. According to the Securities Industry and Financial Markets Association (SIFMA), as of June 2013, the total outstanding debt financed with U.S. bonds is $38.7 trillion consisting of $11.3 trillion in Treasuries, $9.4 trillion in corporate debt, $8.1 trillion in mortgage-related debt, $3.7 trillion in municipal bonds, $2.5 trillion in money market funds, $2.1 trillion in federal agency securities, and $1.6 trillion in asset-backed securities.

How and Why Do Investors Buy Bonds?

Bonds are not traded on an exchange and investors are not able to buy and sell them through a broker as easily as equities (stocks). Many individual investors invest in the bond markets by investing in bond mutual funds or bond exchange-traded funds (ETFs). Some large individual investors and institutional investors buy individual bonds directly in their portfolios.

Bonds provide diversification to an all-equity portfolio because of their lower risk compared to equities. With their periodic interest payments, bonds are a source of regular income in a portfolio and hence are preferred by many investors.

Surya Mrunalini Pisapati

See also: Asset Allocation; Capital Gains and Capital Losses; Compound Interest/Return; Debt; Interest Income and Payments; Investing

Further Reading

Fabozzi, Frank J. 2007. *Fixed Income Analysis (CFA Institute Investment Series)*. John Wiley & Sons: 1–92.

Budget

A budget is the document that categorizes income received into spending, saving, and investing categories. Individuals, organizations, governments, and corporations all use budgets to monitor their income and expenses. The budget creation process is similar for all entities and involves several discrete stages.

The Consumer Budget

Creating a budget or spending plan may be the consumer's most important money management activity. A budget is the spending plan that integrates the consumer's income and expenses and earmarks funds for the important spending, saving, and investing categories. The initial budget is created by tracking and analyzing spending habits so the individual can accurately predict the amounts for each category. After the budget is created and expenses are recorded, the consumer compares spending with the budgeted amounts for each section. Adjustments are made so that the spending plan is realistic and meets the targeted spending and saving classifications.

Pre-Budget: Track Expenses

It's helpful to keep track of one's expenses for a few weeks to accurately develop a budget, otherwise the budget category estimates will likely be inaccurate.

Maya, a new college graduate, gets her first job and wants to create a budget. After tracking her expenses for a few weeks she finds her $2,700 per month salary doesn't last very long. Taxes, including federal, state, Social Security, and Medicare taxes, eat up $700, leaving $2,000 to pay rent, food, utilities, car payment, gas, entertainment, phone, eating out, charity, saving, clothes, and investing for the future.

Maya spent $750 on rent and utilities. She paid $500 for groceries, eating out, and entertainment. Maya's car payment and insurance were $325 per month with gas consuming another $200. That adds up to $1,775, with just $225 remaining for charity, clothes, and saving. By tracking her expenses for a month, Maya understood why her savings account was low and her credit card bill was not paid in full at the end of the month.

Creating the Budget, or Spending Plan

With prior income and spending in hand, step two in creating a budget involves financial goal setting. Before creating the spending plan, decide on saving and spending financial goals. These might include saving for retirement, saving to buy a home, going out several times per month, saving for a vacation, buying a car, or buying new clothing. Both individuals and corporations must prioritize their wants and needs in order to decide in what order to allocate the limited income or corporate revenue.

After deciding and prioritizing financial goals, the working budget creation begins. The budgeter reviews prior income and spending data and financial goals and uses the information as a guide for the budget.

Maya created a few goals including save for retirement, take a vacation, and buy new clothes. She also wanted to save several months' income for emergencies. In the former example, it was clear that Maya didn't have enough room in her budget for her newly outlined goals. Thus, she needed to reduce spending to make room for her future expenses. By integrating all of her prior spending and goals she came up with a working budget. This is a flexible document, which she will try out and amend as needed.

Maya decides to contribute $200 per month to her workplace 401(k) retirement account. Her boss contributes another $135 per month or 5 percent of her pretax income. This retirement account contribution is made before taxes are taken out and reduces her taxable income. In spite of contributing $200 per month to a retirement savings account, her taxable income only declines $69, which leaves $1,931 for the remaining spending and saving. Maya's rent and utilities remain at $750 but she reduces spending on food and entertainment to $425. After shopping around for more economical auto insurance her monthly auto-related payments were reduced to $290. She decides to carpool and cuts gas spending down to $100. These small changes leave Maya $366 to spend on charity, clothes, vacation, and emergency savings.

That's how the budgeting process works for individuals. Organizations receive revenue instead of income and spend on different categories than individuals, but the budgeting process is similar. After trying out the budget for a month or so, the budgeter reevaluates the spending and saving to make sure the benchmarks are accurate.

Common Budget Guidelines

There is no hard and fast rule about how much of one's income should be allocated to various budget categories, although recommended guidelines exist. In particular, savings and housing guidelines are widely accepted. Federal, state, local, and other taxes cannot be overlooked.

In general, the following approximations are guidelines to help allocate one's income. In order to have money for the future, such as retirement and long-term goals, individuals are advised to save 10 percent of their gross income (before taxes and deductions are subtracted from the paycheck). Housing is widely accepted to equal no more than 30 percent of one's income. It's preferable to keep housing costs closer to 20 or 25 percent if possible. Taxes eat up to 25 or 30 percent of one's income. This figure varies based on many factors including whether one has children or other dependents. Taking the most conservative estimate, after deducting housing, tax, and savings goals, 30 to 40 percent remains for food, clothes, insurance, transportation, entertainment, and miscellaneous expenses.

This hypothetical budget scenario illustrates the importance of consumers carefully considering their expenses, so they are able to live within their means and avoid excess credit or debt.

Monitoring the Budget

There are many ways to keep track of a budget including online tools, computer programs, paper and pencil, and envelopes.

The envelope system is one of the oldest methods of budgeting and consists of placing each category's funds in a separate envelope. When one goes to the supermarket, money is taken from the food envelope. When the envelope is empty, the spending is complete for that category.

Another traditional approach is recording income and expenses in a ledger and comparing the actual spending with the predetermined budgeted amounts.

Online tools allow the consumer to input or even download from the bank, credit, or debit card, income and expenses. The actual spending is compared with the targeted spending and adjustments are made as needed.

A unique budgeting strategy, first described by the well-known financial journalist Jane Bryant Quinn, suggests automatically deducting all saving and investing into the appropriate financial accounts. The individual is free to spend whatever money remains, confident that the future is provided for.

Regardless of which budgeting method is used, it is an ongoing process. As income and expenses evolve, the budget will change as well.

Barbara Friedberg

See also: Banking; Cash; Debt; Online Personal Finance

Further Reading

Kapoor, Jack R., Les R. Dlabay, and Robert J. Hughes. 2009. *Personal Finance*, 9th ed. New York, NY: McGraw-Hill/Irwin.

Capital Gains and Capital Losses

Capital gains and capital losses refer to an increase or decrease in value of a capital asset when compared with its purchase price. A capital asset refers to an investment in a financial asset such as a stock, bond, mutual fund, or other investment vehicle. Real estate is also considered a capital asset. Additionally, today's definition of a capital asset might also include precious gems, gold, silver, and other metals; a car used for commuting; or a stamp collection.

Imagine you bought a home for $250,000 and the next year got transferred across the country and sold the home for $200,000. You have a capital loss of $250,000 less $200,000 or $50,000. The reverse holds true for a capital gain.

There is a long history behind the tax treatment of these capital gains and losses. The tax treatment of capital gains and losses had financial implications in the past as well as today. These tax treatments are important to savers and investors.

History

In the 1900s the income taxes on gains from capital assets were the same as those from ordinary income (Auten, 1999). The definition of a capital asset along with the capital gains and losses applied almost exclusively to fixed (capital) assets (Arnett, 1967). A fixed capital asset is a building or equipment used in business production and which is not "used up." At that time, capital losses were only deductible if losses were associated with the taxpayer's trade or business and only up to the amount of any capital gains.

Capital Gains Fun Facts

According to Angelo Young in a recent *International Business Times* article, not everyone believes investors should enjoy lower tax rates on capital gains profits. Bill Gross, former manager of the world's largest bond fund at Pimco (Pacific Investment Management), believes the 15 percent capital gains rate should be equivalent to the earned income tax rate.

Consumers can avoid capital gains taxes when they sell their home. Single home sellers can make up to $250,000 tax-free profit when they sell a home. Married couples can shield up to $500,000 capital gains profits from their home sale.

The Revenue Act of 1921 changed the capital gains and losses tax treatment by dividing assets into short-term and long-term. Simply, a short-term gain and loss is the profit or loss that is garnered when an asset is sold within one year of purchase. Assets held longer than one year are subject to long-term tax treatment. Normally, taxes are lower and investors benefit by owning assets longer than one year.

World War II and the Revenue Act of 1942 changed the capital losses treatment and consolidated the tax treatment of short- and long-term losses. A five-year carry forward was created so that net capital losses could be used to offset capital gains and up to $1,000 of ordinary income in succeeding years. A *loss carry forward* is an accounting term that allows prior years' losses to be used in subsequent years to offset profits, thus reducing taxable income.

During the 1960s through 1970s new tax laws affecting capital gains and losses were enacted. The Revenue Act of 1964 repealed the five-year loss carryover for capital losses and replaced it with an unlimited loss carryover. Net losses, however, were still deductible against only $1,000 of ordinary income in any given year.

From 1986 to 2002, previous tax treatment laws over capital gains and losses were amended once again. One legal change during that 16-year period included the Taxpayer Relief Act of 1997, which changed the capital gains tax treatment by lowering the maximum tax rate on long-term capital gains income to 20 percent (and creating a 10 percent maximum capital gains tax rate for individuals in the 15 percent tax bracket). Today, the capital loss treatment remains unchanged.

Present

At present, under current income tax law, a capital gain or loss is the result of a sale or exchange of a capital asset. Property held for less than a year is considered short-term, otherwise the gain or loss is considered long-term.

Any short-term gain in excess of a short-term loss is taxed at ordinary income tax rates. Assets held for longer than one year are subject to long-term capital gains and losses tax treatment. The long-term capital gains tax rate is usually lower than a taxpayer's ordinary income rate and can range from 15 to 20 percent, depending on the taxpayer's marginal tax bracket. In certain instances, the capital gains tax rate may be higher.

Capital losses offset capital gains, eliminating any tax implications. Long-term capital losses not offset by gains may be used to reduce taxable income up to $3,000 ($1,500 if married and filing separately) with additional losses carried forward indefinitely into later years.

As mentioned earlier, short-term capital gains are taxed at the individual's tax rate and long-term at 15 percent, in most cases. For example, if an investor buys stock for $15,000 and sells it after seven months for $20,000, the $5,000 short-term capital gain is taxed like any other taxable income. However, if it was sold more than a year later, the capital gain will be taxed at the 15 percent long-term capital gain rate (depending on the individual's marginal tax rate).

Taxpayers can elect to avoid taxes entirely on capital gains by holding the securities until death. Then the value of securities is taxed as part of the deceased's estate, and the asset is transferred to the individual who inherits with the cost basis value for the asset equal to current value. This is favorable for taxpayers who want to avoid capital gains tax on the appreciation.

Joseph Krupka

See also: Accountant; Investing; Tax Return, Federal; U.S. Federal Tax System Overview

Further Reading

Arnett, Harold E. 1967. "The Importance of Capital Gains and Losses in Investment Analysis." *Financial Analysts Journal* 23(1); 39.

Auten, Gerald. 1999. "Capital Gains Taxation, from the Encyclopedia of Taxation and Tax Policy." The Urban Institute Web site. Accessed October 21, 2013, http://www.urban.org/publications/1000519.html

"Ordinary or Capital Gain or Loss." IRS.gov Web site. Accessed October 21, 2013, http://www.irs.gov/publications/p544/ch02.html

Young, Angelo. 2013. "Capital Gains Tax: PIMCO Chief Bill Gross Says Era of Taxing Investment Income Lower Than Other Income Should End." http://www.ibtimes.com/capital-gains-tax-pimco-chief-bill-gross-says-era-taxing-investment-income-lower-other-income-should.

Capitalism

Adam Smith (1776) is credited with synthesizing the tenets of capitalism in his book *The Wealth of Nations*, which has become the classic reference for the system's underlying theories and principles. Capitalism is related to personal finance and money management in several ways. First, it is important to understand the basis for the economic environment in which one lives and works. In capitalistic nations, individuals compromise between the benefit of (traditionally) lower taxes and the disadvantage of less social welfare and a smaller public safety net.

Capitalism is a type of economic system in which the majority of property, resources, and means of production are owned privately rather than by the government.

Global Implications of a Capitalistic Society

Managers should understand how differences in economic systems can influence the motivations of their workers, particularly in other countries. Managers in charge of international teams can lead better if they take into consideration how workers in one country may react differently to changes in government regulations. Similarly, the type of economic system of the countries in which a business decides to enter influences its ability to profit from its activities.

More generally, capitalism is based on individual rights and political freedom. In contrast, an economic system based on communism supports public (government) ownership and control of all property and production. In capitalistic nations, the government and economy are separated such that the government has limited control over businesses and the market. The role of the government is to enforce private property rights, support competition through antitrust laws, and create a stable political and fiscal environment. Decisions concerning the production, distribution, and pricing of products and services are market driven instead of governmentally determined. Advanced economies are usually based on capitalism.

The underlying philosophy of capitalism contends that individual entities such as people or businesses have the right to own property and earn profit from their efforts and investments. Proponents of capitalism argue that since people and companies can own property such as land, equipment, and homes, they can influence their own well-being. Thus, capitalism allows for the incentive of personal wealth accumulation that drives people to work harder if they want to improve their economic situation.

In contrast, in communist societies, where funds are accumulated from the owners and producers of goods and services by the government and allocated evenly across citizens, neither individuals nor businesses have the incentive to work harder since their end rewards do not change.

Advantages of Capitalism

Similarly, under capitalism, individuals are able to choose their professions based on their skills and preferences instead of being assigned jobs by the government. In order to maximize individual wealth, people can pair their careers with their expertise. As such, people and businesses are motivated to make the most efficient use of resources, which can result in specialization. Both individuals and businesses can focus on doing the activities to which they add the most value, which increases value creation for the entire economy.

Additionally, individuals have free choice such as options for what to purchase. Businesses decide what to produce and in which markets to compete. The prices of goods and services change in response to supply and demand fluctuations. In turn, businesses must compete for the purchasing decisions of their customers. Thus, businesses have the incentive to match their products and services to the needs and wants of consumers. This competition drives innovation that brings new products and services to the market, increases product quality, and improves the standard of living. Competition between businesses also compels the optimization of production and the reduction of pricing. Capitalism also encourages entrepreneurship as people seek to improve their living standard by meeting market needs. It is argued that capitalism is the economic system that supports market growth since it advances the competition, innovation, and entrepreneurship that drive economies.

Another foundational tenet of capitalism is the minimization of government intervention in commerce. As such, businesses in capitalist countries usually have fewer regulatory constraints than in other nations. This type of government-economy relationship is called "laissez-faire," translated from the French to mean "let do" or "leave to do." Today, laissez-faire is an accepted name for a system with minimal government intervention. On the one hand, this means that the governments of capitalistic countries have less ability to coordinate national economic goals. In practice, businesses optimize performance based on their market environment, not government intervention.

Disadvantages of Capitalism

While capitalism has many benefits, disadvantages are evident. It has been argued that in capitalistic nations, "the rich get richer and the poor get poorer." The ensuing income inequality occurs since the wealthy do not need to overcome the same hurdles that the poor must to increase their assets. Additionally, just as individuals in capitalistic nations have incentives to work harder for material rewards, individuals without the ability to do so are left behind, which can result in higher income inequality than in other types of economic systems. Unlike economic systems in which the government distributes wealth evenly, capitalism does not redistribute assets. Similarly, capitalistic economies tend to have fewer social welfare programs to help citizens in need.

In wealth maximization, businesses direct resources to the opportunities with the most profit-earning potential. This improves the efficient use of capital and assets, but may not meet the needs of the society. For example, under capitalism, pharmaceutical companies may focus on developing drugs with the most lucrative market potential while ailments without such high profit potential are ignored, even though the ailments' influence on society may be much worse.

Another weakness of capitalism is the potentially negative effects of competition. Firms that operate in price-sensitive industries are incentivized to reduce costs to further increase their margins and competitive advantage. The drive to reduce costs increases the potential for workers' rights violations and product quality concerns. For example, firms that find cheaper labor in other countries with fewer workplace safety or child labor regulations may exploit those workers. Businesses may use the least expensive materials to minimize costs even though they reduce the performance of the product.

A system that promotes individual parties maximizing their own well-being also increases the likelihood of negative externalities (e.g., pollution, traffic, or noise). For example, a farm must choose between using pesticides that pollute the groundwater of nearby residents and using farming methods that take more time and money, but do not harm the environment or health of those nearby. Profit maximization rewards the use of the lower-cost materials, regardless of their effect on society.

Capitalism, like any economic model, has its advantages and disadvantages. U.S. workers and managers prize their freedom and independence from extensive governmental regulation. And entrepreneurs are influenced by the economic system in which a firm is started since tax rates and autonomy are greatly influenced by the government's level of intervention.

Jennifer L. Woolley

See also: Tax Return, Federal; Unemployment

Further Reading

Bender, Frederic, trans. 2013. *The Communist Manifesto of Karl Marx and Friedrich Engels.* New York: W. W. Norton.
Smith, Adam. 1776. *The Wealth of Nations.* New York: E. P. Dutton, 1933.

Cash

Cash is legal tender, or an official method of payment, which is used to purchase goods and services. Cash frequently includes short-term debt instruments, which can be converted easily and quickly into cash. These include bank certificates of deposit, money market accounts, bank checking and savings accounts, short-term commercial paper (debt), and U.S. government debt. Paper and electronic checks are another form of cash.

In corporate accounting, cash has a broader definition. It includes additional assets that can be rapidly converted into cash such as customer checks, marketable securities, and even lines of credit.

As society evolves, electronic currency is included under the "cash" heading as well. Current electronic cash systems include prepaid cash cards and debit cards. Prepaid cash cards look like credit or debit cards and are used in lieu of cash. Issued by merchants, credit card companies, or other vendors, cash is loaded onto the card from one's own bank account, in the form of a gift card, or from an outside source. Many government programs use preloaded cash cards to distribute benefits. Universities frequently use cash cards to enable students to pay for meals and other university goods and services with a single swipe. In an accelerating number of instances, cash cards are replacing paper checks.

Popular debit cards are actually a replacement for paper checks and are also used in lieu of cash. Instead of writing a check or paying a merchant with actual currency, the consumer simply swipes a debit card, which immediately transfers cash from a bank account to the merchant's account.

History

Before cash came into existence, barter was used to buy and sell goods and services. A farmer might trade a lamb for an axe and a bushel of barley. The problem with this system was that it was cumbersome. Trading partners needed to be matched up, and what if you didn't want barley, but preferred wheat instead? And what if the barley trader needed a shovel and a hoe, not an axe? Matching trading partners was difficult.

As societies evolved, barter was replaced with a form of cash, a collectively decided-upon item that could be used to buy and sell goods and services. This first iteration of cash needed several universal characteristics. It must be scarce. Imagine using stones as cash, and when a farmer needed a shovel he went to his land and picked up a bunch of stones to use as cash. That wouldn't work. The cash needed to be unique and difficult to copy. Otherwise, one could mold one's own coins or print one's own currency. The cash needed to be easily transportable and durable. Finally, the new cash had to be easily divided and desirable. The money system couldn't be built on $20 bills. What would occur if a trading partner wanted to purchase a small tool worth $3? He would require change. Finally, the cash needed to seem desirable to society. Our money has evolved to represent inherent value. A $100 bill is highly prized, because society agrees upon its worth.

Commodity money was the first form of cash, usually in the form of precious or semiprecious stones, metals, or rare shells. In the recent past, modern cash was linked to actual gold bullion stored in a country.

The introduction of the bank solved the problem of transferring commodity money for trading. Initially, in ancient Mesopotamia and Egypt, the banks were in royal palaces, temples, and state warehouses where guards and security were already in place. Farmers stored their grain and other commodities in the "bank" in exchange for a receipt written on papyrus or clay tablets. These receipts for commodity storage initiated the concept of valuable paper and were the first examples of paper checks.

Coins were first reported in Lydia, Asia Minor, around 640 BCE and minted with electrum, a combination of gold and silver. During the 800s CE, paper money followed, and its growth was spurred by the lack of copper for coins in China. Eventually, paper money became quite popular as European trade expanded. Paper money backed by state governments developed a certain amount of creditability and supported the worth of the paper.

There were problems with paper money. If too much paper cash was printed, then inflation increased and the currency became worthless. The gold standard was introduced to reduce this occurrence and paper money was linked to the gold supply. In the 1800s the gold standard, in use in the United States and abroad, served to stabilize the money supply and keep international exchange rates within a narrow range. This helped the U.S. economy and its trading partners. In 1944 at the Bretton Woods International Conference, currency ceased to be pegged to gold reserves. Today, cash is "fiat money" with no intrinsic value, with its worth decreed by the government.

Cash in the Future

Some say we are headed to a cashless society, but what does that mean? In the present day, cash cards and debit cards are equally as prevalent, if not more so, as cash. Checks are becoming obsolete. By entering your credit card information into a merchant's Web site, instead of paying with cash or check, you electronically transfer the "cash." No money actually changes hands. PayPal and other emerging cash transfer systems also allow immediate payment for a small transaction fee, further reducing the need for actual cash.

Newer cash systems being implemented worldwide include the ability to wave a special card over a machine and electronically transport the payment information. The "MintChip" prototype is under construction by the Royal Canadian Mint. This digital cash replacement is aimed at transactions under $10. Other countries are certain to follow creating this new form of cash.

Mobile payment systems are rapidly being introduced. From Apple Pay to Google Wallet, there are many new payment systems vying to replace cash. Since these mobile payment alternatives are in their infancy, only time will tell which ones survive the early stages. Even the SIM card from one's mobile phone interconnected with a bank card app offers a payment system. With the rapid pace of technological innovation, cash as we previously knew it may one day be eliminated and replaced with chips, cards, and other yet to be discovered methods of payment.

These newer iterations of traditional cash offer convenience. They also present new risks.

As newer cash forms arrive, there are growing dangers. There is an overriding concern about theft and fraud. A bank account may be wiped out if a debit card and personal identification number (PIN) are stolen. Computer hackers continue to challenge the financial system due to their advanced methods of stealing personal information. This leads to identity and financial theft. The electronic currency poses additional safety concerns. No form of cash is 100 percent safe. Fiat cash is subject to physical theft just as electronic cash is subject to other types of theft.

The future remains uncertain regarding the use of cash. At present, there is no indication that the dollar bills and coins in one's pocket will be retired any time soon.

Barbara Friedberg

See also: Banking; Certificate of Deposit; Checking Account: Credit Card; Currency; Digital Currency; Inflation; Liquidity; Money Market Account; Savings Account; Year 1944: Creation of the International Monetary Fund and the World Bank at the Bretton Woods International Conference

Further Reading

Acton, Johnny, and Sean O'Grady. October 16, 2007. "Money Money, Money; The History of Cash." *The Independent.co.uk.* Accessed November 8, 2013. http://www.independent.co.uk/money/spend-save/money-money-money-the-history-of-cash-397015.html

Kapoor, Jack, Les Dlabay, and Bob Hughes. 2009. *Personal Finance,* 9th ed. New York, NY: McGraw-Hill Irwin.

Mills, Carys. April 30, 2013. "Digital Cash Replacement from Royal Canadian Mint in the Works." *Thestar.com.* Accessed November 12, 2013. http://www.thestar.com/business /personal_finance/spending_saving/2013/04/30/digital_cash_replacement_from _royal_canadian_mint_in_the_works.html

Certificate of Deposit

Certificates of deposit (CDs) are a cross between a bank savings deposit and an investment vehicle such as a bond. A certificate of deposit is usually purchased at a bank and includes characteristics of a basic savings account. The depositor places funds in the bank and receives interest payments. The interest rates paid on CDs are usually higher than those paid on savings accounts.

Certificates of deposit, like some investment products, have a term or maturity attached. For example, CDs may be bought to mature in three, six, or nine months or from one year up to several years. At the CD's maturity, like a traditional bond, the holder receives the original or face value back plus the interest earned. If the CD owner wishes to redeem the CD before maturity, the owner sacrifices from a week to three months' interest in exchange for the early withdrawal (called an early withdrawal penalty). Some banks automatically reinvest or roll over the proceeds from the CD at maturity.

Interest Calculation

The interest calculation on a certificate of deposit is important and influences the ultimate return to the investor. There are several methods by which to calculate interest. Annual percentage yield (APY) is the effective annual rate of return and considers the impact of compounding interest or the interest paid on prior interest earned. The annual percentage rate (APR) is calculated using simple interest and does not pay interest on the prior interest received. Thus APY is higher than APR. When comparing CD interest rates, be sure to understand which type of interest rate is stated.

For example, Lily purchases a $1,000 five-year CD at State Bank with a 3 percent interest rate, paid and compounded semiannually (APY). At the end of six months she receives $1,000 x 0.5 x .03 = $15. Add this amount to $1,000 and her CD is worth $1,015 after six months. At the end of year one she receives $1,015 x 0.5 x .03 = $15.23. The value of Lily's CD at the end of year one is $1,015 + $15.23 = $1,030.23.

Had the interest been calculated with the annual percentage rate and not compounded (APY), her CD would have been valued at $1,030 at the end of year one, since the 3 percent return was paid only on the original $1,000 ($1,000 x .03 = $30). With APR interest the CD earns $15.00 every six months. In contrast, with APY interest calculation, each interest payment is greater than the prior one because the 3 percent interest is paid on a growing base.

Safety and Insurance

Certificates of deposit are considered safe investments for several reasons. The redemption amount is clearly stated at the time of purchase and will not vary. For example, buy a $1,000 one-year CD with a 2 percent interest (APR) rate paid at maturity, and in one year the CD can be redeemed at $1,020. There is no risk of losing principal or interest as one might with a stock or bond. The only uncertainty is inflation risk. If inflation increases, then the purchasing power of that $1,020 will decline and the same dollar amount will buy less.

Banks offer insurance to depositors through the Federal Deposit Insurance Corporation (FDIC). All deposits held at insured banks are protected against loss if an insured bank fails. All types of deposits, including CDs, are covered by FDIC insurance up to $250,000 per depositor per bank.

Types of CDs

Historically certificates of deposit were designed as a simple investment. The traditional CD pays a fixed interest rate over a predetermined period of time. At the end of the term, the investor withdraws the money or uses the funds to buy a new CD, called a rollover.

New types of certificates of deposit emerge as the finance industry evolves and consumers demand more sophisticated products. Bump-up CDs answer the concern that interest rates may rise during the tenure of a CD and cause the investor to miss higher yields. These adjustable-rate CDs allow investors to exchange their current interest rate for a higher one if rates on new CDs of a similar term rise during the investment period. This option is usually offered as a one-time rate increase during the life of the CD.

There is a liquid CD for investors willing to trade a lower interest rate for greater flexibility. This account allows the investor to withdraw all or part of the account penalty free. A callable CD gives the bank the right to recall the CD after a set period of time. In contrast with the liquid CD, a callable CD typically pays a higher interest rate in exchange for the uncertainty of the instrument's term. Banks will issue these types of CDs when they are concerned that interest rates will decline.

A zero-coupon CD does not pay annual interest and generally promises a higher interest rate. The CD is bought at a discount to the final redemption value. The interest is calculated by comparing the final payment with the initial amount invested. Although annual interest is not paid, generally tax is due each year on the proportion of reinvested interest.

A brokered CD is purchased in an investment brokerage account and is issued by a national bank. These offerings give investors flexibility to invest outside a hometown or an online bank. In fact, investors can purchase brokered CDs from several banks in their investment brokerage account. Since these CDs are issued by a bank, the FDIC insurance applies. Brokered CDs can be bought and sold from other investors after issue in the secondary market through a brokerage account.

Who Invests in Certificates of Deposit?

A certificate of deposit is a safe investment for the consumer to gain a higher interest payment than from the traditional savings account. These investments are great for targeted expenses. For example, if you are saving money for a down payment on a home in three years, you need to keep the money readily accessible (or liquid) and safe. If you buy a three-year CD, your money will be available when you need it and earning a bit more interest than if you'd left it in the savings account.

Certificates of deposit are among the safest places for consumers to invest their cash for any short- and medium-term (five years or less) financial needs.

Barbara Friedberg

See also: Banking; Bonds; Cash; Investing; Risk; Savings Account

Further Reading

"FDIC Insurance Coverage Basics." Federal Deposit Insurance Corporation Web site. Accessed on August 10, 2013, http://www.fdic.gov/deposit/deposits/insured/basics.html

The Wall Street Journal. December 17, 2008. "What Is a Certificate of Deposit (CD)?" http://guides.wsj.com/personal-finance/banking/what-is-a-certificate-of-deposit-cd/

Checking Account

A checking account, also called a transactional deposit or demand account, is held at a financial institution such as a bank, credit union, or investment brokerage. This basic financial account is the most liquid of all banking alternatives. Liquidity means the funds held in the account are quickly and easily converted into cash. The money in a checking account can be converted into cash or accessed by using paper checks, debit cards, electronic bill pay, other electronic debit forms, and additional methods. The consumer uses a checking account for short-term financial needs such as regular bill paying, emergency expenses, and ready cash.

In the past, the most common way to pay bills was by writing a paper check and mailing or handing it in person to the merchant. The paper check was the standard method used to transfer money out of the checking account. With the advent of electronic banking, paper checks are used with less frequency. In fact, a modern consumer rarely if ever needs a paper check anymore as debit cards, credit cards, and electronic transfer are replacing paper checks.

Although paper checks are less common, the actual checking account remains an important tool for modern money management.

Checking Account Details

A checking account differs from savings, investment, and other types of accounts in several ways. There are many types of checking accounts including specialty checking

---

Six Fun Facts and Cautions about Checking Accounts

It takes three days to get a check posted to your account. If you deposit a check today, don't even think about spending the funds for several days or you may get slapped with an "overdrawn" fee.

Online banking may not be as safe as you think. According to a study at the University of Michigan, out of 214 financial institution Web sites, 76 percent had design flaws, which could hurt you (Samuel).

Watch out: Any fees or overdraft loans that you owe the bank can be deducted from your account to repay the bank.

Ask for a fee waiver. With your first offence you might get it waived. Banks want you happy so you don't flee to another financial institution.

Watch out: Banks are encouraged to promote additional bank services. Only use the services and accounts you need.

Postdating a check, if deposited before the check date, won't help you. The bank goes by the deposit date, not the one written on the check.

---

accounts for students, children, and businesses. Within each type of account there are several classifications: regular, activity, and interest-earning checking accounts.

Regular checking accounts usually allow unlimited deposits and withdrawals. Activity accounts specify the number of monthly transactions and may charge a fee per transaction or a fee over a certain number of transactions. Although most checking accounts do not pay interest, on the occasion when interest is paid on a checking account, there is usually a high minimum balance required.

Fees vary per type of account. Checking accounts may charge a monthly fee, fee per activity, or fee if the account balance is below a certain level. There are also no-fee checking accounts.

Some checking accounts charge fees for specific banking actions. For example, if Joan writes a check for $300 and there is only $100 in her account, she gets charged a fee due to "insufficient funds." This means there is not enough money in her account to cover the $300 check. In order to avoid the possibility of overdrawing her account, Joan may use an "overdraft" service at her bank. This service automatically pays all checks, even if there are insufficient funds in her account. There is usually a small fee for the overdraft protection. But that overdraft protection fee is less than the amount she would have been charged for "overdrawing" her account.

If Matthew has a checking account that allows 20 total transactions per month and he surpasses that limit, the bank will charge a fee. Fees are explained in advance, so the customer needs to understand the type of account and potential fees in order to avoid racking up excessive charges.

Federal deposit insurance, low or no fees, and easy access are common properties of checking accounts. Bank and credit union accounts are insured up to $250,000 for each Social Security number. Financial institutions offer free checking accounts and others with monthly fees. Checking accounts are convenient for electronic deposits and online bill pay. Checking accounts can also be linked with other bank and investment accounts for easy fund transfer.

When a check is deposited or cashed, it must be endorsed or signed by the payee. The payee is the individual to whom the check is written. This action verifies that the correct individual is depositing the check as the bank has the checking account holder's signature on file. Endorsing a check before deposit may also reduce the possibility of identity fraud. Financial institutions employ additional security measures, especially for online banking, to reduce fraud and protect the consumer's funds.

History of Checking Accounts

As early as 100 BCE Roman bankers issued *praescriptiones* similar to a written record, an early form of checks. These eliminated the need for merchants and consumers to carry around heavy bags of coins for trading.

By the ninth century, Middle Eastern traders used a *sakk* or paper record drawn against the merchant's account. The sakk was used as cash replacement in the same way checks are used today. By the 13th century, letters or bills of exchange served the place of checks.

By 1600, Wisselbank of Amsterdam functioned much like modern banks with accounts for withdrawal and deposit, transfer, and bill pay. In 1853 the Bank of England printed banknotes, the true antecedent to the modern check.

During the 1860s, after the U.S. Congress passed the National Banking Act, the use of checks surged. At that time checks were generally restricted to local use. This act laid the groundwork for the national check clearing system of today. From 1939 to 1952, the number of checking accounts in the United States doubled (O'Neil, 2012).

The practice of offering gifts to open accounts began in the 1950s with Regulation Q, also called "the Toaster Rule." Regulation Q was called the Toaster Rule since it was commonplace for banks to offer a gift, usually a toaster, when consumers opened a new account. Regulation Q prohibited banks from paying interest on checking accounts. In 2011, Regulation Q was repealed concurrent with the implementation of the Dodd-Frank Wall Street Reform and Consumer Protection Act.

The age of modern banking began in the late 1950s. In 1959, the first ATM in the United States was installed in Columbus, Ohio. By 1978, Congress signed the Electronic Funds Transfer Act. This law protects consumers using electronic funds transfer including debit cards, automated teller machines, and automatic withdrawals from a bank account. Since 1978, as electronic banking has grown, the use of paper checks has declined.

The Use of Checking Accounts Today

Although checking accounts are widely used, paper checks are less common. According to the Checking Experience Index executive summary (2013), 43 percent of checking account users have no-fee (or are uncertain of the fee) accounts.

Where people bank continues to trend toward the online option. Nationally, checking account holders make 15 transactions per month with 6 of those transactions occurring online. Of all checking account holders, 80 percent use online banking. ATM use is the second most popular banking method with 3.2 transactions per month. Store transactions average 2.3 per month, and mobile is third with 1.5 transactions each month (TD Bank, Checking Experience Index, 2013).

Checking Accounts in Lower Education and Economic Populations

There is a segment of the population that does not use the banking system. Approximately 15 percent of the population do not have a checking account (Lusardi, 2010). Of lower income individuals, 31 percent are unbanked as are 36 percent of those without a high school diploma. As many as 28 percent of African Americans and 30 percent of Hispanics are unbanked.

Checking accounts and the banking industry continue to evolve rapidly along with changes in technology.

Barbara Friedberg

See also: Banking; Budget; Cash; Identity Theft; Interest Income and Payments; Interest Rates; Liquidity; Money Market Account; Savings Account; Year 2010: Dodd Frank Wall Street Reform and Consumer Protection Act

Further Reading

The Financial Brand. 2013. "The State of Checking Account Consumers in 2013." Accessed January 22, 2014. http://thefinancialbrand.com/33346/bank-checking-account-customers-research/

Kapoor, Jack R., Les R. Dlabay, and Robert J. Hughes. 2009. *Personal Finance,* 9th ed. New York: McGraw-Hill Irwin.

Lusardi, Annamarie. 2010. "Americans' Financial Capability." Financial Crisis Inquiry Commission. Accessed January 22, 2014. http://www.astrid-online.it/Dossier--d1/United-Sta/FINANCIAL-1/Forum-to-E/Lusardi_Forum_02_10.pdf

O'Neil, Erin. 2012. "The History of the Checking Account." Accessed January 22, 2014. http://www.banks.com/articles/history-checking-account

Samuel, Neena. "20 Secrets Your Bank Teller Won't Tell You." *Readers Digest.* Accessed March 1, 2014. http://www.rd.com/slideshows/secrets-bank-teller-wont-tell-you/

TD Bank. July, 2013. Checking Experience Index 2013. Accessed January 22, 2014. https://mediaroom.tdbank.com/execsummary

Commodities

Historically, precious metals have been used as the primary form of storing value. Exchanging excess funds for gold, silver, and even diamonds became a common practice after fiat money was introduced. While it is less prevalent in the United States, this practice is still common in developing countries, especially those that have emerged from wars and other conflicts that devastated their economies. So, utilization of commodities is typically associated with instabilities.

Participating in the commodity market does not fit the true definition of investment. Investment requires that the excess funds be used for the purpose of potentially generating more resources or cash flows in the future. Commodities cannot generate any additional value or cash flows in the future. By buying commodities today, you are hoping that someday in the future you can sell the commodities for the same or higher prices. In essence, it is more speculation than investment. Thus, although frequently included as an investment type, commodities are differentiated due to their speculative nature.

Speculation in commodity markets is common and involves many types of commodities. Precious metals such as gold and silver have been used for long periods of time. The advances in futures markets allow many different classes of assets to be used for speculative purposes for individuals who are not directly involved (users or producers are those directly involved) in the commodities.

Agriculture futures such as coffee, wheat, corn, soybeans, lean hogs, and feeder cattle futures are some of the more commonly used futures contracts for those interested in participating in commodities markets. The frozen orange juice market was the background for the cult-classic movie *Trading Places*, starring Dan Aykroyd and Eddie Murphy. A lesser known commodity is also available in the futures market: mung beans. Many people don't know what a mung bean looks like. But it is a very popular agriculture commodity in China. The United States is one of the largest producers of mung beans. You most likely have encountered mung beans and didn't know it. The bean sprouts you see in the supermarket are from mung beans!

The precious metals market is very well developed for gold and silver. Not only can you hold the physical metals, you can also participate in the futures markets. As the world's economy becomes more industrialized, the need for various metals also increases. This has been the driving force behind the growth in other precious metals markets, such as copper, aluminum, and rare metals. These commodities are essential for many industrial products and affect the material cost of the products greatly as their price fluctuates due to fluctuations in demand as the economy expands and contracts.

There are several reasons why someone might want to participate in commodity speculation. First, consider the individual who wants to participate in corn futures because he thinks the corn price might go up. If he has uses for corn, then buying corn futures allows the buyer to lock in the price today. Likewise, if you're a producer of corn, you can lock in a selling price for your products today. But if you're neither a producer nor a user, the only way you can profit is if the other side is wrong about the price movements in the future. By buying corn futures (establishing a long position), you're betting that the producers are wrong about the future price and that you're providing an insurance policy for the price of corn for the producers. Likewise, if you established a short position in corn futures, you can only make money if the future corn price turned out to be lower. So, if you make money, either the users are wrong about the price in the future, or other speculators are wrong. Either way, by participating in the commodity markets, you essentially became an insurance underwriter for the commodity price.

The traditional argument for including commodities in an investment portfolio is that these commodities typically have a low correlation with the stock and bond markets. But using past correlation relationships as a guide to asset allocation is dangerous. The reason is that this correlation relationship can change drastically as more and more people participate in these markets. Since most of these markets are relatively small in size, an additional small outflow/inflow of funds can have a large effect on price movements. Furthermore, the historic return for commodities is poor by any standard. Even with the recent surge in the gold price, gold's historic return is no better than inflation. Other more recent commodities provide a return not much higher than for medium-term U.S. Treasuries.

The reasons for the low return over the long run are many. But the main reason is that most investors are led into these commodities when their prices have risen drastically. When more funds are put into these markets, the price for the related commodities might rise in the short to intermediate term, but that could be driven by increases in demand from mutual funds and not changes in fundamental values. As the fundamentals eventually set in, the price will reflect the real demand and price momentum could reverse.

Participation in commodities markets is also incredibly risky. The risk comes from two sources: leverage and ease of market manipulations.

To participate in commodity futures markets, you do not have to put up 100 percent of the funds for any specific contracts. Each commodity futures contract has its own requirements, set by the futures exchange it is traded in. The typical requirement is less than 20 percent (there is a much lower margin requirement for gold). So, your position will have at least 400 percent leverage. That means if the price declined by less than 20 percent, your initial investment could be completely wiped out.

Market manipulations, while less common due to increases in market regulations and enforcement, is nonetheless a real danger for small investors who choose to participate in commodity futures. The movie *Trading Places* is based on the story of a large futures broker manipulating the frozen orange juice futures by issuing false weather reports. The brokers attempted to illegally profit from the resulting price changes in the orange juice commodity futures prices.

The Brazilian government cornered the coffee market in the 1910s. The Hunt brothers (the Lamar Hunt Trophy awarded to the winner of the NFL's AFC division champion was funded by one of the brothers involved) were found guilty of cornering the silver market in the 1970s. More recently, the Vitol Group, a large hedge fund in the commodity market, was sued by the U.S. Commodity Trading Futures Commission for manipulating the oil futures market.

Furthermore, commodity markets typically generate a higher degree of interest only after a large price surge. Since the oil price surge in 2006, most commodities reached their historic price level. What is the chance of the price continuing to grow at such a high rate? Not likely. So, there is also an elevated chance of high negative returns.

Due to the high degree of risk and low returns, the commodities markets, unlike what traditional finance theory suggests, are not ideal for individual investors. There are more and more mutual funds and exchange-traded funds that are specialized in the commodity markets. These funds typically have lower risk than investing in the actually commodity or the futures markets. Still, the level of risk in these funds is very high. Some of these funds are also leveraged (they can do so due to regulatory loopholes) and present significantly higher risk.

Leo H. Chan

See also: Derivatives; Hedge Funds; Inflation; Investing; Risk

Further Reading

Eichenwald, Kurt. December 21, 1989. "2 Hunts Fined and Banned from Trades." http://www.nytimes.com/1989/12/21/business/2-hunts-fined-and-banned-from-trades.html

Kirkland, Joel. January 17, 2014. "Price-Rigging Probes Jammed by Oil Industry Bid to Protect Its Secrets." http://www.eenews.net/stories/1059993123

The New York Times. May 25, 1914. "How Brazil Cornered the World's Coffee Market." http://query.nytimes.com/mem/archive-free/pdf?res=F70A17F63B5E13738DDDAF0A94DD405B828DF1D3

Compound Interest/Return

Compound interest is created when interest that is added to the principal of a deposit or loan also earns interest. Over a period of time, compounding can greatly magnify the amount of debt owed or savings accumulated. An understanding of this principle will help investors and consumers appreciate the importance of saving and the need to avoid debt.

Importance of Compound Interest

Compound interest is widely believed to be one of the most powerful forces in the universe. Indeed, some claim that Albert Einstein once said that compound interest was the eighth wonder of the world and remarked that "he who understands it earns it . . . he who doesn't . . . pays it."

When we invest money, we receive interest on the original amount invested (known as the principal). If we choose to add the interest to the principal (rather than withdraw and spend it), it also earns interest along with the interest paid on the principal. This is known as compounding. It is an important concept to understand because it shows the importance of investing early and the power of reinvesting the interest earned. Money subject to compound interest will grow to a large sum over a long period of time. Compound interest is particularly important when it comes to deciding whether to postpone saving; if individuals delay, they may not enjoy the full benefits of this powerful force.

Suppose that you invest $1,000 at 10 percent interest. At the end of the first year, you will receive $100 interest on your $1,000 investment. If you reinvest the interest, the $100 interest is added to your original investment of $1,000, and so your investment at the start of the second year is now $1,100.

In the second year, the interest on your investment is $110 (10 percent of $1,100). You earn $10 more interest because your investment is worth $100 more than the amount in the first year.

In the third year, your investment will grow to $1,210 and the interest earned will be $121. With compounding, the interest earned grows with time—$100 in the first year, $110 in the second year, and $121 in the third year. Consequently, the value of your investment grows exponentially with the passage of time. The money value of the increase is not so much in the early years, but it is very large in the later years.

In contrast, if you choose not to reinvest the interest, your original principal will earn *simple* interest of only $100 each year. A $1,000 investment will grow by just $100 each year. After two years, your investment will be worth only $1,200 (compared to $1,210 with annual compounding). However, over a long period of time the differences between simple and compound interest can be enormous. Another simple example can demonstrate this: at 15 percent simple interest, $100 grows to $550 in 30 years, while at 15 percent interest compounded annually, $100 grows to $6,621 in 30 years, a difference of $6,071.

The frequency of adding interest, or compounding, can affect the amount of interest accrued. Interest can be added more frequently than once a year—it can be monthly, quarterly, semiannually, or annually. This is known as compounding frequency. The greater the frequency, the higher the amount of interest earned.

Suppose two banks offer two interest options: bank A pays interest monthly and bank B pays interest annually. With interest added monthly, $1,000 at 10 percent will give you $104.71 of interest in year 1, while $1,000 at 10 percent with interest added annually will you $100 of interest, a difference of $4.71. However, over 30 years this can lead to a huge difference: $1,000 with 10 percent added monthly grows to $19,837 while $1,000 with 10 percent added annually grows to $17,449, a difference of $2,388.

Compound interest richly rewards those who invest early. The benefit of investing early can be illustrated by the story of twins: Hannah and Ellie. Hannah started work after leaving university at the age of 21 and began investing $1,000 per annum with compound interest of 8 percent per year. Ellie also left university and started work at the same time, but she failed to set up a saving plan because she liked to party and buy clothes. Hannah stopped saving at age 30 when she left her job to have a baby. She left her savings to grow but did not invest any more. Ellie, on the other hand, started saving $1,000 per year, earning 8 percent compound interest per year.

By the age of 65, Hannah has accumulated a bigger pot of savings. Although she has only paid in $10,000 over 10 years, her investment is now worth $231,324 because her investment has had 44 years of growth. Although Ellie has paid a total of $35,000 over the 35 years, her investment is now worth less than Hannah's ($186,102) because of the shorter period of investment. The lesson is clear—the sooner you start saving, the better.

People often think that investing only makes sense if you have a lot of money to begin with. This is not true and compounding works on any starting sum. Whether it is on a large or small sum, compounding works its magic and gives the same impressive percentage increase.

Borrowing and Compound Interest

While compound interest can work miraculously when you save, it can have a ruinous effect when you borrow. For example, if you borrow $1,000 over 30 years at 10 percent per annum, the total amount you will have to repay is $17,449, which is more than 17 times the original amount borrowed.

Here, it might be worthwhile to distinguish between good and bad debt. People often borrow money to buy real estate because this is perceived as a good debt as its value is likely to grow over time. Although borrowers will have to repay more than the amount they owe, they take the risk with the hope that their home asset will grow more in value and they can still make a profit. Bad debt, on the other hand, refers to assets whose value depreciates over time (e.g., cars, vacations, paying off other debts), and so money borrowed to acquire these types of assets will not enable individuals to accumulate wealth.

Compound interest, then, is a double-edged sword: it can help those who invest early to build a significant sum of money over a long period of time, and it will punish those who borrow money for a lengthy period. The lessons are clear: when it comes to saving, save early and leave it to grow as long as possible. When it comes to borrowing, borrow as little as possible but repay with speed.

Lien Luu

See also: Banking; Consumer Credit/Debt; Debt; Dividend Income; Interest Income and Payments; Interest Rates; Investing; Loans; Time Value of Money

Further Reading

Binswanger, J., and K. G. Carman. December 10, 2010. "The Miracle of Compound Interest: Does Our Intuition Fail?" *CentER Discussion Paper Series No. 2010-137.* http://papers.ssrn.com/sol3/papers.cfm?abstract_id=1742342

Lofthouse, S. 1996. *How to Fix Your Finances: A Guide to Personal Financial Planning.* Hoboken, NJ: John Wiley & Sons.

Madura, J. 2014. *Personal Finance*, 5th ed. Upper Saddle River, NJ: Pearson Prentice Hall.

Condominium

The condominium form of real estate ownership is a relatively new type of residential living. A condominium is a common-interest community. Owners purchase a condominium with a mortgage (or cash) and pay property taxes, just like single-family homeowners. A condominium is considered real property and the owners possess a deed or ownership document to the property.

The ownership structure defines a condominium, not the style of the condominium home. Frequently condominiums are considered a type of home, yet this is inaccurate. Condominium living takes many forms. Frequently, condominiums are individually owned units in a multiunit building, although a condominium may be a paired home or single family home as well. A condominium can be similar to a one-floor apartment, a several-story townhome, or even a detached single-family home.

The community is governed by rules and regulations and enforced by an association, similar to a small town. Specifically, a condominium consists of a real estate development in which the units are individually owned. Each condominium owner is liable for monthly association fees, which pay for current and future common-area repairs and maintenance.

Ownership typically includes the interior of the property including the paint and all inside fixtures. Another differentiating element of the condominium is that the common areas are not individually owned but owned by the condominium community. This includes all common areas, the yard and exterior grounds, and any recreational areas.

The Condominium as a Legal Entity

Condominiums are owned through a common-interest community and operate with collective governance principles, which impose regulations on the property owners. This type of governing system is a "private government," voted on by the membership or condominium owners.

Three legal documents are required when creating a condominium development. The first document, called a "declaration," must be recorded before building begins. The declaration describes the property, association parameters, and the obligation of owners to belong to the community association.

The Covenants, Conditions, and Restrictions (CCR) document, frequently a part of the declaration, describes the responsibilities of the community members. The third document is the bylaws, which outline how the property may be used and what the condominium homeowners can and cannot do with their property. The bylaws are less formal than the CCRs and both documents may be quite extensive and comprehensive. These documents are interrelated with the duties of the condominium association.

The bylaws might state that window coverings are restricted to a certain color in order to maintain a consistent exterior appearance. Pet ownership and behavior can also be stipulated in the condominium rules. Noncompliance with the rules may result in fines and legal action.

History of the Condominium

Condominiums are a newer form of property ownership. Condominiums began gradually after World War II and didn't become popular until condominium-enabling statutes were formed. In 1961, Arkansas passed the first condominium-enabling legislation in the United States. By 1963, 33 additional states had passed condominium-enabling laws. Just four years later, in1967, 49 states had condominium legislation.

In the early 1960s there were fewer than 500 condominium communities. By 1970 growth began to explode. Common-interest communities grew rapidly between 1970 and 1990 from 10,000 to 150,000. Naturally, individual unit growth accelerated as well. By 1987 individual condominium unit ownership grew to 4.2 million with over 7 million homes by 1999 (Ross-Harrington, 2009).

Advantages and Disadvantages of Condominium Ownership

The popularity of condominium ownership over the years is due to its benefits. Urban cities are crowded with growing populations and limited space, thus, real estate ownership is quite expensive. A condominium in an urban area offers a housing alternative with amenities such as pools and facilities that would otherwise be unaffordable to individual residents. Even in less expensive cities, cost is a benefit of condominium ownership. Due to the multiunit construction, residents frequently experience lower-cost housing in a condominium than would be available in a single-family detached home.

Condominiums are often selected due to the lower maintenance requirements. In contrast with detached home ownership, condominium owners enjoy minimal exterior maintenance duties. For individuals uninterested in maintaining a large yard or pool, a condominium is an economical alternative. The monthly dues pay for the community landscaping, pool, and other amenities.

As opposed to renters who are prohibited from making significant home renovations, a condominium owner can upgrade the interior of the unit with a new kitchen or bathroom. Additionally, renters are subject to rising rents. Although the maintenance fees may increase over time in a condominium, the monthly mortgage payment (of a fixed mortgage) is stable.

A negative factor of condominium ownership may be the covenants and restrictions. There are many rules and regulations for the residents. For example, should an owner want a large dog and the complex only allows pets under 35 pounds, that owner cannot have the big dog. Another restriction might impact the pool hours. If the pool closes at 10:00 p.m., residents cannot go swimming at 11:00 p.m. Gardeners who desire expansive plantings may have to forgo their ideal garden due to community planting restrictions.

Condominium owners who choose to rent out their individual units may experience problems as well. There can be restrictions on owners' opportunity to rent out their units. Or, there may be a limited percentage of rental units allowed in the complex. In the markets today, approximately one-third of all condominiums are rented out (Ross-Harrington, 2009). This large percentage of renters may also create unique problems.

As cities continue to grow more populous, condominium ownership is certain to own a large position in the residential real estate market. In fact, office and commercial condominiums are a growing segment of the commercial real estate market.

Barbara Friedberg

See also: Debt; Homeowners and Renters Insurance; Interest Rates; Mortgage; Real Estate; Tax Return, Federal; Year 2007–2008: Subprime Housing Crisis and Mortgage Meltdown

Further Reading

Kapoor, Jack R., Les R. Dlabay, and Robert J. Hughes. 2009. *Personal Finance,* 9th ed. New York: McGraw-Hill/Irwin, 283.

Ross-Harrington, Jonathan D. 2009. "Property Forms in Tension: Preference Inefficiency, Rent-Seeking, and the Problem of Notice in the Modern Condominium." *Yale Law & Policy Review* (Fall): 187–221.

Consumer Credit/Debt

A consumer debt is defined as borrowing money now to purchase goods or services. The consumer debt is incurred using a credit card or a store payment plan. An individual can buy anything with a credit card, such as clothes, electronics, or a dinner out, and incurs consumer debt until the balance due on the credit card is repaid. The terms *consumer debt* and *consumer credit* are sometimes used interchangeably, although they have slightly different meanings. Specifically, debt is an obligation incurred by the consumer. Consumer credit is offered to the borrower to buy now and pay later. Both terms involve buying consumer goods today with the obligation to pay for the items in the future.

Consumer credit is easily identified as money borrowed to purchase consumer goods with a credit card or payment plan. For example, a credit card gives the holder credit to buy goods and services up to a certain amount. This credit is actually a loan or debt. Consumer credit does not include borrowing money to buy a home, but does include the big-screen television in the home's family room. In general, consumer credit is used for purchases that depreciate (decline) in value such as a car, personal goods, or items that are consumed such as a restaurant meal or vacation.

Problems with Consumer Credit/Debt

It is quite easy to obtain a credit card to purchase goods and services on credit. The problem arises when the bill arrives. Payments are due every month for charges made on a credit card or payment plan. If the charges incurred during the month are not paid in full at the end of the month, the consumer is required to pay a portion of the total amount due, called a *minimum payment*. Any amount that is not paid in the month the charge is incurred is carried over into the following month. The credit card company adds additional interest to the total charges. The cycle continues and every subsequent month that the bill is not paid in full, additional interest is incurred. Consumers who choose to pay the minimum on a credit card or payment plan and continue to accumulate additional consumer debt may ultimately pay double or more than the cost of the original charge.

There is a nationwide epidemic of failure to pay credit card bills in full. Many citizens continue to add to their consumer debt/credit over time and end up owing a lot of money to the credit card companies. The Federal Reserve Bank keeps track of consumers' debt as compared with their disposable (after-tax) income. This household debt service ratio (DSR) is considered an estimate of what percentage of a homeowner's or renter's after-tax income goes toward consumer debt repayment. For example, homeowners' consumer debt as a percentage of total disposable income ranged from 4.81

percent in 1982 to 6.39 percent in 2005. Renters had much higher consumer debt levels according to the Federal Reserve Board's "Household Debt Service and Financial Obligations Ratios" (2013). According to the Federal Reserve Bank, in the first quarter of 2013, aggregate consumer debt was $2.7 trillion. The 2013 consumer debt level is $.58 trillion, above its trough of $2.12 trillion in the first quarter of 2004. These debt levels include student loans, credit card debt, auto loans, and delinquencies.

Consumer credit and debt are integrated into societal consumption patterns in the modern world.

Barbara Friedberg

See also: Bankruptcy; Budget; Credit Card; Debt; Debt Collection; Debt/Credit Counseling; Delinquency; Interest Rates; Online Personal Finance; Rent to Own

Further Reading

Household Debt and Credit Report," Federal Reserve Bank of New York, retrieved July 16, 2013. http://www.newyorkfed.org/householdcredit/

"Household Debt Service and Financial Obligations Ratios," Federal Reserve Board, last modified June 17, 2013. http://www.federalreserve.gov/releases/housedebt/

Credit Card

A credit card is a small plastic card issued by a bank, financial institution, or merchant, which enables the cardholder to purchase goods and services with borrowed funds. Interest on the amount of payment begins one month after purchase. If the card user pays the amount owed within the first billing cycle, there are no interest charges. Credit cards have higher interest rates (around 19 percent per year) than most consumer loans.

Credit cards have become prevalent across all realms of both U.S. and international developed markets. Unfortunately, their overuse can lead one to accumulate excess debt and cause financial problems.

History

Lending money with a card began in the 1800s when store owners and agricultural enterprises in conjunction with financial institutions offered credit. By the beginning of the 1900s hotels and large department stores created paper "charge" cards for their important customers. These designated "creditworthy" customers used the cards in the issuing merchant's store in the same way consumers use credit cards today with a predetermined upper credit limit.

Sears was one of the first companies to use a credit card to increase sales and the strategy worked very well. Long before the Internet, Americans received a Sears Catalog with pictures of toys, tools, tractors, and every kind of household product sold in the Sears stores. With the innovation of credit cards, people could buy anything they wanted from Sears immediately—and pay for it later with interest.

General-purpose, as opposed to store-based, credit cards began in 1949 when Diners Club created their nationwide network card. Cardholders could charge goods and services from network members. Diners Club cards, initially designed for wealthy individuals to pay for entertainment and travel expenses, became successful. In spite of the 7 percent fee charged to merchants by Diners Club, the vendors enjoyed greater spending from card users than from those who paid with cash.

As with most successful concepts, Diners Club inspired many competitors. By the late 1950s, Bank of America jumped into the credit card business with a national card. At that time, interstate banking laws prohibited banks from operating outside of state borders. Creatively, Bank of America circumvented the interstate banking laws with the credit card and reached a large national customer network. As the national network grew more complex, Bank of America separated its credit card business into what is now known as the Visa network.

In 1966 the MasterCard network emerged to compete with Visa. The credit card industry continues to grow with extensive competition for consumers. Today, according to Akers et al. (2005), most Americans as well as members of developing countries hold at least one credit card. In 2001 approximately 76 percent of families had a credit card. Today, 92 percent of families with incomes over $30,000 have a credit card with the average for all households reaching 6.3 cards.

How Do Credit Cards Work?

To obtain a credit card a consumer completes an application, and the issuing company does a quick "credit check" to determine the applicant's ability to make the credit card payments. If the credit card company believes the applicant can repay the borrowed funds, then a credit card is issued with an upper spending limit.

The credit card is a plastic card with the customer's name and account numbers on the front. The account numbers, specific to each cardholder, apply to the credit card's network, bank, and account. On the back there is a signature box, partial account number, and a three- or four-digit card identification security number along with a magnetic code strip.

This is how a college student might get his first credit card: Joachim completes a credit card application and the issuing company checks his credit and possibly his work history. If Joachim has a part-time job and is attending college, the bank will likely approve him for a credit card. Since his income is low, the card might have an upper limit of $800. That means Joachim can make purchases up to $800. Those with higher incomes and greater credit histories usually receive higher credit limits.

Every month, the cardholder receives a statement via mail or online with the list of purchases, fees, and the amount owed along with the due date for payment. If the full balance of the card is paid off every month, no interest fees are charged. If a partial payment is made on the bill, interest begins to accrue or build up. If the consumer continues to pay only part of the total bill, more interest accrues, and eventually the individual ends up owing a lot more money than he initially charged.

Advantages and Disadvantages of Credit Cards

Credit cards are convenient as they eliminate the need to carry cash. Using a credit card responsibly can help the consumer build a credit history. A good credit history is important if one wants to borrow money to buy a home or car. Some credit card companies protect the cardholder from false charges in case the card is stolen and do not hold the cardholder responsible for most of the charges made by the thief.

Many credit cards also offer rewards such as cash back, airline miles, or gift cards. Using a credit card is also a method of keeping track of expenses.

Credit cards allow consumers the opportunity to buy more than they can pay off in one month. This is both an advantage and a disadvantage. The advantage is that it boosts the consumer's spending power and can serve as a help during times of unexpected expenses. The disadvantage of buying more than one can pay off in a month means that the consumer pays a very high interest rate on the unpaid credit card balance.

A major disadvantage of credit cards is that they make it easy to incur large amounts of debt. For example, some consumers charge a lot over the holiday season and end up paying the bills months after the holiday festivities are over.

Many merchants such as hotels and rental car companies require consumers to have a credit card on file in order to rent a car or stay at a hotel. This is a disadvantage if the consumer doesn't have a credit card.

In short, using a credit card responsibly by paying off the balance every month is a convenience. Let the balance build up for many months and the convenience is converted into a serious financial disadvantage.

Barbara Friedberg

See also: Cash; Credit Report and Reporting Agencies; Credit Score; Debt; Interest Income and Payments; Year 2010: Dodd-Frank Wall Street Reform and Consumer Protection Act

Further Reading

Akers, Douglas, Jay Golter, Brian Lamm, and Martha Solt. Federal Deposit Insurance Corporation Web site. "FDIC Banking Review; Overview of Recent Developments in the Credit Card Industry." Updated November 1, 2005. http://www.fdic.gov/bank/analytical/banking/2005nov/article2.html

Credit (or Bond) Rating Agency

In the finance world, it's important for investors to trust institutions that issue bonds and fixed-income debt. After all, if an individual or institutional investor purchases a 30-year bond for $1,000, which promises to pay a 5 percent coupon or interest rate, the investor must be certain that the issuer will be solvent and available to make the interest payments for the next 30 years.

The Rating Agencies' Contributions to the Year 2007–2008 Subprime Housing Crisis and Mortgage Meltdown

The rating agencies were deemed to be above reproach. The rating grade accuracy, up until recently, was not questioned. Yet, during the financial crisis of 2007, the rating agencies were accused of and subsequently settled major lawsuits over their inaccurate ratings.

For the first time ever, S&P and Moody's settled suits claiming that investors had been misled by their ratings. Since 2008, the legal firm of Robbins Geller Rudman & Dowd had fought a $700 million fraud and negligence claim against the rating agencies. The firm ultimately settled for $225 million with a group of institutional plaintiffs that included King County, Washington, and the Abu Dhabi Commercial Bank. The legal suits accused the rating agencies of collusion and, along with Morgan Stanley Bank, of selling subprime debt that was destined to default. This was one of over three dozen cases that claimed that the credit rating agencies helped the sales of toxic mortgage-backed securities (which contributed to the 2007–2008 mortgage meltdown).

During their investigation, Robbins Geller Rudman & Dowd uncovered inflammatory documents that helped investors. Matt Taibbi (2013) of *Rolling Stone* wrote that the rating agencies, Moody's and Standard & Poor's, "have for many years been shameless tools for the banks, willing to give just about anything a high rating in exchange for cash."

The same Taibbi article went on to report that an important S&P analyst stated, "As you know, I had difficulties explaining HOW we got those numbers since there is no science behind it." Finally, Taibbi reported, there were many incriminating e-mails in which executives and analysts for the rating companies admitted that their business model was corrupt.

It is widely accepted that the rating agencies, by inaccurately ranking highly very risky mortgage-backed securities, which should have been rated lower, were major contributors to the economic problems of the latter part of the first decade of the 21st century.

Credit ratings, also called debt or bond ratings, give fixed-income debt issuers a score determined by their financial strength. This rating helps investors understand the likelihood of receiving their interest payments for the duration of the bond, with high credit ratings indicating financially stronger companies and low credit ratings denoting weaker ones.

Credit Ratings Overview

All major debt issuers, from companies, to city and state governments, as well as sovereign countries that issue bonds, are analyzed by the rating agencies. After in-depth analysis of the entity's creditworthiness, it is given a credit grade or score. The raters investigate the economic conditions of a country when deriving the rating for a sovereign nation. A rating agency might also examine the political condition of a country. War-torn and economically unstable countries would receive lower credit ratings on their debt than would a more stable country such as the United States.

As discussed in the Bonds entry, corporations, cities, states, and countries all borrow money. These entities borrow from the public and large institutions by selling bonds. Bonds function similar to a loan, only the lenders are the individuals who buy the bonds.

For fixed-income investors to feel confident in purchasing the debt, they must understand what they are buying. That is where the rating agencies come in. These agencies review the entities who issue corporate bonds, municipal bonds, government bonds, along with a stock-bond hybrid called preferred stock.

There is an inverse relationship between ratings grade and possibility of default. Higher-rated securities have a lower risk of default. For example, Standard & Poor's credit rating scale begins with AAA, the highest available grade (AA+ is the next highest), on down to C and D ratings. Those debt securities with ratings below BBB– are considered to be the riskiest and are called speculative or junk bonds. Only the most risk-tolerant investors should invest in the lower-grade debt.

History of Credit Rating Agencies

In 1913, John Knowles Fitch founded the Fitch Publishing Company. *The Fitch Stock and Bond Manual* and *The Fitch Bond Book* reported financial statistics used by the investment industry. In 1924, Fitch introduced the AAA through D rating system. These grades, from highest to lowest, laid the groundwork for modern investment product ratings.

Other players in the ratings industry include Moody's Investors Service, which published *Moody's Manual* in 1900. This book included statistics and information about stocks and bonds. The modern iteration of this early organization was initiated in 1914 with the creation of Moody's Investor's Service. In the 1970s Moody's began rating all types of debt instruments including short-term government bonds, called commercial paper, and bank deposits. Moody's continues today as one of the premier rating agencies.

Standard & Poor's also began over 100 years ago when Henry Varnum Poor first published *The History of Railroads and Canals in the United States* in 1860. This publication was the predecessor to the securities analysis and reporting of today. In 1906, Standard Statistics published corporate bond, sovereign debt, and municipal bond ratings. In 1941, the two companies merged and formed the well-known Standard & Poor's Corporation. Although retaining the Standard & Poor's name, in 1966 the company was bought by the McGraw-Hill Companies. In addition to ratings, Standard & Poor's (S&P) creates many tools for securities analysis including the gold standard of major stock market indexes.

Ratings Drill Down

The three prominent bond rating agencies, Standard & Poor's, Moody's, and Fitch, each uses its own letter-based rating system. Although similar, with A ratings being higher than D ratings, the specific grades for each company vary. Bonds are rated at issue and subsequently reviewed periodically to determine whether a rating change is warranted (based on changes in the issuing entity).

Ratings are very important to issuers as well as bond buyers. If a bond is expected to receive a high rating, then the interest paid by the organization to the bond buyers is

Credit or Bond Rating Agency Table

	Investment Grade				Not Investment Grade						
	Highest	High	Upper Medium	Medium	Not Investment Grade	Speculative Medium	Speculative Lower	Speculative Risky	Speculative Poor	No Payments/ Bankruptcy	In Default
Moody's	Aaa	Aa1, Aa2, Aa3	A1, A2, A3	Baa1, Baa2, Baa3	Ba1	Ba2, Ba3	B1, B2, B3	Caa1	Caa2, Caa3	Ca/C	—
Standard & Poor's	AAA	AA+, AA, AA–	A+, A, A–	BBB+, BBB, BBB–	BB+	BB, BB–	B+, B, B–	CCC+	CCC, CCC–	—	D
Fitch	AAA	AA+, AA, AA–	A+, A, A–	BBB+, BBB, BBB–	BB+	BB, BB–	B+, B, B–	CCC	—	—	DDD, DD, D

Source: http://www.investopedia.com/articles/bonds/09/bond-rating-agencies.asp

lower than for a comparable entity with a lower credit rating. The lower the interest rate payments, the lower the cost of borrowing for the company. Clearly, an entity prefers to pay less in interest than more.

For example, if Company XYZ receives a credit rating of AAA, then it might pay 3 percent interest on a 10-year bond. If Company LMN receives a credit rating of C, it might have to pay 4.5 percent interest on a 10-year bond in order to entice investors to purchase the debt. The reason for this interest rate discrepancy is because investors must be compensated with higher interest payments for buying riskier bonds.

Barbara Friedberg

See also: Banking; Bankruptcy; Bonds; Debt; Investing; Risk; Year 2007–2008: Subprime Housing Crisis and Mortgage Meltdown; Year 2010: Dodd-Frank Wall Street Reform and Consumer Protection Act

Further Reading

Finney, Denise. August 13, 2009. "A Brief History of Credit Rating Agencies." Investopedia/ articles/bonds/09/history-credit-rating-agencies.asp

Frankel, Alison. 2013. "Moody's, S&P Settle Lawsuits over Debt Vehicle Ratings." As reported in Robbins Geller Rudman & Dowd LLP, http://www.rgrdlaw.com/news -item-165.html

Investopedia. "Bond Rating Agencies." Accessed May 31, 2014. http://www.investopedia .com/terms/b/bond-rating-agencies.asp

Investopedia. "Definition of 'Credit Rating'." Accessed May 31, 2014. http://www .investopedia.com/terms/c/creditrating.asp

Taibbi, Matt. 2013. "The Last Mystery of the Financial Crisis." *Rolling Stone.* http://www .rollingstone.com/politics/news/the-last-mystery-of-the-financial-crisis-20130619

Credit Report and Reporting Agencies

A credit report is a tool used by lending institutions such as banks to determine if you are a good risk and will pay back the loan you are applying for. The credit report contains information on your past and current financial transactions and payment history that involves debt, such as credit cards and loans. Additionally it will include information on judgments and past credit inquiries from credit-granting institutions.

You are allowed to get one free credit report a year from each of the reporting agencies. You may also request a report when you are denied credit. The credit reporting agencies are the companies that compile the data for your credit report and provide the information to banks and other institutions for a fee.

What Is on a Credit Report?

A credit report contains information related to your ability to pay back money that you borrow. It includes the following items:

Personal identification information—This includes your name, address, Social Security number, and phone number. It may also contain information from your past such as former names, addresses, employers, or people with whom you have a credit relationship, such as your spouse.

Outstanding debts—These are debts that you have not paid off in full. Examples are mortgages, car loans, student loans, and credit cards.

Past debts—Any debts that you have finished paying off will continue to show on your credit reports. For example, once you have paid off a car loan, it will remain on your credit report as a debt paid in full. If you do not pay it in full and instead use a settlement, then the report will indicate that the debt was settled and closed.

Payment history—Your credit report will show if you made your payments on time, or late. Typically it will show on time, 30 days late, 60 days late, and 90 days or more late. After that point, it typically will be moved to a collection status such as "referred to collection," repossession, or charged off. These last classifications indicate you have not paid the debt as you had originally agreed to do.

Positive information on your payment history will typically stay on your report indefinitely and negative information will go away after seven years. Bankruptcy will stay on your report for 10 years.

Available credit (utilization)—Your report will show how much you have available on revolving credit. Available credit is considered the available credit line minus your outstanding balance. Thus if your credit line is $20,000 and your balance is $5,000, you have available credit of $15,000.

The lower your utilization, the better it is for your credit score, and lenders look on this favorably. If you are maxed out (borrowed to the full limit) on your credit cards and are applying for more, it is not a good sign.

Public records—Your credit report will also include any items that are on the public record such as tax liens, court judgments, and bankruptcies.

Credit inquiries—Anytime someone checks your credit, it will show up on your credit report.

Dispute statements—If there is an item that you disagree with on your report, you can file a dispute statement, and this will show up on your credit report. The credit-granting company with whom you have the dispute may also include their statement of what happened with your dispute on the credit report.

Types of Debt

There are three types of credit that will appear on your credit report:

Revolving credit—When you don't have a final end date for paying off the debt, you are allowed to continually use the credit, pay it off, and then take out more. Examples of revolving credit are credit cards and home equity loans.

Installment loan—This type of loan has a fixed loan amount, a fixed payment, and a fixed payoff date. Examples are auto loans and mortgages.

Open debt—This is the least common among the types of debts, but includes debts that must be paid in full every month. An example of this are some of the cards offered by American Express. There is no credit limit, but you have to pay in full every month.

Purpose of a Credit Report

The purpose of the credit report is to help companies determine if you are a good credit risk. The report is also used by insurance companies, some employers when you are applying for a job, landlords, and when granting military security clearance. When used by these companies and institutions it is typically to determine if you are responsible and pay your debts.

For some jobs such as in the banking industry employers want to ensure that you are able to handle the constant interaction with money and can responsibly manage it for others. In the military it has been shown that most unethical or illegal acts are in order to gain money to pay off debts.

Credit Score

The credit report itself does not say you are a good or a bad risk. It is up to the lending institution to take the information from the report and make their own decision on your creditworthiness.

In an attempt to make this easier, a credit score was created to attempt to summarize your ability to pay. This is also known as your FICO score. This score is not part of your credit report. Companies pay extra to have this score given to them in addition to your credit report. When you get your annual free report it will not include your credit score unless you pay an additional fee for access to the score.

Reporting Agencies

Your credit report is compiled by a credit reporting agency, also known as credit bureaus. There are three major agencies: Experian, Equifax, and TransUnion.

Each one gathers information from lending agencies and public records to compile your report and score. While each company typically has very similar information about your credit history, there may be small differences between each of the reports and the scores that the agencies report to lending institutions.

These agencies are for-profit companies and make money by selling your reports to lending institutions and others that want the information. You do have to grant the company requesting the credit report permission to access your report; they cannot simply request it. For example, if your landlord wants to run a credit report, you must sign an authorization form for the landlord to be able to do so.

Lending institutions are not required to report any information on your debts, but do so voluntarily to help create a complete picture of an individual's credit.

The reporting agencies are monitored by the Federal Trade Commission (FTC).

Disputing Information on the Credit Report

If you pull your credit report and determine that information is false, then you can request that the reporting agencies remove it from your report.

In order to do this you must submit a request. Then the agency has 30 days to verify the information or to remove the information.

It is, however, possible that the information may show up at a later time. This occurs when the bank or lending institution has the wrong information on their files. After the agency has removed the information, the bank will re-report the data and it will show up again on your report. In order to guarantee that this debt will not show up again, you must work with the lending institution to remove the bad information from their files.

In today's society, maintaining a good credit history is an important personal finance skill. It allows you to more easily buy a home, borrow to purchase a vehicle, rent an apartment, and sometimes be hired for a job.

Andrea Travillian

See also: Bankruptcy; Consumer Credit/Debt; Credit Card; Credit Score; Debt; Debt Collection; Delinquency Loans; Mortgage

Further Reading

Consumer Financial Protection Bureau. "Credit Reports and Scores." Accessed March 12, 2014. http://www.consumerfinance.gov/askcfpb/

Debt.org. "How Being in Debt Affects Military Clearance." Accessed March 18. http://www.debt.org/veterans/military-security-clearances/

Equifax. "How Long Does Information Stay on My Credit Report?" Last modified May 10, 2010.http://blog.equifax.com/credit/faq-how-long-does-information-stay-on-my-credit-report/

Experian. "How Utilization Rate Affects Credit Scores." Last modified October 30, 2013. http://www.experian.com/blogs/ask-experian/2013/10/30/how-utilization-rate-affects-credit-scores/

Credit Score

A credit score is a widely accepted method of determining the consumer's creditworthiness or ability to repay borrowed funds. Several companies provide this credit vetting service to financial institutions. FICO, short for Fair Isaac Corporation, is the most popular credit scoring system.

Credit is an important part of personal finance and modern money management. Credit is given when consumers borrow money to buy goods and services today, to be paid back in the future. When credit is awarded, the consumer takes on debt or the responsibility to pay back the amount borrowed in the future.

The lending company, which issues the credit, needs to ensure that the loan will be repaid in a timely manner along with the accumulated interest. How does the lender decide how much credit or access to cash to give the consumer?

A high credit score has broad implications for the consumer. Borrowers with higher credit scores receive access to larger amounts of credit with lower interest rates. This impacts borrowing for a vehicle, a home, or smaller items bought with credit cards.

Individuals with lower credit scores have greater difficulty obtaining credit and are considered more risky borrowers. Due to their lower creditworthiness, these borrowers pay higher interest rates and encounter greater difficulty in obtaining credit.

For example, a prospective home buyer with a credit score below 600 is ineligible for a prime or preferred interest rate on a mortgage. Due to their lack of creditworthiness, these borrowers get their mortgage from a subprime lender and must pay a higher interest rate on their subprime mortgage.

Credit Score Basics

There are three major credit bureaus in the United States, Experian, TransUnion, and Equifax. Usually, the credit scores from each agency are similar. Lenders, collection agencies, and court records supply information for the consumer's credit report. Since information is reported at different times to each agency, and the formats vary for each credit bureau, credit scores are not identical between agencies.

Each of the credit reporting agencies might have marginally different information about the consumer. Further, each credit bureau calls the credit scores by different names. For example, TransUnion calls a credit score the Precision Score. Consumers should check their credit report and score with each credit reporting agency to investigate inconsistencies and errors.

Credit scores range from a low of 300 to a perfect score of 850. The scores are computed by integrating a variety of information and comparing it with similar data from hundreds of thousands of past credit reports. Simply, the credit score provides an estimate of future credit risk or ability to repay debt.

Credit scores fluctuate with changes in the input information. Thus, a credit score demonstrates a borrower's creditworthiness at a particular point in time.

What Information Influences the Credit Score?

The credit score is derived from the information contained in the consumer's credit report. There are four broad categories in the credit report: personal information, accounts summary, inquiries, and negative items. The personal information identifies the consumer and includes address, birthdate, and Social Security number.

The accounts summary lists current and previous credit accounts. Examples of accounts summary items include bank credit cards, store credit cards, mortgage loans, and car loans.

Inquiries tell who has requested a consumer's credit record. The negative items include late payments, delinquencies, and bankruptcies. The more negative items on a credit report, the lower the credit score.

The impact of one piece of information on a credit score is difficult to quantify. Lenders weigh components of a credit score and credit history according to their own standards.

According to Fair Isaac Corporation, there is an approximate breakdown of the importance of each category of information on a credit score. Payment history is weighted 35 percent, length of credit history is valued at 15 percent, types of credit in use and new credit each contribute 10 percent to the total, and amounts owed contribute 30 percent.

Credit Score Facts

Paying off bills on time helps one's credit score. When a payment is missed, it's important to make the payment as quickly as possible and continue to make future payments in a timely manner. Even if an account with a missed payment is closed, the information remains in the credit history because the payment history includes previous and current payment records. Credit scores are seriously hurt by bankruptcies, foreclosures, suits, wage attachments, liens, and judgments.

Opening more credit accounts doesn't necessarily decrease one's credit score. Nor does closing old accounts necessarily increase one's credit score. Multiple credit inquiries within a limited time period usually don't significantly impact one's overall score. When searching for a loan, it's expected that the consumer will compare rates by checking several lenders. In general, a mix of credit accounts, all in good standing, where the amount of debt is not approaching the full debt limit but is well below, will positively impact one's credit score.

When an individual is turned down for credit, the Equal Credit Opportunity Act (ECOA) gives him or her 30 days to find out why credit was denied. Within 60 days after being declined credit, the consumer is given access to a free credit report.

Healthy Credit Score Practices

Pay all credit accounts on time. Keep balances on credit cards relatively low and avoid using all available credit. Don't open many credit accounts rapidly. Pay off debt instead of moving it around. Only open credit cards you need and will use.

Consumers are advised to check their credit report and credit scores annually in order to spot errors. The government requires each of the three credit agencies to provide the consumer with a free credit report annually. This report can be obtained at annualcreditreport.com.

Barbara Friedberg

See also: Bankruptcy; Consumer Credit/Debt; Credit Card; Credit Report and Reporting Agencies; Debt; Debt Collection; Debt/Credit Counseling; Interest Income and Payments; Liabilities; Loans; Year 2010: Dodd-Frank Wall Street Reform and Consumer Protection Act

Further Reading

Board of Governors of the Federal Reserve System Web site. "Credit Reports and Credit Scores." Accessed December 17, 2013. http://www.federalreserve.gov/credit reports/

My Fico Web site. "Understanding Your FICO Score." Last modified November, 2011. http://www.myfico.com/Downloads/Files/myFICO_UYFS_Booklet.pdf

Credit Union

A credit union is a type of financial institution that allows you to deposit your money and take loans, similar to a bank. However, unlike banks, credit unions have a different organizational structure. The main distinction is that they are nonprofit and member owned. The focus of a credit union is to provide a low-cost source of loans and banking services, while at the same time promoting community and education among its members.

Credit unions are regulated by the government entity that grants them a charter. A charter is a license to operate as a financial institution. Charters are issued by the state government in the state where the credit union is located or by the federal government.

History of Credit Unions

The first credit union was started in the 1850s in Germany by Franz Hermann Schulze-Delitzsch. He started the credit union in the cities as a way for shopkeepers, traders, and artisans to pool money for mutual benefit.

The idea behind pooling money is that a group of people could put their money together and those that needed to borrow could do so, while those that had extra could earn additional money by loaning it out to the others. Thus, the businesses that were in the middle of a slowdown could borrow for a reasonable amount from those businesses that were doing well.

In the 1860s another German, Fredrich Wilhelm Raiffeisen, took the concept to the rural areas and started credit unions for the poorer common workers that were not able to use traditional banks.

These unions had special structures that allowed seasonal employees to make payments on loans when income was coming in and not make payments when there was no income. In the early days all positions at the credit unions were volunteer except for the cashier.

By the end of the 19th century credit unions had spread throughout Europe. The first official credit union in the United States started in November 1908 in Manchester, New Hampshire. As of today there are more than 6,900 credit unions throughout the United States and more than 55,000 worldwide.

How Credit Unions Are Different from Banks

While banks and credit unions offer many of the same products and services, credit unions vary in the structure, the purpose of the institution, and other features. Following are the main differences.

Profit—Banks are for-profit institutions with the money going to the owners or shareholders of the bank. Credit unions, on the other hand, are nonprofit. Once the costs of running the credit union and excess capital requirements are reached, the profits are returned to the members.

Profits are typically returned in the form of higher interest rates (which they call dividends), lower fees for products, and lower interest rates on loans. Some credit unions even use the overage to offer additional services and benefits, such as scholarships and member appreciation days with giveaways.

Management structure—Credit unions are governed by their members, who are the owners. Members each get one vote to elect the board of directors, no matter how much money they have in their accounts.

For day-to-day operations, credit unions hire traditional banking employees to hold positions such as tellers, managers, and loan officers. In most cases, the credit union members elect the governing board of directors. This board steers the strategy and decision making of the credit union. The board reviews interest rates, sets policies, approves budgets, and hires the CEO/president who runs the credit union on a daily basis.

The committees are typically appointed by the board of directors. Typical committees include a credit committee and a supervisory committee.

Banks are governed by employees, shareholders, and outside directors. The board is elected by the shareholders, where the number of shares you own determines how many votes you get. Not everyone that is on a management board or committee is an actual customer of a bank, whereas all managers of a credit union are account holders in the credit union.

Insured and governed—Banks and credit unions are overseen and backed by different government entities. Federally chartered banks are under the control of the FDIC (Federal Deposit Insurance Corporation). Credit unions fall under the NCUA (National Credit Union Administration).

Just as customers of banks have insurance from a government agency to protect the depositors' funds against the banks closing, credit unions also ensure their members' deposits. Credit unions are insured by the National Credit Union Share Insurance Fund, which is run by the NCUA.

Who can join—At a bank, anyone can open an account as long as he or she meets the financial requirements set forth by the bank. Credit unions, however, have nonfinancial requirements that are instead focused on where you work and live.

For example, to join a credit union, you might be required to live, go to school, or work in a specific county or city. Or if it is a company credit union, then you may be required to work for that company. After you meet those requirements the required opening deposit is much lower than at a traditional bank. Instead of $100 to open an account, you typically need around $5.

Once you are a member you have lifetime membership even if you move or change jobs. Once you have membership your immediate family members may also join even if they do not meet the requirements on their own.

Products

Like a bank, credit unions offer checking accounts, savings accounts, loans, certificates of deposit, ATMs, and more. There are some minor differences in the product names, although this is changing to create greater consistency within the financial industry. Here are some of the naming variations between banks and credit unions:

A checking account is a share draft account.
A savings account is a share account.
Certificates of deposits are share term certificates.

Additionally, some credit unions have begun adding outside services such as insurance and investment management.

Fees remain one of the biggest differences between credit unions and banks. Most deposit accounts do not have any monthly fees, unless they offer special benefits. Additional services such as wire transfers, cashier's checks, and statement research are less expensive at credit unions than at traditional banks. For example, a wire transfer at a credit union costs approximately $10, whereas the banks charge about $30.

Credit unions are a competitive alternative to traditional banks for great cost savings. Plus they serve an often ignored segment of the population with fewer financial resources. Credit unions, by offering low fees and smaller account opening requirements, are better able to serve their members.

Andrea Travillian

See also: Banking; Certificate of Deposit; Checking Account; Interest Rates; Investing; Loans; Money Market Account; Savings Account

Further Reading

Credit Union National Association. 2014. Accessed March 6. http://www.cuna.org
Credit Unions for You. "How to Start Up a New Credit Union." 2014. Accessed March 6. http://www.creditunionsforyou.com/start.html
World Council of Credit Unions. "2012 Statistical Report." Accessed March 6. http://www.woccu.org/publications/statreport

Cryptocurrency *(see Digital Currency)*

Currency

Currency is the money we carry in our pocket or keep in our bank account. In its narrow definition, currency is the same as money—a way of storing value or a means of exchange for goods and services. The actual object of money may be physical tokens—whales' teeth, diamonds, gold—or a written record accepted and backed by some sort of guarantee, which could be issued by a bank or a government.

When the token is a coin or printed note declared by a state to be legal, the currency is known as a fiat currency. Where it is backed by a central bank with legal power to create money, it is a sovereign currency.

To enable trade between groups, a satisfactory standard is needed so that exchanges satisfy both parties to the trade. Currency's many forms are evolving.

Tokens

For many years, currencies were based on rare metals—gold, silver, or copper, for example—where the value was the intrinsic value of the metal. This enabled international trade. Large amounts of gold or silver are difficult to transport. Thieves and robbers plagued those who transported the valuable metals. Carrying large amounts of currency is risky, so "promissory notes" were devised where a bank "promised to pay the bearer" the amount denoted.

The actual commodity (gold) would be in a safe place such as a bank vault until the note was presented. Being able to exchange banknotes for gold is known as a gold standard. The value of U.S. paper currency was officially tied to gold from 1879 to 1933 according to Craig K. Elwell (2011). Today the value of paper currency is not pegged to any precious metal.

Gold Standard

The main advantage of a gold standard is price stability—money is limited to the amount of gold held by the central bank, which controls price inflation. Exchange rates can be fixed with respect to currencies that also use a gold standard, and it protects the rights of those who own the gold.

On the other hand, variations in the market price of gold can lead to short-term sharp variations in a currency. About 10 percent of gold is used in industry for manufacturing and other uses, so there may be shortages or gluts in price due to supply and demand. The gold standard also grants excessive power to individuals, companies, and states that already own or mine gold, denying it to the rest and limiting economic growth along with government's ability to steer an economy. Last, it can be very deflationary. Deflation refers to falling prices, usually caused by a shrinking supply. Excessive deflation may lead to falling profits and declining employment. Further perils of deflation include lost income and increasing loan defaults.

At different times, some nations have gone back to the gold standard but they have always reverted after a short while. The last country to use gold to back its currency was Switzerland, which had 40 percent reserve holdings, abandoning it in 2000.

Inflation

Overall economic activity is controlled by varying the interest rate the central bank charges when lending money to retail banks. Too much money with too little demand will lead to price inflation while too little money and too much demand will lead to a slump and recession.

Massive inflation is clearly bad—money needs to be spent before prices rise and the value of money in bank accounts drops. This occurred in Germany after World War I but also in parts of Eastern Europe in the 1990s, when people lost their savings.

Reducing prices may seem to be a good idea but many areas in business have fixed costs, such as rents fixed by contract. Recession quickly forces such businesses into bankruptcy and closure, with loss of jobs affecting the wider economy.

Most economists favor a small amount of price inflation in an economy, typically 2 to 3 percent, to enable differentials to be ironed out and so that no major part of an economy is in recession.

Valuation

A currency has an international value in relation to other world currencies. For example, in February 2014 US$1 could be exchanged for 0.74 euro or 1 euro could purchase US$1.37.

In the past, these values have been fixed by international accord or imposed by one nation on another. But since the 1980s, major currencies have been allowed to float, which means values change from day to day. A currency floats or adjusts based on supply, demand, and various other economic factors. Specifically, the value of one country's currency versus another's will change. Continuing with the former example, although US$1 purchases 0.74 euro today, in a day or a month, that same US$1 might purchase 0.72 euro or 0.79 euro.

Currency values are further adjusted based on the perception of the domestic economy by currency traders. For example, the U.S. trade deficit and budget deficit (signs of economic weakness) have caused the U.S. dollar to weaken against the euro. This weakening means the dollar buys fewer euros than in the past.

A strong currency may seem to be desirable because businesses and individuals can buy overseas or import goods and services with ease, but it makes exporting, including tourism, difficult. For example, the country with the stronger currency is more expensive to visit than the one with the weaker currency. A weak currency means the opposite: imported goods and services become more expensive, but exporting and tourism become easier and more affordable.

Central Banks

In a fiat currency, the amount of money available is theoretically unlimited and needs to be controlled by the central bank, which is the Federal Reserve Bank in the United States. It is theoretically impossible for a nation with a sovereign currency to become bankrupt. However, it is possible for a nation that shares a currency with other nations, such as in the Eurozone, to become bankrupt, even where the nations agree to share a currency, if the central bank cannot—or will not—step in to support a bank. This has been one of the fundamental problems of the Eurozone debt crisis.

Some money creation is essential for an economy because money is always being destroyed by natural disasters, accidents, wear and tear, or waste. But the rate of creation of new money is crucial in managing the economy.

Excess money creation ultimately leads to inflation and the value of the currency declining. Even modest excess creation of money will lead to some reduction in value, but that can be useful to aid economic recovery. Therefore, central banks are either under political control or at least subject to targets of inflation, unemployment, growth, or some other economic stability measures.

Alternative Currencies

New forms of currency independent of governments have been devised based either on trust networks with a central gateway to the "real" world (such as a bank), or peer-to-peer cryptographic systems, which are not centralized but are based on public-private key signed transactions. Further, currencies using trusted brands have also been suggested.

Bitcoin is an example of a peer-to-peer currency with no central bank involvement. All transactions are carried out within the network.

The financial environment is also testing additional currency replacement means of payment. Apple Pay and Google Wallet are two of the recent payment systems looking to bypass cash, credit cards, and debit cards.

None of these alternative currencies or payment systems has gained widespread acceptance. Further, there are regulatory issues, particularly for peer-to-peer systems as they lack central authority. Moreover, there is concern that alternative currencies are used for money laundering, criminal activity, and terrorism. In addition, they are a means of avoiding taxes.

Although backed by the underlying currency, financial transactions today are frequently carried out with debit and credit cards, replacing the need for cash or currency on hand.

Maria Nedeva

See also: Banking; Cash; Digital Currency; Federal Reserve Bank; Liquidity; Savings Account; Year 1944: Creation of the International Monetary Fund and the World Bank at the Bretton Woods International Conference; Year 1999: Introduction of the Euro to World Financial Markets

Further Reading

Bernstein, Peter, and Paul A. Volker. 2008. *A Primer on Money, Banking and Gold,* 3rd ed. Hoboken, NJ: Wiley.

Elwell, Craig K. June 23, 2011. "Brief History of the Gold Standard in the United States." *Congressional Research Service.* http://www.fas.org/sgp/crs/misc/R41887.pdf

Kemp-Robertson, Paul. July 2013. "Bitcoin. Sweat. Tide. Meet the Future of Branded Currency." *TED Global* YouTube video. http://www.ted.com/talks/paul_kemp _robertson_bitcoin_sweat_tide_meet_the_future_of_branded_currency.html

Levinson, Mark. "Guide to Financial Markets." *The Economist—Guide to the Financial Markets.pdf.* Accessed October 24, 2013. https://docs.google.com/file/d/0B_ Qxj5U7eaJTZTJkODYzN2ItZjE3Yy00Y2M0LTk2ZmUtZGU0NzA3NGI4Y2Y5/ edit?usp=drive_web&urp=https://www.google.com/&pli=1&hl=en#

Debt

The obligation to repay borrowed money is called a debt. Individuals, corporations, and nations all borrow money and incur debt.

Debt is used by individuals and corporations to buy things they could otherwise not afford. There is a written agreement when one party borrows from another. This agreement specifies how much money is borrowed, from whom, to whom, and the repayment terms. Debt repayment usually includes interest payments as well. How the interest is calculated and repaid is also specified in the initial borrowing agreement.

There are various types of debts including secured, unsecured, and revolving debt. Consumers take on debt when they use a credit card to purchase a dinner at a restaurant and don't repay the credit card bill in full at the end of the month. A corporation takes on debt when they borrow $1 million in order to expand their business internationally.

When a consumer borrows $100,000 from a lender to buy a home, he or she takes on a legal agreement to repay that money. This particular type of debt is called a mortgage.

This entry will discuss the various entities that borrow and incur debt such as individuals, companies, and nations. Types of debt will be covered. Finally, national household debt will be discussed.

Types of Debt

Secured

Secured debt requires the borrower to give the lender collateral or real goods or property (security) if the borrower fails to repay the debt. A mortgage loan is secured by the property, as collateral. If the borrower fails to repay the loan, then the bank takes possession of the real estate. If a pawnbroker loans someone $100, he expects collateral in exchange for the loan. In that case the collateral might be jewelry or other valuable property.

Corporations might pledge real property as well for a secured loan. A corporation might also pledge their financial securities, such as stocks and bonds, as collateral.

Unsecured

An unsecured loan is not secured by an underlying asset such as real estate, jewelry, or physical property. Credit card debt is unsecured as are medical or utility bills. In this case, if the borrower defaults on the loan, there is no home or jewelry or vehicle to seize.

With unsecured loans, if the borrower fails to make the debt payments within the agreed-on time period, then the lender must use other remedies to collect the amount owed. The lending party might sue in court for the unpaid debt. If the lender wins the suit, the lending party may be allowed to garnish or take a part of the debtor's future wages.

Because unsecured debt carries higher risk than secured debt, unsecured loans usually charge higher interest rates. For example, one might obtain a vehicle loan for 5 percent whereas the interest on a credit card can be as high as 18 or more percent.

Revolving

Revolving debt, frequently called "revolving credit," gives the borrower, either corporations or individuals, access to credit should they need it in the future. Revolving debt is also called a line of credit.

In some cases the borrower pays a commitment fee and then is allowed to use the available funds as needed. The amount available is agreed on when the original contracts are initiated.

There are various types of revolving credit including signature loans (which don't require collateral but simply the borrower's signature), credit cards, and home equity lines of credit, to name a few. Credit cards also offer a type of revolving debt. This type of debt is more complicated than a typical loan. The lender approves the borrower for a specific amount of money or credit limit. This amount is determined by the borrower's perceived ability to repay the debt and considers the borrower's income, assets, and other debt. As the consumer or company repays the debt, the repaid amount is available to borrow again.

Home equity lines of credit and overdraft protection for checking accounts are also considered revolving debt. The interest payment and fees on this type of debt may be variable instead of a fixed interest rate, which stays the same for the life of the loan.

What Is the Difference between Debt and Liabilities?

Frequently the terms *debt* and *liabilities* are used interchangeably to mean an amount owed to another. More specifically, debt has a narrower definition than liabilities. In this instance debt refers to monies borrowed with their terms formalized in a written document. Debt is not a synonym for liability when used to describe types of insurance.

Corporate Debt

Corporations frequently borrow in order to grow and expand. A limited amount of corporate borrowing, sometimes referred to as leverage, gives companies a greater amount of financial resources to use in order to grow the company more rapidly. It is a widely accepted business practice for companies to borrow in order to grow.

The percentage of debt as compared with the amount the company owns (equity) should remain within certain constraints so that the company can afford to repay the debt in a timely manner. There are acceptable industry-wide debt percentages. For example, a utility company with a great amount of guaranteed monthly utility payments made by consumers can afford to borrow more than a small start-up company with uncertain revenue projections.

National Debt

Nationalities, just like individuals and corporations, borrow money to pay for things they could not otherwise afford. In the case of the U.S. government, the national debt includes public debt such as the Treasury securities (Treasury bonds, notes, and bills) issued by the government. The purchasers of these debt securities are the ones loaning money to the government. This debt might be used to help fund wars, pay for government programs, or for a variety of governmental uses.

When the U.S. government lacks sufficient funds from tax revenues to pay for government obligations, it must borrow the deficient amount (or deficit) by issuing Treasury securities. Not only do U.S. citizens, corporations, and other governmental entities purchase the Treasury bonds, notes, and bills, but foreign individuals and governments also buy these securities. That is how the United States develops some financial dependence on international entities.

Consumer Debt Levels in the United States

As previously discussed, debt is a useful tool to finance large purchases such as homes and cars as well as assist when times are tough. When layoffs or unexpected expenses emerge, consumers use debt to help make ends meet.

According to Vornovytskyy, Gottschalck, and Smith (2011), in 2011, 69 percent of U.S. households held debt. Although 69 percent may seem like a great amount of debt, it represents a decline in household debt from 2000 when households with debt hit a peak of 74 percent. Although the percentage of households with debt decreased during the decade, the median amount of debt has increased. In 2000, the median debt level per household was approximately $50,971, whereas in 2011, the approximate median amount of debt per household rose to $70,000. This increase was caused by a 30 percent rise in both secured and unsecured debt.

The increase in debt may have positive and negative implications. On a positive note, more debt may indicate an increase in consumer confidence. Individuals may feel the economy is growing, their employment is secure, and they are willing to borrow for new homes, cars, and additional consumption.

The negative impact of increased debt levels includes financial as well as mental health risks. When a household incurs a greater amount of debt relative to its income, there is a repayment risk. In general, total debt percentage, when compared with gross income, should remain below 43 percent, according to the Consumer Financial Protection Bureau. Should the consumer encounter financial problems such as a job loss or unanticipated medical expenses, the debt repayment could be in jeopardy.

Home foreclosures and bankruptcies are caused when individuals have greater debt than they can repay. Individuals are at risk for financial difficulty when unexpected expenses occur if they have taken on too much debt.

In sum, debt, when used responsibly, is a tool to enable individuals, companies, and countries to smooth out consumption and pay for expenses they would otherwise be unable to afford.

Barbara Friedberg

See also: Accountant; Banking; Budget; Consumer Credit/Debt; Credit Card; Credit Report and Reporting Agencies; Credit Score; Debt/Credit Counseling; Delinquency;

Liabilities; Liquidity; Loans; Margin; Treasury Securities; Year 2007–2008: Subprime Housing Crisis and Mortgage Meltdown; Year 2011–2012: European Debt Crisis

Further Reading

Consumer Financial Protection Bureau Web site. "Debt-to-Income Ratio? Why Is the 43% Debt-to-Income Ratio Important?" Accessed April 15, 2014. http://www.consumerfin ance.gov/askcfpb/1791/what-debt-income-ratio-why-43-debt-income-ratio-import ant.html

Investopedia Web site. "Debt." Accessed April 15, 2014. http://www.investopedia.com /terms/d/debt.asp

U.S. Department of the Treasury Web site. "National Debt." Accessed April 15, 2014. http://www.treasury.gov/resource-center/faqs/markets/pages/national-debt.aspx

Vornovytskyy, Marina, Alfred Gottschalck, and Adam Smith. "Household Debt in the U.S.: 2000 to 2011." Accessed April 15. http://www.census.gov/people/wealth/files/Debt%20 Highlights%202011.pdf http://www.treasury.gov/resource-center/faqs/markets/pages /national-debt.aspx

Debt Collection

A debt is an obligation of a consumer to repay borrowed funds to a lender or vendor. A debt collector is anyone whose job it is to obtain debt repayments. Individuals who fail to pay their bills may be subject to debt collection. Initially, the lender attempts to collect the amount due from the borrower. A lender includes the credit card company for a retail store or national company, a bank, a vendor of services such as a cable company, a medical provider, a lender such as a mortgage company, or any business with whom the borrower has conducted a business transaction on credit. In sum, a lender is any type of organization that issues credit cards, sells goods or services on credit, or makes loans.

This entry groups lenders and businesses together and calls the creditor a lender. If the lender is unsuccessful in receiving the monies owed, he or she may transfer the debt to a debt collection agency or attorney whose job it is to collect or recover all or part of the amount of money owed.

When a consumer fails to pay the department store credit card bill, after a few months, the bill is transferred to a debt collector who attempts to collect the debt. This process occurs when an individual has financial problems and stops making payments or underpays the amount owed to the lender.

The Fair Debt Collection Practices Act

The federal Fair Debt Collection Practices Act (FDCPA) governs how debt is collected. This law was enacted to eliminate abusive debt collection practices. In the past, debt collectors engaged in abusive practices that led to personal bankruptcies, marital instability, loss of jobs, as well as invasions of individual privacy.

Debt Collection Horror Stories

Goldman Schwartz, a Texas-based debt collector, was shut down by the Federal Trade Commission for using scare tactics to force people to pay their debts. Some of their methods included calling repeatedly and stating "we can take you to jail" or "we'll send the sheriff's department to your job and take care of this the hard way." Both of those statements are clearly against the law.

If the former allegations were not enough, according to CNN Money, Goldman Schwartz told the debtors that when they went to jail, police would take their children into government custody. They also posed as a law firm in order to scare consumers into paying.

One consumer accused the firm of going to her workplace and informing her co-workers he was going to arrest her and that the colleagues would have to pick her out of a lineup.

Rumson, Bolling and Associates was fined more than $700,000 for threatening to dig up the dead bodies of the debtors' children if they did not pay their funeral bills. This company also allegedly threatened to kill a consumer's dog and then arrest her.

Clearly, not all debt collectors are following the law.

This law requires debt collectors, within five days of initial contact, to provide the consumer in writing with the amount of the debt, the name of the creditor to whom the debt is owed, and a statement that purports the debt is valid. If the consumer does not dispute the debt within 30 days, the debt is assumed to be valid.

If the consumer disputes the debt, it must be done in writing within 30 days of first contact. At that point, the debt collector is required by law to obtain verification of the debt in writing and mail it to the consumer. The verification must include the amount of the debt as well as the name of the original creditor to whom the debt is owed.

Debt Collectors May Not Engage in Abusive Practices

FDCPA clearly prohibits debt collectors from harassing, oppressing, or abusing anyone while attempting to collect a debt. Debt collectors can't lie in their attempts to collect debts. For example, collectors cannot misrepresent themselves as attorneys or officers of the U.S. government, nor can they falsely claim that the debtor will go to prison. Debt collectors may not call you at work, or early in the morning, or late at night. Nor can debt collectors levy additional interest, fees, or charges on top of the debt unless permitted to do so by state law or under the terms of the original credit contract.

Unless the debt collector sues the individual and wins a judgment, the collector may not garnish the creditor's wages. If the borrower believes the collector violated the law, the borrower has one year in which to sue a debt collector in state or federal court. The debt collector may also be reported to the state attorney general's office for abusive practices.

Debt collection is used when a borrower fails to pay money owed. This practice is regulated by the government and must be practiced in accordance with the law.

Barbara Friedberg

See also: Consumer Credit/Debt; Credit Card; Credit Report and Reporting Agencies; Credit Score; Debt; Debt/Credit Counseling; Delinquency; Mortgage

Further Reading

Ellis, Blake. February 6, 2013. "Debt Collection Horror Stories." *CNN Money Website.* http://money.cnn.com/2013/02/06/pf/debt-collection/

Federal Trade Commission, Bureau of Consumer Protection Business Center. "Fair Debt Collection Practices Act." Amended July 2010. Accessed June 28, 2013. http://business.ftc.gov/documents/fair-debt-collection-practices-act

Federal Trade Commission, Consumer Information. 2013. "Debt Collection." Accessed June 28. http://www.consumer.ftc.gov/articles/0149-debt-collection

USA.gov. 2013. "Debt Collection; Know Your Rights." Accessed June 28. http://www.usa.gov/topics/money/credit/debt/collection.shtml

Debt/Credit Counseling

Credit counseling (sometimes referred to as debt counseling) is designed to help those in need of assistance with a declining financial situation. Credit counseling assists those who are behind in their credit card payments, living paycheck to paycheck, have difficulty saving money, receiving calls from collection agencies, facing bankruptcy, or experiencing other financial difficulties. Credit counselors advise consumers on managing money, budgeting, saving, debt, and assist in creating a money management plan. There are both for-profit and nonprofit agencies to help with financial problems.

Debt and Credit Statistics

The BankAmericard (now known as Visa), issued in 1958, was the first national general-use credit card allowing balances to be paid over time.

As of March 2012, 39 percent of Americans carried credit card debt from month to month.

As of April 2014, total U.S. outstanding consumer debt was $3.18 trillion.

The average age at which Americans expect to be debt-free is 53.

As of April 2012, 55 percent of males carried a credit card balance.

As of April 2012, 60 percent of females carried a credit card balance.

In 2011–2012, the average college student's outstanding credit card balance was $755.

As of June 30, 2013, MasterCard had 144 debit cards in the United States and 336 million cards in the rest of the world.

As of March 31, 2013, Visa had 428 million debit cards in the United States and 906 million cards in the rest of the world.

As of February 2014, the average APR (annual percentage rate) on a credit card with a balance on it was 13.14 percent.

(Source: Ray, Daniel P., and Yasmin Ghahremani. "Credit Card Statistics, Industry Facts, Debt Statistics." Updated June 11, 2014. http://www.creditcards.com/credit-card-news/credit-card-industry-facts-personal-debt-statistics-1276.php)

Credit cards, payday loans, and a variety of loans are widely available today. This ready credit encourages individuals to borrow in order to buy items they cannot afford. Additionally, emergency expenses such as unexpected medical bills create financial hardship. When an individual's bills become delinquent and expenses surpass income, credit counseling is a solution for help with financial problems. Additionally, those facing bankruptcy are required to seek credit counseling.

For example, credit (debt) counseling may be needed in the following situation. If an individual charges a large amount on a credit card and does not pay the total amount due at the end of the month, interest is applied to the unpaid balance. If the bill is not paid in full in subsequent months and more charges are added, additional interest accrues. When this debt, combined with other debts, increases each month, without the likelihood of paying the complete debt due, then credit counseling services can instruct the consumer in how to manage debt and finances.

How to Locate a Credit Counselor

A reputable credit counseling agency will send free information about itself and its services without requiring any information from the consumer. Credit counselors can be found at universities, military bases, credit unions, housing authorities, the Consumer Financial Protection Bureau (CFPB), and branches of the U.S. Cooperative Extension Service (for those in rural locations).

It is usually preferable to choose a nonprofit credit counseling service, although nonprofit does not mean free. Additionally, it is important to understand that there are unscrupulous business people posing as credit counselors at both for-profit and non-profit credit counseling organizations.

After locating a credit counselor, check the state attorney general's office and local consumer protection agency to determine whether complaints have been filed against the agency. The U.S. Department of Justice maintains a list of approved credit counseling agencies by state. Even if an agency is included on the Department of Justice's approved list, it is important to review its fees and services to ensure they are appropriate.

The consumer must ask questions of the credit counselor to understand their services. For example, "What services do you offer?" "Do you offer a plan to help with both current and future financial problems?" "What are the fees and what if I cannot afford the fees?" "Are you licensed?" "What are the qualifications of the counselors?" "How are the counselors paid?" (Beware if counselors are paid more if the consumer signs up for special services or if the counselor requests special contributions to the firm.)

Typical Credit Counseling Services

Basic services include budgeting, designing a financial management plan, and teaching basic money management skills. The agency may recommend a debt management plan (DMP) if the consumer has excess debt. The credit counselor works with the creditors to arrange a payment plan and possibly lower interest rates and fees. With a

DMP, the consumer deposits a predetermined amount of money with the credit counseling organization. The agency pays the unsecured debts, such as credit card bills, student loans, and medical bills, with the deposit. Consumers must follow up with creditors to confirm that the debt payment arrangement described by the credit counselor is valid.

On occasion, the credit counselor may recommend bankruptcy. Although nonprofit credit counselors usually do not offer debt settlement, it is an alternative. This occurs when a for-profit credit counselor negotiates with the creditors for a lump sum payoff of the debt. This payment is usually lower than the full amount owed. Debt settlement can be risky for the consumer with high fees, lack of transparency, and unscrupulous counselors.

Credit counselors are useful for consumers with significant financial problems. An alternative to credit counseling is for the consumer to handle their own financial situation. The consumer may call the creditor and attempt to negotiate his or her own repayment plan. Additionally, there are a wealth of online free resources for assistance with financial education and problems such as the National Foundation for Credit Counseling (NFCC) and the MyMoney.gov Web site.

Barbara Friedberg

See also: Bankruptcy; Budget; Consumer Credit/Debt; Credit Card; Debt; Debt Collection; Delinquency; Interest Rates; Online Personal Finance

Further Reading

Federal Trade Commission. "Choosing a Credit Counselor." Last modified November, 2012. http://www.consumer.ftc.gov/articles/0153-choosing-credit-counselor

MyMoney.gov. U.S. government financial education Web site. Accessed July 9, 2013. http://www.mymoney.gov/Pages/default.aspx.

National Foundation for Credit Counseling. Accessed July 9, 2013. http://www.nfcc.org/

Ray, Daniel P., and Yasmin Ghahremani. "Credit Card Statistics, Industry Facts, Debt Statistics." Updated June 11, 2014. http://creditcards.com/credit-card-news/credit-card-industry-facts-personal-debt-statistics-1276.php

USA.gov. "Credit Counseling Services." Last modified June 27, 2013. http://www.usa.gov/topics/money/credit/debt/out-of-control.shtml

U.S. Department of Justice. "List of Credit Counseling Agencies Approved Pursuant to 11 U.S.C. 111." Accessed July 7, 2013. http://www.justice.gov/ust/eo/bapcpa/ccde/cc_approved.htm

Deficit

A deficit is when you have more cash leaving your account than coming into the account. You can determine if there is a deficit by taking your cash inflows and subtracting your cash outflows. If the difference is a negative number, then you have a deficit.

Governments can and do frequently go bankrupt due to a long-term sustained deficit that they were unable to correct. Since 2008 13 local governments in the United States have gone bankrupt:

- Gould, Arkansas—April 2008
- Vallejo, California—May 2008
- Westfall Township, Pennsylvania—April 2009
- Washington Park, Illinois—July 2009
- Prichard, Alabama—October 2009
- Central Falls, Rhode Island—August 2011
- Boise County, Idaho—March 2011
- Harrisburg, Pennsylvania—October 2011
- Jefferson County, Alabama—November 2011
- Stockton, California—June 2012
- Mammoth Lakes, California—July 2012
- City of San Bernardino, California—August 2012
- City of Detroit, Michigan—July 2013

In addition to local governments going bankrupt, nations have also gone bankrupt. Countries that have had to declare bankruptcy in the past include Argentina, Iceland, Germany, Russia, Great Britain, and Pakistan.

For example, if you are bringing in $1,000 a month in income and your expenses are $1,200 a month, then you have a deficit of $200 a month. The concept of a deficit can be found anywhere that there is money going in and out, including but not limited to personal finances, corporate finances, and government finances.

How Deficits Are Financed

When there is a deficit you need to somehow pay for the difference in the cash coming in and the cash going out. Most entities have three ways to finance the difference. They are equity, existing savings, or debt. Governments have the added ability to create additional money supply to pay their existing bills.

Having a deficit might be sustainable for a short amount of time, but in the long run it will create a situation that is only escapable through bankruptcy. This happens because after you use all the existing savings, you must turn to debt to continue to cover a deficit.

Debt comes with a payment that must be made every month. As you borrow and increase your payments, your expenses increase, making the deficit every month even bigger, which in turn creates more debt and more payments. Eventually the debt payments become so big that creditors will no longer allow more debt. This in turn ends the ability to borrow to cover the deficit. The final outcome is that someone will not get paid as there are no available funds to cover the deficit. It is a vicious cycle that can only be corrected by increasing the cash coming in every month to a point above the cash going out every month, thus eliminating the deficit.

Personal Deficit

If you are creating a deficit on a personal level, you may begin by paying for it with your existing savings. Once your savings have run out, then you will have to utilize debt to manage the difference, including credit cards and other loans.

Eventually your debt payments combined with your existing expenses will become too big and no additional credit will be given to you. At this point you will approach bankruptcy as you are no longer able to pay all your expenses. You can, however, eliminate the deficit by bringing in more income.

Corporate Deficit

A corporate deficit occurs when a company is not selling enough to cover their costs. Their revenue minus costs is less than what is needed to pay the bills.

A company has three ways of covering the deficit. They can utilize existing savings, borrow to cover the difference, or they can sell shares of stock, otherwise known as equity, in the company to raise more money.

As with personal debt, a company cannot maintain a deficit for a long time, as savings will dry up, debt providers will not continue to loan money, and possible new shareholders won't be interested in buying into the company due to the high debt levels. This will cause the company to either go through bankruptcy to rework the existing debt or to close the doors permanently.

Government Deficit

A government deficit occurs when incoming funds from taxes do not cover the expenses incurred. A government can cover the deficit by using savings if they have any, issuing bonds as a debt instrument to borrow money, or by printing new money.

Government savings may occur from one part of the government bringing in more than they need to cover their own costs. This money can then be reallocated to other branches to cover their expenses. This was done with the Social Security surplus funds; they were shifted to other areas to cover costs, in the form of bonds issued to the Social Security trust.

The government issues its own debt in the form of bonds, instead of using credit cards and other loans. Depending on the type of bond, the government either has to pay interest on an ongoing basis, or all at once when it pays back the borrowed amount. Either way, it increases the expenses of the government the same way a loan to an individual would.

Printing new money is the least desirable of the options available to the government, since printing money or increasing the supply of money causes inflation. Inflation raises the price of goods and consequently eliminates the benefit of the new printed money as the amount of goods each dollar will buy, goes down.

Governments or countries may also experience a trade deficit. This is when a country is importing more goods than it is exporting, thus more dollars are leaving the country than are coming in. This can cause an increase in the price of goods coming into the country if the countries holding the currency decide to sell. This has no direct relationship on the expenses of a government, but instead is indirect as the cost of items increases.

How to Eliminate a Deficit

In order to eliminate a deficit you must do one of two things: increase the incoming cash flow or decrease the outgoing money. On a personal level this is increasing income and decreasing your expenses. On a corporate level this is increasing revenues or lowering costs. With a government deficit, they can increase taxes or decrease their spending to get the desired reduction in the deficit.

Andrea Travillian

See also: Bankruptcy; Bonds; Budget; Cash; Consumer Credit/Debt; Credit Card; Debt; Inflation; Loans; Social Security; U.S. Federal Tax System Overview

Further Reading

About.com. "Why Not Just Print More Money." Accessed March 24, 2014. http://economics.about.com/cs/money/a/print_money_2.htm
Billshrink.com. "10 Governments That Went Bankrupt." Accessed March 24, 2014. http://www.billshrink.com/blog/6799/10-governments-that-went-bankrupt/
Congressional Budget Office. June 1, 2004. "The Outlook for Social Security." Accessed March 24, 2014. http://www.cbo.gov/publication/15712
PBS.org. "Which American Municipalities Have Filed for Bankruptcy?" Accessed March 24, 2014. http://www.pbs.org/newshour/updates/municipalities-declared-bankruptcy/

Deflation

Deflation occurs when prices fall instead of rising as they do in inflation. Deflation makes the value of your dollar higher tomorrow than it is today, thus people do not want to spend money today, and instead prefer to wait to buy items in the future as the price continues to drop. For example, if prices are falling and today one dollar will buy you five pieces of gum but tomorrow one dollar will buy you seven pieces of gum, then you would wait to buy gum because your dollar will have more purchasing power in the future.

How Deflation Occurs

Deflation typically occurs for three reasons: a decrease in demand, an increase in operating efficiency, or a reduction in the money supply. When deflation does occur there may be one or several reasons that contribute to the downward pricing pressure.

The most common cause of deflation is a decrease in demand. When demand for a product or service goes down, the company selling the item will be forced to lower the price in order to sell the product. For example, if a company ordered too many winter boots, when spring comes around they may have to lower the price of the unsold boots to get customers to purchase them. Those boots are no longer worth what they were when it was cold.

While this example is for a single product, this can occur on a national level with most prices decreasing. This has occurred a handful of times in the history of the United States, with the most recent being in the recession of 2008–2009.

Deflation can also occur when there are great improvements in the efficiency of production or delivery of goods. For example, when a new technology first comes out it is expensive. As the manufacturers perfect the process, the costs to produce the item decrease, thus the sellers can lower the price to consumers and maintain their profit.

The automobile is an example of this improved efficiency. Until Henry Ford created the assembly line it took days and sometimes months to make a car because they were made one at a time. The assembly line allowed them to make cars in a matter of hours, thus lowering the overall cost to produce the item and allowing more to be made.

Deflation can also occur because of a decrease in the money supply. The money supply is the amount of monetary assets available in an economy at a specific time, in other words, how much cash is available in checking accounts and available for access through tools such as bank loans. As the amount of money available for consumption decreases, the ability to pay for goods and services decreases, thus decreasing demand and lowering prices.

Impacts of Deflation

When we encounter deflation across the entire economy a few things are impacted, including unemployment and wages. There's a decline in the desire of consumers and businesses to spend, and debtors have greater difficulty repaying their obligations. As prices fall, people become less willing to purchase items. They know the price will go lower; therefore they question why they should spend $5 today when next week that same item might be $3.

Another way of saying this is that your dollars are worth more tomorrow than they are today, so you want to save as much cash as you can. Unfortunately, as this occurs it worsens the deflationary cycle, also known as a deflationary spiral.

When no one is buying, the retailers must lower the price if they want to get the product to move off the shelf. This makes buyers want to wait, which makes the retailers have to lower the price even more. It becomes a cycle that is hard to stop.

As this desire to spend declines, it leads to unemployment and falling wages. Since the factories don't have to run as much to produce products that are not selling, there is no need for workers to run the plants and therefore they are laid off.

With fewer people working, demand decreases again as those that are not working are not able to buy as much with no money coming in. The deflationary spiral continues to worsen. This will also decrease the level of wages being paid by employers, since when unemployment is high, wages decline as more workers are willing to work for lower wages.

Finally, those that owe money on loans find that the burden of their debt is consuming more of their dollars. Since debt represents items they purchased earlier, those items become more expensive because money is worth more today than it was yesterday. Thus they must also reduce spending in order to make up for the increased portion of their dollars going to debt repayment, yet again decreasing the level of demand for goods.

How to Stop Deflation

There are a few ways to get out of the deflationary spiral including increasing government spending and increasing the money supply. In order to create more demand for goods and services, government and the Federal Reserve Bank may use a mixture of these tools to get demand moving. By increasing spending on the government's side they increase the demand for goods and services immediately, allowing retailers to sell their products.

An example of a government initiative to increase spending during a deflationary cycle occurred during the Great Depression. The federal government started a program called the Works Progress Administration, which built public works projects. These projects not only increased demand for products used in construction, but also employed workers. These workers could then increase their spending because of an increase in their wages. The new spending by government and increased wages for consumers helped stop the deflation of the Great Depression.

The government can also increase the money supply by modifying reserve requirements for banks, lowering interest rates to encourage borrowing and lending. The Federal Reserve can also purchase bonds on the open market, thus injecting more money into the system for people to spend. Many believe that deflation in a society is more devastating than inflation. In sum, neither high levels of deflation or inflation are desirable.

Andrea Travillian

See also: Banking; Bonds; Federal Reserve Bank; Inflation; Interest Rates; Time Value of Money; Unemployment; Year 1930s: The Great Depression

Further Reading

Federal Reserve Bank of San Francisco. "What Is Deflation and How Is It Different from Disinflation?" Accessed March 25, 2014. http://www.frbsf.org/education/publications/doctor-econ/1999/september/deflation-disinflation-causes

The New York Times. "Why Is Deflation Bad?" Accessed March 25, 2014. http://krugman.blogs.nytimes.com/2010/08/02/why-is-deflation-bad/?_php=true&_type=blogs&_r=0

Swanenberg. August 2005. "Macroeconomics Demystified." New York: McGraw-Hill.

Delinquency

A bill is said to be delinquent if it is not paid on time. Every financial obligation that is not paid immediately has a deadline. For example, a rent payment might be due on the first day of the month or a credit card payment might have to be paid by the 15th of the month.

If the payment is not made on time, the creditor has rules that outline when the payment is considered delinquent. For example, even though a mortgage payment is due on the first of the month, in most cases, there is a grace period of two weeks (or until the 15th of the month) before the payment is delinquent. There are no consequences to the borrower as long is the mortgage payment is made before the 15th of the month.

Although some payments must be made in full by a specific date, such as rent or mortgage payments, there are others that remain current (not delinquent) if a partial payment is made. Most credit cards allow the borrower to pay a percentage of the bill. When a partial payment is acceptable, the amount due is called a "minimum payment" and is a small percentage of the total. If the consumer elects to pay only part of the credit card bill, the remainder rolls over into future periods and accrues interest.

When Does a Payment Become Delinquent?

A payment is delinquent as soon as the due date is passed. Practically, the borrower has a certain amount of time before that late payment is reported to a credit bureau. Typically, for a monthly bill, after the second payment is missed the individual's payment is considered 30 days past due or delinquent. The borrower and the delinquent payment are usually reported to the credit bureau after the third payment is missed and the bill is 60 days delinquent. This practice gives the consumer a short period of time to rectify financial mistakes before the account is turned over to the credit reporting agencies.

Consequences of Delinquent Payments

Our financial system would not work well if there were no consequences for late payments. The consequences for delinquencies help businesses obtain enough cash in a timely manner to deliver their goods and services. For example, if a mortgage company doesn't receive debt repayments on time from borrowers, there won't be enough money to lend to other consumers. This will hurt both the mortgage company as well as potential borrowers.

For consumers, late payments are deleterious to their credit score. Almost every adult has a credit score on file with the credit reporting agencies. When a consumer has a delinquent payment and that payment is reported to the credit bureau, that consumer's credit score will fall. Lower credit scores make it more difficult to get a loan, an apartment, a future credit card, a mortgage, and even a job. If consumers with lower credit scores do manage to obtain credit, they will pay a higher interest rate than consumers with higher credit scores. This is because the credit issuer is taking a bigger risk lending money to individuals with lower credit scores.

Delinquency Law

The Credit Card Accountability Responsibility and Disclosure Act of 2009 was implemented to extend the Truth in Lending Act. These laws govern lending policies and help to increase fairness and transparency in lending.

Sample provisions of the Credit Card Act cover posting the late payment deadline, the due date of the bill, and whether interest rates are increased for late payments. Consumers must also be informed in writing of the amount of any fees assessed for late payments as well as notice of when the fee goes into effect.

How Delinquent Payments Impact Credit Scores

The Fair Isaac Corporation (FICO) score is the most widely used measure of credit-worthiness. The FICO score is a number that indicates a borrower's credit risk. This score is widely used to determine the likelihood that a borrower will repay a debt.

The credit score ranges from 300 for the poorest credit score to 850 for a perfect credit score. A FICO score between 300 and 580 is considered very poor. A score between 580 and 640 is poor. A fair credit score falls between 640 and 700, and a good score falls between 700 and 750. The best or excellent credit score is between 750 and 850.

The MyFico Web site illustrates how various scenarios impact a borrower's credit score. For example, an individual with a 30-day delinquency and a credit score of 680 can see a drop of 60–80 points in the credit score from 680 to 600–620. An individual with a credit score of 780 and a 30-day delinquency might see the score drop to 670–690 or from 90 to 110 points. Although bankruptcies and foreclosures are the largest drags on credit scores, delinquencies are quite harmful.

Rebuilding a damaged credit history and consequently the credit score takes time and attention to credit habits. It takes time for credit missteps to age out of the credit report. Missed payments remain on a credit report for 7 years. Bankruptcies remain on the consumer's credit report for up to 10 years. Tax liens, litigations, or judgments can remain on a credit report for 7 years.

Money management and personal finance tenets teach consumers to keep debt to a minimum and pay all bills in a timely manner. Allowing accounts to remain unpaid has both short- and long-term consequences and can impact many aspects of consumers' financial and personal lives. In the event that one cannot pay a bill on time, it is advisable to contact the creditor in an attempt to arrange a payment plan in order to avoid a negative mark in one's credit file.

Barbara Friedberg

See also: Bankruptcy; Budget; Compound Interest/Return; Consumer Credit/Debt; Credit Card; Credit Report and Reporting Agencies; Credit Score; Debt; Debt Collection; Debt/Credit Counseling

Further Reading

Credit Card Accountability Responsibility and Disclosure Act of 2009. Public Law 111–24. May 22, 2009. http://www.gpo.gov/fdsys/pkg/PLAW-111publ24/pdf/PLAW-111publ24.pdf

Credit Karma Web site. "What Is a Good Credit Score?" Accessed February 27, 2014. https://www.creditkarma.com/faq/what-is-a-good-credit-score

My Fico Web site. "Credit Report Q & A." Accessed August 22, 2013. http://www.myfico
.com/crediteducation/questions/credit_problem_comparison.aspx

Derivatives

Derivatives are unique financial instruments. In fact, these investments receive their
value from an underlying asset, typically stocks, bonds, or loans. The derivative itself
is actually a contract between two individuals. An investor in a derivative does not own
the underlying asset but profits (or loses) from the movement up or down in the price
of the underlying asset.

This is a complicated financial product with benefits for individual investors, professional investors, corporations, and speculators. The derivative products, with their
frequent media mentions, are important additions to the modern personal finance
glossary.

Derivative Example

The payoff of a derivative investment depends on the value of other assets. For example, a call option gives the holder the right to purchase an asset such as a stock at a
prespecified price on or before a certain date. The profit comes from the sales price of
that option on the expiration date of the derivative contract. If the sales price on the
expiration date is higher than the call option exercise price, then the call holder can buy
the asset at the lower (option exercise) price and sell it for a profit at the higher market
price.

Assume Facebook (FB) stock is selling for $68 per share in March and you believe
the stock is going to rise in price. You don't want to shell out $6,800 to purchase 100
shares. You decide to buy a call option. The call option will give you the option to buy
FB shares at a predetermined price before a specific date. According to the call option
chart, you can buy the $67.50 May 14 call for $6.20. What this means is that for $6.20
× 100 or $620, you have the right to purchase 100 shares of FB stock for the strike
price of $67.50 any time between March and May 14.

If the price of FB is $75 on May 13, you decide to exercise the option and purchase
the shares for $67.50 per share, or $6,750. You can then turn around and sell the shares
for the market price of $75 per share, or $7,500. This yields a profit of $7,500 − $6,750,
or $750. But you must also subtract the $620 cost of the call options. Thus your net
profit for these transactions is $750 − $620, or $130.

This scenario suggests you would have made more money had you purchased the
stock outright. Well, in this situation that is true. But what if you purchased the stock
outright and it fell in price from $68 per share to $60 per share? In that case, you would
have lost $6,800 − $6,000 or $800.

There are many different types of derivative transactions, from buying and selling
(or writing) calls to buying and writing puts. Puts give the option holder the right to sell
a stock at a predetermined price during a specific time period. Buying a put is

sometimes considered insurance for investors who believe the market is going to decline in value, but don't want to sell their shares.

Who Invests in Derivatives?

Derivatives are used by corporations to hedge financial risks arising from variations in foreign exchange, interest rates, and commodity prices. Depending on the type of the contract, derivatives can trade on exchanges (like stocks) or can trade over the counter (OTC), which is unregulated, unlike the exchanges. Individuals and corporations use derivatives as insurance to protect their investment portfolio from a downward shift in prices or to speculate for future profits.

What Are the Various Types of Derivatives and How Do They Work?

Forward/Futures Contracts

Forward or futures contracts are contracts between two counterparties wherein one party agrees to buy an asset/commodity at a predetermined price at a future date and the other party agrees to sell it. This helps investors to hedge the prices of their assets.

For example, a corn chips manufacturing company enters into a forward contract to buy a bushel of corn for $100 in two months from a corn farmer. At the end of two months, if the market price bushel of corn is $105, the farmer's loss is $5 and the company's gain is $5. If the market price is $95, the farmer's gain is $5 and the company's loss is $5. In either case, the price of $100 determined two months earlier helps the company lessen the impact of fluctuating corn prices on its bottom line. This transaction also helps the farmer put a floor under the price of corn he will sell in the future, protecting a specific profit level.

Though the underlying contract structure is the same for forward contracts and futures, they differ in the following way: Forward contracts are customized contracts between two parties that have a counterparty risk (risk of default on payment) and trade over the counter between private parties. Futures contracts are liquid, trade on exchanges, and have very low counterparty risk (counterparty is the exchange on which the futures contract is traded and is not another investor).

Option Contracts

Options are an extension of futures contracts with an exercise option embedded. An option contract gives the buyer the option to buy or sell a security at a predetermined price (strike price) at a predetermined date (maturity), and the cost of entering this contract is called the option premium.

Option contracts fall into two categories, puts and calls. A call option is the option to buy at a predetermined price, and a put option is the option to sell at a predetermined price. For an investor who wants to take a bet on the directionality in the price of a certain security, options are a cheap way of speculating instead of buying the underlying security.

An investor who believes that IBM (trading at $175) will trade above $180 in two months will buy a call option and is said to be long call. An investor who believes that the IBM stock will trade below $180 will sell the option and is said to short or write the call. The seller of the call gets the option premium, which is also the price of the option. The price of an option is dependent on the strike price, fluctuations in the price of the security, time to maturity, risk-free rate, and dividends paid.

For an investor who wants to limit the downside risk on a security, buying a put option acts as insurance. If a current holder of IBM stock (trading at $175) believes that IBM might trade down to $165 in two months, he or she will buy a put option at $165 with expiration in two months and will pay an option premium (the value of the put option) to the seller (or writer of the option contract). If IBM went down to $160 in two months, the put option buyer sells the stock for $165 and makes a gain of $5 (less the option premium paid). If the stock traded up to $180, the put option buyer's loss equals the premium paid and the option expires worthless.

The put option buyer is said to be long put and the put option seller or writer is said to be short the put. Thus, a long put is equivalent to buying insurance to limit downside price movements while a long call is equivalent to buying a stock with unlimited upside potential.

Options are widely used by portfolio managers to hedge portfolio exposure, to bet on the direction of certain securities, to generate income (from premiums), and to create complex option structures that provide a return profile in line with their hedging needs.

Swaps

Swaps are the derivative instruments that allow for transfer of an asset or liability between two counterparties. The most common types of swaps are interest rate swaps and currency swaps. Interest rate swaps allow for swapping of interest rate payments between two parties including fixed to floating swap, floating to fixed swap, and floating to floating swap.

A company that has floating-rate loans (those are loans for which the interest rate owed on the loan may go up or down) on its balance sheet would want to swap them for a fixed payment schedule if it expects interest rates to increase. This helps lessen the interest expense for the company. Similarly, a company with fixed-rate liabilities would want to swap them for a floating-rate payment schedule in case of falling interest rates.

Currency swaps are used by companies that derive their revenue from multiple countries (i.e., multiple currencies) and would like to hedge (or protect) their exposure to various currency fluctuations. For example, a multinational company with business branches in Germany and Mexico will enter into currency swaps in euros (to hedge revenues coming from Germany) and pesos (to hedge revenues coming from Mexico). This provides the company with more certainty about its revenues and helps the company keep track of future earnings.

Derivatives are financial instruments that help the financial community smooth out risk and increase potential profit (or losses) for the speculator. Many parties in the financial community benefit from the opportunity to use derivatives. Unfortunately, there is also occasional misuse of these complex financial instruments.

Surya Mrunalini Pisapati

See also: Commodities; Hedge Funds; Index Mutual Funds; Interest Rates; Risk; Stock Market; Stocks

Further Reading

Black, Fischer, and Myron Scholes. 1973. "Options and Corporate Liabilities." *The Journal of Political Economy* Vol. 81, No. 3 (May–June).

Hull, John C. 2011. *Options, Futures and Other Derivatives*. Prentice Hall.

Markowitz, Harry. 1952. "Portfolio Selection." *Journal of Finance* (March 1): 77–91.

Digital Currency

Digital currencies (or cryptocurrencies) are created by a complex algorithm and stored electronically. There is no government control or monitoring. All transactions and storage are governed by protocols set when these currencies are established. The most popular and largest in valuation is Bitcoin, which was conceptualized by Satoshi Nakamoto in a paper published in 2008. An article in March 2014 claimed to have found the true identity behind the most popular digital currency, but the person cited denied such association. These digital currencies all have one common goal: to be used as a method of payment using peer-to-peer networks, bypassing financial institutions. These digital currencies, however, are not money in the traditional definition. They are more like commodities (such as gold and silver). To understand why these digital currencies are not money, we have to understand what money is.

In economics, money has three essential functions. First, it is used as a unit of accounting (or measurement). Second, it is used as a medium of exchange. Third, it is used as a store of value.

The first function of money is easily fulfilled by digital currencies and most other commodity moneys. For any commodity to be considered "money" in terms of the function as a unit of measurement, all it needs is some form of agreement on the measurement. This is the main reason for gold and silver to have served as commodity moneys for most of human history.

The second function is where it gets a little more difficult for digital currencies to gain mainstream acceptance. Unless these digital currencies can be used to make daily transactions, it will be difficult to accept them as money. While there have been efforts to make purchases with digital currencies in some online retailers and even some physical stores (digital price tags), these types of currencies are largely limited to transactions that are linked to the digital world. Imagine you are going grocery shopping in the fresh food markets in Vietnam, and you can see how well these types of currencies would function. The large volatility in price also makes these currencies a poor choice for the method of payments for businesses that are increasingly demanding more precision in production and sales planning.

The high degree of variation in value for digital currencies also makes them a poor form to store value. Take Bitcoin's "price" as an example. It started off with a value of a few cents and skyrocketed to over $1,000 in a matter of a few years. Within a year, the value can fluctuate between a few hundred U.S. dollars to more than a thousand. Imagine that you work for a company that accepts Bitcoin as payment for the goods and services you provide and your compensation is also in Bitcoin. Since the value of Bitcoin fluctuates frequently, the amount of income available to you also fluctuates widely. Imagine that you go to a restaurant and you have to decide what to order, or if you have enough money for a tip, depending on the value of the Bitcoin you have. It is simply impractical. The problem gets deeper if you think about long-term planning in the world of highly volatile value. Hyperinflation and deflation are major problems for any economy. Having a highly volatile currency is like having hyperinflation and deflation all the time. An economy will simply stall.

Furthermore, for goods or services to have value, a certain amount of resources have to be put into them. Once those goods and services are created, their value might change depending on the supply and demand for them. But in general, only goods that can generate more cash flow/value in the future should see their price go up in the future. Goods that have limited supply could see their value increase if the demand for them increases. If there are many people bidding on a limited supply of certain goods that generate less value than the selling price, we have a speculative bubble.

We must also note that Bitcoin has a price. So, the value of a Bitcoin still depends on the value of existing currencies. The value of Bitcoin changes based on the last price in which a transaction/exchange was made at one of the Bitcoin exchanges. If Bitcoin is to replace all other currencies, the value of all goods and services will be measured in Bitcoin. In that case, Bitcoin will become another good with its value depending on the relative values of other goods and services. In that scenario, we will be back to a barter system, with Bitcoin serving as the reference value/unit. In a barter system, credits cannot be created easily. The complex capital markets we have today would not be possible under such a system.

Controversies

Due to the nature of the transmission mechanism originally intended, Bitcoin became a tool for illegal drug trades, money laundering, and many other illegal activities. The biggest online illegal drug dealer, Silk Road, was shut down by authorities in October 2013. Silk Road used only Bitcoin for transactions and charged commission in Bitcoin. Silk Road 2, the reincarnation of Silk Road, was shut down for a different reason in February 2014. Hackers attacked Silk Road 2 and stole all the funds (in Bitcoin). Hacker attacks were also the reason behind the closure of the biggest Bitcoin exchange, Mt. Gox, in February 2014. Another Bitcoin exchange, Flexcoin, also closed in March 2014 for a similar reason. The closure of these exchanges caused large variations in value of Bitcoin. More importantly, they showed that Bitcoin is far less secure than the believers claimed. Hacker attacks on these online exchanges or businesses that utilize Bitcoin are similar to bandits robbing trains or banks that carry gold or silver.

Should You Invest in Bitcoin?

From what we have discussed so far, Bitcoin is not money or any currency. Instead, it is a speculative asset that varies in value depending on demand and supply. In other words, Bitcoin can be viewed as an alternative asset. And it was defined as such in March 2014 by the Internal Revenue Service. Should an average investor invest in such an asset? The famed investor Warren Buffett advised investors to stay away from Bitcoin. He might have good reasons for that. There are two main driving forces behind the value of Bitcoin. First, different exchanges have different values for Bitcoin, and the variation in value is not small. The value of gold or silver is fairly standardized because they have established exchanges with rules and regulations on setting proper value, depending on market transactions. Bitcoin has no such mechanism. Second, demand and supply (or speculations) are the main driving force in variation of value for Bitcoin. The surge in value from 2012 to 2013 was due to a large influx of speculators. Many believe that Bitcoin reached a speculative bubble in late 2013 and is likely to be worth far less in a matter of months. For prudent investors, it is best to stay away from unregulated assets with extreme volatility. Bitcoin is such an asset.

Conclusion

Digital currency is a new class of speculative asset that has emerged quickly in recent years. While a more efficient payment system might emerge in the future, Bitcoin isn't ready for daily use. It will require regulatory changes in financial systems around the world in order to make this type of currency practical. Until then, the value will continue to fluctuate widely. Because there is competition to be the most dominant digital currency, most of the existing ones will likely have no value once the development stage is settled.

Leo H. Chan

See also: Cash; Currency; Federal Reserve Bank

Further Reading

Clinch, Matt. February 25, 2014. "Bitcoin Exchange Mt. Gox Closed 'For the Time Being.'"http://www.nbcnews.com/business/markets/tbitcoin-exchange-mt-gox-closed-time-being-n37896

The Economist. November 30, 2013. "The Bitcoin Bubble." http://www.economist.com/news/leaders/21590901-it-looks-overvalued-even-if-digital-currency-crashes-others-will-follow-bitcoin

Goodman, Leah M. March 6, 2014. "The Face Behind Bitcoin." http://mag.newsweek.com/2014/03/14/bitcoin-satoshi-nakamoto.html

Leger, Donna L. March 25, 2014. "IRS: Bitcoin Is Not Currency." http://www.usatoday.com/story/money/business/2014/03/25/irs-says-bitcoin-is-property/6873569/

Nakamoto, Satoshi. 2008. "Bitcoin: A Peer-to-Peer Electronic Cash System." https://bitcoin.org/bitcoin.pdf

Watts, William. March 14, 2014. "Warren Buffett: Don't Dump Stocks on China or Ukraine and Stay Away from Bitcoin." http://blogs.marketwatch.com/thetell/2014/03/14/warren-buffett-dont-dump-stocks-on-china-or-ukraine-and-stay-away-from-bitcoin/

Disability Insurance

Disability insurance protects a worker's current and future earnings. There is both government and private insurance to assist the disabled worker.

The worker's earnings are his or her most valuable asset. Any injury, illness, or medical condition, be it a mental disorder or a physical incapacity, leading to a permanent or temporary disability can be more disastrous to an income earner and his or her financial dependents than death. Family breadwinners, the self-employed, and those with substantial debts are particularly exposed.

Disability insurance protects those who are disabled to the extent that they can no longer perform the main functions of their work and must forego their income. The proceeds from disability insurance replace the disabled worker's income and pay for daily living expenses, significant medical expenses, and rehabilitation expenses. A disability occurs when the worker is physically or mentally disabled, has been in a debilitating accident, or has suffered an injury and/or serious illness.

U.S. Social Security Disability Insurance

The government offers Social Security Disability Insurance, which pays benefits to workers who become disabled if the worker is "insured." To become insured under the Social Security program, the worker must have worked in jobs covered by Social Security and have a medical condition that meets the Social Security definition of disability. Additionally the worker must have been unable to work for at least one year because of a disability. These benefits usually continue until the worker can return to the workforce.

Private Disability Insurance

Many companies offer disability insurance policies that grant more lenient coverage rules and offer the policyholder the opportunity to receive benefits earlier than with Social Security Disability Insurance.

The most important feature of any disability insurance policy is how the policy defines a "disability." This definition can vary from insurer to insurer. The consumer should avoid policies whose definitions and types of benefits offered are not easily understood. As a general rule, the more ambiguous the definition of "disability," the more open the definition is to interpretation by the insurance company. Unclear and ambiguous policy language may lead to difficulty collecting compensation for a disability.

Disability insurance benefits include paid sick leave, short-term disability benefits, and long-term disability benefits. After an individual is deemed disabled and unable to complete his or her job duties, the insurance company pays a percentage of the claimant's income as a monthly benefit. Periodic payments are paid after the waiting period (14 days is common) and over a benefit period (which varies in duration for each policy).

The waiting or elimination period ranges from 30 to 90 days. During the waiting period the claimant will need other sources of income such as an emergency fund, sick leave, or annual leave benefits for support while waiting for benefits to be paid. The longer the waiting period a claimant has opted for when purchasing the insurance, the lower the premiums. The maximum benefit amount payable can vary between 50 and 80 percent of the insured's gross earnings prior to the disability event.

Types of Disability Insurance

The different types of disability insurance available include short-term disability (STD) insurance, long-term disability (LTD) insurance, and critical illness insurance. These types of coverage consist of regular payments to someone who suffers a disability and cannot work.

Short-Term Disability and Long-Term Disability

Short-term disability coverage pays for disabilities of up to two years. In actuality, most short-term policies pay for six months of coverage. Short-term disability policies have a waiting period of between zero and 14 days before the benefit becomes available to the claimant, with a maximum benefit period of between two to five years.

Long-term disability policies have a waiting period that may range from 30 days to 360 days with a maximum benefit period ranging from a few years to usually age 65, after which Social Security income benefits become available. Long-term disability insurance generally covers injuries and treatments lasting at least 30 days.

Some policies have residual (additional/rider) benefits such as guaranteed renewable or noncancelable policy features. Guaranteed renewable policies give the claimant the right to renew the policy with the same benefits and not have the policy canceled by the insurer. The insurer has the right to increase the premiums as long as it does so for all other policyholders. Noncancelable means the policy cannot be canceled by the insurer, except for nonpayment of premiums. A cost of living rider will ensure that the benefit payments keep up with inflation. All disability policies waive premiums during the disability.

Not all employers offer disability insurance. Even if an employer offers disability insurance, the coverage may be insufficient. In these cases, individuals may choose to insure themselves with an individual disability insurance policy. Professional associations frequently offer group disability insurance policies to their members.

Critical Illness

Over the course of a lifetime, an individual is more likely to suffer from a serious illness for a short duration and survive, than die prematurely. In this scenario, the individual and his or her family may suffer severe financial consequences while the disabled person is unable to work and is recuperating during treatment.

Critical illness or trauma insurance policies pay a lump sum rather than regular income payments in the event that someone is disabled as a result of a dreaded illness. A dreaded disease is defined as a heart attack, stroke, bypass surgery, and cancer. This type of disability insurance pays a benefit on the occurrence of the dreaded disease event, provided the definition of the disability is satisfied.

This insurance is distinct from short- and-long term disability insurance. Critical illness disability insurance provides protection for those who are temporarily disabled and cannot make a claim for illness or injury under their medical, short-term, or long-term disability insurances.

The critical illness lump sum payout can be used for many expenses such as paying off the mortgage, covering daily living expenses, funding future income needs, and contributing to retirement savings, while the person is ill and not able to work. Fortunately, critical illness disability payments do not just cover medical costs (Gjertsen, 1998).

Disability Insurance Cautions

Buyers beware: Some insurance policies define an individual as disabled if he or she is unable to perform the duties of "any occupation," justifying charging low premiums.

For example, if a university engineering professor becomes disabled and holds a policy that only applies if the professor is unable to work in "any occupation," here's what might occur. Assume the professor has a very mild stroke that doesn't impact him physically, but leaves his memory and mind minimally impaired. Due to the mental incapacity, the professor is not competent to teach engineering coursework. But, since he returns to physical competence, he is able to perform physical-type work such as being a checker in a grocery store.

The grocery store clerk job is not similar to his former job as an engineering professor. His disability would not pay out because although he is unable to teach engineering courses, he can still work in another field. His policy states that in order to receive benefits he must be unable to work in *any* role.

The superior insurance policies are usually more expensive because they pay benefits if someone is unable to perform the usual duties of his or her *"own occupation,"* which is the current role the individual performed prior to the disability. Consumers must carefully compare the various disability insurance options available, especially if the insurer is offering lower premiums compared to its competitors.

Workers Who May Be Ineligible for Disability Insurance

Those individuals in hazardous occupations, such as pilots and flying or diving instructors, may be uninsurable for disability insurance. High-income earners are subject to payment ceilings for disability benefits as well. The modern consumer is well served to insure against disability along with other more common types of insurance coverage.

Angelique N. S. McInnes

See also: Life Insurance; Social Security; Umbrella Insurance

Further Reading

Gjertsen, L. A. 1998. "Brokers Surveyed on Disability Cover." *National Underwriter/ Property & Casualty Risk & Benefits Management* (Vol. 102, No. 6): 33.

Lavandeira, E. A. 1995. "Cover Yourself!" *Hispanic* (Vol. 8, No. 8): 62.

Richardson, B. C. 2011. "Planning for Business Continuation." *Advisor Today* (Vol. 106, No. 1): 18–19.

Ruquet, M. E. 2012. "Survey: 9 in 10 Would Pay for Disability Insurance, If They Knew What It Was." *National Underwriter/P&C* (Vol. 116, No. 15): 8.

Sargent, D. 2008. "Give Staff a Safety Net." *Credit Union Magazine* (Vol. 74, no. 8): 52.

Social Security Web site. "Benefits for People with Disabilities." Accessed March 17, 2014. http://www.ssa.gov/disability/

Teale, J. 2008. *Insurance and Risk Management.* Milton: John Wiley & Sons Australia.

Wiskowski, J. 2008. "Study Finds Gap in Employee Understanding of Disability Insurance." *National Underwriter/Life & Health Financial Services* (Vol. 112, no. 4): 18–26.

Discount Rate

The discount rate has several meanings in personal finance. In one case, the discount rate refers to the interest rate that is used in discounted cash flow (DCF) analysis to determine the present value of future cash flows. The discount rate in DCF analysis takes into account not just the time value of money, but also the risk or uncertainty associated with future cash flows. The greater the uncertainty of future cash flows, the higher the discount rate. In simpler terms, this means the discount rate is an interest

Discount Window Borrowing during the Global Financial Crisis

The Fed's discount rate is an administered rate set by the Federal Reserve Banks, rather than a market rate of interest. Use of the Fed's discount window soared in late 2007 and 2008, as financial conditions deteriorated sharply and the Federal Reserve took steps to provide liquidity to the financial system. Discount window borrowing increased to a record $111 billion at the peak of the global financial crisis in October 2008, while the Federal Reserve's board of governors set the discount rate at a post–World War II low of 0.5 percent on December 16, 2008.

rate used to help analysts understand what an investment might be worth today, given a known understanding of its future value.

The discount rate also refers to the interest rate that is charged to commercial banks and other depository institutions for loans received from the Federal Reserve Bank's discount window. There is discussion as to the relationship of the discount rate to the interest rates that borrowers and savers pay or earn with their money. The research on this topic is inconclusive.

There is even a third meaning of the term *discount rate*. It is the rate used by pension plans and insurance companies for discounting their liabilities. This rate is less of a concern for modern consumers.

Discount Rate in Discount Cash Flow (DCF) Analysis

How can we determine the present value of future cash flows? Or, what is an investment worth today, given that we know what the future payments will be? This might pertain to an investment such as a bond with known interest or coupon payments.

Here is a simple explanation of how the discount rate is used in DCF analysis. Suppose that you expect to receive $1,000 in one year. But you want to know what that payment's value is today. To determine the present value of this $1,000, or what it is worth to you today, you would need to discount it by a particular interest rate. The discount rate is usually a market interest rate you might expect to earn if you were to invest a sum of money for one year today. Assuming a discount rate of 10 percent, the $1,000 in a year's time would be equivalent to $(1,000 / [1.00 + 0.10]) = \$909.09$ to you today. If you expect to receive the $1,000 in two years, its present value would be $\$826.45 = (\$909.09 / [1.00 + 0.10])$.

The Federal Reserve Bank Discount Rate

The Federal Reserve Banks offer three discount window programs to depository institutions: primary credit, secondary credit, and seasonal credit. Each has its own interest rate.

The Federal Reserve Bank, which is charged with helping the economy to remain stable, uses its discount window to help the credit and banking markets remain stable. It helps the banks maintain sufficient reserves so that if there were to be a large demand by depositors to withdraw their funds, the bank would always have access to ready cash to satisfy the depositors' withdrawal requests.

Under the primary credit program, loans are extended for a very short term (usually overnight) to depository institutions that are in sound financial condition. The secondary credit is available to institutions that are not eligible for primary credit. They may apply for secondary credit to meet short-term liquidity needs or to resolve severe financial difficulties. Seasonal credit is extended to relatively small depository institutions that have recurring intrayear fluctuations in funding needs, such as banks in agricultural or seasonal resort communities.

The discount rate charged for primary credit (the primary credit rate) is set above the usual level of short-term market interest rates. The discount rate on secondary credit is above the rate on primary credit. The discount rate for seasonal credit is an average of selected market rates. Discount rates are established by each Reserve Bank's board of directors, subject to the review and determination of the board of governors of the Federal Reserve system. The discount rates for the three lending programs are the same across all Federal Reserve Banks except on days around a change in the rate.

The Relationship between the Discount Rate and Market Interest Rates

As consumers, we're more concerned with the market interest rates, which are those rates that consumers receive on their savings account deposits. Borrowers are also concerned with the lending rates for their mortgage, student loan, or credit card debt. As consumers, it's helpful to understand what causes changes in market and lending rates and how we might predict the future market rates.

According to an article by Daniel L. Thornton, written for the St. Louis Federal Reserve Bank, there is widespread acceptance by money market analysts that the discount rate is a method that the Federal Reserve Bank uses to impact the economy and market interest rates. Since 1982, this belief has further solidified, given the strong relationship changes in the discount rate and changes in market interest rates.

In spite of these widely held beliefs about the relationship between the discount rate and market interest rates, Thornton, in "Discount Rate and Market Interest Rates: Theory and Evidence" (1986), posits that changes in the discount rate actually have no effect on market rates. He discusses that they may hint at upcoming changes in the Federal Reserve Banks' use of other strategies to impact the economy and interest rates. He further suggests that changes in the discount rate, in lieu of indicating a change in the market rate, may actually follow market interest rate changes.

So, the discount window is the lender of last resort to member banks. The discount interest rates move in line with other market rates but do not necessarily foreshadow changes in market interest rates.

Ramya Ghosh

See also: Banking; Cash; Debt; Federal Reserve Bank; Interest Rates; Liquidity; Loans; Year 2007–2008: Subprime Housing Crisis and Mortgage Meltdown

Further Reading

Federal Reserve Bank of New York. "Discount Window." Accessed May 27, 2014. http://www.newyorkfed.org/banking/discountwindow.html

Madigan, Brian, and William Nelson. July 2002. "Proposed Revision to the Federal Reserve's Discount Window Lending Programs," *Federal Reserve Bulletin.* http://www.federalreserve.gov/pubs/bulletin/2002/0702lead.pdf

Thornton, Daniel L. 1986. "The Discount Rate and Market Interest Rates: Theory and Evidence." The Federal Reserve Bank of St. Louis. August/September. https://research.stlouisfed.org/publications/review/86/08/Discount_Aug_Sep1986.pdf

Dividend Income

A dividend is a transfer of part of a company's earnings to its shareholders (stockholders). In general, the dividend is stated in terms of a percentage of the current market price. This is referred to as the dividend yield. For example, if a stock is selling for $10 per share and pays a dividend of $0.50 per share, the dividend yield would be 5 percent (0.50 × 10). Investors in mutual funds also receive dividends passed through from the individual stocks and/or bonds held within the mutual fund.

Investment Income

When investing in stocks, investors can realize gains in two ways. The first type of gains are called capital gains and are calculated as the difference between the sale price of the stock and the buy price of the stock. In other words, capital gains are realized when the price of stock appreciates and the shares are sold. If the stock price depreciates, the investment in the stock will yield a loss. For example, on January, 1, 2014, an investor buys the stock ABC at $12.00 per share. The investor sells the stock at $25.00 per share one month later. The capital gain for the investor is calculated as $25.00 – $12.00 = $13.00. The investor realized a profit of $13.00 per share or a percentage gain of 108 percent ((25 – 12)/12).

The second type of gain that an investor can realize when buying a stock is the dividend income. From the investor's standpoint, dividend income is an amount of cash received per share of stock held. For instance, if the dividend associated with stock ABC is $2.00 per share, the investor will receive $2.00 for every share of stock ABC held. The total gain for the investor will be the sum of the appreciation of the stock and the dividend income. Continuing with the same example, if the investor realizes $13.00 in capital gains and $2.00 in dividend gains, this results in a total of $15.00 of profit for every share of stock held.

Dividend Income: What Does It Represent?

From an investor's perspective, the dividend income is an additional source of gain when investing in equities. In order to invest in stocks that offer dividend income opportunities, it is important to be familiar with the concept of dividends. A public corporation is a firm that has the ability to raise money in the public capital markets by allowing public investors to own shares of its firm, called stocks. Dividends are cash payments that public corporations pay to these public investors as a return on their capital investment in the firm. A person who buys a share of stock in a public company becomes a part owner in the firm and thus may be entitled to certain regular payments, such as dividends.

Investors inject capital into the firm in the form of equity. This capital allows the firm to run its operations and invest in growth opportunities. The firm makes profits in the form of revenues. After subtracting all the operational and financial costs associated with these revenues, the company is left with the final profit, called net income. If the net income is a profit, the company will retain a portion of it. The part of earnings that a corporation keeps and doesn't pay out to shareholders is called retained earnings. The residual amount of net income not retained in the firm will be paid out to investors in the form of dividend payments. The percentage of net income paid out to investors is called the payout ratio.

For example, company ABC realized net income of $200 million in 2013. The company's management decided to retain 45 percent of the earnings to invest in new projects in 2014. The amount of retained earnings is $90 million. As a result, the payout ratio is equal to 55 percent and the amount of dividends paid out to investors is $110 million. The dividends are divided proportionately among all of the shareholders. If the company has 55 million shareholders, then each will receive a $2.00 per share dividend.

The retained earnings can vary tremendously depending on growth and investment opportunities offered to the firm. If the management thinks that an investment opportunity will return significant value for the shareholders, they might decide to retain all the earnings instead of paying cash dividends to the investors. Mature companies usually pay more dividends than younger growth companies. For investors looking for dividend income as a primary source of investment gains, investing in mature companies with a history of dividend payments could be a good option. Investors need to keep in mind that a history of dividend payments is not a guarantee of future dividend payments.

Valuing a Company Based on Dividend Payments

For mature companies who have been consistently paying dividends to investors, the dividend cash flows can be used to value a company, or in other terms to calculate the intrinsic value of the stock. Investors will seek to invest in stocks that are undervalued by the market or, in other terms, stocks that are selling cheaper than their intrinsic value. One way to calculate the intrinsic value is to calculate the present value of expected future dividend payments. In order to complete this calculation, investors need to forecast future dividend payments based on historical data for the firm. Readers interested in this calculation should consult literature on the dividend discount valuation model.

Taxation of the Dividend Income

Dividends can be taxed either as ordinary income at ordinary income tax rates or at the preferred long-term capital gains tax rate. Please consult the IRS Web site for comprehensive information on the taxation of dividend income. The taxation of dividend income has been criticized because of the double-taxation problem. Indeed, the company pays corporate taxes for profits realized, and the investor pays taxes for dividend gains, which is a double taxation that shareholders have to bear.

Dividend income gives investors a cash flow as long a firm continues to profit and to return part of those proceeds to investors.

Yousra Acherqui

See also: Capital Gains and Capital Losses; Investing; Stock Market; Stocks

Further Reading

Damodaran, Answath. "The Dividend Discount Model." Accessed April 10, 2014. http://people.stern.nyu.edu/adamodar/pdfiles/eqnotes/ddm.pdf

IRS Web site. "Topic 404—Dividends." Accessed April 10, 2014. http://www.irs.gov/taxtopics/tc404.html

Draft Account *(see Checking Account)*

Equities *(see Stocks)*

Estate Planning

Estate planning is the roadmap for distribution of one's financial and personal assets upon death. An individual creates an estate plan while living. The estate planning strategy makes it clear and easy for the remaining beneficiaries to carry out the deceased's wishes with respect to his or her financial and property holdings.

Six Famous People Who Died without a Will

Jimi Hendrix died in 1970 and conflict over his estate went on until 2000. Not only were there problems with his existing assets, but the ongoing royalties of his estate created more headaches for those unraveling the mess of his estate.

Pablo Picasso, the world-famous artist, died in 1973 at the age of 91. His assets included precious artwork, five homes, cash, gold, and bonds. His estate cost $30 million and took six years to settle among six heirs.

Michael Jackson, who died in July 2009, was initially thought to have died without a will. Later, a will was discovered. Similar to Jimi Hendrix's, his estate continues to generate money; in fact, during the year following his death, his estate earned over $424 million.

Steve McNair, murdered NFL player of the Baltimore Ravens, Tennessee Titans, and Houston Oilers, died without a will in 2009 at age 36. He was murdered by an alleged girlfriend who committed suicide after killing McNair. He had no will.

The nation's 16th president, Abraham Lincoln, was the first president to be assassinated (1865) and the first president to die without a will. Even a lawyer like Lincoln made the estate planning error of dying intestate.

Steig Larsson, Swedish author of *The Girl with the Dragon Tattoo* series, died intestate of a heart attack in 2004. He died at age 50 before experiencing the full success of his books and subsequent movies. Swedish law prevailed and divided his estate between his brother and father, leaving his partner of 32 years, Eva Gabrielsson, with nothing. Subsequently, the family left her the couple's apartment. Conflict continues between the heirs and Gabrielsson.

Understanding Estate Planning

First, let's look at a brief overview of the legal terms used when setting up an estate plan. The deceased is the individual who has died. The beneficiary(ies) are the individuals who received the deceased's possessions. The will is a document that is created by the living person to describe his or her wishes upon death. The executor of the estate is an individual who carries out the directives of the will. Probate is the court process of proving the validity of a will. A lawyer usually draws up a will and creates an estate plan.

For individuals with few assets, estate planning is simple and usually involves completing a will and having the will signed, witnessed, and possibly notarized. In simple cases, an individual may create his or her own will by hand or with an online program.

People with greater amounts of wealth, assets, and more complex finances usually have complicated estate plans. These plans involve not only a will, but trusts in order to ensure that their assets are treated in the way they prefer.

Estate Planning Functions

An estate plan can have narrow or broad implications. The estate plan lays out how assets are distributed upon death. There are various goals of an estate plan. The most simple of those is the will, which instructs how to distribute the deceased's assets.

More detailed estate plans can be structured to smooth out the legal probate process. The estate plan simplifies the legal process by using trusts and other legal tools. In this way the plan protects an individual's wealth from undue taxes and expenses. In other words, money, property, and financial assets can be maximized while minimizing their estate tax burden.

An estate plan usually names a guardian for minor children. If a couple dies and leaves behind young children, the estate plan tells the court who should care for the children. This is very important because without this section, it is left to the courts to decide who should care for the children. Without a named guardian for the minor children, there is no assurance that the children's guardian would be in accord with the deceased parents' wishes.

Another function of an estate plan is for medical issues. A living will/advance health care directive addresses end-of-life medical treatment wishes. This document instructs medical providers and family members regarding end-of-life care. For example, if an elderly individual cannot breathe on his or her own, the medical directive in the estate plan might advise the doctor to remove the breathing assistance. A "do not resuscitate" directive is common for the elderly as well. This means that if the individual suffers a heart attack or a medical procedure that stops the heart, the individual does not wish to be revived.

The durable medical power of attorney is sometimes referred to as a "health care proxy" or "health care surrogate." This document, contained within an estate plan, names an individual to make medical decisions in the event the person is not able to make those decisions for himself or herself.

Power of attorney is another document included in an estate plan. The power of attorney gives someone else the power to act on your behalf. The power of attorney responsibilities may be limited to specific circumstances or more comprehensive in nature, covering all decisions. For example, when the elderly lose mental functioning or under certain prescribed circumstances, the power of attorney document names someone to act in their stead. Frequently, married couples name the other partner in their power of attorney documents.

What Happens If Someone Dies Intestate (Without a Will)?

The state has laws of descent and distribution. These laws map out who receives the deceased person's property. The chain of distribution usually begins with the spouse and/or living children and next goes to other family members if there is not a living spouse or children. It is preferable to have a will in order for the deceased person's property to pass according to his or her wishes.

How Does an Estate Plan Impact Probate?

Probate is a two-part process in which the will is submitted to the probate court in order to be proved valid. The second part of the probate process is the appointment of an estate administrator to collect and distribute the assets to the designated heirs.

There are disadvantages to the probate process and some individuals use estate planning strategies in order to avoid probate. There are several reasons to attempt to avoid probate. First, the legal probate process is publicly recorded. Many individuals don't want public disclosure of the details of their estate. Further, the probate process can also be slow and expensive in some states.

In order to avoid probate, there are legal techniques and instruments that can be used, although these strategies can be expensive. For example, trusts can be set up to pass assets to beneficiaries without going through probate.

How Do Trusts Fit in an Estate Plan?

A trust is a legal entity that "holds" assets on behalf of its beneficiaries. The trust has rules or provisions that define the document.

Estate planning uses a variety of trusts such as a testamentary trust, living trust (either revocable or irrevocable), generation-skipping trust, and others. A lawyer can explain the advantages and disadvantages of each type of trust. In especially complicated situations life insurance, charitable trusts, and other more sophisticated tools are used.

Although frequently considered a tool only for the wealthy, trusts are also useful in estate planning to help young parents who want to protect their children in the case of the death of both parents. For example, a young couple with children could create a trust for the benefit of their children in case they die while their children are minors. This trust could describe how their assets would be handled and who would attend to their affairs and the care of their minor children.

Estate planning is not a one-time activity. As individuals and families evolve, so must their estate plans. As families grow and age, the estate plan needs to change.

Barbara Friedberg

See also: Life Insurance; Power of Attorney; Probate; Wills and Trusts

Further Reading

Bostwick, Heleigh. 2011. "10 Famous People Who Died Without a Will." http://www.legalzoom.com/legal-headlines/celebrity-lawsuits/10-famous-people-who-died

Estate Planning Council of Tompkins County. 2014. "What Is Estate Planning?" Accessed January 5. http://www.estateplanningcouncil.org/planning.cfm

UW College of Law. 2014. "Frequently Asked Questions about Estate Planning." Accessed January 5. http://www.uwyo.edu/law/experiential/practicums/faq.pdf

Federal Open Market Committee *(see Federal Reserve Bank)*

Federal Reserve Bank

Founded in 1913, the Federal Reserve System is the central bank of the United States of America. It includes 12 regions and was created to maintain a stable monetary and financial system. The Federal Reserve banking system is frequently referred to as the Fed.

Its duties are categorized into four sections. The first task of the Fed is to implement the national monetary policy. Monetary policy manages the money supply of the country, which influences interest rates. The goal of the monetary supply management is to maintain reasonable levels of inflation, promote maximum employment, and maintain moderate long-term interest rates. Second, the Federal Reserve System protects consumers' rights and oversees and regulates the banking system. The third responsibility of the Fed is to maintain stability in the financial markets and handle systematic risks, which occur occasionally in financial markets. Finally, the Federal Reserve serves as the U.S. banking systems' bank by providing financial services to member banks, the U.S. government, and foreign official institutions.

How the Federal Reserve Bank Is Structured

The board of governors in Washington, D.C., and 12 regional Federal Reserve Banks give the Fed a national economic perspective. The board of governors of the Federal Reserve System are appointed by the president of the United States for overlapping 14-year terms. The members of the board of governors and presidents of several other branches (appointed on a rotating basis) comprise the Federal Open Market Committee (FOMC). This central committee oversees the main function of the Fed, the open market operations. The open market operations influence monetary and credit policies.

How Is Monetary Policy Implemented?

The major method of controlling monetary policy is through the federal funds rate. This is the interest rate charged to depository institutions at the Federal Reserve Bank. This interest rate has a subsequent impact on the level of most other interest rates charged by banks and purveyors of credit.

For example, when you take out a loan at the bank to purchase a car or make a home improvement, you are charged interest on the borrowed funds. In the same way, when your bank borrows money from the Fed, it pays interest to the Federal Reserve Bank. The amount of interest charged is called the federal funds rate. If the Fed funds rate increases, it's likely that the interest rate you are charged on a car loan will go up as well, as it costs the bank more money to borrow funds.

The Fed influences the demand for and supply of money in the following ways. An important goal of the Fed is to impact the level of balances the member banks hold at the Federal Reserve Bank. This in turn will influence the lending behavior of banks. By purchasing or selling securities, such as U.S. Treasury bonds, notes, and other issues, it indirectly influences interest rates. For example, selling Treasury securities increases the availability of funds in the market, thereby driving down interest rates with the excess supply of funds. Lower interest rates encourage consumers to borrow and spend, thereby increasing economic growth.

By raising or lowering the reserve requirements or percentage of money that banks must keep on hand, the Fed can influence the amount available for lending. For example, although you deposit $10,000 in a bank, in reality some of that money will be lent to other customers. The reserve requirement states the percentage of your total deposits that must remain in the bank.

Banks are required to hold additional funds or contractual clearing balances, on top of their reserve requirements, at the Fed. Similar to the prior examples, this influences the amount of money the depository bank has left to lend out and subsequently the interest rates it will charge.

The final method of influencing interest rates is through discount window lending. The federal funds rate is the interest rate, set by the Fed, at which members lend and borrow funds. The Fed lends money to member banks, and the interest rate charged to the member banks has a relationship to the interest rate those member banks will charge their borrowers.

Supply and demand influences interest rates, just like other commodities. If a bank has a greater supply of funds due to lower reserve requirements, interest rates will be lower. Conversely, if a bank has fewer funds available for lending, this relative scarcity of lendable cash will drive interest rates up.

Member Banks

The U.S. banking system is divided into three groups. These three groups are classified by which governing body charters them and whether they belong to the Federal Reserve System. National banks are charted by the federal government and are legally members of the Federal Reserve System. State-chartered banks are both Federal Reserve member banks (state member banks) and those that are not.

Monetary Policy and the Economy

The Federal Reserve decisions impact not only banking in the United States but internationally as well. A change in short-term interest rates influences long-term interest rates on Treasury notes, corporate bonds, mortgages, and auto and other consumer loans. Interest rate directions go beyond borrowing and lending, but also influence how investors perceive the future economy. When long-term interest rates are higher than short-term rates, consumers believe we will experience a normal pattern of economic growth. Interest rate movements also impact stock market values, which in turn influence consumers' net worth or household wealth. For example, lower interest rates suggest a strong economy with higher corporate profits due to lower borrowing costs. This scenario of lower interest rates with higher corporate profitability can also lead to increased hiring and greater national employment levels.

The increased demand for goods and services drives prices and wages upward. Thus, lower interest rates and economic expansion eventually lead to higher prices and inflation. This pattern highlights the inherent difficulty in the Fed's goals of maximizing employment and minimizing inflation.

Although the Federal Reserve's duties appear straightforward, monetary policy is an inexact science. Decisions are made in response to economic events. The Fed policies are widely debated in economic circles. For example, during the mortgage crisis and subsequent recession of the mid 2000s the Federal Reserve acted to reduce interest rates to the lowest levels seen in decades and to buy the toxic debt on the books of U.S. banks. These efforts by the Fed illustrate how the organization attempts to circumvent a depression and reignite economic growth. In 2013, controversy continued regarding these monetary policy decisions. Although the economy avoided a recession, the ensuing economic growth as well as job growth have been slow.

Monetary goals are clearly stated in the law, yet how to achieve these goals is not. The FOMC has discretion in its methods. Furthermore, the results of Fed actions are not immediate and only observable in the future. This lag between Fed actions and economic results adds to the controversy that surrounds most Fed decisions. The more the public understands the goals of maximum employment and stable prices, the easier it is for the Federal Reserve Banking System to implement its policies.

Barbara Friedberg

See also: Banking; Bonds; Cash; Compound Interest/Return; Consumer Credit/Debt; Inflation; Interest Income and Payments; Interest Rates; Investing; Risk; Savings Account; Treasury Securities

Further Reading

Board of Governors of the Federal Reserve System. 2005. "The Federal Reserve System; Purposes and Functions, Ninth Edition." U.S. Federal Reserve System Publication. Washington, D.C. http://www.federalreserve.gov/pf/pdf/pf_complete.pdf

Financial Advisor

A financial advisor is an individual who provides financial advice or guidance to customers for compensation. Financial advisors provide different services, including investment portfolio management, tax planning, retirement planning, insurance planning, and estate planning. These professionals help their clients meet and manage their most important financial goals in life. A fundamental goal of financial advisors is to increase clients' net worth over time, while protecting them from risks such as loss of income due to disability, premature death, and long-term care expenses.

History

Financial advising began in the period following the Industrial Revolution. In the United States this period was marked by a change in the structure of business organizations. Business was transformed from owner-operator entrepreneurs to the public corporate structure seen today. An investor class developed as individuals began to commit capital to companies to gain financial returns. In general, investors have no say in direct managerial decisions, thus they lack pertinent information about the organization in which they have invested. This trend created a need for the financial world to make advice and information available to investors.

The first steps toward creating a professional class of financial advisors were taken by existing financial institutions and professionals, such as securities brokers and dealers. It was soon apparent that a conflict of interest existed as many firms that were acting as both suppliers and advisors were abusing investors by offering advice designed more to aid the sale of the securities in which the firms and professionals had a particular interest, rather than suggesting securities that would best suit the needs of the investors. As a consequence of the need for trained and unbiased assistance, financial advising firms and individuals evolved.

Following the end of World War I, the new profession spread rapidly. As abuses from investment companies and investment trusts became frequent, the U.S. Securities and Exchange Commission (SEC) started an investigation that led to the Investment Advisors Act of 1940. The act required all investment advisors to register with the SEC, with the exception of lawyers, accountants, engineers, teachers, registration publications, magazines, and financial newspapers.

On December 12, 1969, Loren Dunton, Lewis Kearns, and 11 other individuals with various backgrounds and interests in financial products and services gathered in Chicago. For two days, they laid the groundwork for an institution that was to become the College for Financial Planning, a credential that would evolve into the Certified Financial Planner (CFP) certification. This membership organization subsequently became the International Association for Financial Planning (IAFP). The IAFP is one of the two entities that came together in 2000 to form the Financial Planning Association (FPA), the other one being the Institute of Certified Financial Planners (ICFP).

On July 21, 2010, President Barack Obama signed into law the financial regulatory reform bill known as the Dodd-Frank Wall Street Reform and Consumer Protection Act as an outcome of the financial crisis of 2007–2008. The act provides new requirements for the registration of investment advisors and affects investment advisors, financial planners, as well as Certified Public Accountants (CPAs).

Types of Financial Advisors

Financial advising is a broad concept with different types of professionals and varying domains of expertise. A certified financial planner offers broad-based financial advice and prepares financial plans for his or her clients. The kinds of services financial planners offer varies. Some financial planners assess every aspect of a client's financial life—including savings, investments, insurance, taxes, retirement, and estate planning—and then helps the client develop a detailed strategy or financial plan for meeting all of the financial goals. These professionals must pass an extensive, 10-hour examination and meet other education and ethics requirements to attain the credential.

A chartered financial consultant (ChFC) specializes in insurance and estate planning and is trained to meet the advanced financial planning needs of individuals, professionals, and small business owners. The ChFC has knowledge of the key financial planning disciplines, including insurance, retirement planning, investments, estate planning, and income taxation.

Other professional financial advisors include registered investment advisors (RIA). A RIA is registered with the Securities and Exchange Commission or a state securities regulator and can manage investment portfolios. Certified public accountants is are especially qualified to help with tax planning.

Fee Structures

Some financial advisors charge a fee as a percentage of the client's account value. This is one of the most common ways that a financial or investment advisor is compensated. As the account value grows, the advisor makes more money. If the account value declines, the advisor makes less money. In this way, the financial advisor has an incentive to grow the account value and to minimize losses.

Some advisors are compensated by commissions. When the client purchases a financial product such as a stock, annuity, or insurance, the advisor receives a commission. This is one of the most common ways a financial salesperson charges for services. Some of these people are good financial advisors; some are just good salespeople. Their advice can be influenced by the way they are compensated.

Other advisors receive a combination of fees and commissions. They often use the term *fee-based*. It is important to understand the difference between a fee-only advisor and a fee-based advisor. A fee-only advisor does not collect commissions based on product sales.

Consumers with specific financial questions may hire a financial advisor compensated by an hourly rate. This can be a great way to pay for financial advice if you are willing to implement the advice on your own. For example, you may pay a financial advisor an hourly rate to tell you how to allocate the investments in your 401(k) plan. Then you would be responsible for actually making the changes the advisor suggested.

Just like attorneys or accountants, financial advisors' hourly rates will vary widely. Expect to pay a higher hourly rate for experienced advisors or advisors with a specialty.

When you need a project completed, such as an initial retirement plan, it may make sense to pay a flat fee to have someone crunch the numbers and help you understand all the moving parts that go into creating an accurate retirement plan projection. The fee should be quoted upfront, along with a clear description of what will be provided for that fee. Ask if follow-up meetings or questions are included.

Those with a more complex situation, such as ongoing stock options to be exercised, a small business, rental properties, or a need for regular income from investments, may benefit from paying a quarterly or annual retainer fee for ongoing advice. Since a retainer fee is not tied to the value of investments or generated by the purchase of any specific investment, the client is assured of receiving objective advice. A written contract details the fee structure and services provided. The best way to understand financial advisors' services and fee structures is to ask.

Joseph Krupka

See also: Accountant; Interest Income and Payments; Investing; Life Insurance; Net Worth; Online Personal Finance; Retirement; Tax Return, Federal; Year 2010: Dodd-Frank Wall Street Reform and Consumer Protection Act

Further Reading

Nissen, W. G., and M. K. Buckingham. 2011. "New Investment Adviser Requirements of the Dodd-Frank Act: What CPAs Should Know." *Journal of Accountancy* 211(1): 34–41.

Ritchin, L. 2009. "Financial Planning Pioneer Lewis G. Kearns on the 40th Anniversary of the Profession." *Journal of Financial Planning* 22(12): 14–16.

Snider, S. 2013. "What You Need to Know About Financial Planners." *Kiplinger's Personal Finance* 67(5): 71.

U.S. Securities and Exchange Commission. 2008. "Financial Planners," last modified August 20, 2008. http://www.sec.gov/answers/finplan.htm

Wilsey, H. 1949. "The Investment Advisers Act of 1940." *Journal of Finance* 4(4): 286–297.

Fixed Income *(see Bonds)*

Flexible Saving Account

A flexible saving account, also called a flexible spending account (FSA), is a workplace-provided account into which employees contribute money before federal income taxes and the employee portion of Social Security tax (pretax) are calculated. Once a worker sets up an FSA, the employer then deducts that amount in installments from the employee's pay each pay period and deposits the money into the worker's FSA.

By either name, the accounts usually are referred to as FSAs. Account owners can use the pretax dollars to pay specific out-of-pocket costs.

Companies are allowed, but not required, to offer employees both medical expense FSAs and dependent or child care FSAs. An employee can enroll in one account, both, or neither. When carefully established and managed, the accounts can save individuals tax dollars and cover costs, such as uninsured expenses, that they would normally pay out of pocket.

Medical FSA Rules

By opting to open a medical FSA, a worker can set aside up to $5,000 to help pay health care costs that are not covered by insurance. A medical FSA owner either presents covered cost receipts to the account administrator and is reimbursed for the expenses or pays for the eligible expenses using a plan-issued debit card. Even if a debit card is used, workers should retain receipts in case the employer or tax officials have questions about a reimbursement's eligibility.

Qualified medical expenses that are eligible for FSA reimbursement or payment via debit card generally are those costs listed in the FSA's plan description. Most employers use the medical costs listed in IRS Publication 502, "Medical and Dental Expenses."

Common eligible health care expenses detailed over more than 12 pages in the publication include insurance co-payments made with after-tax income, treatment co-payments, deductibles, eye surgeries (such as Lasik), extra pairs of prescription eyeglasses and contact lenses, chiropractor treatments, travel costs for treatment, birth control pills, and pregnancy test kits. In addition, prescription drugs and over-the-counter (OTC) drugs may be reimbursed from or paid for directly with FSA funds. However, a tax law change effective with the 2013 tax year requires that an FSA owner get a prescription from a doctor for OTC medicines before the account money will cover those costs.

The IRS periodically updates the qualifying medical expenses list. An FSA account owner should check the IRS Web site and double-check with his or her FSA administrator before making questionable medical purchases or receiving services to ensure he or she will be covered.

Child Care FSA Rules

By opting to open a dependent-care FSA, a worker can set aside up to $5,000 to help pay some of the costs incurred in placing children in day care while the parent or parents are at work. If both married spouses work and each has access to a child care FSA, the $5,000 limit applies to them as a couple; one spouse can open a $5,000 FSA or they can split the limit between themselves.

A child care FSA operates like a medial FSA. Once an employee decides what amount, up to the limit, he or she wishes to contribute to the account, the employer deducts that amount in installments from the employee's gross pay each pay period before taxes are calculated and sends it to the FSA. The money then is used to pay the child care provider or reimburse the parents for their out-of-pocket expenses.

Free Money from FSAs

Another advantage of FSAs is that a reimbursement request can be fulfilled before the account has enough money to cover the cost. For example, a medical FSA owner breaks his wrist in February and requires surgery. The injured employee's workplace health insurance covers most of the surgical costs, but because the injury was incurred early in the benefits year, he had to pay a $2,000 deductible. Also because of the timing, the worker had only contributed to his medical FSA for two months, or $833 toward his eventual $5,000 annual total.

Tax law, however, allows for the worker to be reimbursed for the full $2,000 deductible costs because he is enrolled for a $5,000 FSA total contribution. Even if the worker leaves his job before he contributes the amount already paid by the FSA, he won't have to repay the money.

Use or Lose FSA Money

FSAs, however, do have a major downside. If an account holder ends a benefits year with excess money in the account, the money is forfeited to the employer. This is known as the "use it or lose it" rule. It also is why many workers undercontribute to their FSAs.

Employers are allowed to offer FSA owners a grace period of two and one-half months, or until March 15 for benefits plans that operate on a calendar year, to ensure eligible medical expenses use the prior year's excess funds. But this is an employer option, not a requirement of its employee benefits offerings. Workers should make sure they understand when their FSAs must be used so that they don't inadvertently lose some of their contributions.

Life Changes Allow for FSA Changes

Once an employee chooses an amount for an FSA, no changes are allowed unless there is a major life change. Valid life changes for both medical and child care FSAs are a change in marital status (e.g., marriage, divorce, death of spouse, legal separation, or annulment); dependents added or lost via birth, adoption, placement for adoption, or death; employment status change on the part of the employee, a spouse or dependents (e.g., change in worksite, switching from part-time to full-time or vice versa, or job loss); residency change; and a dependent's eligibility change (e.g., reaches a birthday beyond the eligibility age or is no longer a full-time student). In these cases, an FSA owner can and should adjust the contribution amount to the saving plan to ensure that it has enough funds to cover expected costs, but not so much as to lose unused money.

Kay Bell

See also: Health Insurance; Tax Deferral; Tax Return, Federal

Further Reading

Cuddington, John T. February 2, 1998. "Optimal Annual Contributions to Flexible Spending Accounts: A Rule-of-Thumb." Economics Department, Georgetown University, Washington, D.C. http://128.118.178.162/eps/game/papers/9802/9802001.pdf

Ebeling, Ashela. 2012. "New Healthcare Flexible Spending Account Rules for 2013, Use-It-Or Lose-It Still Undecided," *Forbes Magazine* (Nov. 16). http://www.forbes.com/sites/ashleaebeling/2012/11/16/new-healthcare-flexible-spending-account-rules-for-2013-use-it-or-lose-it-still-undecided/

"Health Savings Accounts and Other Tax-Favored Health Plans, Publication 969." Department of the Treasury Internal Revenue Service, last modified January 30, 2013. http://www.irs.gov/pub/irs-pdf/p969.pdf

"Medical and Dental Expenses Publication 502." Department of the Treasury Internal Revenue Service, last modified December 10, 2012. http://www.irs.gov/pub/irs-pdf/p502.pdf

Van de Water, Paul N. June 5, 2012. "Limitation on Use of Tax-Advantaged Health Accounts Should Not Be Repealed." Center on Budget and Policy Priorities Web site. http://www.cbpp.org/cms/?fa=view&id=3789

Flexible Spending Account *(see Flexible Saving Account)*

Government I Bonds *(see Inflation-Protected Investments)*

Gross Domestic Product (GDP) and Gross National Product (GNP)

The *gross domestic product (GDP)* is the monetary value of goods and services that a country produces in one year. The GDP includes production by both citizens and foreign residents inside the country. Specifically, the GDP is the total spending by consumers, governments, and businesses as well as net exports. The measure provides an indication of the overall spending in a country.

The *gross national product (GNP)* is the amount of goods and services that a country produces in one year including that produced by its citizens located in other countries, but not including foreign residents inside the country's borders. More precisely, the GNP is the total amount of consumer spending, government spending, business investment spending, and net payments to foreigners for producing goods and services.

The subtle difference between the GDP and GNP pertains to the definition of the country's production either by geography or citizenship, respectively. For example, the output of a Brazilian company manufacturing products in the United States would be included in the U.S. GDP but not the U.S. GNP. The U.S. production from the same Brazilian company would be included in Brazil's GNP.

The GDP and GNP include transactions that have a monetary value, but do not include volunteer or household work, illegal or underground deals, and unreported cash transactions. For instance, the GDP and GNP would include the sale of jam at a grocery store, but not jam made for friends and family. Thus, these measures capture only financially based transactions on established markets, recorded and monitored by the government.

The GDP and GNP are often used as measures of the size and health of a country's economy. The changes in these measures from year to year indicate a country's economic growth or contraction. The period of time during which the GDP growth rate increases is considered an economic expansion. A country is considered to be in a recession when its GDP contracts for two consecutive quarters; a contraction with a GDP decrease of more than 10 percent is considered an economic depression.

Purchasing Power Parity

For purposes of comparison, the GDP and GNP figures of countries are converted to a common currency using nominal exchange rates. One difficulty in using the GDP or GNP to assess and compare the economies of countries is the relative values and buying power of domestic currencies, which can make GDP and GNP figures seem better or worse than they actually are. By converting these figures into one common currency, one falsely assumes that currency buying power is the same in all countries. In other words, the GDP and GNP conversion using official exchange rates does not show what a local currency can buy in its home country.

Purchasing power parity creates an apples to apples comparison of the purchasing power of a country's currency. Converting GDP and GNP figures using a country's purchasing power parity (PPP) exchange rate, which adjusts the exchange rate to account for the buying power of a domestic currency, simplifies the comparison and allows for more useful evaluations between countries. For example, India's GDP converted using the nominal exchange rate was only $1,824 billion, which placed it as the 10th largest in the world. Yet, according to the International Monetary Fund (IMF), India had a GDP of $4,711 billion in 2012 when converted with the PPP, which made it the third largest national economy in the world. Thus, the buying power of India's currency is higher than its official exchange rate would indicate. (Dividing the GDP converted with the PPP by the GDP converted by the nominal exchange rate indicates a PPP of 2.6.)

The *GDP per capita* is the gross domestic product divided by the number of people living in the country. This measure takes into account the relative size of a country and is used to compare the economic health of citizens across countries. Although it is often considered as one measure of a country's standard of living or its citizens' well-being, the GDP per capita does not evaluate how much money an individual actually receives or the distribution of the GDP among citizens. The GDP and GNP per capita also do not measure personal income. This is particularly apparent in countries where the middle class is shrinking and the poor population is growing. Also, since the GDP and GNP per capita measures are averages across citizens, they reduce the ability to perceive the extremes of wealth in a country. A country may compare favorably with others even if there is a small population of extremely wealthy or prosperous individuals and a large poor population. The buying power of a country's currency is also an important factor. Thus, it is important to consider multiple measures of economic health when comparing countries.

The GDP and GNP take on more personal meaning when one considers how the measures are used by government and regulatory organizations. When the GDP of a country is not growing, businesses are not increasing outputs or profits. Policymakers may act to stimulate the economy by reducing interest rates, purchasing long-term bonds, increasing government spending, or cutting taxes. The reasoning follows that an economic stimulus motivates individuals and businesses to increase spending. Likewise, if the GDP is expanding faster than expected, policymakers may attempt to reduce economic output to avoid excessive inflation.

In general, countries aim to maximize their GDP. This has created situations that call into question the validity of these measures. Some argue that a few governments prop up or artificially increase their GDP to appear competitive in the global market arena. Mechanisms to artificially increase the GDP include spending government funds on useless projects. However, even if a government were to use such tactics, the effects are short-lived since the activity is not sustainable in the long run.

Jennifer L. Woolley

See also: Capitalism; Deflation; Inflation; Interest Rates

Further Reading

International Monetary Fund. 2013. Accessed May 16. http://www.imf.org
Organisation for Economic Cooperation and Development. 2013. Accessed May 16. http://www.oecd.org
The World Bank. 2013. Accessed May 16. http://www.worldbank.org

Health Insurance

Health insurance helps the consumer pay for medical costs. As former Minnesota governor Jesse Ventura stated, "Health insurance should be a given for every citizen." Finally, with the recent implementation of the Affordable Care Act (ACA) all citizens have access to affordable health insurance.

Health insurance covers the insured for medicine, visits to the doctor and emergency room, and hospital stays as well as other medical expenses. The amount and type of coverage, the copay charges (portion paid by the insured), the deductible (how much the insured must pay before the insurance contributes), and the cost are determined by the policy.

Until 2014, health insurance in the United States was optional. If one didn't have health insurance through an employer or an individual policy, there was no requirement or law that one must purchase a health insurance policy. Without insurance, the uninsured were expected to pay for all health care charges, such as doctor visits, with their own funds.

With the passage of the Affordable Care Act (ACA) and its implementation in 2014, health insurance is required for all Americans. In order to facilitate the health

---

Demographic Health Statistics for the U.S. Population

- 61 percent of adults aged 18 years and older were in either excellent or very good health.
- 27 percent of adults were in good health.
- 12 percent of adults were in fair or poor health.
- Health condition was better for younger individuals and deteriorated with age.
- 49 percent of African American adults had excellent or very good health compared with 63 percent of Caucasians and 64 percent of Asian Americans.
- Level of education was positively correlated with health status: 74 percent of adults holding a bachelor's degree or higher were in excellent or very good health.
- 38 percent of adults with less than a high school degree reported excellent or very good health.
- In 2010, 73 percent of those under age 65 with private health insurance had excellent or very good health compared with 55 percent of adults without health insurance coverage.
- 41 percent of those under age 65 with Medicaid health insurance had excellent or very good health.
- Only 6 percent of those under age 65 with private health care insurance reported fair or poor health.
- Married adults were less likely to report fair or poor health than adults who were widowed, divorced, living with a partner, or had never married.

Source: 2010 National Health Interview Survey (NHIS).

---

insurance selection process, the U.S. government (www.healthcare.gov) and the individual states have new insurance marketplace Web sites.

Understanding Health Insurance

Health insurance makes paying for health care costs more affordable. With a health insurance policy, the consumer pays a portion of the total health care costs. So how does health insurance work?

The consumer signs up for a policy, either individually, through the U.S. government marketplace, the state marketplace, or through his or her employer. This policy is similar to other types of insurance. The policy describes in detail the medical coverage provided as well as the co-pays the consumer must pay for treatment. Policies vary from a bare-bones, high-deductible plan, to a more extensive one that covers vision and prescription drugs. The policy costs and co-pays also depend on the policy details.

After purchasing the health insurance policy, the individual joins other members in the same plan. All health insurance plan members belong to a risk pool. Individuals in the risk pool consist of those higher risk participants who are in poor health (likely to need a lot of medical care) and lower risk individuals with good health. The insurer takes into account the risk profiles of its members and calculates how much it will cost to pay for the expected medical expenses of the plan participants.

Those calculations are used to determine the per-member monthly rate or premium charge.

Health insurance provides a shared cost format. The plan member pays a monthly premium (sometimes the employer pays all or part of the premium on behalf of the employee), and the member also pays additional out-of-pocket costs for services received. The plan member's out-of-pocket fees may be a co-pay, deductible, and/or coinsurance.

A co-pay is a predetermined amount the consumer pays for doctor and emergency room visits as well as for prescription medicines. This is different from coinsurance where the insured pays a percentage of the cost of the medical care. An annual deductible is a predetermined out-of-pocket amount the insured is required to pay before the insurance company pays for any medical claims.

Types of Health Insurance Plans

There are hundreds of various health insurance plans. This section will discuss the three most common types of health plans.

A health maintenance organization (HMO) frequently charges lower monthly premiums and out-of-pocket costs in exchange for allegiance to a predetermined group of medical providers. Normally, HMO participants have a primary care physician. Any referrals and treatment needed from specialists must go through the gatekeeper primary care physician.

A preferred provider organization (PPO) offers more flexibility than an HMO, along with higher costs. A PPO offers a network of member doctors, specialists, and hospitals. PPOs do not require the member to go through the primary care physician for a referral to a specialist. The plan member may see in-network providers for a lower cost than for seeing an out-of-network medical professional.

The consumer-directed health plan (CDHP), often called a high-deductible plan, usually requires greater initial out-of-pocket expenses than the HMO or PPO, with lower monthly premiums. For example, the high-deductible plan may require the consumer to pay up to $2,500 or $5,000 out-of-pocket before the health plan payments kick in. A health savings account is a tax-advantaged account (with special tax benefits regulated by the Treasury Department) available to participants with CDHP plans. These accounts allow users to pay for medical care with pretax dollars. This type of plan may be offered in conjunction with an HMO or PPO.

Government Health Insurance Programs

The government offers public insurance for the elderly and lower-income members of the population. Medicare is the federal government health insurance program for citizens age 65 and older as well as the disabled. Medicaid, jointly funded by the federal and state governments, is the health insurance program for the poor. The State Children's Health Insurance Program (SCHIP) is a special type of health insurance for children. Even if parents do not meet income thresholds for Medicaid, SCHIP ensures that children's medical needs are covered. See the Medicare and Medicaid entries for more detailed coverage.

Penalties for Lack of Health Insurance

With the advent of the ACA, those without health insurance face penalties. Since the government created low-cost health insurance and provides financial assistance to those who cannot afford health insurance, there is a penalty to those without insurance.

Most individuals are required to have health coverage or pay a penalty. If one didn't have coverage in 2014, the penalty was a fee of 1 percent of one's income or $95 per adult ($47.50 per child), whichever is higher. The fee was due on the 2015 income tax return. Some people are eligible for an exemption from the fee, based on income levels or other factors.

Must an Employer Provide Employees Health Insurance?

Many employers offer health insurance as a benefit to their employees. In fact, the ACA requires employers with a minimum of 50 full-time employees (or equivalents) to offer health insurance to its full-time employees and their dependents. If employers do not provide the required health insurance, they must make a special tax payment called the Employer Shared Responsibility Payment (ESRP).

Employers with fewer than 50 full-time employees aren't subject to ESRP. If these employers wish to offer their employees insurance, the government offers a special marketplace, the Small Business Health Options Program (SHOP). The SHOP marketplace offers plans designed for small businesses and their employees. As an added incentive for employers, those with fewer than 25 employees may also qualify for tax credits if they buy insurance through SHOP.

Finally, health insurance is now available to all U.S. citizens at an affordable cost. There are opportunities for all consumers to select a suitable plan from the wide range of health care providers.

Barbara Friedberg

See also: Affordable Care Act; Disability Insurance; Medicaid; Medicare; Obama, Barack, President of the United States

Further Reading

BlueCross BlueShield of Illinois Web site. "Health Plans and Provider Networks." Accessed June 25, 2014. http://www.bcbsil.com/getting_started/health_insurance/types_plans

Centers for Disease Control. 2012. "Summary Health Statistics for U.S. Adults: National Health Interview Survey, 2010." January. http://www.cdc.gov/nchs/data/series/sr_10/sr10_252.pdf

Healthcare.gov Web site. Accessed June 25, 2014. https://www.healthcare.gov/

Hedge Funds

Hedge funds are private pooled funds that make investments in equities (stocks), bonds, and derivatives. The hedge funds are similar to mutual funds in that they are pools of capital collected from investors. The capital is invested on behalf of the investors by a dedicated investment team consisting of portfolio managers and analysts. Hedge funds are less regulated than mutual funds and do not have to disclose their NAV (net asset value = sum of value of all investments in the fund less expenses) on a daily basis. They are also not traded on a stock exchange like stocks and exchange-traded funds (ETFs). Investors can invest in hedge funds by contacting the fund team directly.

In order to invest in a hedge fund, high net worth investors have to meet certain income and assets criteria. Before investing in a hedge fund, prospective investors complete a worksheet detailing all their assets including stocks, real estate, physical commodities (such as gold), commodity contracts, or derivatives.

There are two categories of private investors: accredited investors need a net worth of at least $1 million; qualified purchasers need $5 million in investments excluding a business and primary residence. There may be other requirements to invest such as a commitment to leave funds in the fund for an allotted time period.

These guidelines have been put in place to discourage small investors from putting all their savings into hedge funds. Hedge funds are riskier than mutual funds given their lack of liquidity (not traded on an exchange) and their lack of transparency (hedge funds do not have to report their asset values or the underlying holdings on a daily or weekly basis). All of these participant requirements are enacted by the SEC to protect the investor as these funds are loosely regulated.

Hedge Fund Fees

The fee charged by a hedge fund to manage the money is made up of two components: management fees and incentive fees. Management fees are fixed annual fees charged as a percentage of an investor's investment with the fund. For example, if an investor invested $1,000,000 with a hedge fund that charges a 2 percent management fee, the management fee paid to management by the investor for the year is $20,000. Most hedge fund managers charge management fees between 1 and 2 percent.

Incentive fees are the performance-based fees charged as a percentage of the hedge fund's profit. If the above hedge fund charges a 20 percent incentive fee and generates a 10 percent return in a year, the profit for the investor is $100,000 and the incentive fee paid by the investor to the fund is $20,000. Most hedge funds charge incentive fees between 10 and 20 percent.

Some hedge funds charge an incentive fee beyond a hurdle rate. Assume the above hedge fund has a hurdle rate of 6 percent. The incentive fee is calculated on the profit generated above this hurdle rate. The excess profit in this case is 4 percent or $40,000, and the incentive fee paid by the investor to the hedge fund is $8,000.

Another common feature of the hedge funds is charging incentive fees with a high water mark, that is, in case of negative returns in a particular year, the fund cannot charge incentive fees the next year until it recoups the loss from the previous year. For example, if a fund generated a 5 percent loss in year one and generated a profit of 12 percent in year two, the fund can charge incentive fees only on profit equaling 7 percent of returns generated in year two. This 7 percent incentive fee is the difference between the 5 percent loss in year one and the 12 percent gain in year two. The fund is said to have reached the high water mark in year two when it recoups the losses generated in year one.

Hedge Fund Strategies

The strategies used by hedge funds vary by the types of assets the funds invest in and with the complexity of the strategies. The aim of many hedge funds is to generate absolute returns, that is, returns that are independent of the market movements. They aim to make a profit even when the stock and/or bond market returns are negative. Funds achieve this by creating strategies that are less, or not at all, correlated with the markets.

Many hedge funds trade in derivatives (futures, options) and by short selling. Derivatives are a type of financial security contract between two individuals who receive a payoff according to the movements of an underlying asset. This topic is further discussed in the entry on derivatives.

Short selling is a strategy whereby a short seller investor believes that the price of a security will go down. That short seller investor will borrow the security and sell it at its current price. The investment company finds a stock to borrow either from its own inventory or a client account. When the price falls, the short seller investor buys back the security in the market and the difference between the higher selling price and lower buyback price is the profit for the short seller investor.

Short selling has received bad press due to the structure of the investment contract. A short seller benefits when stock prices decline. The press suggests that the short seller may be benefiting from others' misery (i.e., loss in security value).

Some of the common strategies include long/short equity (buying and short selling equities); market neutral equity (buying and short selling securities such that the total market exposure equals zero, that is, for every dollar of security bought there is a dollar of security sold short; distressed credit (buying bonds that are near or in bankruptcy); global macro (buying and selling across equities, bonds, futures, and options to take advantage of global trends like a rise in consumerism in emerging markets, a rebound in the European economy, etc.).

Hedge funds are investments for wealthy and sophisticated investors due to their high fees and risky characteristics. Although reported in the news, these investments are only a small component of the overall investment world.

Surya Mrunalini Pisapati

See also: Bonds; Derivatives; Investing; Liquidity; Mutual Funds and Exchange-Traded Funds (ETFs); Risk; Stock Market; Stocks

Further Reading

Collimore, Thomas. 2013. "Hedge Fund Strategies for Individual Investors." CFA Institute Web site. http://www.cfainstitute.org/learning/investor/Documents/hedge_funds.pdf

Griffin, John M., and Jin Xu. 2010. "How Smart Are the Smart Guys? A Unique View from Hedge Fund Stock Holdings." *CFA Digest* (Vol. 40, February).

Homeowner's and Renter's Insurance

A pillar of modern personal finance is protecting one's assets. Whether one lives in a home or apartment, renters and homeowners need financial protection against perils that may arise unexpectedly. The perils might include theft, fire, or potential for litigation occurring over accidents or mishaps in or around the home.

In the United States there are seven forms of homeowner's insurance that range in name from HO-1 through HO-6 and HO-8 (there is no HO-7). Each of these levels offers a different package of protection. For example, the HO-1, the most basic homeowner's policy, covers fire but not damage due to frozen pipes. If there is a mortgage on the property, the mortgage company will require a minimum level of coverage in order to protect their investment in the property.

Homeowner's and renter's insurance offer that necessary protection. Homeowner's insurance differs from renter's insurance in that it may cover different perils with different amounts of insurance coverage. Additionally, a homeowner must protect the building structure whereas a renter only needs to protect the apartment's contents, not the building itself. Condominium insurance is a combination of both homeowner's and renter's insurance because condominium property owners do not possess the exteriors of their dwellings.

Homeowner's Insurance

The likely perils that may damage a property are hail, wind, lightning, falling trees, tornadoes, vandals, water, theft, fire, explosion, vandalism, riot, and perhaps even a falling aircraft. Most homeowners purchase a homeowner's insurance policy to cover insurable events that may occur in or around their home that would culminate in a financial loss. Although the homeowner's insurance policy will normally reimburse the homeowner for rebuilding expenses, there are other costs to consider as well.

After a catastrophic event, while the home is being rebuilt or repaired, the occupants of that home incur living expenses that are over and above their usual costs. In this circumstance, the homeowners may be temporarily unable to live in their home and may be forced to pay for alternative accommodation such as hotel expenses, clothes, and meals at restaurants (Norton 2009). For these reasons homeowner's insurance comes in handy to assist them in recovering some of these additional unforeseen expenses.

A standard homeowner's insurance policy is often a package deal. Not only is the home itself insured, but also structures on the property, such as garages, barns, sheds, gazebos, and fencing are insured. Trees, plants, and shrubs may also be covered under standard homeowner's insurance.

Items that are covered in the homeowner's policy may include personal possessions that occupants of the house may keep in and around their home. So if an occupant's furniture, electronics, clothing, sports equipment, and other personal items are stolen or destroyed by fire or another insurable disaster, the insurance company will pay a sum of money as specified in the policy document so that they may replace or repair the lost or damaged belongings. Ideally the insurer places the claimant in the same position financially as they were before the calamitous event.

In the unforeseen event of any bodily injuries or property damage caused to a homeowner's guests while visiting the owner's property, the homeowner's policy will cover it. A homeowner's insurance policy may also insure them for their legal liability to third parties. The personal liability portion of the homeowner's insurance policy covers homeowners against lawsuits or legal judgments in favor of members of their family or other third-party individuals who are not the occupants of the property.

The homeowner's policy pays for the cost of defending the homeowner in court and any court awards. In most cases, there is an agreed limit the insurer will pay (Teale 2008).

If a friend or neighbor is injured in an insured homeowner's home, then medical expenses can be paid to the injured party without a liability claim being filed against the homeowners. If a homeowner's children or dog accidentally ruins the neighbor's expensive rug, the homeowner's policy will cover these perils, but not if they destroy the rug within the homeowner's own home. If the policy allows for off-premises coverage, then the insurance will cover property such as binoculars stolen during a vacation away.

Casual and occasional workers such as babysitters or neighborhood children mowing the homeowner's lawn are generally covered by the standard homeowner's policy. Permanent full- or part-time domestic employees or contractors such as plumbers, electricians, home health caregivers, or gardeners are not covered by a homeowner's policy.

It is very important that homeowners do not underinsure their property. This means insuring it for less than replacement value or for less than the amount sufficient to rebuild the home in the event of a disaster even though it may only need to be repaired. A home is rarely insured for its market value since the market value also includes the land.

There are some disasters that may cause damage to a home that are not covered by private insurers. Federal and state governments are left to make provision for these events, such as damage by disease, or other natural perils such as earthquakes, tornadoes, hurricanes, and of course flooding, whether caused by bursting levies, overflowing rivers, or a spring thaw.

Poor maintenance or general wear and tear on a home are not covered, because the homeowner is responsible for any maintenance-related damage to the house. If the toilet backs up or the sump pump fails, no homeowner's insurance will cover it. Instead coverage for these natural perils and poor maintenance are purchased as two additional distinct policies rather than covered under a homeowner's policy.

Homeowners of expensive antique furniture, furs, jewelry, silverware, artworks, or other valuables, such as coin and stamp collections or baseball memorabilia, will not be covered by homeowner's insurance. They need to purchase a special personal property endorsement or "floater" to cover these items' full appraised value up to a dollar limit in the event that they are lost, stolen, or destroyed.

Renter's Insurance

Renter's insurance is frequently overlooked, yet it is equally as important as homeowner's insurance. Renter's or "tenant's insurance" provides the same coverage as homeowner's insurance, with the exception of coverage for the structure of the home itself (Johnson & Sykes 2005). A renter's policy costs correspondingly less than a homeowner's policy, since only the personal property items are insured and not the real estate.

Although landlords buy insurance to protect the structure of rental units against loss, a homeowner's policy doesn't protect tenants' personal property (Foong 2012). Standard renter's insurance typically protects renters against loss of personal property to theft and other perils such as liability, fire, vandalism, lightning, and water damage caused by overflowing bathtubs and unreported water leaks that have caused substantial damage. The personal possessions component will reimburse tenants for loss of personal property, and the external living expenses coverage will pay residents for living expenses and accommodation costs if they should be evacuated temporarily as a result of a fire or some other disaster. The liability component of renter's insurance protects the residents of the rental against damages caused to third parties that may lead to a lawsuit.

Renter's insurance does not cover property losses due to floods, earthquakes, sewer backups, and hurricanes. So additional specific policies or endorsements to protect property from damage or loss caused by those threats should be purchased, especially if the renter does not have the means to replace or pay for such losses.

Some landlords, as part of the lease or rental agreement, may force residents to purchase renter's insurance and provide proof of a certificate of insurance prior to moving in (Nelson 2007). The greatest benefit of tenant insurance to landlords is the ability to recover the costs of repairs and replacement for damages from the resident's insurance company should the resident cause destruction to the rental property.

Deductible

Both homeowner's and renter's insurance require the policyholder to pay a deductible before the insurance company pays for a claim. The deductible is set at the time the policy is purchased and ranges from $250 to $1,000. The higher the deductible, the lower the cost of the policy. That is because with a high deductible, the insurer assumes that small claims will be paid by the homeowner, and the insurance company will make lower overall financial outlays.

Angelique N. S. McInnes

See also: Condominium; Risk; Umbrella Insurance

Further Reading

Foong, K. 2012. "Owner Beware." *Multi-Housing News* (Vol. 47, No. 9): 53–54.

Unknown. 2013. "Home Insurance: Are You Really Covered?" *Consumer Reports* (Vol. 78, No. 10): 22–23.

Johnson, E. R., and T. A. Sykes. 2005. "Getting Renter's Insurance." *Black Enterprise* (Vol. 36, No. 2): 161–161.

Nelson, P. 2007. "Renters Insurance: Planning for Trouble." *Counseling Today* (Vol. 49, No. 10): 44–44.

Norton, R. D. 2009. "10: Where Do You Want to Live?" *Economic Education Bulletin* (Vol. 49, No. 7): 71–76.

Teale, J. 2008. *Insurance and Risk Management*. Milton: John Wiley & Sons Australia.

Human Capital

Human capital is the idea that intelligence and skillfulness make humans valuable. Human capital is the concept that people or workers are a type of asset just like financial, physical, and other types of capital. This implies that companies and even countries can invest in people just as they invest in other types of capital.

Early Human Capital Ideas

The United States at the start of the 20th century first saw the notion expressed that the country's people exemplified its prosperity. Near the conclusion of the 20th century, the world acknowledged that academia is important for technology implementation as well as economic expansion (*New England Economic Review*, 2002). The debate between whether people can or cannot be seen as capital continues to thrive. As research and theories continue to evolve, some questions may arise. Perhaps businesses have overlooked or underestimated the power of human capital, and with contemporary exposure maybe human capital will override the strength of physical capital, such as land, buildings, and equipment. In addition, an important question is whether the business world and other entities can come to a sound balance within their business realms between both physical and human capital.

Researchers can trace the notion of human capital back to the 17th century. In about 1691, Sir William Petty (1623–1687) put worth on workers and assessed the worth of human capital to show England's strength. Petty appraised the price of lives taken by way of warfare and other deaths. In 1853, William Farr (1807–1883) described the current worth of an individual's net future profits as profits minus living expenditures. Farr then posited that the net future profits signified prosperity in the same manner as tangible possessions, and governments ought to tax them in a similar manner.

In 1867, Theodore Wittstein said that law courts ought to use Farr's current worth of net future profits to decide reimbursement for requests in terms of life that has been taken away. In 1930, Alfred Lotka (1880–1949) and Louis Dublin (1882–1969), who both worked in insurance, became interested in Wittstein's idea in order to decide the quantity of life insurance that a person should buy. The two men's labor went beyond Wittstein's current worth of net future profits to contemplate death statistics (Kiker, 1966).

Human Capital and the Business World

The business world placed emphasis on human capital during the 1950s and 1960s, when labor economists started to view matters in reference to labor force quality. Businesses spent funds on training and academic education. Business leaders pondered whether the training and education would positively enhance efficiency as well as incomes. After these pioneers of human capital, various other people developed the idea of human capital in terms of economics. They did this by considering the myriad of ways that people are an investment that brings forth a return. Many others also acknowledged the idea but did not want to perceive people in the same way as physical commodities because of sentimentalism (Berry, 2007).

Throughout the decades, people have employed what contemporaries refer to as the claim of human capital theory to tackle many matters pertaining to civic courses of action. Major topics related to human capital include the influence of countries, the outcomes of migration, investments in as well as supervision of well-being, well-being investing, economic expansion, and academic procedure and investing. Human capital economics, like other sciences, is mobile and continues to progress. During any period, it is the product of what occurred beforehand (Kiker, 1966). In Nick Schulz's (2012) essay, "Human Capital in a Global Age," he notes that economists have been striving to evaluate the importance of human capital today. One particular estimate was that the whole stock of human capital in the United States was worth more than $700 trillion. This number was far in excess of the estimate that the physical capital stock was worth $45 trillion.

In *The American*, Gary Becker and Kevin Murphy (2007) maintained that greater rates of return on capital signify higher production in the economy. This inferred statement is valid for human capital just as it is for physical capital. The primary effect of greater returns on human capital might suggest that there is broad wage inequity. Young men and women may reverse this trend over time by investing more in their human capital.

Michael Schrage (2012) provides a wider viewpoint in *Who Do You Want Your Customers to Become?* In this book, Schrage stressed how inspiring creativity signifies a special type of human capital investment that people do not currently notice. He argued that maybe innovators' main assets are not their workers but their consumers. The importance is on how investment is in terms of the consumer, which involves focusing on and elevating the consumer's proficiency level. Perhaps these attributes are the solution to whether an entity is going to prosper. Schrage continued by explaining that consumers' human capital plays a vital role in a business. Increasing the human capital of consumers and clientele is as cost-effective, fiscally sound, and tactically important as overseeing the human capital of employees in the firm. Innovation creates a newfangled prosperity in terms of human capital. Consumers and clients obtain new abilities as well as new communication standards, causing an increase in value.

How Important Is Human Capital?

Formal economic theory as well as empirical studies have regrettably undermined and belittled the importance of consumers' human capital in innovation achievement. Fruitful innovators have indulged in quality and quantity simultaneously, and this intertwining of the two has created an upsurge in the human capital stock of their consumers or clients. This is proof that their success is due to their innovations making their consumers or clients indispensable (Salam, 2012).

People currently emphasize the important nature of businesses in many ways. Research demonstrates that businesses migrate from a status of above average to superior because of the qualities and emphasis that the businesses place on the workers themselves. This is done through the all-inclusive business entity that involves leadership. *Fortune*'s America's Most Admired Companies is an exclusive list because the peer groups' ranks depend on their perception of human capital as the top aspect. These companies emphasize worker aptitude, management quality, and origination and civic obligation. The focal theme is that investors and business personnel adore entities who place prominence on the human capital aspects of their entities (Phillips, 2005).

The concept of human capital in the United States will continue to be controversial to many with reference to its importance in comparison to physical capital. One sound question may involve the following: If all American business entities incorporated an identical model in terms of the amounts of all measured input including human capital so that equality of work is acknowledged, would this action be considered a fair practice or a socialistic state of affairs?

Scott Glenn

See also: Capitalism; Gross Domestic Product (GDP) and Gross National Product (GNP)

Further Reading

Becker, G. S., and K. M. Murphy. 2007. "The American. The Upside of Income Equality." Accessed January 4, 2014. http://www.american.com/archive/2007/may-june-magazine-contents/the-upside-of-income-inequality

Berry, J. 2007. "Cutter Consortium. The Cutter Edge. The Origins of the Human Capital Concept." Accessed March 2, 2014. http://www.cutter.com

Kiker, B. F. 1966. "A Brief History of Human Capital. The Historical Roots of Human Capital." *Journal of Political Economy*.

Langelett, G. 2002. "Human Capital: A Summary of the 20th Century Research." *Journal of Education Finance* 28(1), 1–23.

Pace, A. 2013. "Human Capital Solutions for the 21st Century." *T+D* 67(5), 64–66.

Phillips, J. 2005. "The Value of Human Capital: What Logic and Intuition Tell Us." *Chief Learning Officer* [serial online] 4(8), 50–52. Retrieved April 14, 2014 from Business Source Complete, Ipswich, MA.

Salam, R. 2012. "The Agenda. Brief Thoughts on Human Capital Investment." *National Review Online*. http://www.nationalreview.com

Schrage, Michael. 2012. *Who Do You Want Your Customers to Become?* Harvard Business Review Press.

Schultz, N. 2012. "Human Capital in a Global Age." *Business Horizon Quarterly*. http://www.aei.org/article/society-and-culture/immigration/human-capital-in-a-global-age/

"What Produced the Human Capital Century?" 2002. *New England Economic Review*, 6. Retrieved February 4, 2014 from EBSCOhost database.

Identity Theft

Identity theft (*ID theft*) and *identity fraud* are terms used to refer to all types of crime in which an individual wrongfully obtains and uses another's personally identifiable information in some way that involves fraud or deception, typically for economic gain. The terms are used interchangeably. *Identity fraud* is the umbrella term that refers to a number of crimes involving the use of false identification, though not necessarily using another person's identification. *Identity theft* is the specific form of identity fraud that involves using the personally identifiable information of another individual. Identity theft as a form of fraud may directly affect the life of the victim whose identity is stolen. In addition to defrauding the victim, third parties (such as creditors, employers, insurance providers, etc.) may also be harmed.

Current federal law defines identity theft as a federal crime. Specifically, when someone knowingly transfers, possesses, or uses, without lawful authority, a means of identification of another person with the intent to commit, or to aid or abet, or in connection with, any unlawful activity. Identity theft is also defined by federal regulations as "fraud committed or attempted using the identifying information of another person without permission." Identity theft can therefore both facilitate and be facilitated by other crimes. For instance, identity theft may enable crimes such as bank fraud, document fraud, employment fraud, or immigration fraud. Obviously, identity theft and fraud may be furthered by crimes such as robbery or burglary.

Different Forms of Identity Theft

There are various forms of identity theft and fraud. Financial identity theft occurs when identity thieves access their victims' bank accounts and credit/debt account records. Individual victims are often protected under the Electronic Funds Transfer Act (EFTA), but financial institutions suffer billions of dollars in losses each year.

Medical identity theft as well as insurance identity theft, are two types of ID theft that not only impact the victim's finances, but carry potentially life-threatening consequences as well. When someone receives health care using another's insurance benefits, this may preclude the true insured person from receiving needed care in the case of an emergency. The World Health Organization has identified this as an information crime that can kill and one of the most difficult forms of ID theft to fix.

Criminal identity theft occurs when an ID thief uses the victim's identity during the committing of a crime and is subsequently caught and processed under the name of the victim. It becomes very difficult for the victim to eradicate his or her name from "the system." For example, the victim's credit record may be damaged due to the malfeasance of the criminal.

Driver's license identity theft occurs when one's wallet or purse is lost or stolen. Thieves sell the stolen ID to someone who then continues to acquire other forms of identification in the victim's name.

Social Security identity theft occurs when another individual uses someone's Social Security number in order to work legally. The thief may be an illegal immigrant or an American citizen who is trying to avoid detection by the authorities. The problem emerges when the victim tries to collect government benefits or file a tax return. To monitor this potential form of theft, individuals should review their annual Social Security Administration statement to ensure that only their wages are being reported to the Social Security Administration.

Child identity theft occurs when an adult, often a family member, uses the child's information to create accounts in their name. The child will not learn about this type of ID theft until he or she attempts to apply for student loans or other credit when older. Often, the information comes to light when the young adult is denied the loan due to a bad credit history. Parents should begin monitoring children's credit reports at age 16, which gives parents time to repair any damage from an ID thief.

ID Theft Impact

According to a report prepared by the Congressional Research Service in 2010, over 8 million Americans were victims of identity fraud, and the average victim incurred a direct cost of $631 as a result of the ID theft. The report found identity fraud costs at the highest level since 2007.

According to the Department of Justice, the total financial cost of identity theft was nearly $17.3 billion over a two-year period covering 2009–2010, with almost 25 percent of identity theft victims suffering an actual out-of-pocket financial loss from their victimization. Almost half of the victims reported having to spend at least one day working to resolve the financial and credit problems associated with their identity theft, and 3 percent continued to experience problems related to the fraud more than six months after discovering it.

Victims of identity theft should immediately contact both their local police and the Federal Trade Commission to file reports. Next they should contact all of the three major credit bureaus to report the fraud; ask for a freeze on their credit report, which will prevent any potential new creditors from opening a new account; and ask for a copy of their credit reports. The victim should then contact the creditors and financial institutions that have been impacted by the fraud and inform them that an identity thief has taken over the account or that the account was created in their name but without their knowledge.

ID Theft Prevention

The U.S. Department of Justice has created an education program called SCAM, standing for Stingy, Check, Ask, and Maintain. Consumers should be stingy or cautious about those with whom they share personal identifying information. They should check their financial information such as bank and credit card statements regularly for any unusual activity. Consumers should ask for a copy of their free credit report annually, which they are entitled to under the FACT Act, and look for any accounts that are not theirs. Last, they should maintain careful financial records. All bank and credit card statements should be kept for a minimum of one year.

Consumers should keep all their important financial and legal papers secure and shred documents with sensitive financial and personal information before disposing of them. It is also important to limit any personal information carried in purses and wallets. Avoid carrying birth certificates and Social Security cards on your person in case of loss or theft.

Leslie E. Linfield

See also: Consumer Credit/Debt; Credit Card; Credit Report and Reporting Agencies; Credit Score; Debt; Debt/Credit Counseling; Social Security

Further Reading

American Bar Association Web site. "Bankruptcy." Accessed October 15, 2013. http://www.americanbar.org/groups/public_education/resources/law_issues_for_consumers/bankruptcypros.html

Federal Trade Commission Web site. "Consumer Information: Privacy & Identity." Accessed November 5, 2013. http://www.consumer.ftc.gov/topics/privacy-identity

Tabb, Charles Jordan. 1995. "The History of the Bankruptcy Laws in the United States." *American Bankruptcy Institute Law Review* (Vol. III, No. 5): 5–51.

U.S. Department of Justice Web site. "Identity Theft and Identity Fraud." Accessed November 5, 2013. http://www.justice.gov/criminal/fraud/websites/idtheft.html

Index Mutual Funds

According to the U.S. Securities and Exchange Commission (SEC), an index fund is "a type of mutual fund or unit investment trust (UIT) whose investment objective typically is to achieve approximately the same return as a particular market index, such as the S&P 500 Composite Stock Price Index, the Russell 2000 Index or the Wilshire 5000 Total Market Index." An index fund attempts to achieve its investment objective primarily by investing in the securities (stocks or bonds) of companies that are included in a selected index.

History of the Index Fund

The index fund originated in the early 1970s when Wells Fargo implemented the first models of index accounts for the pension fund of Samsonite Corporation. Wells Fargo's strategy, which was based on an equal-weighted index of New York Stock Exchange equities, didn't get the intended success. The strategy was abandoned in 1976 and replaced with a market-weighted strategy using the Standard & Poor's 500 Composite Stock Price Index (Bogle, 2006).

In 1973, Burton S. Malkiel, a Princeton University professor, released a book named *A Random Walk Down Wall Street*. In his book, Dr. Malkiel suggested "[a] new investment instrument: a no-load, minimum-management-fee mutual fund that simply buys the hundreds of stocks making up the market averages and does no trading." Dr. Malkiel's book led to calls by many financial observers for index funds to be formed. Dr. Samuelson, a professor of finance at MIT, wrote "Challenge to Judgment," an article that appeared in the *Journal of Portfolio Management* in the fall of 1974. Charles D. Ellis, president of Greenwich Associates, wrote a seminal article entitled "The Loser's Game" in *The Financial Analysts Journal* for July/August 1975. Both articles implicitly opened a challenge for someone to start an index fund. In 1975, boosted by Dr. Malkiel's book and the articles from Dr. Samuelson, Ellis, and others, John Bogle, founder of the Vanguard Group, launched the first broad-market index fund for retail investors.

How an Index Fund Is Structured

When an investor purchases a share of an index fund, he or she is purchasing a share of a portfolio that contains the securities in an underlying index. The index fund holds the securities in the same proportion as they occur in the actual index, and when the index decreases in value, the fund's shares decrease as well, and vice versa. The only time an index buys or sells a stock is when the index itself changes (either in weighting or in composition). Index funds have ticker symbols and are traded on all major exchanges.

Index funds are available for most indexes. Some index funds replicate broad market indexes, and some replicate indexes that only contain securities with special characteristics, including minimum financial ratios, participation in a certain industry, geography, or other distinctions. The Standard & Poor's (S&P) 500 includes 500 of the most important U.S. company stocks. It is frequently referred to as the benchmark of the U.S. stock market. There are thousands of other indexes tracking various regions and industries.

The performance of an index fund usually does not exactly match the actual index's performance. This is because index funds charge management fees, which reduce returns, and because the fund's weighting in particular securities may not perfectly match the weighting of the securities in the actual index. The degree to which the fund and the index returns differ is called tracking error. Although the first index funds tracked stock investments, today there are index funds comprised of bonds, commodities, real estate, and most financial asset classes.

Advantages of Index Funds

Index funds are a popular way to participate in the stock market and diversify a portfolio. Index funds have several major advantages over direct ownership of the underlying securities.

Index funds provide the investor with broad diversification. Each index fund represents an interest in an underlying basket of securities. This allows investors to easily gain broad exposure to a large group of companies. This diversification also makes index funds much less volatile than individual securities. Foreign index funds in particular make diversifying internationally less difficult and expensive; they also offer exposure to entire foreign markets and market segments.

Index funds have lower fees than actively managed funds. Buying and selling shares of an index fund is far less expensive than separately buying and selling a basket of underlying shares. Also, the decision of which securities to invest in is determined by the index rather than by active management. This is why index funds usually have minimal expense ratios and are often more affordable than other diversified investment vehicles. However, many have required minimum investment amounts and front- or back-end loads (or commissions), making them impractical for some investors.

Other benefits of index funds include liquidity and the opportunity to compound growth or increase cash flow from the dividend payments. Index fund shares are bought and sold on major exchanges every day, and many funds trade hundreds of thousands (and in some cases millions) of shares per day. Buying and selling shares of an index fund can be faster and more convenient than buying and selling the underlying shares. Many index funds pass through the accumulated dividends paid by their underlying stocks. Over time, these dividends can add up to a significant sum.

Some index funds track broad U.S. equity market indexes. Meanwhile, others track specific sectors or industry groups. Still others represent an interest in baskets of foreign stocks. And finally, others invest exclusively in the bond market. The index fund varieties make it easy to implement a particular investment strategy.

Index funds have tax benefits over actively managed mutual funds. Since shares are bought or sold only when the underlying index adjusts, these funds don't incur as many taxable gains as their actively managed counterparts might.

Studies have proven that over time, the average mutual fund typically fails to beat the broad indexes. With this in mind, index funds are a great way to capture broader-market returns. For adherents to the efficient market hypothesis, which states that it is impossible to outperform the broad stock market over the long haul, index funds can be a way to optimize portfolio returns. In his article "Behavioral Perspectives on Index Funds," Keith Redhead states that the average actively managed fund underperforms index funds. Redhead also states that the use of index funds could help to avoid the perception of loss, unrealistic expectations, inappropriate choice criteria, loss of dividend income, and emotional attachment to investments.

Disadvantages of Index Funds

An investment in an index fund could lose money over short or even long periods. The share price and total return may fluctuate within a wide range, like the fluctuations of the underlying assets. As with all investments there are tax liabilities incurred on dividends and capital gains. Additional risks may also impact fund performance.

Newer Varieties of Index Funds

The first modern index funds were market capitalization weighted. The percentage of each company in the index fund was determined by the company's size or market capitalization within the index. Today newer varieties of index funds offer equal weight where each company is owned in the same amount. Specialized index funds use specific factors to create index funds as well.

In addition to index mutual funds, a newer variety of index funds is called exchange-traded funds (ETFs). Index funds may also refer to ETFs in addition to mutual funds. Like a mutual fund, ETF index funds are comprised of a basket of underlying securities representing an index. Unlike a mutual fund, they trade on a stock exchange throughout the day and can even be bought on margin. Last century's newly designed index funds have become the cornerstone of modern investing strategy today.

Joseph Krupka

See also: Asset Allocation; Behavioral Finance; Bonds; Capital Gains and Capital Losses; Commodities; Compound Interest/Return; Dividend Income; Investing; Liquidity; Mutual Funds and Exchange-Traded Funds (ETFs); Opportunity Cost; Real Estate Investment Trust (REIT); Risk; Stock Market

Further Reading

Bogle, J. C. 2006. "The First Index Mutual Fund: A History of Vanguard Index Trust and the Vanguard Index Strategy." *Bogle Financial Markets Research Center*. http://www.vanguard.com/bogle_site/lib/sp19970401.html

Gastineau, G. L. 2002. "Equity Index Funds Have Lost Their Way." *Journal of Portfolio Management* 28(2): 55–64.

Kostovetsky, L. 2003. "Index Mutual Funds and Exchange-Traded Funds." *Journal of Portfolio Management* 29(4): 80–92.

Landis, D. 2008. "Own the Market with Index Funds and ETFs." *Kiplinger's Personal Finance*, 50–53.

Redhead, K. 2010. "Behavioral Perspectives on Index Funds." *Journal of Financial Service Professionals* 64(4): 54–61.

U.S. Securities and Exchange Commission Web site. "Index Funds." Last modified May 14, 2007. http://www.sec.gov/answers/indexf.htm

Individual Retirement Account (IRA) *(see Retirement Accounts)*

Inflation

Inflation is an economic concept that describes an increase in the general price level for goods and services. The increase in prices leads to a decrease in the purchasing power of money. In other words, we can view inflation as either an increase in price level, or a decrease in purchasing power. Thus, it is important to understand some of the basic issues on the construction of the price level index and how changes in the construction will affect purchasing power differently. A discussion about hyperinflation and the impact of hyperinflation on productivity is also included.

Inflation is an important measure for investors because the risk-free interest rate is approximately the sum of the real growth rate and the inflation rate. So, the inflation rate will play a large role in determining the rate of return for investments.

To understand inflation, we must first understand the reference price level index. In the United States, inflation is measured by the Consumer Price Index (CPI). Inflation is defined as changes in the CPI. The CPI is produced by the Bureau of Labor Statistics (BLS). A basket of possible consumer goods and services that best represents an average U.S. household is created from the year 1990 census data (the base year set by the BLS; this date changes infrequently). Each item in the basket has a point value. Changes in a particular item's price level multiplied by the point value results in the effect of a price change for that particular item.

The basket is determined by a survey of two-week purchasing habits of 7,000 U.S. families over two years. According to the BLS, the broad categories are:

- Food and beverages (breakfast cereal, milk, coffee, chicken, wine, full-service meals, snacks)
- Housing (rent of primary residence, owner's equivalent rent, fuel oil, bedroom furniture)
- Apparel (men's shirts and sweaters, women's dresses, jewelry)
- Transportation (new vehicles, airline fares, gasoline, motor vehicle insurance)
- Medical care (prescription drugs and medical supplies, physicians' services, eyeglasses and eye care, hospital services)
- Recreation (televisions, toys, pets and pet products, sports equipment, admissions)
- Education and communication (college tuition, postage, telephone services, computer software and accessories)
- Other goods and services (tobacco and smoking products, haircuts and other personal services, funeral expenses)

It is important to note that not every item in the basket is purchased by every family in the survey. In fact, some will never purchase any of those items. So, price increases in some of those items will have very little impact on the rest of the population. Take the cost of college education as an example. The cost of attending college has been going up at a rate more than twice the general level of CPI increases. Thus, the cost of a college education will have no impact on a family with no one going to college during this period. Likewise, a family with two children in college will likely feel the large impact of college tuition increases. Depending on which goods and services one purchases, inflation impacts individuals and families to differing degrees.

We can think of a few other examples where inflation will affect individual families differently. New vehicles, gasoline, and car insurance will have little impact on someone who lives in an urban setting with available public transportation options, and therefore has no need for car ownership. In contrast, most low-income families spend a large portion of their income on food and other basic necessities. Thus, price increases in basic necessities and food will have a much higher impact on them than on a family with a higher income level.

So, depending on a family's consumption habits, inflation will affect the purchasing power of individual families to differing degrees. Since most families do some form of price comparison and change their consumption habits by substituting higher price items with lower price items that are similar, the broad-based CPI has been criticized. In response, the BLS created what is known as the chained CPI, which takes into account the substitution effect. So, the chained CPI will result in a lower inflation rate. Some entitlement programs are considering using the chained CPI as the basis for adjustment. A new measure more reflective of the actual cost of living called the Cost of Living Index (COLI) is being proposed as a substitute. But the COLI also has its shortcomings. It is based on the relative cost of living of typical mid-level households in more than 300 cities in the United States. Mid-level households are not the norm in the United States anymore. Both new measures are facing criticism.

Moderate Inflation versus Hyperinflation

A moderate level of inflation is generally seen as a good thing for the economy. Producers will only produce more goods and services if they know they can sell those goods and services for higher prices in the future. So, a moderate level of inflation will encourage production growth. A moderate level of inflation is approximately 3 percent. If inflation is too low or in negative territory (deflation), the monetary authority will generally relax monetary policy to induce a higher level of inflation.

Hyperinflation, whereby the price level increases at a rapid rate, could hinder economic activities. Since inflation reduces purchasing power, in a hyperinflationary period, the income and wealth of households will decline rapidly. During a period of hyperinflation, one of the key functions of money (a store of wealth) is essentially gone. So, consumers will try to spend their money as quickly as possible, and thus exchange their income for food and other basic necessities as soon as they get their paycheck. This not only requires a constant demand on people's time (everything from waiting in lines to buy things to constantly changing the prices on all the items), it will also increase the velocity of money. The velocity of money refers to the speed with which money changes hands. According to the quantity theory of money, an increase in velocity will result in a higher price level. So, this will induce a vicious cycle.

After World War I, Germany had an inflation level of more than 2 billion percent a year for an extended period. The value of money was not worth the paper it was printed on. As a result, the economy was basically destroyed. Images of people rolling around a cart full of money looking for bread to buy still bring chills to some folks from the older generation. The more recent example is the Brazilian economy from 1980 to 1997. The CPI went from 4 to 5,080,300,000,000! Something that cost $1 in real dollars in 1980 would cost $1 trillion in 1997!

By late 1997, inflation was under control in Brazil and the economy started to recover very quickly. With modern knowledge about the effect of monetary policies on inflation, periods of hyperinflation like those experienced by Germany and Brazil likely are not going to happen again in developed countries.

Conclusion

Inflation is an important piece of data for investors in that it informs one about the lowest level of return one must obtain in order to maintain the purchasing power of one's wealth or income. Inflation, however, affects purchasing power differently across demographics and consumption habits. While hyperinflation is bad for the economy, a low level of inflation or deflation is also bad for the economy. And since the risk-free rate is tied to the inflation rate, knowing the inflation rate will help you understand the real rate of return for various risky investments. Having a better understanding of this important piece of data creates more informed consumers and assists investors in making better financial decisions.

Leo H. Chan

See also: Deflation; Federal Reserve Bank; Greenspan, Alan, 13th Chair of the U.S. Federal Reserve Board; Gross Domestic Product (GDP) and Gross National Product (GNP); Retirement; Risk; Year 1970s to 1980s: Economic Problems and the United States

Further Reading

Bureau of Labor Statistics. Consumer Price Index. http://www.bls.gov/cpi/

Bureau of Labor Statistics. "Consumer Price Index Data Quality: How Accurate Is the U.S. CPI?" August 2012. http://www.bls.gov/opub/btn/volume-1/pdf/consumer-price -index-data-quality-how-accurate-is-the-us-cpi.pdf

Heakal, Reem. May 2, 2010. "What Is the Quantity Theory of Money?" http://www .investopedia.com/articles/05/010705.asp

Margolin, Emma. April 5, 2013. "How the 'Chained CPI' Works—and Why Critics Call It a Benefits Cut." http://www.msnbc.com/hardball/how-the-chained-cpi-works-and -why- critics

Inflation-Protected Investments

Inflation is the rate at which the prices of goods and services increase. When prices rise, the consumer's purchasing power declines. In other words, as inflation increases and prices increase, the same dollar amount purchases fewer goods. Inflation touches the entire society. This is a problem for savers attempting to amass funds for retirement and future consumption.

Anyone who needs to divert current income into savings for a future expense may be hurt by inflation. For example, if you are saving money for college expenses 10 years in the future and your bank pays interest of 3 percent, you assume that at the end of 10 years that 3 percent interest rate would grow your initial funds at 3 percent per year. If inflation during that period was 4 percent per year, at the end of the savings period, your money would purchase less than when you started. Although you receive a 3 percent return on your funds, subtract 4 percent per year inflation and your actual purchasing power declines approximately 1 percent (3 percent return less 4 percent inflation rate = −1 percent).

Inflation-protected investments were created by the U.S. government to provide savers with investment products that protect savings from a decline in real value and purchasing power. There are two types of inflation-protected investments: Treasury Inflation-Protected Securities (TIPS) and government I savings bonds (inflation adjusted). By investing in these secure government products the consumer is promised a return that keeps pace with the government-calculated inflation rate.

Government I Savings Bonds

Treasury Inflation-Protected Securities (or TIPS)

Treasury Inflation-Protected Securities are marketable securities similar to a bond investment. This means one can buy or sell them to other investors before their final maturity date. The maturity date is the predetermined date when the purchaser receives the full amount due (principal). TIPS' principal or face value changes with inflation and deflation as calculated by the nonseasonally adjusted Consumer Price Index (CPI-U). For example, if inflation increases, then the principal value of the TIPS increases by the same amount. So with increases in inflation, you are assured that the value of your TIPS bond also increases in value.

There is a second part to the return on a TIPS investment. When purchased, the TIPS have an interest rate that remains fixed for the entire period of ownership. This interest rate is paid semiannually on the adjusted principal amount. For example, purchase a five-year TIPS bond for $1,000 with an interest rate of 1 percent. If inflation increases, the 1 percent interest is paid semiannually on the increased principal amount. In the event of deflation, the 1 percent interest is paid on the reduced principal amount. At maturity, which in this case is five years, the TIPS owner receives either the upwardly adjusted principal or the original principal amount in the case of zero inflation or deflation. Additionally, this protects the consumer against deflation as one never receives less than the original principal amount.

Federal tax is due on the semiannual interest payments and inflation adjustments in the year that they occur. Interest is subject to federal tax and exempt from state tax.

How to Buy TIPS: Denominations and Maturities

TIPS are sold in denominations starting at $100 on up to $5,000,000. Their maturities are 5, 10, and 30 years, and they can be bought at auction through the treasurydirect.gov Web site or from a bank or investment broker. TIPS (previously issued) are also available in the secondary market. The secondary market means investors buy and sell the TIPs securities in a similar way that investors buy and sell stocks and bonds. In other words, TIPs may be held until maturity or sold in the secondary market at any time prior to maturity.

I Savings Bonds

Similar to TIPS, I savings bonds are designed to provide a savings vehicle that protects consumers' funds from erosion due to inflation. Although I bonds' purpose is the same as TIPS, the investment I bond is designed uniquely. I bonds combine two interest rates, with a fixed rate of return assigned at the bonds' creation. The second interest rate is calculated semiannually and is based on changes in the nonseasonally adjusted Consumer Price Index (CPI-U). Interest is compounded semiannually and earned monthly. The published value of the bond does not show the previous three months of interest. Although the purchaser receives no semiannual interest payments, as TIPS holders do, the final redemption value includes all of the previous interest payments.

The I bonds' value changes each month as the interest is calculated and applied to the principal amount. Unlike TIPS, ownership is neither transferable nor able to be traded on the secondary market. I bonds may be redeemed anytime after 12 months at the treasurydirect.gov Web site or a bank. If I bonds are redeemed prior to five years, the seller loses the previous three months' interest accrued. The principal and all interest due is paid at redemption.

Taxes are not due on I bonds until they are redeemed, although the consumer may opt to pay taxes annually. Interest is subject to federal tax and exempt from state tax.

How to Buy I Savings Bonds: Denominations and Maturities

I bonds may be purchased electronically at treasurydirect.gov Web site. They are offered in denominations of $50, $100, $200, $500, $1,000, and $5,000. There is a limit to the amount of I bonds an individual may buy each year. Investors may purchase up to $10,000 worth of I bonds annually and up to an additional $5,000 with a tax refund.

Education Considerations for I Savings Bonds

The Education Savings Bond Program stipulates that if the savings bond proceeds are used to pay qualified higher education expenses at an eligible institution in the same year that the bonds are redeemed, the savings bond interest is exempt from federal tax. Additional information regarding this provision is available in IRS Publication 970.

Barbara Friedberg

See also: Banking; Bonds; Compound Interest/Return; Inflation; Interest Income and Payments; Interest Rates; Investing; Risk; Treasury Securities

Further Reading

TreasuryDirect Web site. "Comparison of TIPS and Series I Savings Bonds." Accessed August 2, 2013. http://www.treasurydirect.gov/indiv/products/prod_tipsvsibonds.htm

TreasuryDirect Web site. "I Savings Bonds." Accessed August 2, 2013. http://www.treasurydirect.gov/indiv/products/prod_ibonds_glance.htm

TreasuryDirect Web site. "Treasury Direct TIPS in Depth." Accessed August 1, 2013. http://www.treasurydirect.gov/indiv/research/indepth/tips/res_tips.htm

TreasuryDirect Web site. "Treasury Inflation-Protected Securities (TIPS)." Accessed August 2, 2013. http://www.treasurydirect.gov/indiv/products/prod_tips_glance.htm

Interest Income and Payments

Interest is a form of rent paid for the use of money for some period of time. For example, when a consumer deposits money into a savings account, the bank pays the consumer a percentage of the deposit as an interest payment for the opportunity to use those funds while they are on deposit at the bank. In accounting, *interest income* is a term used on an income statement for reporting the interest earned on an asset normally in a bank savings account, certificate of deposit, or other investment.

Another way to look at the interest concept is through the economic term of *opportunity cost*. The one who makes a deposit loses other possibilities to use the money, thus the interest is compensation.

In contrast, when one borrows money from a bank or other lender, there is a cost to the borrower. The borrower must make interest payments to the lender in exchange for receiving the loan. In general, the more risky the borrower, the higher the interest rate she or he is charged.

Interest rates are generally set in the market by the economic forces of supply and demand. Additionally, the Federal Reserve Bank influences interest rates due to their monetary policy. It is customary for a bank to pay savers a lower interest rate than they charge borrowers. The difference between the interest income received from the bank (or lender) and that paid to the bank by the borrower is called the spread. The spread is one of the ways a bank makes money.

History

According to Paul John, in 5000 BCE, using food as money for lending or borrowing was normal in Middle Eastern civilizations. They viewed interest as appropriate because purchased seeds and animals could "reproduce themselves." One grain of seed could produce a plant with over 100 new grain seeds, so farmers could easily repay the grain with "interest" in grain after the harvest. When animals were lent, the interest was paid by sharing in any new animals born. Anything loaned had regeneration power and the interest was a sharing of the result.

In the ancient developing urban communities of Egypt, Assyria, and Sumeria, interest payments evolved. These communities traded in agricultural and metallic commodities, mainly barley and silvers. The interest charged on loans of metals was paid in additional metal. This created a problem. The ancients treated materials as living animals with the means of reproduction. But metals are unproductive, they have no powers of regeneration, and any interest must come from another source.

In ancient times as well as today, there are some who take advantage of borrowers by charging unusually high interest rates. In the royal household, the largest lender and charger of interest set the standard rates for several commodities. This solved the problem of metals' lack of regenerativity, but there was no oversight over interest rates. In fact, farmers who were unable to get out of debt due to a poor harvest might lose their land, or be forced into slavery to repay their debts. The Solon Reform prevented debtors from going into bondage and modified the usury system. Since then, lenders have been watched to prevent their charging excessively high interest rates.

Revenue Act of 1913: Interest Income Is Taxed

The Revenue Act of 1913, also known as the Tariff Act, Underwood Tariff Act, or Underwood-Simmons Act, was the first decision to tax interest income on the federal income tax return. Following the 16th Amendment, it was signed into law by President Woodrow Wilson on October 3, 1913. In addition to taxing individuals' interest income, the Revenue Act also imposed a flat 1 percent tax on a corporation's net income including interest income. The federal tax rate for interest income for individuals varied from 1 to 7 percent. However, most individuals were free from tax because of the $3,000 personal exemption, which was greater than most people's income at that time.

Tax Issues

Interest income is subject to tax in three ways: taxable as ordinary income, nontaxable, and tax deferred. Interest income is earned on deposits at banks and credit unions, on money market funds, on bonds, and on loans, such as seller-financed mortgages. This type of interest is taxed as ordinary income, subject to the ordinary income tax rates for federal and state tax returns.

Interest on U.S. Treasury bonds and savings bonds are taxable on an individual's federal return, but are tax-free at the state level. Interest on municipal bonds is tax-free at the federal level. Municipal bond interest is usually tax-free at the state level if it is invested in the bondholder's state of residence.

Generally, interest income is taxable when it is actually paid. However, there are some situations when tax payment on interest income is deferred to a future tax year. Tax deferral is a major reason to save in a workplace retirement account. The interest income earned in a retirement account such as a 401(k) or traditional IRA compounds and grows, free of tax obligation until the moneys are withdrawn at retirement, when tax payments are due. Interest income and interest payments are integrated into modern commerce, saving, lending, borrowing, and investing.

Joseph Krupka

See also: Banking; Certificate of Deposit; Compound Interest/Return; Consumer Credit/ Debt; Credit Union; Debt; Federal Reserve Bank; Interest Rates; Loans; Opportunity Cost; Retirement Accounts; Savings Account; U.S. Federal Tax System Overview

Further Reading

Pope, Thomas R., Kenneth E. Anderson, and John L. Kramer. 2012. *Prentice Hall's Federal Taxation 2012—Individuals*. Upper Saddle River, NJ: Prentice Hall.

"Topic 505 Interest Expense," IRS.gov. Last modified April 15, 2013. http://www.irs.gov/ taxtopics/tc505.html

Interest Rates

When one thinks of interest rates, it's often aligned with the interest received from a savings account. But there is a lot more to the interest rates topic than just the interest one receives from savings. Broadly defined, interest is the compensation lenders (or consumers) receive for giving up their excess funds. On the other side of the transaction, interest is the amount charged to the individual or organization for use of the borrowed money. So, there are interest rates for lending and interest rates for borrowing. The specific rates all tie in to the riskiness of each transaction. Since these transactions are typically conducted through an intermediary (such as a bank), the intermediary takes a small percentage of the compensation/cost. So, the actual cost to borrowers might be drastically different from the compensation to the lenders.

Lending Risk

In any form of lending, there is always an associated risk. The biggest risk is default risk. Default risk depends on many factors. The more protections put into a loan, the lower the default risk. Likewise, the better the financial condition of the borrowers, the lower the default risk will be. That's the main reason behind credit scores. Credit scores are the basis for determining the interest rate for most consumer loans.

Liquidity Risk

The second biggest risk is liquidity risk. Liquidity has many forms. The first is maturity or length of the loan. The longer the maturity, the higher the liquidity risk. The second liquidity risk is the ability to resell the loan. Traditionally, the U.S. Treasury securities have the best liquidity because the market is huge and there are plenty of buyers and sellers for these securities on any given day. Small consumer loans and municipal securities are thought to be less liquid. But the advance in securitization (the process of bundling a large number of small loans into a new class of security) has changed that quite a bit.

Interest Rate Risk

The third risk is the variability of the interest rate itself (interest rate risk). As most loans are for a fixed rate and a fixed term, changes in the interest rate change the value of the cash flow characteristics of these loans. That can lead to an increase or decrease in the value of these loans. Loans with longer maturity will be affected more, all else being equal, than shorter maturity loans. That's the reason why longer maturity loans typically are the most costly. Since the risk-free interest rate is typically tied to inflation and the economic growth rate, there are long-term U.S. Treasuries that have coupon payments that are tied to the inflation rate. These are called Treasury Inflation-Protected Securities (TIPS). In the housing market, the adjustable-rate mortgage (ARM) is a common tool for dealing with interest risk. Typically, the ARM is tied to the London Interbank Offer Rate or LIBOR (more on that later).

How Are Interest Rates Determined?

All interest rates are tied to one of a few basic base rates. These base rates are some-times known as index rates. The most commonly known rate is the risk-free rate. The risk-free rate is the rate of return for investing in short-term U.S. Treasury securities. Short-term U.S. Treasuries are thought to be default-free, and thus they carry very little risk. So, by buying short-term U.S. Treasuries, one is essentially lending money to the U.S. government for a short period of time. The return depends on the price (demand) for U.S. Treasuries. Historically, this rate has been around 3 percent on average. It was as high as 14 percent during the late 1970s and early 1980s. But that was an unusual period in history. During the 2008 financial crisis, the yield on Treasuries declined drastically. The risk-free rate went down to almost zero (it was 0.01 percent for an extended period of time) due to aggressive purchases by the Federal Reserve and other institutional investors (money market mutual funds, for example).

The other widely known interest rate is the discount rate set by the Federal Reserve (the Fed). There is a large amount of misunderstanding about this rate. The discount rate is not a rate anyone can get. It is only available to member banks of the Federal Reserve system. The Fed allows member banks to borrow funds from the Fed to meet reserve requirements on a short-term basis (overnight). So, this rate has almost no practical importance for average investors. But since most other rates are based on this rate, the rise and fall of this rate will indicate the direction for all other interest rates.

Since the discount window loans are only for a short-term basis, most banks actu-ally borrow from other banks if they need additional reserves. The rate member banks charge each other is the Fed fund rate. This rate is higher than the discount rate. The Fed fund rate is important because most adjustable-rate mortgages are based on the prime rate, which is set by banks by adding a markup to the Fed fund rate. The prime rate's role was replaced by the LIBOR. The LIBOR has been the most widely used index rate for more than a decade. Presently, almost all floating-rate instruments/assets are based on LIBOR. For example, a typical 5/1 ARM (adjustable-rate mortgage) will have the first rate adjustment five years after the mortgage is initiated, and the adjust-ment will be based on the average of the one-year LIBOR rates over the last three months. This is an important rate for homeowners who have adjustable-rate mortgages. Like the risk-free rate, the LIBOR was at a historic low during the period 2009 to 2013 (following the 2008 financial crisis).

In 2013, it was discovered that all major global investment banks were involved in a LIBOR rate-fixing scheme. The rate-fixing scheme defrauded investors and mortgage-backed security writers out of hundreds of billions of dollars. The FDIC is pursuing legal actions against the banks involved.

After the cost side of interest rates follows a discussion about the compensation side of interest rates. The most important rule in investment is that return and risk are inversely correlated. So, the level of risk associated with a certain investment will play a large role in determining the return. Investors can get a risk-free return by investing in risk-free assets such as the Treasury bills. Other close to risk-free assets are gener-ally found in money market instruments. Since most money market instruments are in large denominations (1 million or more), typical small investors can only participate through money market mutual funds. Since there is a small chance of default in money market instruments, the return is a bit higher than for U.S. Treasury bills. It is important that investors know the cost associated with investing in money market mutual funds. There is a management fee associated with these funds. After fees are taken out, the typical money market mutual fund return is almost zero today. Certificates of deposit (CDs) and other types of bank-offered fixed-term instruments provide a little higher returns, but not by much.

It's useful for savers and investors to understand that interest rates go up and down. In spite of the fact that from approximately 2007 through 2014, interest rates were at historically low levels, there is no guarantee that they will remain near zero. In fact, it's likely that as the economy improves from the 2007–2009 recession, interest rates will trend upward.

Investors interested in higher compensation for their savings/investments should consider long-term U.S. Treasuries and corporate bonds. Corporate bonds are rated by credit rating agencies such as S&P, Moody, and Fitch. Investment-grade corporate bonds typically return about 6 to 8 percent, depending on credit rating. On average long-term U.S. Treasuries return about 4 to 6 percent, depending on maturity. These figures average to about half of what the historic return is for the broad equity market. But they are typically very safe and subject to very little price risk. Low-cost mutual funds are the most effective tools for investors interested in these instruments.

A knowledge of interest rates and the influences on their movements is helpful for the consumer. Both the borrower and lender benefit from understanding interest rate properties and history.

Leo H. Chan

See also: Banking; Bonds; Certificate of Deposit; Compound Interest/Return; Consumer Credit/Debt; Credit Card; Dividend Income; Federal Reserve Bank; Inflation-Protected Investments; Interest Income and Payments; Loans; Savings Account; Treasury Securities

Further Reading

BBC News. February 6, 2013. "Timeline: Libor-Fixing Scandal." http://www.bbc.com/news/business-18671255

Raymond, Nate. March 14, 2014. "FDIC Sues 16 Big Banks for Rigging Libor Rate." http://www.huffingtonpost.com/2014/03/14/fdic-banks-libor_n_4965875.html

Investing

In economics, investing is defined as the act of purchasing goods that are not consumed today but will be used in the future to create wealth. In finance, an investment is a monetary asset purchased with the idea that the asset will provide income in the future or appreciate in value and be sold at a higher price. In simple words, investing is how you make your money grow, or appreciate in value so you can meet your long-term financial goals.

Investing Is Not the Same as "Speculating" or Gambling

It is important not to equate investment with speculating or gambling. Investing usually involves the creation of wealth whereas speculating is often a zero-sum game; wealth is not created. Investing is not gambling either. Gambling is putting money at risk by betting on an uncertain outcome with the hope that you might win money. True investing doesn't happen without some effort on your part. A good investor performs a thorough analysis and commits capital only when there is a reasonable expectation of profit. Yes, it still involves risk, and there are no guarantees, but investing is more than simply hoping that luck will favor you.

Examples of investments, in the economic sense, would include going to college to earn your degree, purchasing a computer for your business, or building a factory to produce goods. In the financial sense, investments include the purchase of bonds, stocks, or real estate property. There are many reasons to invest. Investing allows us to achieve financial goals like buying a car or paying for college, beat inflation, and reach retirement.

The earlier you start investing, the more money you will have and the faster you will reach your financial goals. Investing garners the power of compound returns. Compound returns is the process of one's money growing and making money on top of the original sum. For example, if one invests $2,000 a year for nine years starting at the age of 21, assuming a 10 percent interest rate, at age 65, the investment of $18,000 will be worth around $763,000. On the other hand, if you wait until age 30 to start saving and then save $2,000 a year every year until you are 65, then you will only have $542,048.73, a difference of $220,000 from the alternative when you started investing at the age of 21.

Financial Market Investing Options

You can choose from many investing options. This includes investing money in stocks, bonds, mutual funds, or real estate, or starting your own business. No matter which method you choose for investing your money, the goal is always to put your money to work to earn additional income.

The stock market is one option for investing money. One who invests in stocks of a company buys a share of that company. The value of each share depends on how profitable the company becomes. Compared with savings accounts, stocks tend to offer a higher rate of return on the initial investment. But stocks are relatively more risky because, unlike a savings account, the stock is not insured by the Federal Deposit Insurance Corporation (FDIC). Individual company stock prices tend to go up and down based on many factors including the merits of the company, the psychological tenor of the overall stock market, and supply and demand.

Buying bonds is another investing option. A bond is an agreement or a loan between the issuer (a company, municipality, or other type of entity) and the person buying the bond (the bondholder). The bondholder essentially loans a certain amount of money to a government agency, municipality, or corporation and earns interest on the loan.

The term of a bond is given as a fixed rate at the time of issue and expires on the specified maturity date. At that time, the issuer must pay the bondholder the face value of the bond. Throughout the term of the loan, the issuer also pays interest to the bondholder. The interest amount is set when the bond is issued. Bonds can vary in term length. They can be as short as three months or as long as 30 years. Bond interest is also called a "coupon" payment. Usually, the longer the term on the bond, the higher the interest rate the bondholder receives.

Mutual funds are another type of investment. Mutual funds are created when money is put in a pool of money from other investors to create a large portfolio so everyone benefits from bigger profits. Most funds buy a variety of investments like stocks, bonds, or other securities. Due to such a variety of different investments in one mutual fund, there is lower risk than investing in individual stocks and bonds because if one investment has a poor return, another can make up for that loss.

In investing in the financial markets, the investor makes money when she sells a stock, bond, or mutual fund for more than she paid as well as when she receives interest or dividend payments. If the investment does not increase in value, the investor may lose money when the stock, bond, or mutual fund is sold for less than the purchase price.

Real Estate Investing

Many individuals look to real estate as another investment in which to grow their funds for the future. Investors who do not want to buy an individual home or apartment building and rent that property out to tenants may invest in real estate through an investment called a Real Estate Investment Trust (REIT). REITs are actually financial securities that combine the ownership of many real estate properties and then sell individual slices of ownership, or shares, to individuals. REITs come in several varieties including those that only invest in shopping centers, office buildings, or even just the mortgages of certain types of property.

For those who want to buy actual real estate as an investment in order to increase their wealth, there is a certain degree of knowledge, risk, and time involved in buying, renting out, and managing the real estate investment. For example, if Kris wanted to buy a two-family apartment building as an investment, she would need to save money for a down payment and go to a lender for a mortgage loan. Kris would need to examine the rental income and expenses as well as evaluate future rental income and expenses. Before purchasing the rental investment property, she'd need to make sure that the income would be enough to pay for the expenses with some left over for profit. Investors may consider real estate–type investments to diversify their portfolios.

Barbara Friedberg

See also: Asset Allocation; Behavioral Finance; Bonds; Capital Gains and Capital Losses; Compound Interest/Return; Dividend Income; Hedge Funds; Index Mutual Funds;

Inflation-Protected Investments; Margin; Mutual Funds and Exchange-Traded Funds; Portfolio Management; Real Estate Investment Trust; Retirement Accounts; Stock Market; Stocks; Systematic Market Risk; Time Value of Money

Further Reading

Hudspeth, Christian. February 21, 2013. "Ask the Expert: What's the Best Way to Start Investing When You're Young?" *Yahoo Finance Website.* http://finance.yahoo.com/news/ask-expert-whats-best-way-122056581.html

Smart, Scott, Lawrence Gitman, and Michael Jehnk. 2013. *Fundamentals of Investing* (12th ed.). New Jersey: Prentice Hall.

Liabilities

The term *liabilities* has personal, business, and insurance connotations. In personal and business uses, liabilities and debt both mean all obligations or amounts owed. On occasion, these terms may be used interchangeably. At other times debt has a more narrow definition and only includes funds borrowed and formalized with a written contract.

Insurance liability refers to fault or legal responsibility. Liability insurance protects the policyholder from a variety of personal and business risks.

Personal Liabilities

A personal liability is a financial obligation one repays out of one's personal assets. For example, the home mortgage is a personal liability the consumer has to repay to the lender for the amount borrowed to purchase a home. In this case liability and debt mean the same thing.

Secured liabilities are loans guaranteed by collateral. If the loan is not repaid, then the lender has the legal right to take possession of the asset. For example, a vehicle loan is secured by the car or truck. If the borrower doesn't make the loan payments, the lender has the right to repossess the vehicle.

An unsecured liability may be considered a promise to pay. Should the borrower default or fail to pay back the financial obligation, the lender has the right to sue the borrower for the unpaid balance. The lender may eventually be repaid from the borrower's other assets or future wages.

Business Liabilities

In general, a company's liabilities are the amounts owed to lenders as well as payments to vendors and suppliers. Simply, a company's liabilities are bills or payments due to others. In business a liability might have the term *payable* in its title.

Liabilities and the Balance Sheet

In business and accounting, a balance sheet is an important financial statement used by business managers and accountants to describe the financial picture of a company at a specific point in time. The balance sheet includes three major categories: assets, liabilities, and equity.

The business balance sheet is comparable to an individual's net worth statement (a document that shows an individual's assets less liabilities; the resultant figure shows the individual's financial worth). In sum, the balance sheet, like the net worth statement, includes a company's assets (any item of value owned by a corporation or individual that can be converted into cash) less their liabilities and net owner's or shareholder's equity or the economic value of the company.

The liabilities section of a balance sheet normally includes current and long-term liabilities or amounts owed. The current liabilities are short-term obligations due within one year such as a short-term loan or note payable. Accounts payable, wages payable, and interest payable are also considered short-term liabilities. Long-term liabilities include long-term loans and other financial obligations due in more than one year.

On the balance sheet, after liabilities are subtracted from assets, the value of the company remains. Just as with personal liabilities, a corporation needs to keep liabilities within a certain range for the company to remain profitable.

Liabilities Example

This example shows how liabilities fit in with a family's financial picture and can be generalized to a company's financial balance sheet as well. The assets owned by the Patel family include a car, a home, and money and investments in savings and retirement accounts. These assets are worth $500,000.

The family's liabilities include a home mortgage, a car loan, and a small amount of credit card debt. The total amount of their liabilities equals $275,000.

The Patels' net worth is $225,000. This figure is obtained by subtracting their liabilities ($275,000) from their assets ($500,000). The net worth is the sum of their financial worth, similar to a company's equity. This financial illustration shows how liabilities fit in an overall representation.

Insurance Liability

In business accounting and personal instances, liability means financial obligation. In insurance terms, liability refers to risk. Usually, liability insurance protects individuals from financial and legal risks.

A liability insurance policy protects the individual or business from the risk of suit arising from malpractice, injury, or negligence claims. In most cases, this insurance pays for both legal costs and financial payouts for which the policyholder is legally responsible.

For example, most states require vehicle owners to purchase liability insurance. That way, when a driver A's car hits driver B's car, injuring car B's driver and passenger, driver A's liability insurance will pay for the medical and vehicle repair bills.

Business liability insurance pays the damages when a customer falls, twists her ankle, and sues the company. Business liability insurance might also protect the business owners if an employee is injured while performing work duties.

Liability in the broad sense means responsibility. One might have financial responsibility to repay a debt or legal responsibility to pay for an injured person's medical charges (if the insured was the cause of the medical expense). In modern money management today, well-informed consumers will understand this concept with relation to their personal finances as well as its business and insurance applications.

Barbara Friedberg

See also: Bankruptcy; Budget; Credit Card; Debt; Life Insurance; Risk; Umbrella Insurance

Further Reading

Accounting Coach Web site. "Liability." Accessed April 12, 2014. http://www.accounting -coach.com/terms/L/liabilities

Accounting Coach Web site. "What Is the Difference Between Liability and Debt?" Accessed April 12, 2014. http://www.accountingcoach.com/blog/what-is-the-difference-between-liability-and-debt

Investopedia Web site. "Liability." Accessed April 12, 2014. http://www.investopedia.com/terms/l/liability.asp

Investopedia Web site. "Liability Insurance." Accessed April 12, 2014. http://www .investopedia.com/terms/l/liability_insurance.asp

Life Insurance

Life insurance is a product created to protect family members from the loss of income when the family's primary earner (or earners in the case of a two-income family) passes away. When the owner of the life insurance is the individual, the proceeds are paid to the policy's nominated beneficiaries or the insured's estate, where no beneficiaries are nominated. In some cases when the insured has been diagnosed with a terminal illness confirmed by at least two medical practitioners, the insurer may also pay out the sum insured. Not only does life insurance coverage apply to breadwinners and individuals, there are many business owners who need a life insurance policy for the survival of their businesses in the event of a key employee's death.

Life Insurance: Why It Is Important

Should the main income earner of a family die, the surviving family members may end up facing huge debts they cannot repay. Without an income or means of support, a death could leave the remaining family members destitute. Without life insurance, the surviving spouse and financial dependents could face a lowered standard of living, insurmountable bills and expenses, and even bankruptcy.

Life insurance, as with most other insurances, is purchased as protection for the beneficiaries, similar to homeowner's insurance. Breadwinners should also be insured in the unfortunate and unforeseen event they die prematurely.

Life Insurance Terms

A life insurance policy will specify the policyholder (person who purchased the insurance cover), the insured (person whose life is covered), the insurer (insurance company that provides the cover), the beneficiary (person who receives the proceeds of the insurance payout), the amount of the premium, and the amount of the sum insured. Premiums are the regular payments the policyholder agrees to pay to the insurer to transfer the risk of death of the insured to the insurer. Premium payments can remain the same for the duration of the policy, referred to as level premiums. Alternatively premiums may increase periodically, usually annually, in a stepped fashion and are thus called stepped premiums.

In addition to basic life insurance coverage, there are additional options included in an insurance policy, called riders. Riders are the additional benefits that can be purchased and added to a standard life insurance policy. Riders can take the form of additional life insurance amounts or supplemental benefits, such as for accidental death. An accidental death rider provides a supplemental payment if the insured dies as a result of an accident.

Types of Life Insurance Policies

There are three main types of life insurance policies or products to protect the different risk protection needs of individuals, families, or businesses ("Life Insurance" 2008; Sargent 2008; Zinkewicz 2002). Permanent insurance (whole of life and endowment policies), term life (temporary) insurance, and universal life are discussed here.

Permanent Insurance

Besides providing a death benefit, this type of policy also builds up equity in the form of a surrender value (cash value) that accumulates over the life of the policy. The policyholder receives the surrender value of the policy on his or her death, at the maturity date of the policy if no disaster befalls them, when the policy lapses, or if the policyholder cancels the policy, whichever occurs first. The policy lapses when the policyholder stops paying the premiums.

The investment component consists of premiums less expenses and less the cost of the insurance coverage. The cash value comprises the face value of the policy (the amount of money the person is insured for) plus any bonuses. Bonuses are the return on the investment component of the policy that has accrued over the life of the policy.

Whole Life Insurance

There are two main types of traditional permanent insurance policies, whole life policies and endowment policies. Whole life insurance offers permanent insurance for the policyholder's entire life, with higher premiums than term life policies (discussed later in the entry). They provide death benefits comparable to term life, along with additional benefits. For example, the surrender value and premiums terminate after a certain predetermined period. The contract detailing a whole life insurance policy may allow the policyholder to take out a loan against the cash value accumulated.

As long as the premiums are maintained, a whole life insurance policy offers a guaranteed payout to the beneficiaries of the policyholder. The whole ife policy pays a benefit when the insured person dies and has a maturity date ranging from 85 to 95 years old or older. Therefore, these types of policies can outlive the life of the insured. For this reason most payments tend to occur on death rather than at maturity.

Endowment Insurance

Endowment insurance policies are similar to whole life policies, with one exception: the two have different maturity periods. Endowment policies have short- to medium-term maturity dates and generally do not outlive the life of the insured person.

The endowment policy pays the face value of the policy on a fixed date or on the death of the insured, whichever comes first. The benefit may also be paid on cancellation.

The endowment life insurance policy is used to meet certain future expenses such as college tuition or buying a retirement home. The maturity dates can be set for a specific term, such as 10 years, or can be set to mature when a beneficiary reaches a certain age, such as 21 or retirement age, 65.

Term Life Insurance

Term life policies provide a payment in the event of the death of the life insured within a specified term. Unlike permanent insurance, there is no investment component to term life insurance. It is solely an insurance product.

The simple term life policy remains in effect as long the annual premiums are paid. The annual premium amount can be set at purchase for a specific length, such as 10, 15, or 20 years. This is called level term. This means the insured person knows how much the annual fee will be for the specific amount of insurance purchased.

The premiums are fairly low-cost, making them more affordable than many other types of life insurance policies. The insurance value is guaranteed to last for the specified term as long as the insured pays the annual premium. Unlike the permanent life policies, term life contains no investment component. When the policy is canceled or lapses, there is no surrender value (cash value). A claim from these polices only occurs when the death event occurs. Term policies are normally purchased to provide financial security to the surviving family of a breadwinner at death.

Universal Life Insurance

Universal life is a combination of low-cost insurance with a side investment funded by additional premium payments from the insured. These policies are for insureds who plan to keep the policy long-term. Universal life insurance policies need to be in force for at least 15 years to be eligible for any return on the investment. Those who benefit most from this type of life insurance usually need life insurance into their seventies.

By maintaining the policy for at least 15 years the savings portion has enough time to accumulate into an investment. With a universal life insurance policy, the policyholder has some control over the investment decisions. The policyholder also has some latitude regarding the amount of the premium, how much cash value accumulates, and how much death benefit will be given to the beneficiary. Furthermore, the death benefit may increase over time as the policy builds value.

A variable universal life policy gives the insured the responsibility of choosing the types of investment products to accumulate a cash value. The underlying investments supporting a variable life policy increase the risk of loss of some of the value due to the possibility that the investment performance will be less than expected.

Group Life Insurance

Group life insurance (group wholesale life insurance or institutional life insurance) is a type of term life insurance that covers a group of people, usually employees of a company or members of a union or association. Group life insurance is typically part of an overall employee benefits package. On occasion, a certain coverage level is paid for by the employer, with increased coverage available to individual employees.

Individual proof of insurability is not normally a consideration in the underwriting. Instead, the underwriter considers the size, turnover, and financial strength of the group. Contract provisions attempt to exclude the possibility of adverse selection. Group life insurance often includes a provision for a member exiting the group to buy individual coverage.

Angelique N. S. McInnes

See also: Annuity; Compound Interest/Return; Disability Insurance; Dividend Income; Estate Planning; Health Insurance; Investing; Loans; Probate; Wills and Trusts

Further Reading

Cordell, David M., and Thomas P. Langdon. 2009. "Life Insurance in Times of Uncertainty." *Journal of Financial Planning* (Vol. 22, No. 9): 32–37.

Johnson, I. Richard, and Paul A. Randle. 1995. "Evaluating New Life Insurance Products." *CPA Journal* (Vol. 65, No. 9): 30.

"Life Insurance." *Best's Review* (2008): 32–33.

Richardson, Brian C. 2011. "Planning for Business Continuation." *Advisor Today* (Vol. 106, No. 1): 18–19.

Sargent, D. 2008. "Give Staff a Safety Net." *Credit Union Magazine* (Vol. 74, No. 8): 52.
Zinkewicz, P. 2002. "New Compact Would Cover Life Products." *Insurance Advocate* (Vol. 113, No. 26): 2.

Liquidity

The liquidity concept traverses the personal and business finance categories. Liquidity refers to an individual's or corporation's access to cash or assets that can be quickly converted into cash. For example, bank certificates of deposit and cash in a checking or savings account are liquid assets. Assets that can be easily bought or sold are considered liquid. Another term for liquidity is *marketability*.

Liquidity is important in daily life. Consumers need ready access to cash to meet regularly scheduled bills and financial obligations as well as unexpected expenses such as car repairs or medical bills.

Corporations need available liquid cash in order to meet ongoing expenses such as payroll and cash for accounts payable. The company also needs a certain amount of liquidity available for other business uses.

Which Assets Are Considered Liquid?

Obviously, cash held in checking and savings accounts is liquid. Money market mutual funds and money market bank accounts are also used as cash substitutes. But there are other types of financial assets that are also easily converted into cash. These short-term financial obligations include a class of investments called short-term marketable securities. Short-term Treasury bills and notes (types of government bonds) are liquid. Corporations also issue very short-term debt, maturing in less than six months. These types of financial assets, called commercial paper, are readily converted into cash.

Consumers and Liquidity

When consumers plan their spending, saving, and budgeting, liquidity is an important concern. While some expenses occur frequently, such as rent, utility, and grocery bills, others are less frequent. Individuals need to maintain sufficient liquidity to pay for emergency car repairs, medical bills, occasional insurance, and other periodic expenses.

When applying for a home mortgage, lenders examine the prospective borrowers' liquidity and access to capital. In general, lenders expect consumers' debt expenses including mortgage, student loan, and consumer debt to fall below approximately 40 percent of the borrowers' gross income. This relationship between debt levels and liquidity is of concern to both lenders and borrowers. The lender wishes to ensure the borrower has enough liquidity to pay the loan payments. The borrower also is concerned with their own cash availability and cash flow.

This illustration demonstrates the importance of how liquidity relates to personal finance and money management. For example, the Martinez family is planning their monthly spending and saving and wish to calculate their liquid cash, after all expenses.

Mr. and Mrs. Martinez earn $7,500 per month, gross. They pay $2,000 per month in city, state, and federal taxes. This leaves them $5,500 to spend (or net spendable income). After paying rent, food, transportation, insurance, entertainment, miscellaneous expenses, and retirement account contributions, the Martinez family have no liquidity remaining. They spend all of their take-home pay.

This lack of liquidity is a problem as it leaves no cushion for unexpected expenses or additional funds for deposit in an emergency fund. The solution to unexpected expenses for the Martinez family is to use their credit card as an emergency fund. The lack of liquidity causes the family to incur debt because of the excess interest charges on the unpaid balance of their credit card. The family has a very small savings account without sufficient liquidity to cover all of the unexpected or infrequent expenses.

The Martinez family is not unlike many American working families. Consumers such as the Martinez family must understand their liquidity position and how to maintain sufficient accessible cash for living expenses.

Liquidity Related to Investing

Assets that can be easily bought and sold are considered liquid. This liquidity assumes there is a ready market of buyers and sellers. In general, stocks, mutual funds, and exchange-traded funds (ETFs), which trade in the public markets such as the New York Stock Exchange, are liquid. If an investor owns shares of Apple stock and would like to sell the shares, there is a pool of investors ready to purchase the shares on the popular NASDAQ stock exchange. Most stocks are easily converted into cash.

In contrast, there are certain financial or investment assets that are "illiquid." These "thinly traded" stocks and bonds from smaller companies lack the interest that the larger companies enjoy. When an investor holds an illiquid security, it may take extra time to sell the asset, and there may be a large "spread" (or difference) between the buy and sell prices.

Corporate Liquidity Ratios

When investors buy stock in public companies and the companies analyze their own financial condition, liquidity ratios help calculate whether a firm has enough ready cash. There are standard metrics or ratios that companies use to measure their ability to handle particular financial scenarios. The following liquidity ratios may have various acceptable levels based on the industry. Due to the differences in both cash coming in and the need for cash, a large retail store such as Target would have different liquidity needs than a utility company.

The current ratio or working capital position takes the company's current or short-term assets (cash, marketable securities, receivables, and inventory) and compares them to the current liabilities (notes payable, debt due within the year, accrued expenses, and taxes). This ratio shows whether the company's short-term cash is sufficient to cover short-term obligations. A higher ratio shows better financial strength.

The current ratio is one of the most widely used financial ratios, yet it can be misleading as it may not be easy to convert inventory into ready cash. Thus, the quick ratio can be a tighter ratio to better measure a company's financial solvency.

The quick ratio, sometimes called the acid test ratio, is an indicator that measures the relationship between a company's most liquid assets (such as cash, short-term investments, and accounts receivables) and their current liabilities. A higher ratio indicates that the firm is better able to handle financial obligations.

Why Liquidity Is Important

As the financial crisis in 2007 demonstrated, there are severe financial ramifications when both consumers and the banking industry lack liquidity. In the case of homeowners and banks, the financial crisis could also be considered a liquidity crisis. After the housing boom of 2005–2006, many homeowners' adjustable rate mortgage payments increased, making it difficult for the homeowners to make their mortgage payments. This lack of liquidity led to mortgage delinquencies, foreclosures, and personal bankruptcies.

As previously mentioned, companies also need to maintain appropriate liquidity levels. If a company lacks sufficient liquidity to pay its short-term obligations such as repaying loans, paying its employees, and paying bills, the company may experience a liquidity crisis. If this situation is not quickly resolved with cash, the company may need to file for bankruptcy.

At the beginning of the 2007 financial crisis, banks improperly managed their liquidity and experienced great financial problems and stress. Banks need to lend money at higher interest rates than they pay depositors in order to make a profit. Yet banks also need to hold enough reserves to pay depositors under a variety of withdrawal scenarios.

In the middle of the first decade of this century, when many of homeowners defaulted on their loans, subprime lenders (those who lent to less financially stable individuals) filed for bankruptcy, due to lack of liquidity. Many larger banks, which had purchased the mortgage loans from the smaller banks that originally granted the loans, later offered a form of the loans to investors as securities (called mortgage-backed securities). These larger banks also experienced financial problems because when the homeowners defaulted on their loans and stopped making their payments, these large banks were not receiving the expected mortgage payments. Thus, the banks didn't have enough money coming in to pay out to the owners of the mortgage-backed securities. These liquidity issues were some of the major contributors to the 2007–2008 subprime housing crisis and subsequent mortgage meltdown.

Tools for Individuals to Manage Liquidity

The world of online personal finance has come up with many tools to help individuals monitor and manage their liquidity needs. There are many online companies that offer budgeting, saving, and financial monitoring software for computers. One of the most popular personal finance and liquidity management tools is mint.com, an online version of the grandfather of personal finance tracking software, Quicken (published by Intuit). There are other online companies that help consumers track and manage debt as well as their credit score. With all of the easily accessible and free money management tools, consumers have access to assistance with all of their liquidity concerns.

Barbara Friedberg

See also: Banking; Bankruptcy; Bonds; Budget; Cash; Certificate of Deposit; Consumer Credit/Debt; Credit Report and Reporting Agencies; Credit Score; Delinquency; Investing; Liabilities; Mortgage; Online Personal Finance; Real Estate; Risk; Savings Account; Year 2007–2008: Subprime Housing Crisis and Mortgage Meltdown

Further Reading

Bank for International Settlements Web site. 2013. "Basel III: The Liquidity Coverage Ratio and Liquidity Risk Monitoring Tools." January. http://www.bis.org/publ/bcbs238.pdf

Brunnermeier, Markus K., and Lasse Heje Pedersen. 2009. "Market Liquidity and Funding Liquidity." *The Review of Financial Studies* (22): 6.

Investopedia Web site. "Liquidity." Accessed May 16, 2014. http://www.investopedia.com/terms/l/liquidity.asp

Investopedia Web site. "Liquidity Ratios." Accessed May 16, 2014. http://www.investopedia.com/terms/l/liquidityratios.asp

Mint Web site. Accessed May 18, 2014. https://www.mint.com/

Loans

A loan is money that is borrowed today to be repaid in the future. A loan usually has a defined term during which the money must be repaid. The borrower pays the lender interest in exchange for the use of the money loaned. The money borrowed is referred to as principal. The money is usually paid back in regular installments, often monthly payments.

The interest payments are the reason that the lender makes a loan. In most cases, loans are enforced by a contract to ensure that the lender receives the money that is owed.

Types of Loans

There are two main categories of loans—secured and unsecured loans.

Secured Loans

A secured loan is one in which the borrower promises an asset as collateral. Collateral is the borrower's promise of an asset as security for repayment of the

Payday Lenders Controversy

Payday loans are a type of short-term loan used to "make ends meet" and fund unexpected expenses. They are one of the fastest growing financial sectors and are known for high-interest-rate, short-term loans.

The controversy surrounds the allegation that payday lenders take advantage of low-income borrowers or those who have had financial troubles. These lenders thrive on borrowers who roll over their loans from pay period to pay period and may end up paying annual interest rates of up to 500 percent (Hisrich, 2004).

Payday lenders may offer cash advances on yet-unreceived income such as future tax refunds or paychecks. The proponents of payday lenders claim they are offering a service to an underserved portion of the population.

loan. If the borrower defaults or doesn't repay the loan, the lender takes possession of the collateral. Such assets might include a car, stocks, gold, or property. This collateral is protection for the lender in case the borrower defaults—fails to repay the amount borrowed along with the interest agreed on—on the loan. If the borrower does default, he or she gives up whatever collateral is pledged to the lender, who then owns it.

A common secured loan is a mortgage. A mortgage is used by many people to purchase a house. The institution from whom the money was borrowed (often a bank) is given a lien on the house's title until the mortgage loan is paid off completely. If the borrower is unable to meet the monthly payments on this mortgage and stops paying back the loan (this is referred to as defaulting), the institution would have the right to the house and be able to sell it again to get the money it is owed by the borrower.

Another popular secured loan is a car loan. This works in the same way as a mortgage loan except the length of the loan is much shorter—a mortgage loan is typically between 15 and 30 years, whereas a car loan is usually between 5 and 7 years in length.

Unsecured Loans

Unlike secured loans, unsecured loans are monetary loans that are not secured against the borrower's assets, or collateral. The interest rates on these types of loans are always higher compared to those on secured loans since the lender is taking on more risk as the borrower does not have to put up collateral to obtain this loan. The two main types of unsecured loans are credit cards and student loans.

A credit card allows the cardholder (or borrower) to purchase an item with the promise of the borrower repaying the credit card company with much interest added to the original amount borrowed. If the credit card balance is paid in full within the prescribed time period, usually 30 days, there are no interest charges.

Unsecured Education Loans

A student loan is money borrowed to pay for college. There are two basic types of student loans—federal (government) loans and private loans. Federal student loans are ideal because they usually have a low interest rate and are available to students who may not have much of a credit history. There are two types of federal student loans: Stafford loans or Perkins loans.

Stafford loans are made available to college and university students to supplement personal and family resources, scholarships, grants, and work-study. Nearly all students are eligible to receive Stafford loans regardless of their credit history. Stafford loans may be subsidized by the U.S. government or unsubsidized depending on the student's need.

Stafford loans have many benefits. They have a low fixed interest rate—during the 2011–2012 school year some rates were as low as 3.40 percent. They have borrowing limits up to $20,500 per year depending on degree status and years in school. You do not have to repay these loans while enrolled in school, and acceptance for obtaining this type of loan is not based on credit history. In addition, there is a six-month grace period (the six months after the student leaves college) before the student must start repaying this debt.

The Perkins loan program provides low-interest loans to help needy students finance the costs of postsecondary education. Students attending any one of approximately 1,700 participating postsecondary institutions can obtain Perkins loans from the school. Each school's revolving Perkins loan fund is replenished by ongoing activities, such as collections by the school on outstanding Perkins loans made by the school and reimbursements from the U.S. Department of Education for the cost of certain statutory loan cancellation provisions.

Perkins borrowers are eligible for loan cancellation for teacher service at low-income schools and under certain other circumstances. Students may defer repayment of the loan while enrolled (at least half-time) at a postsecondary school. Borrowers who have difficulty repaying a Perkins loan should contact the school where they received the loan to find out if they are eligible for a deferment or forbearance based on economic hardship or other circumstances.

Loan Guidelines

There are loans available for many additional purposes from a wide variety of lenders. Loans can be obtained from banks, finance companies, social lenders (Internet platforms where individuals lend to other individuals), and payday lenders. When lending or borrowing money, it is important to understand the terms of the loan, repayment requirements, amount of interest due, and when interest is due.

In summary, a loan is an amount of money borrowed (by a borrower) from another person or institution (the lender) in order to pay for something that the borrower does not have the cash to pay for in full. The borrower agrees to repay the loan in a set amount of time and, in most cases, the amount he or she pays back exceeds the initial amount borrowed due to the interest charged on the loan.

Danny Kofke

See also: Banking; Consumer Credit/Debt; Credit Card; Credit Score; Credit Union; Debt; Debt Collection; Debt/Credit Counseling; Delinquency; Interest Income and Payments; Interest Rates; Liabilities; Mortgage; Social Lending or Peer-to-Peer Lending

Further Reading

Dominguez, Joe, and Vicki Robin. 1999. *Your Money or Your Life.* New York: Penguin, 182, 313.

Hisrich, Matthew. 2004. "The Payday-Loan Controversy." *The Freeman: Ideas on Liberty.* October. http://www.fee.org/files/docLib/1004ThePayday-Loan.pdf

Margin

The term *margin* has several different meanings and applications related to personal finance. Business, accounting, economics, finance, investment, and banking all use the term. The meaning of margin varies along with the discipline in which it is used.

Business and Accounting

In business and accounting, margin refers to profit as a percentage of sales generated by a corporation. This is referred to as profit margin and shows how much money is left over after costs are subtracted. In this situation, a larger margin is better and means greater profit.

There are three basic classifications for margin depending on the profit calculation technique used. *Gross profit margin* refers to profitability after deducting only the costs of goods sold (COGS). COGS is an accounting term and usually refers to the cost of raw materials and labor expense.

Operating profit margin measures profitability after excluding all overhead costs (these costs include rent, utilities, etc.) and administrative (such as salaries) and selling (vehicle, advertising, and other costs) expenses. Operating profit margin also excludes COGS.

Finally, *net profit margin* measures profitability after subtracting taxes and interest expense resulting from debt incurred by a corporation as well as the exclusions from gross and operating profit margins. Net profit margin shows the true percentage of profit after deducting all expenses.

Higher profit margins are superior to lower and demonstrate how effective a company is at controlling costs. All other factors being equal, when comparing two companies in the same industry, if Company A has a profit margin of 15 percent and Company B has a profit margin of 19 percent, then Company B would be considered a more profitable company than Company A. After all, a company prefers to keep a larger percent of the sales revenue from the product or service.

Economics

In the context of economics, margin means extra. It can be illustrated by a simple example. The first sandwich you eat when you are extremely hungry will provide a certain level of satisfaction (this satisfaction is referred to as utility), but the second sandwich might achieve a different level of satisfaction (this different level is what we mean by marginal). That concept can also be applied to money and the utility achieved from consumption. Each additional unit of consumption achieves a different utility or level of satisfaction and is referred to as *marginal utility*.

To generalize, margin is the excess benefit or cost that results from inducing a certain level of change. This concept has an important implication for personal finance. If you get a raise in your allowance or salary, how much of that will you spend (consume) and how much will you save? Generally, if you get a small increase, you will spend most of it, but with a greater increase, you will tend to save more than you spend, and that is referred to as the *marginal propensity to consume*.

Finance and Investment

In the context of finance and investment, margin is the deposit an investor needs to place with a broker when the investor borrows money in order to buy a security (such as a stock or bond). In this sense, margin is similar to collateral. If the value of the security drops significantly, the investor has to deposit more cash, that is, increase the margin, or sell part of the securities purchased. In the United States, the Federal Reserve Board's Regulation T states that investors can borrow up to a maximum of 50 percent of the purchase price of the securities bought on margin.

The percentage provided by the investor from his or her own money (equity) is called the initial premium. Self-regulatory organizations like the New York Stock Exchange require a minimum amount of equity to be maintained in the account. This is referred to as the maintenance margin. The maintenance margin required is equal to 25 percent of the security purchase price. If the security price drops, the broker will issue a margin call that requires additional funds to be deposited by the investor.

Investors choose margin trading because it allows a means to purchase more securities with less money. This is helpful when the market is moving up and a security purchased on margin increases in value. This allows the investor to realize a higher return (given a smaller initial investment) than if he or she had purchased the security totally with cash. But if the market drops, the investor will suffer greater losses than from an all-cash purchase. The losses can force the broker to sell part or all of the security to meet the margin call requirements for the security that declined in price.

Banking

In the banking world, margin refers to the difference between the value of collateral pledged against a loan and the amount of the loan provided by the bank. This amount is sometimes called "haircut." Collateral is an asset; real like a building or financial like a stock or bond. This asset secures one's borrowing in case of default. If a borrower defaults on the loan, the lender can sell this collateral to collect the value of the loan.

Usually a bank extends a loan for less than 100 percent of the collateral value. This requires market assessment of the volatility of the collateral value. The ratio is referred to as loan-to-value ratio. Different types of collateral require different margin levels. The larger the margin or "haircut," the more secure the loan is. This concept is applied to protect against two types of risks: the risk of a decline in the value of the collateral or the risk of the inability to liquidate the collateral without great loss (Chapman et al., 2011).

Yasmine H. Abdel Razek

See also: Banking; Bonds; Investing; Loans; Stocks

Further Reading

Chapman, James, Jonathan Chiu, and Miguel Molico. 2011. "Liquidity Provision and Collateral Haircuts in Payments Systems." *Bank of Canada Review* (9): 13–20.

Interactive Brokers Web site. "Introduction to Margin: Margin Accounts." Accessed July 7, 2013. https://www.interactivebrokers.com/en/?f=margin

John Wiley & Sons [database online]. "Buying Stocks on Margin." Accessed July 23, 2013. http://www.dummies.com/how-to/content/buying-stock-on-margin.html

Key Bank Web site. "Collateral." Accessed July 26, 2013. https://www.key.com/html /collateral-bank-lending-process.html

Library of Economics and Liberty Web site. "Margins and Thinking at the Margin." Accessed July 23, 2013. http://www.econlib.org/library/Topics/College/margins.html

Titman, Sheridan, Arthur J. Keown, and John D. Martin. 2011. *Financial Management: Principles and Applications*, 11th ed. Pearson, 88–90.

Medicaid

Medicaid is a U.S. government health care program for lower-income citizens. The federal program is integrated with individual Medicaid state programs. Medicaid includes a special program to help lower-income children called the Children's Health Insurance Program (CHIP). Parents of children who receive CHIP benefits are not necessarily Medicaid recipients.

Medicaid and CHIP cover approximately 60 million Americans. Those insured with Medicaid include children, pregnant women, parents, seniors, and individuals with disabilities. States are required by federal law to cover certain population groups, called the "mandatory eligibility groups," and federal law offers states the option to cover other population groups or "optional eligibility groups." After meeting the federal coverage guidelines, many states grant expanded coverage above the federal minimums, especially for children's support.

Ancillary Problems and Issues with Medicaid

According to attorney Laura Hermer of the University of Texas Medical Branch, in difficult economic times tax revenues decline whereas Medicaid financial demands increase. The Affordable Care Act allows states to decrease benefits and provider reimbursements, further damaging Medicaid recipients.

There are 26 states that asked the Supreme Court to examine the Affordable Care Act's Medicaid expansion to determine whether it is "unconstitutionally coercive." A group of Republican governors requested that Medicaid be "block-granted." This means that states could allocate funds as they saw fit to finance a wide range of services, not just Medicaid.

Medicaid Eligibility

The Affordable Care Act of 2010 designated the national Medicaid maximum eligibility level at 133 percent of the federal poverty level. The 2014 eligibility level for Medicaid for a family of four is $31,720.50. This is the maximum income level for a family of four to be eligible for Medicaid benefits. The federal poverty level is updated annually to ensure that the eligible citizens are covered.

In addition to income level criteria, there are additional eligibility requirements for Medicaid recipients. To receive Medicaid, individuals need to meet certain federal and state guidelines regarding residency, immigration status, and U.S. citizenship documentation. In some cases, states may apply for waivers to cover individuals who aren't ordinarily eligible for Medicaid benefits.

Medicaid Benefits

The Medicaid benefits are divided into two categories: mandatory and optional. Mandatory benefits include inpatient and outpatient hospital services as well as early periodic screening diagnostic treatment (EPSDT). This benefit is important for children under age 21 to ensure that youth obtain appropriate health care services to facilitate their physical, dental, and mental health. Further mandatory benefits encompass nursing care, home health services, physician services, laboratory and x-ray tests, family planning, nurse midwife care, as well as transportation to medical care.

The optional benefits are provided at the states' discretion. States elect whether to offer prescription drugs and physical, occupational, speech, and respiratory care services. Podiatry, optometry, dental, chiropractic, and related services are also optional. At present, all states provide prescription drug programs.

Similar to the copays required by many health care plans, states may also require co-pays or cost sharing for Medicaid enrollees. The most vulnerable groups, children and pregnant women, are exempt from most out-of-pocket costs.

States also may charge higher co-payments when individuals visit a hospital emergency department for nonemergency services. This requirement is in place as some lower-income individuals tend to use emergency room services in lieu of other types of clinics and medical facilities.

Long-Term Services and Support

The elderly are particularly at risk for depleting their financial resources due to excess medical costs. After the elderly have exhausted their financial resources, they may need to rely on Medicaid for medical care and other life maintenance support services.

The Medicaid program may also cover institutional care, home care, and community-based long-term care and support. As the population continues to age, the Medicaid program may be stressed as it is expected to cover more eligible elderly citizens.

The institutions caring for the elderly Medicaid recipients are residential and cover all care for the admitted occupants. The care includes room and board. The caregiving institutions must meet certain standards, be licensed, and be certified by the state. Other names for these facilities are nursing homes, extended care facilities, and senior citizens' homes.

Community-Based Long-Term Services and Support

These services are designated for individuals with disabilities and chronic conditions. The care for citizens with disabilities and chronic conditions strives to maintain their independence and a reasonable level of health and quality of care. There are partnerships and programs to assist these candidates.

Long-term community-based services and support also vary from state to state, but maintain certain characteristics in common. Medicaid attempts to allow the program recipients to maintain control and decide where and with whom they live as well as the services they receive. The services strive for a high level of quality and are coordinated with all providers. Finally, due to the multicultural nature of our citizens, the services are sensitive to the participants' individual cultural needs. In sum, the government attempts to promote self-respect, control, and independence for service recipients.

How Are Medicaid's Bills Paid?

As previously stated, Medicaid is funded by the federal and state governments. The federal government pays each state a percentage payment, called the federal medical assistance percentage (FMAP). The average FMAP is 57 percent, but it ranges from a low of 50 percent in wealthier states to 75 percent in states with lower revenues. The maximum regular FMAP is capped at 82 percent. The states negotiate payments to providers such as managed care organizations to deliver the Medicaid services.

Children's Health Insurance Program (CHIP)

The CHIP program covers approximately eight million children in families with incomes too high to receive Medicaid benefits, but who cannot afford private medical insurance coverage. This program became law in 1997.

Similar to the Medicaid program, CHIP is funded by both the federal and state governments. The federal government designed the contribution rate to be favorable to the states in order to benefit a greater number of uninsured children.

The Affordable Care Act improved federal CHIP funding by 23 percent. This brings the federal matching rate for CHIP to 93 percent. States have the option of operating CHIP independently of Medicaid, as an arm of the Medicaid program, or as a combination of both types.

Medicaid is an example of a taxpayer-funded service to provide for the well-being of citizens who cannot afford health care for themselves or their children.

Barbara Friedberg

See also: Affordable Care Act; Health Insurance; Medicare; Social Security

Further Reading

Hermer, Laura. "Federal/State Issues in Medicaid: Current Controversies." Accessed May 27, 2014. http://onlinemj.luc.edu/symposium/Hermer.pdf

Medicaid.gov Web site. Date accessed May 21, 2014. http://www.medicaid.gov/Medicaid-CHIP-Program-Information/By-Topics/By-Topic.html

Medicaid.gov Web site. "2014 Poverty Guidelines." Accessed May 20, 2014. http://www.mediaid.gov/Medicaid-CHIP-Program-Information/By-Topics/Eligibility/Downloads/2014-Federal-Poverty-level-charts.pdf

Medicare

Medicare is a U.S. government–run insurance program that helps offset the costs of medical care. The program assists individuals over age 65, as well as certain younger people with disabilities, permanent kidney failure, or Lou Gehrig's disease (amyotrophic lateral sclerosis). The Medicare program applies to working and nonworking individuals. Since Medicare only partially covers medical expenses, an integral extension of the program is the opportunity to purchase a Medicare supplement policy (Medigap) from a private insurance company to cover some costs not included in Medicare.

The Centers for Medicare and Medicaid Services at the Social Security Administration implements the program. Medicare is partially financed by the payroll taxes paid by workers and employers. The other part of Medicare funding is paid by premiums deducted from retirees' Social Security checks.

History of Medicare

President Lyndon B. Johnson signed the Medicare and Medicaid programs into law on July 30, 1965. The program was created to provide health insurance for those over age 65 at a time when insurers were not insuring senior citizens. The greatest medical financial concern during the era of Medicare's creation was that an insurmountable hospital bill would destroy an individual's finances. Medicare was originally created in the paradigm of the private insurance system in place in the 1960s. The private insurance offered fewer choices and assisted with much lower medical costs than we experience today. There is controversy that as health care has evolved, Medicare changes have not kept up.

Parts of Medicare

Medicare Part A is the hospital insurance. It helps cover inpatient hospital care, skilled nursing facility care, hospice care, and home health care. You usually don't pay a premium for Part A coverage if you or your spouse paid Medicare taxes while employed. Another name for Part A is premium-free Part A. Those ineligible for Part A may be able to purchase this coverage.

Medicare Part B is the medical insurance portion. This part of Medicare covers a portion of the costs associated with doctor and other health care provider visits. Part B also offsets the costs of outpatient care, home health care, durable medical equipment, and some preventive services. Most Medicare recipients pay the standard monthly Part B premium (or charge). The Part B premium or charge is deducted from the individual's Social Security payment. Private companies offer a Medicare supplement insurance policy (Medigap) to help pay additional charges not already covered under Medicare Part B.

Medicare Part C or Medicare Advantage is sponsored by Medicare-endorsed private insurance companies. Part C includes all benefits and services of Parts A and B and usually adds prescription drug coverage (Part D) as well. For an extra cost, Medicare Advantage may also include additional benefits.

The fourth part of Medicare, Part D, covers prescription drugs. This program is also supported by Medicare-chosen private insurance companies.

Where Medicare Is Lacking

There are many health care services not covered by Medicare. For example, Medicare does not cover routine dental care, eyeglasses, hearing aids, and most long-term care. Nursing home care is not covered for Medicare patients but may be available for the poor under the Medicaid program for consumers with less than $2,000.

As with most government services, there are debates and criticisms about Medicare. The concerns, according to studies by the National Academy of Social Insurance (NASI) Study Panel on Medicare Financing, suggest that Medicare leaves the elderly with large out-of-pocket costs and expensive supplemental insurance. The research estimates that the typical Medicare-eligible individual spends approximately 19 percent of his or her income on medical care and insurance. There is a projection that this medical percentage could rise to 30 percent of income by 2025 if health care costs continue their current trajectory.

Medicare, Demographic Trends, and the Future

The National Academy of Social Insurance in "The Future of Medicare" offers some startling statistics. As the baby boomer generation (born between 1946 and 1965) ages, Medicare will be pressured. There are data to suggest that by 2030, Medicare enrollment will double to approximately 80 million. Compound that projection with the decline in available workers supporting retirees, and there is the potential for a large shortfall in Medicare funding.

In 2010, Medicare spending totaled about 3.6 percent of the gross domestic product (GDP). By 2030, the percentage of GDP spent on Medicare is expected to increase to 5.1 percent, according to the National Academy of Social Insurance. In 2014, the Affordable Care Act gave Medicare recipients expanded benefits such as preventive services, cancer screening, and yearly "wellness" visits, without out-of-pocket charges.

The Medicare funding projections will impact both government and consumer spending in the future. With health care costs growing faster than the rate of inflation, modern money management requires consumers to be educated about this health care insurance topic for themselves and family members.

Barbara Friedberg

See also: Affordable Care Act; Gross Domestic Product (GDP) and Gross National Product (GNP); Health Insurance; Retirement; Social Security; U.S. Federal Tax System Overview

Further Reading

Centers for Medicare and Medicaid Services. "Medicare and You 2014." Accessed September 22, 2013. http://www.medicare.gov/publications/pubs/pdf/10050.pdf

Medicare.gov Web site. "The Affordable Care Act & Medicare." Accessed March 4, 2014. http://www.medicare.gov/about-us/affordable-care-act/affordable-care-act.html

National Academy of Social Insurance Web site. "Medicare." Accessed September 20, 2013. http://www.nasi.org/learn/medicare/

Money Market Account

A money market account is a type of savings account that promises higher interest payments in exchange for a larger deposit. A bank money market account is also known as a money market demand or deposit account (MMDA). This type of bank account, in addition to requiring a larger minimum deposit base than a traditional savings account, may have additional restrictions such as a limited number of monthly transactions. Banks vary in the amount of required minimum deposits from $500 on up. The interest rate usually increases for larger deposits.

In 2013, with historically low interest rates, the higher rates offered by money market accounts didn't seem too enticing. An online bank money market account might pay 0.85 percent interest. During previous decades, when market interest rates were higher, money market accounts paid rates from 5 to 10 percent.

As with all bank accounts, bank money market accounts are insured by the Federal Deposit Insurance Corporation (FDIC) up to the legal limit. In 2013 the FDIC insurance amount was $250,000 per depositor, per insured bank for each account. In other

Historical Money Market Interest Rates—the Highs and Lows

Money market interest rates fluctuate along with market interest rates. For a bit of historical perspective, the following chart illustrates the returns of taxable money market funds starting in 1975 in five-year intervals.

Money Market Yields Table

1975	1980	1985	1990	1995	2000	2005	2010	2014
6.36%	12.68%	7.71%	7.82%	5.48%	5.89%	2.66%	0.04%	0.70%

Notice how money market account rates peaked in 1980 at 12.68 percent and fell to less than 1 percent in 2010. It's important to note that those returns are not inflation adjusted. What that means is that the real return or the return after inflation is subtracted will be much lower than the nominal return (without an inflation adjustment) listed in the chart above.

For example, in 1975 inflation was 9.20 percent, in comparison with the inflation rate of 3.38 percent in 2000. One of the lowest inflation rates during the entire time period was the 1.64 percent inflation rate recorded in 2010.

In sum, interest rates bounce around quite a bit. In order to understand the real purchasing power of interest rate returns, they need to be considered in light of the inflation rate.

words, as long as one doesn't have more than $250,000 in the bank account, one is fully insured. For credit union members, the National Credit Union Association (NCUA) also insures money market accounts up to $250,000.

Money Market Extra—MMAX

For those with assets above $250,000, this type of account offers insurance otherwise unavailable due to the account's size. These accounts are usually created for corporations and commercial enterprises. The commercial customer deposits the large amount, such as $500,000, with the bank. The money is then divided into two $250,000 accounts and placed in distinct banks within the Institutional Deposit Corporation (IDC) network. Consequently, the $500,000 is eligible for FDIC insurance. There are other restrictions on this type of account including a limited number of withdrawals.

Money Market Mutual Funds

Frequently confused with money market bank accounts, money market mutual funds are another type of higher yielding cash investment. Money market mutual funds are not the same as bank money market accounts.

A mutual fund is an investment that combines a pool of money and then places these funds in securities as determined by the fund charter. Quite simply, the money market mutual fund invests in money market instruments. Money market instruments are generally very short-term commercial paper or debt instruments of corporations and governments. Money market mutual funds are the safest of all debt securities (possibly with the exception of Treasury bills).These short-term loans pay higher interest rates than a bank due to slightly higher additional risk.

Although not insured by the FDIC like money market bank accounts, money market mutual funds are very safe. They are regulated by the Securities and Exchange Commission (SEC) and normally invest in only very secure and short-term (maturities of less than 120 days) debt securities.

Historically money market mutual funds' value remains consistent at one dollar per share. Due to the nature of the underlying commercial paper, the true value of each share occasionally drifts below or above one dollar. Most investment companies have agreed to keep the value at one dollar per share in spite of minor underlying deviations in value.

Advantages and Disadvantages of Money Market Bank and Mutual Funds

Both of these types of accounts offer higher returns than traditional savings accounts. They are quite liquid and the money can be accessed quickly. These are great investments for the cash portion of an investor's portfolio. Many people use these types of accounts instead of a savings or even checking account.

Minimum account balance requirements may be a deterrent for some. The limited number of allowed transactions can hinder those with a need for extensive check writing and monthly transactions. Fees accrue if the minimum balance is not met or if the maximum number of transactions is surpassed.

Interest rates on these accounts are influenced by current market interest rates. In times when market interest rates are low, so are the rates on both types of money market accounts. Fortunately for savers, when market interest rates increase, so will the returns on money market accounts and funds. Money market accounts are a viable option for savers looking to best interest rate returns from traditional bank savings accounts.

Barbara Friedberg

See also: Asset Allocation; Banking; Bonds; Cash; Checking Account; Credit Union; Interest Income and Payments; Liquidity; Mutual Funds and Exchange-Traded Funds (ETFs); Online Personal Finance

Further Reading

Federal Deposit Insurance Corporation Web site. "FDIC Insurance Coverage Basics." Accessed November 15, 2013. http://www.fdic.gov/deposit/deposits/insured/basics.html
McMahon, Tim. 2014. "Historical Inflation Rate." Accessed March 4, 2014. http://inflationdata.com/Inflation/Inflation_Rate/HistoricalInflation.aspx
National Credit Union Association Web site. "NCUA Share Insurance, Fund Information, and Reports." Accessed November 15, 2013. http://www.ncua.gov/DataApps/Pages/SI-NCUA.aspx

U.S. Census Bureau. "Money Market Interest Rates and Mortgage Rates." Accessed March 4, 2014. http://www.census.gov/compendia/statab/2012/tables/12s1197.xls

Mortgage

A mortgage is a type of loan made to individuals to enable them to buy assets such as real estate. The loan is then secured on the asset until the debt is fully repaid. Many financial institutions offer mortgages and each has its own criteria, but the underwriting process is similar. Mortgages can be a powerful instrument to help individuals build personal wealth and an understanding of how they work can enable investors and homebuyers to exploit this benefit.

How a Mortgage Works

A mortgage is usually the biggest financial commitment individuals take on. It is a loan to help individuals buy a house and it is repaid over a long period of time, normally 15 to 30 years. The cost of a house is likely to be several times more than a family's annual salary, and so the payments are spread over a long period of time to make the house purchase affordable.

However, the longer the period of repayment, the greater the total amount payable. Suppose you take out a loan of $100,000 at 6 percent fixed interest over 30 years. The monthly payment is $599 and the total amount repayable is $215,838, as the interest charge is $115,838. In comparison, if you borrow the same amount for 20 years, the monthly payment will be higher ($716) but you will save $43,895 of interest. A shorter term loan means the homeowner pays less total interest.

How Much Can a Buyer Afford?

Meeting regular mortgage payments is an important obligation, and failure to do so can lead to foreclosure when the lender takes back the property and forces its sale to repay the loan (Frasca, p. 233). As a rule of thumb, financial planners suggest that a home price should be no more than two times the total gross annual household income and that all of the monthly household debt payments (including the mortgage loan) should be no more than about 40 percent of the total monthly gross income. These rules of thumb do not apply to everyone and the buyers' spending habits and lifestyles should also be considered (Madura, p. 266).

Mortgage Lenders

Mortgages are offered by a variety of institutions, including commercial banks, mutual savings banks, mortgage companies, and savings and loan associations. They each have their own criteria and the interest rates may vary. The borrowers can contact the lending institutions directly or they can employ a mortgage broker to help them find a suitable mortgage. It is important for borrowers to compare deals because a small difference in interest rate can result in significant savings. On a $100,000 30-year mortgage, a 0.50 percent reduction in the interest rate can save you more than $12,000 of interest over the life of the loan (Frasca, p. 224).

The mortgage market is highly competitive, with lenders offering a wide range of products. Choosing a mortgage is an important decision because a typical mortgage is repaid over a long period of time, and the amount individuals pay back can be as much as three times the original amount borrowed.

Factors Affecting Mortgage Rates

The cost of the mortgage is determined by the interest rate, which in turn is affected by the buyers' credit rating and the amount of down payment they put down. Typically, a high down payment and a good credit score can lower the interest rate because the risk of the loan to the lender is lower.

Borrowers can make mortgage payments more affordable by spreading the payments over a longer period of time, which will result in lower monthly mortgage payments but the overall costs of borrowing will be higher. The typical homebuyer puts down a 20 percent down payment and borrows over 30 years on a fixed-rate mortgage. However, with mortgage insurance buyers may be able to obtain a mortgage with as little as a 5 percent down payment (Frasca, p. 224).

Annual Percentage Rate (APR)

The annual percentage rate (APR) gives an important indication of the overall costs involved. It takes into account the interest rate and other credit charges (such as mortgage insurance and loan origination fees) into a uniform measure of cost. The APR, rather than the initial interest rate, gives individuals a better tool to compare the overall cost of the mortgages offered by different providers.

Types of Mortgages

Fixed-Rate Mortgages

Choosing the type of mortgage is one of the most important decisions individuals make when seeking a mortgage. There are essentially two options: fixed rate or adjustable rate. The decision will be determined by buyers' risk attitude as well as their personal circumstances.

Many people prefer a fixed-rate mortgage because it gives borrowers a sense of stability as the interest rate and monthly payments remain the same over the life of the loan. Fixed-rate mortgage loans are available with a variety of repayment terms, with 30-, 20-, and 15-year fixed-rate mortgages being the most popular. For example, if you borrow $100,000 at 6 percent for 30 years, you would have the same monthly payment of $599 over the entire 30-year period. Part of each payment will go to the repayment of the principal (the amount owed) and part will go toward payment of interest on the principal.

Pros and Cons of Fixed-Rate Mortgages

The main advantage of a fixed mortgage rate is that the individual is protected against future increases in mortgage rates. Also, it is easier to budget as the monthly payments remain the same.

On the other hand, the main disadvantage is that the interest rate on fixed-rate mortgages tends to be higher than on adjustable-rate mortgages because fixed-rate mortgages pose a higher risk to lenders, and so they have to factor in this risk by charging higher rates (Frasca, p. 225). Individuals will also not be able to benefit from a fall in interest rates with a lower future payment. In addition, some fixed-rate mortgages might have a penalty attached if the loan is paid off or sold before the end of the period.

Adjustable-Rate Mortgages (ARM)

Adjustable-rate mortgages (also known as variable- and flexible-rate loans), as the name suggests, mean that the interest rate on the loan is not fixed. Adjustable-rate mortgages tend to have a lower initial interest rate than standard fixed-rate mortgages. The difference between the initial rate on fixed and variable loans can vary widely and has ranged between 0.05 and 2 percentage points in recent years (Frasca, p. 226).

The interest rate on an adjustable-rate mortgage is usually tied to an easily trackable popular interest rate such as the London Interbank Offered Rate (LIBOR). Additionally, the loan rate varies on a variety of schedules from yearly to an ARM loan whose rate remains the same for 5 or 10 years and then varies annually after that time.

Pros and Cons of Adjustable-Rate Mortgages

The main advantage of adjustable-rate mortgages is flexibility. If individuals sell their home and move, they can repay the debt without worrying about paying a penalty. If interest rates fall, borrowers can take advantage of this situation. Additionally, if borrowers don't expect to remain in the home for more than a few years, they will benefit from the lower interest rates and payments of an ARM versus a fixed-rate loan.

Mortgage Application Process

When individuals apply for a mortgage, the lender will be assessing two important factors: their ability and their likelihood of repaying the loan, and the assessed value of the property as security for the loan. In order to determine the borrower's ability to repay the loan, the lender requires documentation to verify employment history, creditworthiness, overall financial situation, as well as a look at the borrower's payment history and credit score.

The property's valuation must be assessed in order to determine the loan amount. Also, in the event that the borrower is unable to repay the loan, the lender needs to ensure that they can sell the property to repay the loan. It is therefore important that the property offers a good security for the loan.

Refinancing

If interest rates decline and individuals have a mortgage, they may wish to refinance their loan. They may want to do this to take advantage of a lower rate, or to take equity out of their home to carry out home improvements, buy a new car, pay off unsecured debts, or meet other financial needs. Refinancing is only possible if the property has risen in value or a higher loan-to-value mortgage can be obtained. "Cash out" refinancing means that customers will increase their borrowing and the new loan will be more than the original mortgage, resulting in a higher new monthly payment.

The ability to take out a mortgage makes real estate an attractive investment because investors can take advantage of the benefits of leverage. Taking out a mortgage is a big financial commitment, but if used effectively, it can be a powerful tool to build personal wealth.

Lien Luu

See also: Banking; Condominium; Debt; Interest Income and Payments; Interest Rates; Loans; Real Estate; Rent to Own; Year 2007–2008: Subprime Housing Crisis and Mortgage Meltdown

Further Reading

Frasca, Ralph R. 2009. *Personal Finance: An Integrated Planning Approach*, 8th ed. New Jersey: Prentice Hall.
Madura, Jeff. 2014. *Personal Finance*, 5th ed. New Jersey: Prentice Hall.

Mutual Funds and Exchange-Traded Funds (ETFs)

Mutual funds and exchange-traded funds (ETFs) are pooled investment vehicles used by investors to invest in a variety of asset classes. Instead of an individual investing in a specific stock or a bond, mutual funds and ETFs collect a pool of capital from many investors and invest on behalf of these investors. Investors are charged a management fee for this service, referred to as the expense ratio.

Mutual Funds

Mutual funds are a way for an investor to participate in the stock, bond, or real estate investment market with a small amount of money. Investors pool their money and the fund company manages and invests those funds according to the specified investment policy of the mutual fund. Over the last 20 years, mutual funds have become very popular with more than 80 million people (one-half of all U.S. households) invested in them.

There are many varieties of mutual funds with a wide range of objectives. Index fund mutual funds have become quite popular recently with the manager investing in approximately the same companies as those in the popular stock and bond indexes. For example, the Standard & Poor's 500 stock index measures the price movements of the

500 most important companies in the United States and is widely duplicated by stock index mutual fund companies. The S&P 500 is not an investable index, that is, an investor cannot directly invest in the S&P 500 index, thus the mutual fund companies offer the opportunity for investing in that and many other popular stock market indexes.

Actively managed mutual funds attempt to beat the returns of index funds with additional security analysis and strategies. There are many actively managed funds with a variety of managers, strategies, fees, and approaches.

Exchange-Traded Funds (ETFs)

ETFs are a relatively new form of investment vehicle. An ETF is very similar to a mutual fund, yet it trades during the day like a stock on organized exchanges. Unlike a mutual fund whose net asset value (NAV) is calculated once per day at the end of the day, an ETF's price changes throughout the day based on supply and demand.

Originally ETFs were created to pool investors' dollars and earmark the moneys in funds designed to track a stock or bond or proprietary index. For example, SPY (SPDR S&P 500 ETF Trust) is designed to track the performance of the Standard & Poor's 500 (S&P 500) index. Investors are able to gain exposure to the S&P 500 index by investing in the SPY ETF, which replicates the index such that the returns generated from the index and the ETF are similar.

As ETFs gained in popularity, the variety of ETFs expanded. Thus, by using ETFs, investors are able to access a wide range of strategies for their portfolios, including sector-specific exposure (XLF—SPDR Financial Select Sector ETF), country-specific exposure (MCHI—iShares MSCI China ETF), region-specific exposure (VGK—Vanguard FTSE Europe ETF), market capitalization–specific exposure with leverage (TZA—Direxion Daily Small Cap Bull 3X, i.e., leveraged three times), and commodity-specific exposure (GDX—Market Vectors Gold Miners ETF). A tremendous benefit of these funds is their low expense ratios and the ability to buy or sell them on traditional stock exchanges throughout the day.

Fund Accessibility and Costs

Investors can access mutual funds and ETFs through a brokerage account, just as they can access stocks. Many investment companies offer mutual and exchange traded funds.

In comparison to actively managed mutual funds, the cost of investing in index mutual funds and ETFs is lower for investors, given their structure, which provides for tax efficiency. Holdings in ETFs generally are not bought and sold as frequently as those in actively traded mutual funds, thereby keeping capital gains taxes lower than in actively managed mutual funds.

The expense ratio varies across mutual funds. In general, index mutual and exchange-traded funds have the lowest expense ratios. Some mutual funds also charge sales and distribution fees (load), charged either upfront at the time of purchase (front load) or when shares are sold (back load). A mutual fund could have different share classes for investment, each with a different minimum investment and expense ratio. Investors have to invest the minimum investment amount in order to invest in a particular mutual fund.

Types of Mutual and Exchange-Traded Funds

Investors are able to access a wide variety of types of investments through mutual funds and ETFs. As a result, these vehicles have seen a large amount of investor fund inflows since they were launched. The most common classification in these vehicles is based on the asset class in which the vehicle invests. Simply put, asset class refers to the type of financial asset contained in the mutual fund; for example, stocks, bonds, real estate, commodities, or other.

Equity funds invest in stocks. Some stock funds are categorized according to the size of the company or market capitalization (current share price times the number of shares outstanding): large-cap (over $10 billion), mid-cap ($2 billion to $10 billion), small-cap ($250 million to $2 billion) and micro-cap (less than $250 million). Within each of these market capitalizations, the strategies vary by style: value, growth, and momentum. Each of these styles represents a distinct investment philosophy. Some of these strategies have an income (dividend) focus while some focus on capital appreciation. These funds can also be classified based on the geographic area that they invest in: domestic funds invest in the securities issued in the United States, international funds invest in securities issued throughout the world, emerging market funds invest in the securities issued in the emerging and frontier markets, and regional global funds invest in companies from across different regions.

Bond funds invest in bonds and may be categorized in many ways. Government bond funds include U.S. Treasury debt. Other types of bond funds carry municipal, corporate debt, convertibles, asset-backed securities, mortgages, and bond derivatives. Within each of these classifications the funds vary by the average maturity of the underlying instruments, by credit quality, and by the amount of income generated. Similar to equity funds, some bond funds have a mandate to invest outside of the United States. Bond funds are an important part of an asset allocation strategy to reduce risk or volatility in the investor's portfolio. Most bond funds pay a quarterly or monthly dividend, which endears them to retirement accounts due to their ability to generate income along with some capital appreciation.

Alternative funds have an investment mandate to invest in alternative asset classes of real estate, commodities, or other types of financial assets. A growing part of alternative funds are the complex strategies that differ from the traditional long-only strategies seen in equity and bond funds. These strategies include long/short equity, long/short credit, managed futures, event-driven, and global macro strategies. These alternative strategies have traditionally existed in a hedge fund structure and have recently seen an explosion within the mutual fund space.

Regulations and Investor Protection

All funds are guided by a prospectus that defines the investment strategy and mandate for the fund. The prospectus also provides other useful shareholder information such as fees charged, biography of management, and investment risks.

All mutual funds and ETFs in the United States are registered with the SEC (Securities and Exchange Commission) and are governed by the Investment Company

Act of 1940. Being regulated entities, these funds have to comply with the SEC regulations regarding liquidity, investor transparency, and fees, all of which have been implemented by the SEC for investor protection.

Surya Mrunalini Pisapati

See also: Asset Allocation; Bonds; Capital Gains and Capital Losses; Derivatives; Dividend Income; Hedge Funds; Index Mutual Funds; Investing; Real Estate Investment Trust; Retirement Accounts; Stock Market; Stocks

Further Reading

Bodie, Zvi, Alex Kane, and Alan J. Marcus. 2011. *Investments*. New York: McGraw-Hill/Irwin.
Bogle, John C. 2009. *Common Sense on Mutual Funds*. Wiley.

Net Worth

The net worth concept applies to both business and personal finance. Net worth describes how much an entity is worth. Determine the net worth of a business by adding the total of the things the business owns (assets) and subtract from this amount the total of what the business owes (liabilities). When it comes to determining an individual's net worth, we do the same thing. We add up all of the things the individual owns and subtract the amount of debt this individual owes. The amount that remains after subtracting the liabilities from the assets is called the net worth.

The Net Worth of a Business

As described above, the net worth of a business—net worth can also be referred to as net assets—is determined by subtracting the total liabilities of the company from its total assets. A company needs to determine its net worth in the event it is sold or forced to close.

For example, assume a company has total assets of $10 million. These assets might include land owned by the company and inventory. Assume the company owes its creditors $5 million—these are its liabilities. These liabilities include an expansion loan for the business and a mortgage on a factory. To determine this company's net worth, subtract its liabilities—in this case $5 million—from its assets—$10 million. The company's net worth is $5 million.

A company's balance sheet shows the net worth. A balance sheet is an accounting document that lists a company's total assets and liabilities along with the net worth. Of course, the balance sheet may not reflect the company's current net worth depending on when it was completed; it shows the value of the company at a particular point in time.

There are advantages and disadvantages when calculating a company's net worth. The biggest advantage is that it is a relatively easy way to determine a company's value, if it were to stop operating. In addition, looking at a company's balance sheet provides this information in an easy-to-read and easy-to-understand format.

A disadvantage is that since a balance sheet is similar to a snapshot, it reflects the company's net worth at a specific point in time. It does not always reflect the current value of a company. In addition, net worth does not always take into account items such as patents and the intellectual property of a company. For example, if one examined Apple's net worth before the iPod came out, one would not count that invention as part of Apple's assets since it was not released yet but was only a part of Apple's intellectual property at that point in time. We now know how valuable this idea was—along with the advent of the iPhone and iPad, which sprang from the popularity of the iPod. If someone determined the net worth of Apple in the summer of 2001 (before the iPod was released), he or she would not have been able to determine the true value of Apple since there was no way to foresee the impact of its intellectual properties.

The Net Worth of an Individual

The purpose of calculating a net worth statement for an individual is similar to that of a business. It is a way to figure out how much money the individual would have if all of his or her assets were sold. In general, personal property, with the exception of vehicles, is not included in the individual's net worth statement because one will not normally sell everything in order to raise money.

Net Worth Table

Assets (What Richard Owns)	
House (current value)	$100,000
Car (current value)	$10,000
Retirement Account	$30,000
Savings Account	$5,000
Checking Account	$2,000
Savings Bonds	$1,000
Total Assets	$148,000
Liabilities or Debts (What Richard Owes)	
House/Mortgage	$100,000
Car Loan	$20,000
Student Loan	$15,000
Credit Card Balances	$10,000
Total Debt	$145,000
Net Worth	
$148,000 – $145,000	$3,000

Net worth is the amount of money you are actually worth after subtracting what you owe from what you own. Many of us think that someone is wealthy if he or she has a lot of stuff. However, the accumulation of stuff can actually lower one's net worth. To illustrate this situation, take a look at a hypothetical example for Richard Stevens.

When completing an individual's net worth, one usually estimates the value of the home and vehicle using comparable sales of similar assets. All of Richard's assets total $148,000. That includes the current value of his home, car, retirement account, savings account, and checking account along with savings bonds he received as a graduation present.

Richard's debts include his home mortgage, which is the exact worth of the home. His car loan is actually greater than the current value of his car. This is because after a car is purchased its value tends to decline or depreciate significantly in the first several years. So the car actually has a negative worth ($10,000 – $20,000) or –$10,000. His additional debt includes student loans and credit card charges, which he does not pay off in full during the month the items are charged. Thus, Richard's total debts are $145,000. Richard's net worth is $3,000, which is calculated by subtracting his liabilities of $145,000 from his assets of $148,000.

If one purchases many things with a credit card and doesn't pay the credit card bill in full at the end of the month, one can amass a lot of debt. If the debts are greater than one's assets, this is called a negative net worth. That is how those who might appear wealthy, because they have a lot of stuff, might actually have a lot of debt and a negative net worth.

Net worth is an important concept for a business and individual. It is the way to measure whether the entity is making financial progress.

Danny Kofke

See also: Accountant; Cash; Investing; Liabilities; Loans; Savings Account

Further Reading

QFinance. "Calculating a Company's Net Worth." Accessed December 1, 2013. http://www.qfinance.com/contentFiles/QF02/hnrfm9bx/13/4/calculating-a-companys-net-worth.pdf

Obamacare *(see Affordable Care Act)*

Online Personal Finance

The digital generation gap is obvious when it comes to personal finance. A nationwide financial survey conducted in March 2013 found that younger investors would rather use a Web site for their financial planning needs than meet with an investment professional. That is not surprising. Young people have grown up with electronic access.

They are comfortable using the Internet for both personal reasons and to achieve professional and financial goals. And as they have made buying products via the Internet a regular practice, they have become more comfortable managing the money they use for those e-purchases with online personal finance tools.

The financial industry received the message. Banks, investment companies, and financial advisers are tailoring their products and services to meet the needs and wants of electronic and fiscally savvy individuals. Financial service providers also are progressing to mobile accessibility, with more personal finance apps being developed for smartphones. The government is even transitioning to electronic transactions for savings bond programs. From budgeting, to shopping, to banking, online personal finance has become a popular approach to handling financial matters.

Many individuals, especially younger people, also utilize a social media approach to their personal finances. They seek Web sites and blogs written by peers where they can share and compare their financial tips, successes, and concerns. In determining whether online personal finance resources are a good match, many of the same evaluation techniques used to determine the credibility and personal fit of traditional money management also must be considered for online personal finance sources.

Focus

One must take a critical approach when evaluating online personal finance resources. Does the online money management tool, Web site, or blog deal with personal finance in general or does it specialize? Some online programs are designed to help individuals save, either for a specific goal such as retirement or for a child's education. Others take a more wide-ranging approach, covering many areas of personal finance.

Features

Does the online money management Web site or management tool offer programs into which users enter personal data? Are the online resources easy to use? Can they be personalized? Does the site offer different scenarios so that users can compare multiple personal finance strategies?

Security

Is the site secure? This is crucial if users are required to enter personal data. What assurances are made regarding the safeguarding of personal information? Does the site have a privacy policy that is made available to users? If a password is required, are strict verification procedures required?

Licenses, Credentials, Credibility

If the site is a corporate one, does it identify the credentials of those supplying information online? Look for the types of featured financial advisors, such as certified financial planner (CFP); Chartered Financial Consultant (ChFC); registered investment advisor

(RIA); certified public account (CPA); Enrolled Agent (EA); personal financial specialist (PSF); or attorney with a special area of concentration. Such certifications also are good clues as to the value of advice provided on personal blogs and Web sites.

User Involvement

Does the program or money management system require a substantial commitment from the user? For example, does the money management system require frequent user inputs? A site that requires frequent updating and user attention is off-putting to some consumers. If there is a community of users, is it moderated and are there clear terms of service guidelines?

Discipline

Dealing with personal finances demands discipline. Instead of receiving paper statements or bills, the data come to the customer's e-mail box. If the recipient does not immediately open or download the documents, they could get lost in a crush of subsequent electronic communications.

Point of View

What is the blog's or Web site's financial point of view? Is it primarily a purveyor of news or does it focus on a specific age, gender, or social or economic philosophy? Is it very personal, sharing the author's own money experiences? Sites that are more personal tend to attract readers with similar tendencies who also want to share. Individuals who are reticent about revealing personal circumstances should look for a more discreet site.

Free or Fees

Are features on the site free or is there a charge to participate? If there is a charge, is it a flat fee or can users select levels of paid involvement? How is payment made? Again, is the payment method secure?

Sponsorship Influence

A corporate personal finance Web site obviously promotes its products. If the online personal finance site or blog is sponsored, does that affect the information or advice that is offered?

Online Personal Finance versus Financial Advisor

Ultimately, the decision whether to rely on online personal finance resources rests on the individual's comfort level, not only with the technology necessary to access sites and online tools, but also the comfort level of dealing with financial issues remotely. In contrast with a face-to-face relationship with a financial advisor, online personal finance demands additional responsibility from the user.

Kay Bell

See also: Banking; Financial Advisor; Tax Deferral; U.S. Federal Tax System Overview

Further Reading

Ary, Eddie J., and Christopher W. Brune 2011. "A Comparison of Student Learning Outcomes in Traditional and Online Personal Finance Courses." *Merlot Journal of Online Learning and Teaching* (December): Vol. 7, No. 4. http://jolt.merlot.org/vol7no4/brune_1211.htm

"Nationwide Financial Survey Finds Fear of the Markets Trumps Fear of Death." 2013. *BusinessWire* (July 24). http://www.businesswire.com/news/onenewspage/20130724005883/en/Nationwide-Financial-Survey-Finds-Fear-Markets-Trumps

Waymire, Jack. 2013. "How to Choose a Financial Advisor." *Forbes* (Jan. 3). http://www.forbes.com/sites/deborahljacobs/2013/01/03/how-to-choose-a-financial-advisor/

Opportunity Cost

Opportunity cost is a fundamental economics concept. Opportunity cost involves making a choice between exclusive options about how to make use of a resource. In other words, opportunity cost involves the decision to give up one or more choices in order to accept a particular choice.

This is generally a personal decision based on the perceptions of the person making the choice. The opportunity cost is then the other possible choices an individual could have made. The concept of opportunity cost is becoming more important in contemporary times as resources become scarcer and people become more aware of choices.

History of the Opportunity Cost Concept

People give credit to Austrian economists for the breakthrough of the concept as well as its initial claim. Known as the father of economic theory, Richard Cantillon (1680–1734), created and made use of the opportunity cost concept. Cantillon's ethical, logical idea did not involve a purposeful expense approach but simply an effort to estimate opportunity cost. This explanation pardons Cantillon from the accusation of being an objective cost theorist and predates the commonly accepted creation of opportunity cost by approximately a century and a half. If many other economic scientists comprehended this, they could possibly have avoided an enormous dead end in the labor theory of value. One of these researchers, Adam Smith (1723–1790), focused on this labor theory of value. This economic concept specifies that the worth of goods or services depend on the work used to produce or complete them (Thornton, 2003).

The early 20th century saw the formalization of the expression opportunity cost or alternative cost concept. During World War I, economist Friedrich von Wieser (1851–1926) posited that whenever the entrepreneur talks of earning expenses, the person's mindset focuses on beneficial means used to attain a particular outcome. However, this also mandates the connected notion of an expense from the individual person's labor (Brue, McConnell, and Flynn, 2010). Opportunity cost forces the individual to decide what to give up in order to make a given choice. If Jill chooses the cherry ice cream, she gives up the opportunity to eat the chocolate ice cream. The opportunity cost of this choice is the chocolate ice cream.

Components of the Opportunity Cost

Opportunity cost does not just involve financial expenditures alone but nonfinancial actions in life as well. This means that it involves not only finances but also individual wants and needs, work and energy, as well as time. Once one understands the assets and liabilities of the potential decision, one may have a better notion in terms of choosing.

It is important to comprehend both the direct expense of life and the indirect opportunity cost. Nobel Prize achiever in economics Milton Friedman said that a free lunch does not exist because opportunity cost influences all decisions. With every possible choice, a person either misses or acquires something.

There are various types of costs in terms of opportunity. For example, people could make choices between going to or completing school and seeking multimillion-dollar professional contracts in the sports or entertainment world. In choosing the entertainment world, this would mean that the person would have to forego the option to finish school or take part in tertiary education. One can say that the opportunity cost for people pursuing a sport or entertainment career is neglecting to go to or finish school. The antithesis of this scenario can be that people weighed the options differently and decided that education was more important than acquiring a profession in the entertainment or sporting world. For this alternate choice, the profession itself and the money that goes with it are the opportunity cost.

Opportunity cost is in the eye of the beholder and depends on the given situation; the choices made will differ from person to person. One person may make the choice to obtain a college education to achieve a certain dream and profession, while another may not see the benefit in doing so due to the costs. After individuals evaluate and weigh the costs of different situations, the results may differ. For example, an individual could choose to ignore the negative results of not attending college and focus on the positive results that come from the proposed decision to seek a dream profession.

In opportunity cost, there are explicit costs that entail a monetary compensation and implicit costs that contain no monetary compensation. Explicit costs entail disbursements of money like wages provided to workers. Implicit costs are the opportunity cost of assets the business's proprietor gives up such as loss of interest income when money is spent instead of invested. Opportunity costs are greater than explicit costs because opportunity costs have implicit costs.

Economists' versus Accountants' Views of Opportunity Costs

Economists as well as accountants use the concept of opportunity cost for different reasons. Economists use opportunity cost to explain the actions of businesses and individuals. Their agenda is to make the most profit by taking the total revenue of the best choice and subtracting the opportunity cost. Accountants use the same process but subtract revenue less the explicit cost.

On the other hand, economic profits are less than accounting profits, because accountants neglect the implicit costs since they are difficult to measure. The accountant cannot value the investment opportunity that was not selected when another financial decision is made (Levitt, 2012).

Tests of Opportunity Cost

Researchers Becker, Ronen, and Sorter (1974) directed a study to decipher if those who made decisions thought about opportunity costs. The study involved free opportunity cost information for individuals taking part in the study who were making decisions. The rationale for this action was to test whether people made use of the free opportunity cost advice during their decision-making process. If the participants did not make use of the advice, then there would be less reason to assume that the individuals would pursue the opportunity cost information when its acquirement was costly.

The outcomes demonstrated that the individuals did react to the free opportunity cost advice when they did not need to pay for it. In some instances, the participants paid no attention to the advice in terms of opportunity cost.

Opportunity Costs and Personal Finance

As the world continues to become more complex with resources becoming scarcer, the need to make sound decisions in all aspects of life will be crucial for individuals, societies, nations, and the world. As contemporary technology and the ability to become more educated throughout the world through swift communication are greater than in the past, the importance to think soundly in life's decision-making process is crucial for all people.

For example, in the 1960s, the fear of global warming was not in question. Yet today, there is great concern regarding the future depletion and proper use today of resources. Therefore, the question is whether countries including the United States make the proper opportunity cost calculations in their energy and policy choices. A serious consideration would be whether individuals and policymakers act to satisfy themselves or group agendas. Again, whether opportunity cost is right or wrong depends on who or what is making the decision.

Over the years, the term *opportunity cost* will provoke a wide range of responses in reference to choice. Decisions today differ from those of years past. What an individual or nation gives up when making a choice continues to impact that person's as well as that nation's financial situation.

Scott Glenn

See also: Accountant; Capitalism; Human Capital

Further Reading

Becker, S. W., Ronen, J., and G. H. Sorter. 1974. "Opportunity Costs—An Experimental Approach." *Journal of Accounting Research* 317–329.

Brue, S. L., C. R. McConnell, and S. M. Flynn. 2010. *Essentials of Economics*, 2nd ed. New York: McGraw-Hill Irwin.

Crompton, J. L., and D. R. Howard. 2013. "Costs: The Rest of the Economic Impact Story." *Journal of Sport Management* 27(5), 379–392.

Hoskin, R. E. 1983. "Opportunity Cost and Behavior." *Journal of Accounting Research* 21(1), 78–95.

Levitt, A. 2012. *The Role of Opportunity Cost in Financial Decision Making.* http://www.investopedia.com

Spiller, S. A. 2011. "Opportunity Cost Consideration." *Journal of Consumer Research*, 38(4), 595–610. doi:10.1086/660045

Thornton, M. 2003. *Richard Cantillon and the Discovery of Opportunity Cost.* Accessed from http://rachive.mises.org

Pension Plans

A pension plan is a type of retirement program where an employer contributes funds for an employee's future benefit. The pool of funds is then invested on behalf of the employee. That allows the employee to receive benefits upon retirement. A pension

Other Types of Retirement Plans

A simplified employee pension plan (SEP) is a relatively straightforward retirement savings scheme. This type of plan allows employees to make contributions on a tax-favored basis to individual retirement accounts (IRAs) owned by the employees. Under such a plan, an employee must set up an IRA to accept the employer's contributions. SEPs are subject to minimal reporting and disclosure requirements.

A cash balance plan is a defined benefit plan that defines the benefit in terms that are similar to those of a defined contribution plan. In other words, a cash balance plan defines the promised benefit in terms of a stated account balance. In a typical cash balance plan, a participant's account is credited each year with a "pay credit" (e.g., 5 percent of compensation from the employer) and an "interest credit" (either a fixed rate or a variable rate that is linked to an index such as the one-year Treasury bill rate). The benefit amounts are not directly affected by increases and decreases in the value of the plan's investments. Thus, the investment risks and rewards on plan assets are borne solely by the employer. The benefits in most cash balance plans are usually protected by federal insurance provided through the Pension Benefit Guaranty Corporation (PBGC).

plan is usually tax exempt. The two main types of pension plans are defined benefit plans and defined contribution plans.

Defined Benefit Plan

A defined benefit plan promises a specified monthly benefit at retirement. This promised benefit may be an exact dollar amount, such as $100 per month at retirement. But usually the benefit is calculated through a formula that considers such factors as salary and length of service. For example, a benefit might be calculated as follows: it might be computed by taking 1 percent of the average salary for the last five years of employment for every year of service with an employer. The benefits in most traditional defined benefit plans are usually protected by federal insurance provided through the Pension Benefit Guaranty Corporation (PBGC).

This type of pension plan is in contrast with other types of retirement plans whose payouts are dependent on returns of the underlying investments in the plan. Employees are required to work for a certain period of time (called a vesting period) before they are eligible to receive benefits in a defined benefit plan. In addition to a monthly payment, these pensioners frequently received a health care insurance plan. In many cases, these benefits were on top of the Social Security benefits the retiree received.

These plans were established in the late 1800s, according to Seburn (1991) in "Evolution of Employer-Provided Defined Benefit Pensions." The early pension plans covered workers in the railroad, banking, and public utilities industries. In 1974, the Employee Retirement Income Security Act (ERISA) was enacted to protect employees' benefit rights in private pensions.

By the 1980s the private pension system assets expanded exponentially. In spite of the growth of the assets in the defined benefit pensions, during the mid-1980s the medium- and large-sized companies that offered these plans began to shift toward private plans that were financed completely by the employees. Since these defined benefit pensions became very expensive to administer, new retirement savings options became available.

Furthermore, with the increase in smaller, service-oriented firms, the number of employer-funded retirement pensions decreased. Today, the individual who works for the same company throughout his or her career and receives an employer-sponsored pension is rare.

Defined Contribution Plans—401(k) and 403(b)

A defined contribution plan does not promise a specific amount of benefit at retirement. Under this type of plan, the employee, the employer, or both contribute to the employee's individual account, sometimes at a set rate, for example, 5 percent of earnings annually. These contributions generally are invested on behalf of the employee. The employee will ultimately receive the balance in the account, which is based on contributions plus or minus investment gains or losses. The value of the account will fluctuate due to the fluctuations in the value of the investments. Examples of defined contribution plans are 401(k) plans, 403(b) plans, employee stock ownership plans, and profit-sharing plans.

A 401(k) plan is a defined contribution plan that is a cash or deferred arrangement. The 401(k) plans can be offered by all employers except governmental employers. Under this type of plan, employees can elect to defer receiving a portion of their salary, which is instead contributed on their behalf, before taxes, to the 401(k) plan. Sometimes the employer may match these contributions. There are special rules governing the operation of a 401(k) plan. For example, there is a dollar limit on the amount an employee may elect to defer each year. Employees who participate in 401(k) plans assume responsibility for their retirement income by contributing part of their salary and, in many instances, by directing their own investments.

The tax benefits to employees who contribute to a defined contribution plan such as a 401(k) are important. For example, if an employee earns $4,000 per month, that employee ordinarily pays tax on the entire amount earned. Yet, if the employee elects to contribute $500 per month to the 401(k) plan, he or she will only be taxed on $3,500 ($4,000 − $500) per month. When the employee retirees and withdraws the retirement savings, the income taxes will be due on the amount withdrawn at that time.

Although the employee owns his or her plan contributions, some employers require the employee to work for the organization for a predetermined length of time before becoming vested or "owning" the employer's contributions. Thus, if the employer required five years for the worker to become vested and receive the employer's contributions, then if the worker left the firm after three years, he or she would be ineligible to receive the employer's portion of the contribution to the pension plan.

A 403(b) plan is similar to a 401(k). The basic difference between the two types of plans is eligibility. The 403(b) plan is limited to 501(c)(3)s or tax-exempt nonprofit organizations. The 403(b) plans are frequently administered by government or nonprofit employers such as K–12 schools and nonprofit colleges and universities. Another substantive difference between the 401(k) and 403(b) plans is that the latter is normally required to fund the investments with annuity contracts and mutual funds.

A profit-sharing plan or stock bonus plan is a defined contribution plan under which the plan or the employer may determine, annually, how much will be contributed to the plan (out of profits or otherwise). The plan contains a formula for allocating to each participant a portion of each annual contribution. This plan is quite flexible in that the contribution amounts can be adjusted annually. This plan offers a secondary benefit. It allows employees to feel as though they have a stake in the future of the company and when the company profits, so do the employees.

An employee stock ownership plan (ESOP) is a form of defined contribution plan in which the investments are primarily in employer stock. Similar to a profit-sharing plan, employees also benefit in the company's growth. When the firm's stock increases, so does the value of the employees' stock options. There are additional tax benefits to both the employer and employee.

There are many other types of pension plans including individual retirement accounts (IRAs), Roth individual retirement accounts, and other varieties of the aforementioned accounts. The government and the financial industry frequently devise new retirement savings alternatives so that workers are not completely dependent on the Social Security system for their future financial well-being.

Ramya Ghosh

See also: Annuity; Capital Gains and Capital Losses; Compound Interest/Return; Estate Planning; Investing; Retirement; Retirement Accounts; Social Security

Further Reading

Brandon, Emily. February 21, 2012. "10 Important Ages for Retirement Planning." *U.S. News & World Report.* http://money.usnews.com/money/retirement/articles/2012/02/21/10-important-ages-for-retirement-planning

Seburn, Patrick W. 1991. "Evolution of Employer-Provided Defined Benefit Pensions." *Monthly Labor Review*, December. http://www.bls.gov/opub/mlr/1991/12/art3full.pdf

TIAA-CREF Financial Services. "Differences Between 403(b) and 401(k) Plans." Accessed May 27, 2014. http://www1.tiaa-cref.org/plansponsors/resources/compliance/403b/resources/faqs/faqs_differences_403b_401k.html?ssSourceSiteId=tcpub

Portfolio Management

Portfolio management describes the activities necessary to manage a pool of investments. The essential basics of portfolio management include defining or identifying investment objectives, identifying resources and limitations, constructing the investment portfolio, and monitoring and revising the portfolio. The first step in investing is perhaps the most important. Most people only think of investment as part of retirement planning. In fact, purchasing a house, saving for one's children's college fund, bequests, and savings for emergencies are all part of one's investment goals. The sooner these objectives are identified, the easier it will be to achieve them.

The earning power of individuals usually follows a pattern known as the income life cycle in economics. In general, one tends to earn less in the earlier stages of adult life and also to accumulate debts during that period. As one improves one's educational attainment and experiences, earning power increases over time as well. This is generally the period when mid-aged adults pay off the debts accumulated in the first phase of life. The increase in earning power eventually diminishes and either stabilizes or declines as one approaches retirement. This is the third phase of the income life cycle. The accumulation of excess income available for investments usually occurs during phases two and three. While earning power and ability to set aside excess income are easiest in the latter part of phase two and most of phase three, the best time to start investment planning is in the latter part of phase one. Due to the effect of compounding, a small amount invested in the early part of phase one will have significantly higher returns than a large amount invested in the latter part of phases two or three. Failure to set investment goals early in life will cost significantly.

Thus, when setting investment objectives, the impact of the time value of money must be taken into consideration. It might be worthwhile to delay some major purchases or spending. Sometimes, it may be worthwhile to take out a loan and not reduce the amount put into investment. One such example is the purchase of a house by taking out a mortgage. The idea that all debts are bad is naïve. Debts that are for consumption purposes are bad. But debts that could improve future income or lower costs are good. College tuition loans (up to a certain point) and mortgages are examples of good debts.

It is also important to set investment objectives that are realistic and practical. One cannot expect a rate of return higher than the market average without the willingness to take on additional risks. Your investment advisor or portfolio manager should be able to help you identify a class of assets that meets your desirable level of risk and return. If you are a member of a board of trustees for an endowment fund or trust, you will need to have an investment policy that guides the portfolio manager on how to invest the fund. The portfolio manager can serve in an advisory role in setting the investment policy, but the main responsibility on this task lies with the board.

Common investment objectives considered in portfolio management include growth of income, stability of principal, income (or cash flow), and capital appreciation. Some of these objectives are mutually exclusive. For example, stability of principal and capital appreciation are mutually exclusive. The role of cash and liquid assets that would meet the spending need throughout an individual's life cycle is also an important factor to consider in setting objectives.

Portfolio Construction and Management

Once the investment objectives and resources are identified, the next step is to construct a portfolio that will achieve those objectives. It is not enough to realize that it is important to invest early. It is also important to identify the asset class that will give you the best return for a given level of risk. The historic average return for stocks is about 9 percent to 12 percent, depending on the market capitalization of the stocks. The average return for corporate bonds is about 7 percent and the average for U.S. Treasuries is about 5 percent. Other asset classes typically have 5 percent or lower returns on average. Given these figures, if you want to achieve more than a 10 percent return, stocks will be your only option. So, if you delay your investment process, you might not be able to achieve your goals without increasing your contributions greatly. Leveraged asset classes (options and futures, for example) are typically more speculative and carry more risk. They are not ideal for most investors.

There are a few special investment strategies that result in higher levels of return. Value investing and contrarian investing strategies both outperform the broad market index by about 2 percent of returns annually. But if more investors are participating in these strategies, their returns will decline accordingly.

Most individuals will likely never utilize the services of an investment professional. Most people have their retirement saving account through their work and just assume that the company will do the work for them. This is one of the biggest mistakes most people make, and they often never find out until it is too late. Most companies utilize the services of one of many mutual fund companies or the wealth management division of a major bank to manage their 401(k) plans. These management companies have no fiduciary duty to the planholders. Typically, it is the human resources department of the company that decides, with advice given by the management company, on the default investment options. The initial options can range from ultra-safe assets such as U.S. Treasuries, or even money market funds, to equity index funds. The most common default nowadays is either a balanced fund or a life cycle fund. A life cycle fund will reset the asset mix automatically throughout an individual's life cycle. As the age of the individual increases, getting closer to retirement, the fund's mix will move more toward bonds and less in equities.

This is a passive investment strategy that will do well for most individuals who have no time or very little knowledge about the various investment options. But the management company has no responsibility to put your investment fund into their best performing funds in certain asset classes. So, the typical life cycle fund often performs below the market average of a portfolio with a similar asset mix. Therefore, it is very important to pay attention to the asset allocation policies for any life cycle funds, and perhaps pick your own set of funds that will match similar risk characteristics. Picking one's own index funds may reduce fees by reducing total expenses.

For the individual investor who has more time and/or knowledge, actively engaging in adjustment in asset allocation may yield better returns in the long run. However, anticipatory changes to asset allocation (known as tactical strategy) can only work if one's timing is right most of the time. This strategy is very difficult even for the most seasoned portfolio manager. Thus, passive strategies with annual rebalancing might be more preferable than active investing strategies. It has been shown that dollar cost averaging (consistent monthly, quarterly, or annual contributions into investment accounts) yields better outcomes than market timing strategies over the long run.

While a passive strategy is preferred over active strategies for portfolio management, revisions must be made when there are major events in an individual's life cycle. Major changes in one's financial condition (getting a higher paying job, being laid off, marriage, divorce, having children, etc.) should trigger revision in one's investment portfolio. Portfolio management requires an overview of one's total investments and is important for both individual and professional investors.

Leo H. Chan

See also: Asset Allocation; Behavioral Finance; Bonds; Capital Gains and Capital Losses; Compound Interest/Return; Dividend Income; Index Mutual Funds; Opportunity Cost; Stock Market; Stocks

Further Reading

Strong, Robert A. 2009. *Portfolio Construction, Management and Protection*, 5th ed. Mason, OH: South-Western.

Power of Attorney

A power of attorney (POA) is a legal document in which an individual gives another person power to act in his or her stead. The person appointed to serve in the place of another is frequently called an attorney-in-fact. The power given may be narrow and limited to one situation, such as signing documents for a real estate transaction, or broad to cover all types of legal transactions. Or, the power of attorney may be durable and last while the individual (principal) is alive and after his or her death.

A power of attorney is effective at execution. When the principal remains competent, the power of attorney may be revoked at any time.

The POA document is an important personal finance concept as it touches on many business and estate-planning situations. This entry will discuss the many types and uses of the power of attorney.

When Is a Power of Attorney Needed?

There are a variety of circumstances when a power of attorney is needed. The case of a sudden illness or accident might cause an individual to be unable to handle financial affairs. This creates the need for a power of attorney. In other expected circumstances, such as when an older adult is losing his or her mental capacities, a power of attorney is created so that a trusted individual can care for and handle the incapacitated principal's affairs.

The POA might be created for a one-time business event when a participant in a transaction is unable to be present to sign documents. In this case, the principal selects another person to serve as his or her agent for this specific purpose.

General, Durable, or Limited Power of Attorney

A general power of attorney gives the person appointed (the agent) the power to manage the principal's assets and financial affairs while the principal is alive. The document gives the agent specific directions, and the document must be signed by the principal while he or she is mentally competent. The general power of attorney may be for a specific period of time and can be revoked by the principal at any time. The general power of attorney ceases on the death of the principal. After the death of the principal, the POA agent is replaced by the executor of the deceased individual's estate.

A durable power of attorney continues after the principal becomes incapacitated and is unable to handle his or her own affairs. The durable POA must specify the terms so that the order continues after the principal becomes unable to handle his or her affairs.

Power of attorney documents are important to execute when an elderly family member is at risk of losing mental capacity. For example, should an elderly parent have difficulty paying bills and handling normal financial decision making, a son or daughter may be appointed to serve in their parent's stead with the power of attorney document. An attorney typically assists the family to decide which type of power of attorney to execute. The power of attorney documents are frequently created when an estate plan and will are generated.

The limited power of attorney is drafted for a specific purpose and a restricted period of time. For example, when a homeowner is buying a vacation home and is unable to attend the property settlement (when the purchase documents are signed), she might give a limited power of attorney to her realtor. In this case, her agent or attorney in fact signs all the legal paperwork required to purchase the vacation home on her behalf. After that one incident, the POA is terminated.

Medical Power of Attorney

As it sounds, a medical power of attorney is created to handle expected medical situations. It may also be called a health care directive or "durable power of attorney for health care" and is designed to carry out one's predetermined health care wishes. This legal document would be executed in the case of accident, illness, or aging and loss of mental capacity.

The medical power of attorney is created to handle medical decisions that the principal is unable to carry out competently. For example, when an incompetent elderly patient is unable to eat and needs a feeding tube, the agent under the health care directive decides whether to authorize this treatment or not.

Another type of document may also be considered in the above example. The "Do Not Resuscitate (DNR)" order, created by a doctor on the request of an individual or family member with power of attorney, is useful when an individual is terminally ill or very elderly. The DNR goes into effect if the individual does not want CPR or other extraordinary measures used to prolong life. In the above feeding tube example, if there is a DNR, the agent may decide that the feeding tube is not compliant with the DNR and is an invasive treatment that will artificially prolong the life of the patient. Thus, the agent will refuse the insertion of the feeding tube.

Financial Power of Attorney

Financial power of attorney gives another the right to handle financial matters on the principal's behalf. The limited power of attorney in the above real estate example granted a limited financial power of attorney.

The durable financial power of attorney is the most inclusive POA and as previously mentioned is in force when the principal is competent and incapacitated as well as during the principal's life and after death. Separate financial and medical power of attorney documents are important as the two types of instructions include quite dissimilar topics and both need great specificity.

Sample Duties and Qualities of a Power of Attorney Agent

The person given a power of attorney is a trusted family member, close confidant, or legal or financial professional. The agent keeps in close touch with family members to discuss the requisite financial and medical care decisions (depending on the type of POA). The agent's duties may be as simple as paying bills and completing tax returns to the more complex tasks of monitoring the principal's financial accounts. The agent needs common sense and a commitment to the best interests of the principal.

The general duties of an agent include paying bills necessary for the principal's maintenance, property, and well-being. If the principal has dependents, the agent may provide support for them as well. All actions must be in compliance with the duties spelled out in the legal POA document.

Organization is important for the agent along with attention to detail. When transactions are made on behalf of the principal, the agent must keep accurate records. After the death of the principal, the agent must remain in compliance with the will and the estate plan of the deceased.

Accepting the responsibility of attorney in fact is a big decision. If an individual does not feel competent to take on the responsibilities, he or she may decline the appointment.

Barbara Friedberg

See also: Estate Planning; Probate; Wills and Trusts

Further Reading

Free Dictionary by Farlex. "Power of Attorney." Accessed May 12, 2014. http://legal -dictionary.thefreedictionary.com/Power+of+attorney

Irving, Shae. "Do-Not-Resuscitate Orders." Accessed May 10, 2014. http://www.nolo .com/legal-encyclopedia/do-not-resuscitate-orders.html

Irving, Shae. "The Durable Power of Attorney: Health Care and Finances." Accessed May 12, 2014. http://www.nolo.com/legal-encyclopedia/durable-power-of-attorney-health-finances-29579.html

Scotia Bank Web site. "Your Duties as Power of Attorney." Accessed May 10, 2014. http:// www.scotiabank.com/ca/common/pdf/spcg/your_duties_as_power_of_attorney.pdf

USLegal.com. "Power of Attorney Law and Legal Definition." Accessed May 10, 2014. http://definitions.uslegal.com/p/power-of-attorney/

Probate

Probate is the legal process, conducted by a court with appropriate jurisdiction, in which the validity of a deceased person's will (if any) is proved and the person's estate (property, debts, and taxes) is administered. "Probating a will" is the act of proving the validity of the will itself; the "probate process" is the legal proceedings followed to administer the estate. In modern times, the terms *probate, probating a will* and *probate process* are often used interchangeably.

History of Probate

Probate, like many aspects of American law, finds its roots in England during the Middle Ages. During this period the ecclesiastical courts established jurisdiction over the inheritance of personal property. With that jurisdiction, the idea developed that courts should determine whether a will was genuine or not. The first secular probate court in the United States was established in Massachusetts in 1784, building on a tradition of secular courts with authority over probate and other matters, which had developed during the colonial period. Probate courts with jurisdiction over the transfer of both personal and real property became well established in the United States during the 19th century, and the modern probate court is often empowered to deal with a variety of other relevant matters.

The Purpose of Probate and the Probate Process

The primary purpose of probate is to demonstrate that a will is valid (or genuine). This avoids fraudulent wills and assures that the deceased person's wishes for the distribution of property and the care of loved ones are fulfilled as directed, at least to the degree possible given the financial assets available in the estate.

Probate provides an orderly and enforceable process for the transfer of personal property, real estate, and other assets from the deceased to the living. It also generally allows for the appointment of guardians and other legal representatives to protect vulnerable dependents of the deceased, such as minor children.

How the Probate Process Works

Upon death, a case is filed with the local probate court. If the person left a will, the individual named as executor in the will (or his or her attorney) will file the case. If the deceased died without creating a will, a situation known as dying "intestate," an interested party such as a family member (or his or her attorney) will file the case.

If there is a will, once the case is filed the executor will probate it, or prove that it is valid. In the vast majority of cases, this is now a routine matter due to the development of "self-authenticating" wills. Generally, a person must sign his or her will in front of at least two witnesses, who in turn also sign the will. During the probate of a will the witnesses must then testify before the probate court that the deceased signed the will in their presence without fraud or undue influence.

With a self-authenticating will, at the same time the person signs the will in their presence, the witnesses sign written statements that the deceased was of sound mind and not under undue influence. If these witness statements are included in the will, the witnesses are not required to testify before the probate court when the will is being probated.

A self-authenticating will is generally admitted by the court unless it is actually being contested (opposed) by someone else, in which case the court conducts a thorough review of the documents, witnesses, and relevant facts. The probate of a will can only be contested on certain grounds, such as fraud, incapacity of the deceased to make a will at the time it was created, or failure to follow the required legal formalities.

Once the will is admitted by the probate court, the executor is recognized by the court as the representative of the deceased person's estate. If the deceased died without a will, the court will appoint an administrator to be the representative of the deceased person's estate.

The executor or administrator will then begin administering the estate. First, the relatives and creditors of the deceased are notified. Then the assets of the deceased must be found, secured, and when appropriate managed to ensure their value is maintained. The probate process can last anywhere from a few months to a year depending on the circumstances.

The outstanding debts of the deceased are identified during the probate process. These debts must be paid off by the estate before any property is distributed, even if property must be sold in order to pay the debts.

Once all of the debts have been identified and paid, the probate court allows the remaining assets to be distributed to the individuals named in the will. If the deceased died intestate, state law will specify who is to receive the property. This is often referred to as "intestate succession." Anyone who inherits or is entitled to inherit property from the deceased by will or by intestate succession is known as an "heir." Once all of the assets have been distributed to the heirs, a final report is filed with the probate court and the estate is closed.

Guardianship of Minor Children

Often a will contains instructions on the appointment of a legal guardian for a minor child of the deceased. In these cases the probate court will investigate to ensure the proposed guardian is qualified and appropriate. If there is no directive for the appointment of a guardian for a minor child, the probate court must determine who the guardian should be based on the best interests of the child.

Estates Not Requiring Probate

Not every deceased person's estate must be probated. There are also circumstances when part of one's assets need to go through probate, and other assets do not. If the deceased used certain estate planning tools to distribute his or her assets after death outside of the probate system, no case may need to be filed. For example, trusts created during one's lifetime may be structured to distribute assets without going through probate. Certain retirement accounts may also have beneficiary statements that pass the assets directly to the individual listed on that form. If an account is titled "joint ownership with right of survivorship," then when one owner dies, the remainder of the account automatically transfers to the other owner. In general, life insurance proceeds do not pass through probate. If the deceased had no assets at death, the probate process is unnecessary.

John C. Linfield

See also: Debt; Estate Planning; Life Insurance; Tax Return, Federal; Wills and Trusts

Further Reading

Christianson, Stephen G. 2001. *How to Administer an Estate: A Step-by-Step Guide for Families and Friends*, 4th ed. Franklin Lakes, NJ: Career Press.

Esperti, Robert A., and Renno L. Peterson. 1992. *The Living Trust Revolution: Why America Is Abandoning Wills and Probate*. New York: Viking Penguin.

Haertle, Eugene A. 1962. "The History of the Probate Court." *Marquette Law Review* Vol. 45, No. 47: 546. Accessed November 15, 2013. http://scholarship.law.marquette.edu/mulr/vol45/iss4/7

Real Estate

Real estate is a significant source of personal wealth for many Americans. Data from the Federal Reserve show that in 2013 a third of U.S. personal wealth (or $20.8 trillion) was held in real estate. While many people make money from real estate, a wrong decision can have adverse financial consequences. An understanding of real estate therefore can help investors make the right investment decisions and avoid costly mistakes.

Definition of Real Estate

Real estate is defined as both the land and its improvements. This could include structures, buildings, crops, or even mineral rights. It is part of the class of investments known as real assets, which include things like commodities and natural resources. They are grouped together as they share many characteristics—they are a "real asset" in that we can touch and feel them, they tend to be more long-term in nature, and they are seen to provide good protection against inflation.

Types of Real Estate

Real estate purchased as an investment provides two forms of potential returns—income and capital growth. Real estate that can be rented (such as office buildings and apartments) generates income in the form of rental payments. In addition, investors can also make a profit from real estate by selling the property for a higher price than they had paid for it (Madura, p. 9).

Real estate can be broken down into several core groups. Residential real estate usually refers exclusively to single-family housing. Commercial real estate has a business purpose rather than personal use. Commercial real estate comes in the following forms: retail, industrial, multifamily apartments, offices, and hospitality.

Retail real estate includes shopping centers and malls. Industrial real estate is used by businesses for production and storage of goods. Industrial real estate includes manufacturing plants, warehouses, and so on. Multifamily real estate includes apartment buildings and usually refers to a residential property with more than four units. Office buildings range from large urban towers to suburban office parks. Hospitality real estate encompasses hotels and resorts.

For many ordinary people, their experience in real estate is likely to involve buying a home for personal use. This is likely to be the largest single purchase individuals will make in their lifetime, and the largest single asset they are likely to own. As their wealth increases, they may wish to invest in commercial real estate to achieve diversification.

Factors Affecting the Value of Real Estate

Buying real estate is likely to be the single biggest investment decision individuals make. Prices of real estate are determined by a wide range of factors, including physical factors such as size, construction, type of property, and location; economic factors such as prevailing economic conditions and job prospects; emotional factors such as desirability and popularity of the area; and the availability of facilities such as schools and transport links (Madura, pp. 270–271).

Location is a pivotal factor in determining the return on real estate investments. In general, real estate with unique features (such as location by a lake, with good view, etc.) tends to achieve higher prices as it is highly sought after. Real estate prices are also affected by economic conditions. The value of real estate in big cities, where there are better job opportunities, tends to be higher as well.

Real estate prices are also affected by the ability to get insurance. Areas prone to natural disasters will be difficult to insure and prices will be affected as a result.

Like all financial assets, supply and demand affect real estate prices. During the recent housing boom in the middle of the first decade of this century, housing prices appreciated rapidly, only to fall dramatically as the trend reversed, foreclosures increased, and elevated housing prices returned to normal levels.

Popularity of Real Estate as an Investment

People like to invest in real estate for several reasons. First, it is a tangible asset—they can feel and touch it—and so it is easier to understand than other types of investments. Unlike other assets such as stocks, real estate also gives investors or owners control as they can add value to it through renovation and further development. Second, as land has a limited supply, real estate should experience significant capital growth in areas with a dense population. Third, real estate is popular because it offers investors protection in times of increasing inflation.

In periods of rising prices, real estate is seen as good protection against inflation because its real value often increases faster than the rate of inflation. In 1970, for example, the inflation-adjusted median price of a home was $25,000. By 1978 the price doubled to $50,000, according to JParsons.net. During the same 1970–1978 period, the Consumer Price Index (CPI) increased from 38.8 to 65.2 for an increase of 40.49 percent. Consequently, housing prices grew faster than inflation.

The ability to benefit from leverage (or gearing) also increases the attractiveness of real estate. Unlike other assets, it is possible to finance the purchase of real estate through borrowing. Mortgage loans allow investors to benefit from leverage, which can magnify the returns when the value of their assets grows.

For example, with a $10,000 down payment, you can borrow $90,000 to purchase a house worth $100,000. If the value of your house goes up by 10 percent, the new value will be $110,000. If you decide to sell the house, you will need to pay off the $90,000 mortgage, leaving you with $20,000 ($10,000 down payment and $10,000 profit). This means a 10 percent rise in the value of the property gives you a 100 percent return on your initial investment. This process of using a small investment and borrowed funds to acquire an asset is called leverage.

The value of real estate can go up and down, and you can lose your money if the value goes down. In the above example, if the property value drops by 10 percent to $90,000, the value of your house is the same as the value of the loan on the property. If you sell, you will only have enough to repay the debt and would have lost your original investment of $10,000. If the property value drops by 20 percent, the house value will be $80,000, lower than your mortgage loan. In this situation you are said to have a negative equity.

Real Estate and Tax Benefits

Home ownership has tax advantages. When a profit is made in selling a home, for example, the first $250,000 of gain (or $500,000 for married couples) is exempted from capital gains tax (providing certain criteria are met, such as two years' ownership). This feature, combined with the general increases in house prices over the years, has made home ownership a very popular investment (Frasca, pp. 96, 214).

Drawbacks of Real Estate as an Investment

Despite its widespread appeal, it is important to be aware of the risks involved in real estate investment. Besides fluctuations in value, real estate is an illiquid asset. The value of real estate can only be converted into cash if you can sell it. The process of selling can be lengthy and costly. In addition, investment in real estate also requires a substantial investment of time and money (Frasca, p. 222).

An alternative way is to invest in real estate investment trust (REIT). REITs pool investments from individuals and use the money to invest in real estate. They commonly invest in commercial real estate such as office buildings and shopping centers (Madura, p. 511). Investing in REITs and home ownership allows investors to gain exposure to different real estate markets and achieve diversification.

Lien Luu

See also: Asset Allocation; Capital Gains and Capital Losses; Condominium; Debt; Homeowner's and Renter's Insurance; Inflation; Interest Rates; Investing; Liquidity; Mortgage; Year 2007–2008: Subprime Housing Crisis and Mortgage Meltdown

Further Reading

Frasca, Ralph. 2008. *Personal Finance: An Integrated Planning Approach.* New Jersey: Prentice Hall.

"Historical Consumer Price Index (CPI-U) Data." *Inflationdata.com.* December 22, 2014. http://inflationdata.com/Inflation/Consumer_Price_Index/HistoricalCPI.aspx?reloaded=true

"Inflation Adjusted House Prices." *JParsons,* accessed December 22, 2014. http://www
.jparsons.net/housingbubble/
Madura, Jeff. 2014. *Personal Finance*, 5th ed. New Jersey: Prentice Hall.

Real Estate Investment Trust (REIT)

Real estate investment trust (REIT) is a type of mutual fund. A pool of capital is collected from investors and invested directly in real estate or mortgages. REITs acquire, develop, lease, and manage real estate properties with the purpose of generating revenues from rents. They are traded on an exchange like stocks or grouped together in mutual funds or exchange-traded funds. For example, Simon Property Group Inc. (NYSE: SPG), the largest U.S. shopping mall owner, owning Simon Malls across the country, is a REIT that buys or builds a shopping mall and generates revenues from the rents collected from leasing out the property to various stores.

In order for a fund (pool of capital) to be qualified as a REIT, it must distribute 90 percent of its income back to the investors in the form of a dividend (also referred to as distributions). Given the periodic distributions, REITs are sought after by investors looking for securities with an ability to generate income along with capital appreciation.

Types of REIT

REITs are commonly classified based on the type of property in which they invest. REITs that invest exclusively in real estate properties are referred to as equity REITs. Within equity REITs there are various classifications.

Retail REITs invest in properties that derive rents from retail stores, that is, regional malls, shopping centers, free-standing stores and so on, which usually have a large anchor store like a grocery, pharmacy, or department store, and several small stores. As investors in these malls, the REITs generate revenues from the rents collected from its tenants. REITs are responsible for the daily maintenance and upkeep of the property. Simon Properties (described above) is a good example of a retail REIT.

Office REITs invest in office buildings and corporate centers and generate revenues from the rents paid by the office tenants. REITs are responsible for daily maintenance and upkeep of the office buildings. In times of recessions, more office buildings become vacant and this impacts the revenues of office REITs. Boston Properties Inc. (NYSE: BXP) is an office REIT that owns several office buildings in major cities like New York City, Washington, D.C., Boston, and San Francisco.

Residential REITs invest in apartment communities and generate revenues from the rents paid by the tenants. Based on their expertise or location, some of the residential REITs focus on one particular geographic area or sector. For example, American Campus Communities Inc. (NYSE: ACC) owns and operates private student housing units across college campuses. Home Properties Inc. owns and operates apartment communities in selected cities in the United States.

Health care REITs invest in real estate serving the health care industry like senior housing communities, assisted living communities, medical offices, hospital buildings, research facilities, and skilled nursing facilities. Healthcare REIT (NYSE:HCN) is a good example of a health care REIT that invests across all of the above-mentioned facilities.

Other types of REITs target specific market niches. Included in these niche REIT investments are lodging and resorts (Hersha Hospitality Trust, NYSE: HT), self-storage properties (Public Storage, NYSE: PSA), farmlands (Gladstone Land Corporation, NASDAQ: LAND), timberlands (Weyerhaeuser Company, NYSE: WY), and data storage centers (Digital Realty Trust, NYSE: DLR).

Mortgage REITs differ from equity REITs. These REITs invest in real estate mortgages and real estate debt, which can be both residential (housing related) and commercial (nonresidential property types).

American Capital Agency Corp. (NASDAQ: AGNC) is a specific type of mortgage REIT that invests in residential mortgages (loans given out to homeowners) for which the principal and interest payments are guaranteed by U.S. government–related agencies like the Government National Mortgage Association (GNMA) or Federal National Mortgage Association (FNMA). Specifically, the lender of a government-guaranteed mortgage sells individual mortgages to the REIT company, which then combines many mortgages together into the REIT security (mutual fund). Investors purchase the REIT, which invests in the government-guaranteed mortgages. GNMA and FNMA give investors in this type of REIT a layer of protection against defaults by mortgage holders.

REITs that invest in both real estate properties and mortgages are referred to as hybrid REITs. For example, Ellington Financial LLC (NYSE: EFC) is a hybrid REIT that invests in residential mortgages, commercial mortgages (property loans issued to commercial properties like offices or warehouses), and other real estate–related securities (derivative instruments related to real estate companies).

Some REITs invest in a combination of the above property types and are referred to as diversified REITs. Vornado Realty Trust (NYSE: VNO) is a diversified REIT that invests in office buildings, shopping malls, strip malls, and lodging properties.

Leasing and Vacancies

For any property, the percentage of property that has been rented or leased is referred to as being leased and the percentage of property that has remained vacant is referred to as the vacancy rate. REITs aim to keep the vacancy rate as low as possible since higher vacancies lead to reduced revenues. A highly vacant shopping center will not drive the same amount of business toward the leased stores as does a fully leased center. This could lead to unhappy tenants. Hence, vacancy rate is an important measure of the quality of property in the real estate space.

REITs add diversification to an investment portfolio along with cash flow through the dividend distributions. Investing in a REIT gives investors an opportunity for exposure to real estate in their portfolio without owning individual real estate properties.

Surya Mrunalini Pisapati

See also: Asset Allocation; Debt; Dividend Income; Index Mutual Funds; Investing; Mutual Funds and Exchange-Traded Funds (ETFs); Real Estate; Stock Market

Further Reading

Block, Ralph L. 2012. *Investing in REITs: Real Estate Investment Trusts*, 4th ed. Bloomberg Press.

Registered Investment Adviser *(see Financial Advisor)*

Rent to Own

The choice of rent to own is different from just renting or purchasing a home or goods in general. When a consumer purchases a home, he or she pays the seller the value of the home. The buyer of the home normally pays part of the price from his or her own funds (the down payment) and part with money borrowed from the bank (a mortgage). The same process occurs when a consumer buys cars, furniture, electronics, and high-cost items. Individuals with poor credit or insufficient funds have an alternative method for obtaining a home, furniture, or electronics.

Rent to Own a Home

This action requires the creation of an agreement between the buyer and the seller involving the payments that are made each month based on the home's worth. In general, a rent payment is agreed on and part of the payment might be allocated to a future down payment.

The contract expiration date depends on the original agreement. Upon expiration of the contract, the renting party can elect to purchase the house at the initial given cost, excluding the equity that the renter has paid into the home.

If the renter declines the option to purchase the house at the end of the contract, the owner has the right to eject the renter and retain the total amount of money that the renter paid into the house. In addition, the owner can also keep the premium option fee agreed on in the beginning for the option to purchase, if the renter does not purchase the house. To make matters even worse for the potential homeowner, in some contracts any tardy payments can result in lost equity.

The renter must understand that there's a possibility that the value of the house might go down substantially during the rental period. If this happens, it means that the renter's fixed payment rates during the renting period result in the seller overcharging the renter.

It's important to consider the inherent risks in the choice of rent to buy and remember that agreements vary depending on the individuals who partake in the contract. Comprehending that contracts differ, renters should make sure that they are on the same page as the sellers. This may even include hiring a lawyer who can weigh the positives and negatives of renting to own (Woolsey, 2009).

Conerly (2013) posited that the decision to rent or buy varies depending on the person. Historically, people considered buying a house as a sound investment given the proper economic conditions. In today's housing market and with an untrustworthy economy leading to uncertain job status, both the desire to purchase a home and the ability to do so are limited. In earlier years, the choice to rent or own was mainly about whether to reside in an apartment or a house. Such is not the case in contemporary times. Ever since about the 1970s, housing has increased in value by an average of approximately 4.5 percent per year. Estimated house values before 1980 displayed 3.0 percent yearly surges in nominal worth and a little over 0 percent once people considered inflation.

Buying a home during sound economic periods appears to be an outstanding investment. With a 20 percent down payment put toward a home, a price upturn of only 3 percent translates into a 15 percent jump in the consumer's home equity, which people see as a money on money return. On the other hand, there is a negative aspect to this. Putting 20 percent down on the home and a 20 percent value regression eliminates the sum of the consumer's equity. Interest in the housing market is deductible but very much overregarded. The compensation of the deductible does not overpower the idea that the consumers are disbursing interest, putting the buyers in a poorer situation than they were in before investing.

Renting in comparison to buying has its advantages as well. With renting, the landlord is responsible for repairs. If people choose to buy, then they have to pay for the repairs. This can get very expensive, especially if the owners need to perform repairs on a regular basis instead of periods spread over a long duration. In the end, renting may save people more money because the expenses are not coming out of their pockets. On the other hand, when one chooses to rent, the ability to *own* the property is not there. This allows the owner the capacity to sell to someone else or increase the rent once the current agreement runs out.

When comparing renting to buying, one must keep in mind that some of the monthly payment goes to pay-off the principal amount of the loan. Another thought in terms of owning a home is that the transaction costs are enormous, and real estate negotiators will make one pay anywhere from 6 to 7 percent commission on a purchase. This makes moving from one house to another very costly, and the decision to buy should depend on how long the buyer plans on living in the house (Conerly, 2013).

Rent to Own Furniture, Electronics, and More

There are establishments that cater to individuals who can't afford to buy certain household items outright. These stores are typically called "rent to own" stores. The ability to rent to own can be beneficial, because the process grants a buyer who may have unsatisfactory credit the ability to acquire certain goods without the full commitment of an outright purchase.

Eligibility for this type of rental agreement differs depending on the specific arrangement. Eligibility usually depends on the buyer's proof of income and individual background. The rent to own business continues to do extremely well in the housing arena even among sustained allegations from purchaser factions and scholars who perceive rent to own contracts as hidden payment agreements. When alleged merely as payment agreements, the inferred annual percentage rates (APRs) are truly high even though the rent to own firms integrate the worth of added services in their computations (Anderson and Jackson, 2001).

In terms of a home, the option of rent to own enables the renter or buyer to indulge in the house purchase procedure without direct lender financing. The actual buyer's expense consists of a rent premium to the owner as well as an optional charge toward the house's overall buying price.

Controversy with the Rent to Own Concept

Anderson and Jackson (2001) cite Hill, Ramp, and Silver (1998); Renuart and Keest (1999); and Swagler and Wheeler (1989) in saying that contemporary economic findings have perceived rent to own arrangements as hidden payment agreements. These are disadvantageous to buyers by their obligation of the unrevealed use of interest rates. Anderson and Jackson also agreed with Walden (1990) in saying that analysts alleged that rent to own contracts produced astonishingly enormous rates of return to the seller or owner even after subtracting sensible business costs. No matter the case, whether one agrees to rent to own or not, the business continues to excel even with the various criticisms that exist.

Scott Glenn

See also: Credit Report and Reporting Agencies; Credit Score; Debt; Mortgage

Further Reading

Anderson, M. H., and R. Jackson. (2001). "A Reconsideration of Rent-to-Own." *The Journal of Consumer Affairs 35*(2).

Conerly, B. (2013). "Should You Buy a House or Rent? The Economics of Homeownership." *Forbes*. Retrieved from http://www.forbes.com/sites/billconerly/2013/11/11/should -you-buy-a-house-or-rent-the-economics-of-homeownership/

Hill, R. P., D. L. Ramp, L. Silver and J. C. Andrews. (1998). "The Rent-to-Own Industry and Pricing Disclosure Tactics." *Journal of Public Policy and Marketing 17*(1): 3–10.

Kapner, S. (2009). "Rent-to-Own Makes a Comeback." *Fortune 159*(12): 22.

Renuart, E., and K. E. Keest. (1999). *The Cost of Credit: Regulation and Legal Challenges*. Boston, MA: National Consumer Law Center.

Swagler, R. M., and P. Wheeler (1989). "Rental-Purchase Agreements: A Preliminary Investigation of Consumer Attitudes and Behaviors." *The Journal of Consumer Affairs 23*(1): 145–160.

Vida, D. (2012). "Servicing the Rent-to-Own Borrower." *Mortgage Banking 72*(10): 86.

Walden, M. L. (1990). "The Economics of Rent-to-Own Contracts." *The Journal of Consumer Affairs 24*(2): 326–337.

Woolsey, M. (2009). "Rent-to-Buy Pros and Cons." *Forbes*. Retrieved from http://www .forbes.com

Retirement

Retirement is a modern phenomenon. It refers to a time when people formally cease to engage in economic activities for a wage and become eligible for Social Security benefits. It is a great paradox that as life expectancy increases, many people are retiring earlier and spending more time in retirement than employment. An understanding of what retirement entails will help individuals prepare for and enjoy this stage in their life.

Retirement Definition

Retirement is an elusive concept and means different things to different people. Traditionally, retirement is seen as a distinctive life stage when we, according to *Webster's Dictionary*, "withdraw from one's position or occupation or from active working life," and a time of inactivity and recovery from years of working. Retirement is seen to represent an abrupt change in the life of the retired, and the concept is portrayed as a dichotomous one—an individual is either retired or not.

The traditional definition of retirement is no longer seen as adequate as it fails to capture the life of retirees in modern society. Although it is common for some people to stop work completely, many Americans are making a gradual transition. Some first reduce their hours of work to part-time status. Others leave a career and then start another, either full or part time, in the same industry and occupation or in a new line of work altogether.

Indeed, the time when people retire now is no longer fixed. It is paradoxical that at a time when life expectancy has increased and people are living longer, many people are retiring earlier and earlier. The working life is now much shortened. Legislation encourages early retirement as the Social Security system allows people to retire early at age 62 if they are willing to take a slight reduction in their monthly pension. Consequently, retirement at age 62 is more common than retirement at age 65 (Johnson, p. 591).

The average number of years spent in retirement has risen as a result. One third or more of life can now be spent in retirement. Those in the military or civil service with options to retire after 23 years of service may spend more years in retirement than employment (Shield, p. 179). This has stimulated the need for retirement planning as a professional service.

Social Security and Retirement

Retirement in the United States is symbolically linked to age 65, which has represented the retirement age (if you were born before 1937) since 1935. However, age 65 is not a retirement age but is the age of full entitlement to U.S. Social Security benefits (Johnson, p. 591).

The full retirement age refers to the age when an individual is eligible to receive full retirement benefits. The full retirement age is graduated, depending on birth year. Those born before 1937 reach full retirement age at age 65. Those born between 1937 and 1942 may receive full retirement benefits at 65 and several months, with the time increasing two months per birth year. Those born between 1943 and 1954 achieve full retirement age at age 66. Individuals born between 1955 and 1959 also add two months per year of additional time before full retirement age. If one is born after 1960, full retirement age is 67.

Beginning at age 62, individuals may receive partial retirement benefits. If you delay receipt of Social Security retirement benefits past full retirement age, you are eligible for a credit that increases your total monthly benefit.

Retirement Age

The growth of retirement as a socially accepted life stage has been facilitated by the growth of state- and employer-sponsored pensions. However, demographic trends are putting public funding under immense pressure. While it is believed the population over age 65 in the United States (about 30 million) will double in the next 40 years, the increase of the population under age 65 will be only 12 percent, and thus the ratio of those employed to those retired will be greatly reduced.

People now are also living longer, with the average life expectancy in the United States at age 81 for women and age 76 for men. This has serious consequences for public finances. When the Social Security Act was passed in 1935, only 15 percent of workers reached the age of 65, whereas in the 1990s more than 80 percent of workers did (Shield, p. 179). In addition, individuals may live anywhere between 5 and 25 years in retirement, and so funding this extensive period has proved very costly.

Expenditure on Social Security benefits to retirees therefore has seen an exponential growth, and it is expected to cost 6.7 percent of GDP in 2015. For those who rely on the government for an income in retirement, this change means that in the future they may have to work longer as there are increasing calls for the retirement age to rise to 68, 69, or even higher. The Bureau of Labor Statistics estimates that nearly 32 percent of Americans aged 65 to 74 will still be in the labor force by 2022, an increase from 20 percent in 2002 and 27 percent today. Changes in Social Security provisions widen the gap between those who have private wealth, which enables them to withdraw from the labor force earlier, and those who have no private provisions and must work longer than before.

Retirement Income

Most people experience a drop in income in retirement. The historic rule is that people need about 60 percent of their final salary to retain their current living standard during retirement and a higher replacement ratio (80 percent) if they intend to pursue an active life in retirement (Frasca, p. 459). On average, retirees only get about one-half to two-thirds of their preretirement income (Harris, p. 275), and many retirees live in poverty.

Many people have an inadequate income in retirement because Social Security was intended to provide a safety net, not the replacement income of a full-time job. In addition, many employer pension schemes are only available to those who work in large companies, and they only provide a portion of workers' former salary (Shield, p. 180). Consequently, those who do not have an adequate income do not retire, and this is made possible by legislation passed in 1986 removing mandatory retirement in the United States (Shield, p. 180). People now retire when they can afford to, while others reenter the labor force after retirement. A recent study shows that 15 percent of retired Americans reenter the labor force, and they tend to be those who are younger, in better health, and have a defined contribution pension plan (Cahill, Giandrea, and Quinn, 2011).

The Retirement Process

Retirement is not a one-off event, but a process. Robert Atchley has distinguished six phases: preretirement, honeymoon, disenchantment, reorientation, stability, and termination of retirement. Individuals may not experience all phases.

Literature in the 1960s often emphasized the negative aspects of retirement, such as economic deprivation and loss of occupational identity and social status. However, in recent years a number of economic and social factors have made the transition to retirement easier and a more rewarding experience. Many products and services cater to this expanding consumer market, including retirement housing, travel services, and senior citizen discounts, which all help to enhance the retirement lifestyle (Harris, p. 272).

Research by Schlossberg also shows that retirement can take many forms, allowing many retirees to engage in an active, fulfilling life. Retirees are classified into several groups: continuers, adventurers, searchers, easy gliders, involved spectators, and retreaters (Dittman, 2004).

Retirement is now seen by many as a time to do things and enjoy life, learn new information and new skills, and help others. Studies on retirement reveal that individuals who have a satisfactory retirement are those with good health and an adequate income (Harris, p. 274; Shield, p. 179).

Research also shows that planning ahead can help and that those who plan for retirement enter their golden years with higher levels of wealth. They are also likely to have a higher level of enjoyment as they have not stumbled into retirement and have planned so that they have the necessary financial resources to live their dreams.

Lien Luu

See also: Estate Planning; Pension Plans; Retirement Accounts; Social Security; Tax Deferral

Further Reading

Atchley, Robert C. 2000. "Retirement as a Social Role," in J. F. Gubrium and J. Holstein, *Aging and Everyday Life*, pp. 115–124. Wiley-Blackwell.

Cahill, Kevin E., Michael D. Giandrea, and Joseph F. Quinn. 2011. "Re-entering the Labor Force after Retirement." *Monthly Labor Review,* June. http://www.bls.gov/opub/mlr/2011/06/art2full.pdf

Dittman, Melissa. 2004. "A New Face to Retirement." *American Psychological Association Monitor* (November), Vol. 35, No. 10. http://www.apa.org/monitor/nov04/retirement.aspx

Frasca, Ralph. 2009. *Personal Finance: An Integrated Planning Approach*, 8th ed. Pearson.

Harris, Diana K. 1990. *Sociology of Aging*. United Kingdom: Rowman & Littlefield.

Johnson, Malcolm L., Vern L. Bengtson, Peter G. Coleman, and Thomas B. L. Kirkwood (eds.). 2005. *The Cambridge Handbook of Age and Ageing*. Cambridge: Cambridge University Press.

Lusardi, Anna, and Olivia S. Mitchell. 2006. "Baby Boomer Retirement Security: The Roles of Planning, Financial Literacy, and Housing Wealth." National Bureau of Economic Research, October. http://www.nber.org/papers/w12585

Quinn, Joseph F. 1990. *Passing the Torch: The Influence of Economic Incentives on Work and Retirement*. Kalamazoo, MI: Upjohn Institute Press.

Shield, Renee Rose, and Stanley M. Aronson. 2004. *Aging in Today's World: Conversations Between an Anthropologist and a Physician*. Oxford, NY: Berghahn Books.

Retirement Accounts

A retirement account is a type of investment account that allows workers to invest today's dollars for use in retirement. There are many types of retirement plans and one can invest in one or several simultaneously depending on one's income level and personal situation. The underlying benefit of a retirement account is to provide tax benefits for the individual to increase his or her net worth for retirement. In general, retirement accounts are structured to give a financial incentive (usually in the form of lower taxes) and encourage workers to save and invest for retirement.

Individual retirement account (IRA), Roth IRA, SEP (IRA), 401(k), and 403(b) are the names of the most common retirement accounts. There are additional retirement account options for small business owners and others.

Retirement accounts are designed to be funded during the individual's working life with the proceeds withdrawn during retirement. There are penalties and tax liabilities for withdrawing funds before retirement or age 59½ (whichever is earlier). This entry will discuss the most common types of retirement accounts: 401(k), 403(b), traditional IRA, and Roth IRA.

Types of Retirement Accounts

401(k) or 403(b)

For-profit companies offer 401(k) retirement accounts whereas 403(b) plans are offered to employees of nonprofit companies such as schools, hospitals, or religious groups. These types of retirement accounts are similar. Their main difference lies with the type of organization offering the plan. The law stipulates the maximum amount one can contribute to these and all retirement accounts annually.

There are several major benefits to 401(k) and 403(b) accounts. Employees contribute a set amount every pay period into the account with "pretax" dollars. In other words, the contribution is taken from one's paycheck before taxes are deducted. The result is lower taxable income. The employee chooses from a menu of various investment options for these funds.

The second benefit is that the money in the account grows tax free. No tax is due during the time the contributions are in the account. This benefit allows the money in the 401(k) or 403(b) account to compound more quickly.

Additionally, some plans allow the account holder to borrow funds from his or her own account. There are regulations governing these withdrawals, and it is generally a poor idea to borrow from a retirement account.

In some organizations, an employer also contributes to the employee's retirement account. In most cases, the employer "matches" the employee's contribution up to a certain percentage. Three to 6 percent are the "matching" benchmarks employers most frequently use.

Compound Returns Increase Retirement Account Balances

Consider this common workplace retirement scenario. Colleen earns $1,000 per week, contributes 5 percent to her retirement account, and receives a matching contribution from her employer of an additional 5 percent. So Colleen contributes $50 per week and her employer contributes another $50 for a total of $100 per week. In one year, Colleen's retirement account contributions equal $5,200.

The financial benefit of investing this money for retirement is massive. Assume Colleen invests in a combination of stock and bond mutual funds, whose average annual return is 7 percent. If Colleen's account contributions continue from age 30 until age 65, she (and her employer) will have contributed a total of $182,000 ($5,200 × 35) after 35 years.

Yet, Colleen's account, invested in stock and bond mutual funds and compounding at 7 percent per year, is worth $769,150 at age 65. Upon retirement, these savings, along with government Social Security income, will provide Colleen with funds to live on during retirement.

There are certain restrictions for these retirement accounts. If you make a withdrawal before age 59½, you may incur a 10 percent early withdrawal penalty as well as any taxes that might be due on the withdrawal.

Traditional IRA

The traditional IRA is another type of tax-advantaged retirement account. An individual and his or her spouse (if filing a joint tax return) can contribute if they have taxable compensation and are younger than age 70½. There are contribution limits for a traditional IRA. In 2014, each individual could contribute up to $5,500 or $6,500 if they are older than age 50. One cannot contribute more money than one earned. If the worker is covered by a retirement plan at work, high-income workers may not be able to contribute the full amount, or at all, depending on their income level.

Unless the worker is not covered by a retirement plan at work, the contributions are made with after-tax dollars. Workers who are not covered by another workplace retirement account may contribute pre-tax dollars to the traditional IRA and receive the same reduction in taxable income as the 401(k) or 403(b) plan participants. As with all retirement plans, once the contributions are made, they are invested and can grow tax deferred until withdrawn at retirement.

Roth IRA

This retirement account is distinct from the other types in that the contributions are always made with post-tax and never pre-tax income. In other words, contributions aren't tax deductible. Unlike other retirement accounts, no tax is due when Roth IRA contributions are withdrawn, in most cases.

If one has taxable income, there is no age restriction for contributing to a Roth IRA. Your modified adjusted growth income must be below certain levels in order to make a contribution.

The contribution levels for a Roth and a traditional IRA are the same and one cannot surpass those amounts in totality. The total amount someone over age 50 in 2013 may contribute to all of a traditional and Roth IRA is $6,500 each.

If moneys contributed to a Roth IRA are rolled over from another type of retirement plan, to avoid penalties, they must remain in the account for at least five years. Additionally, if the Roth IRA funds are withdrawn before age 59½, there may be a 10 percent penalty.

Unlike traditional IRAs, there are no minimum required Roth IRA distributions at any age. In fact, a Roth IRA may be left in place for the heirs of the account owner to inherit.

The Roth IRA is unique in another way. Funds may be withdrawn without penalty before age 59½ if the participant is totally and permanently disabled, uses the distributions to buy a first home, uses the distributions to pay qualified higher education expenses, and in a few other circumstances.

Required Minimum Distributions from Retirement Plans

The law requires most retirement account holders (with the exception of Roth IRA account owners) to take required minimum distributions (RMD) when they reach age 70½ and yearly thereafter. If the account holder does not comply, the amount not withdrawn is taxed at 50 percent.

Since the contributions to these retirement accounts were made with pre-tax dollars, they are taxable on withdrawal. Employees assume that during retirement their income will be less than it was while they were working, and thus they will pay lower taxes than they would have paid on that income without the retirement account.

There are no required minimum distributions for a Roth IRA. If the account owner is over age 59½, there is no penalty to withdraw funds from a Roth IRA; otherwise, as with a traditional IRA, there is an additional 10 percent tax penalty for ineligible early withdrawals.

The limits, types, and constraints of modern retirement accounts are constantly changing and evolving. In general, these tax-advantaged accounts are a cornerstone of modern personal finance.

Danny Kofke

See also: Compound Interest/Return; Estate Planning; Investing; Pension Plans; Retirement; Tax Deferral; Tax Return, Federal

Further Reading

RS.gov. "Tax Information for Retirement Plans." Accessed March 13, 2014. http://www.irs.gov/Retirement-Plans/

Risk

Risks are situations where individuals, families, or organizations are exposed to the possibility of a harmful aftermath through injury, death, or financial loss. Risks are either pure risks or speculative (investment) risks (Day et al., 2013; MacMinn, 2000; Schuchardt et al., 2007; Teale, 2008).

Pure Risks

Pure risks are the possibility of a peril occurring that always results in a financial loss. The main income earner of a family could die prematurely, leaving his or her financial dependents without sufficient income to pay their daily living expenses. This type of pure risk can be transferred to an insurance company or other third party.

Pure risks comprise personal risk, property risk, liability risk, and nonperformance risk. Individuals are vulnerable to personal risks when they face the possibility of death, illness, or injury causing a financial loss. The risk of someone with financial dependents suffering a major trauma so that the person is unable to work and earn an income can ruin the person financially.

Property Risk

Property risk typically occurs when physical assets are stolen, damaged, or destroyed. Two types of property risks are direct property losses and indirect property losses. Direct property losses occur when the property itself is lost, damaged, or destroyed. On the other hand, indirect loss refers to the consequential losses or additional financial costs that occur after suffering initial direct losses.

For example, a direct loss occurs when a driver's car is damaged in an accident and can't be driven anymore. The driver not only faces a direct loss, the damaged car, but also the indirect losses of the additional cost of using public transport, notwithstanding the inconvenience and extra time it takes to travel.

Liability Risk

When someone's actions result in loss to another's property, the upshot is the liability risk of an expensive lawsuit. The liability can arise under statute law, common law, and the law of contract.

The government of a country creates statute law. Common law, which has developed over many years, states that everyone owes a duty of care toward others in certain circumstances. A person should be held responsible for harm or loss caused by failing to observe appropriate standards, including negligence. A liability under contract explicitly or implicitly infers that the parties entering into the agreement accept this liability, such as an employer being liable for an employee if the employee is injured at work. Public liability occurs when a member of the public sues for damages occurring on someone's business premises. A worker suing for damages occurring at a residence where he or she is working is an example of personal liability.

Nonperformance Risk

Nonperformance risk happens when financial losses occur should one party agree to perform a certain service for another and then fail to perform this service completely.

Avoiding Pure Risk

Pure risk is defined as a risk with a certain negative outcome; there is no possible positive outcome. Pure risk can be handled by avoiding it altogether, controlling it, or financing it. Examples of pure risk include premature death due to illness, a natural disaster, or identity theft.

Risk avoidance is the ideal solution. The person facing the peril either removes the offending asset or stops the risky situation from taking place. Sadly, not all risks can be avoided completely, making room for risk control.

Risk or loss control is a method used to either remove the size (magnitude) or reduce the number of times (frequency) of the financial consequences of a loss.

The risk financing approach is to transfer the risk to another party such as an insurance company by way of contract. A second risk financing method is where someone decides to personally carry the risk themselves (risk retention/self-insurance), especially where it cannot be transferred and the cost of handling it themselves is less than transferring it.

Speculative Risk

Speculative risk, also known as investment risk, involves both the chance of a financial loss and, unlike pure risk, the possibility of a financial gain on an investment.

Those who invest money in shares on the stock exchange are exposed to the possibility that the share price of the investment may decrease below the price they paid for the investment, and thus they would experience a financial loss. Investors are averse to realizing losses on their investments. Yet the same investor could experience a gain if the share price rose more than the purchase price. The investor has no control over this. Investors can limit the effects of these risks by avoiding or controlling the risk. Not investing in the share market is a method of risk avoidance.

The risk control method used by investors is called diversification. Diversification is ensuring that the funds are spread over a range of countries, markets, market sectors, companies, or different types of investment products rather than putting "all the eggs in one basket." If one investment performs badly, this will be supported by the other better performing investments.

Using hedging and derivative products is a form of risk financing when facing speculative risks. In order to protect the investment against potential losses or adverse market movements, a hedging strategy uses the performance of one investment to counter losses in another investment.

Derivative financial products comprising options, forward rate agreements (FRAs), futures, and swaps are a form of insurance against speculative risk that lock in existing gains. Assume an investor already holds shares in Coca-Cola and has significant unrealized profit. The investor wants to continue holding the shares but is concerned that a market correction will cause the value of the shares to drop. So the investor purchases an option to gain the right to sell the shares at the current high price sometime in the future. If the share values drop in the future, then the investor can exercise this right and sell the shares at the higher price that was locked in when the Coca-Cola shares were high.

Some risky events may be relatively unimportant and have no significant effect on someone financially. Bearable losses have a severe impact on a person's financial situation, but do not result in bankruptcy. Unbearable losses may result in bankruptcy. The severity and probable frequency of the peril will determine how it should be managed to eliminate or minimize the financial loss.

Angelique N. S. McInnes

See also: Asset Allocation; Bankruptcy; Capital Gains and Capital Losses; Derivatives; Estate Planning; Health Insurance; Homeowner's and Renter's Insurance; Identity Theft; Inflation; Investing; Liabilities; Life Insurance; Stock Market; Umbrella Insurance; Wills and Trusts

Further Reading

Day, John, Paul Banister, Brett Davies, et al. 2013. *Australian Financial Planning Handbook 2012–2013*. Sydney, Australia: Thomson Reuters Australia.

MacMinn, R. 2000. "Risk and Choice: A Perspective on the Integration of Finance and Insurance." *Risk Management & Insurance Review* (Vol. 3, No. 1): 69–79.

Schuchardt, Jane, Dorothy C. Bagwell, William C. Bailey, et al. 2007. "Personal Finance: An Interdisciplinary Profession." *Journal of Financial Counseling & Planning* (Vol. 18, No. 1): 61–69.

Teale, J. 2008. *Insurance and Risk Management*. Milton, Australia: John Wiley & Sons Australia.

Risk Premium

Risk premium is the excess return an investor gets to compensate for the excess risk borne by investing in any particular security other than the risk-free Treasury bill (T-bill). Premium refers to the excess return that an investor receives over a certain benchmark of return. The benchmark is usually the rate of return on an investment in a Treasury bill. T-bills are short-term borrowing instruments that are used by governments to borrow money from the public. Since the government is deemed the least risky issuer in most countries, T-bills are referred to as a risk-free asset.

Risk premium is calculated by deducting the rate of return on the risk-free asset (T-bill) from the expected rate of return on the security under consideration, sometimes called the risky asset. For example, if a company decides to borrow long-term from investors in the capital market, it will sell investors a long-term bond. If the rate of return on that bond (referred to as the coupon rate) is equal to 10 percent and it has a maturity of five years (i.e., investors can get back their invested capital after a period of five years), and if the rate of the T-bill is 3 percent, then the risk premium for the company bond will be 7 percent.

Risk premium = company bond expected return − T-bill rate (risk-free rate)
Risk premium = 10% − 3% = 7%

This 7 percent return in the example should compensate investors for risks associated with investing in that company. Risks include default risk, since the company is riskier than the government and the odds of its default are higher than the government's. Another source of risk is liquidity risk. The company's bond is a longer term instrument (five years versus one year for the T-bill), and thus reselling it in the secondary market might not be as easy as selling a short-term instrument like the T-bill. The secondary market for securities refers to the market where securities are exchanged between investors without the involvement of the original issuers of the securities. The original issuer of a security is only present in the primary market when the security is first offered.

Risk premium was defined by the financial concept of the capital asset pricing model (CAPM) developed by William Sharpe in 1964. Risk premium was categorized into market risk premium (by investing in an asset with a greater than the market level of risk) and security risk premium (the riskiness of an individual security when compared with the overall market). The CAPM determines the level of return required on any investment by adding a risk premium to the risk-free rate of return.

Required return on asset = Risk-free rate + Risk premium

The risk premium has to compensate the investor for investing in financial markets in general instead of investing in the risk-free asset. This is referred to as the market risk premium and is calculated as the difference between the return on the market portfolio (indexed by the return on a broad market index like the S&P 500) and the risk-free rate.

The security risk premium shows how much additional return an investor demands by investing in a specific asset and compensates the investor for purchasing this asset in particular. The security risk premium is determined by multiplying the market risk premium by the security's systematic risk given by beta (a measure of how much a specific security varies in return when compared to the overall market's volatility).

Taking both types of risk premium into consideration, the CAPM equation can be rewritten as follows:

Required return on an asset = Risk-free rate + Beta (market risk premium)

In general, the higher the risk of a security, the greater the risk premium required by the investor. Investors in the equity market purchase stocks, which entitle them to an ownership claim in a company. Equity (stock) holders endure more risk than holders of government bonds and thus should be compensated with higher returns. That explains why government bonds have lower rates of return than stocks. The excess return required by equity holders over holders of government debt is referred to as the equity risk premium.

Equity risk premiums are significant because they are the basis for many of our personal financial decisions such as saving, investing, and choice of retirement accounts. The degree of risk an individual is willing to take, referred to as degree of risk aversion, determines the risk premium required and thus the type of investment that would achieve this. In general, more risky investments carry higher returns and greater risk premiums.

Yasmine H. Abdel Razek

See also: Bonds; Investing; Risk; Stock Market; Stocks; Systematic Market Risk; Treasury Securities

Further Reading

Damodaran, Aswarth. "Risk Premiums: Looking Backwards and Forwards." Accessed August 16, 2013. http://people.stern.nyu.edu/adamodar/pdfiles/country/riskpremiums .pdf

Sharpe, William F. 1964. "Capital Asset Prices: A Theory of Market Equilibrium under Conditions of Risk." *Journal of Finance* (Vol. 19): 425–442.

Roth Individual Retirement Account (IRA) *(see Retirement Accounts)*

Savings Account

A savings account is a type of financial account held at a bank or other financial institution. These accounts protect the consumer's bank deposits and also offer a low interest rate. There are many types of savings accounts and most financial institutions offer a menu of account options. All bank and credit union accounts are insured and protected against loss up to $250,000 for each Social Security number, making these accounts very safe. (Bank accounts are insured by the Federal Deposit Insurance Corporation

Savings Data and Tips

It is widely accepted that consumers should maintain the equivalent of at least three to six months of their salary in a savings account for emergencies. If one's work is unpredictable, a greater savings account balance increases financial stability.

According to the U.S. Bureau of Economic Analysis (as reported in tradingeconomics.com), the personal savings rate (savings rate as a percentage of disposable after-tax income) was 4.3 percent in January 2014. Between 1959 and 2014, the savings rate in the United States averaged 6.83 percent with a record high of 14.60 percent in May 1975. The U.S savings rate fell to an all-time low of 0.80 percent in April 2005.

(FDIC) and credit union accounts are insured by the National Credit Union Share Insurance Fund (NCUSIF).

Savings accounts are considered one of the most liquid investments and allow consumers easy access to their funds. These accounts are frequently linked to a checking account for easy fund transfer. Depending on the type of account, there may be monthly charges or limits on number of transactions. Online banks and financial institutions with saving and checking accounts are becoming more popular and frequently offer higher interest rates due to their lower overhead costs.

Use of a Savings Account

A savings account is where to keep money one needs to access easily for emergencies and unexpected expenses. Unlike a checking account, which is used to pay monthly expenses, a savings account is used to pay for short- and medium-term financial goals as well as unexpected expenses. Consumers use a savings account for vacations, upcoming larger purchases such as appliances, a down payment on a car, or intermittent bills such as semiannual car insurance payments.

Types of Savings Accounts

The regular savings account is easy to set up and use. Linking this account to a checking account at the same bank allows the consumer to quickly transfer funds between checking and savings accounts for sound money management. Many banks allow linked accounts to protect one from accidentally overdrawing the checking account (paying a bill valued at more than the checking account balance).

In spite of the convenience and accessibility of this type of regular savings account, the disadvantage of a basic savings account is low interest payments. It's a wise financial decision to keep some money in a savings account for easy access, but maintain other types of investment and savings accounts for longer term savings needs.

The online savings account serves the same purpose as a regular savings account. These types of savings accounts have no physical building or branch. All business is transacted online, by telephone, and/or by mail. Due to the lack of a physical location, which is more expensive than an Internet location, the bank may pass those savings on to the customer. Online savings accounts frequently pay higher interest rates on savings accounts. Fees and expenses may also be lower than those on regular savings accounts.

Both regular and online savings accounts may offer money market deposit accounts. In general, these accounts pay the highest interest rates of any type of savings account. Money market deposit accounts may limit the amount of monthly transactions. These accounts are quite safe and are insured by the same FDIC or NCUSIF insurance as other types of savings accounts.

This type of savings account is not the same as a money market mutual fund, which is uninsured and available through investment brokerage accounts. In most varieties of savings accounts, consumers receive higher interest rate payments with higher account balances (the balance is the amount in the account).

Disadvantages of Savings Accounts

Due to their low interest rate payments, savings accounts aren't suitable for retirement or long-term goals, which require a large amount of funding. One of the benefits of other types of financial vehicles, such as stock and bond mutual funds, are their higher investment returns.

How to Start Saving

Workers benefit by instructing the human resources office to automatically transfer part of their paycheck into a savings account. This automatic saving is a smart way to build an account for emergencies and short- and medium-term financial goals. Another version of automatic saving is to have the financial institution regularly transfer a set amount from the checking to savings account.

Psychologically, the consumer is less likely to spend money that is not readily accessible. If the funds are transferred into a savings account, it is easier to consider that money "off limits" for discretionary spending.

In summary, a savings account is an account in which money is placed to save for the near future. The focus of this account should not be on earning interest; it is there to pay for unexpected life events and near- to medium-term financial expenses.

Danny Kofke

See also: Banking; Budget; Cash; Checking Account; Interest Income and Payments; Interest Rates; Investing; Liquidity; Money Market Account; Retirement Accounts

Further Reading

Elwell, Craig K. "Savings Rates in the United States: Calculation and Comparison." September 14. https://www.fas.org/sgp/crs/misc/RS21480.pdf

Kapoor, Jack R., Less R. Dlabay, and Robert J. Hughes. 2009. *Personal Finance,* 9th ed. New York: McGraw-Hill Irwin.

Kofke, Danny, 2011. *A Simple Book of Financial Wisdom: Teach Yourself (and Your Kids) How to Live Wealthy with Little Money*. Oregon: Wyatt MacKenzie Publishing.

Social Lending or Peer-to-Peer Lending

Peer-to-peer (P2P) or social lending is a relatively new lending and investing platform in the United States. Started by Prosper Marketplace in 2005, the concept is quite simple. Individuals both borrow and lend money without the use of the traditional financial system. Lending Club and Prosper Marketplace are the dominant players in the social lending platform. Both Prosper and Lending Club are registered with the Securities and Exchange Commission (SEC) and file the required documents.

In the past, financing was available primarily through mortgage brokers, banks, and quick high-interest-rate payday lenders. Borrowers could also obtain high-interest and fee-heavy loans through their credit cards. Through an online peer-to-peer marketplace borrower members may borrow directly from lenders without going through a traditional lender.

Borrowing and Lending with Peer-to-Peer

Borrowers apply for loans to consolidate credit cards, fund a business, pay for a home remodel, or for any number of financial endeavors. Their credit score impacts the interest rate. Borrowers are categorized according to creditworthiness from A to G for Lending Club. Prosper grades loans from AA for those with higher credit scores down to E for those borrowers with weaker credit histories. Those with poorer credit receive higher interest rate loans. The practice of matching higher interest rates with higher risk borrowers is common with traditional and nontraditional lenders.

The terms of loans in the peer-to-peer system range from three to five years. Borrowers can obtain from $1,000 up to $25,000 at Prosper Marketplace and up to $35,000 at Lending Club.

Karen is a typical borrower with a job and credit card debt. She sought a loan from a traditional bank to consolidate her credit card payments. Although Karen had a high credit score, she could not secure a bank loan. She went online, applied for a peer-to-peer loan, and got funded in one week at a rate of 5 percent. Her interest rate was favorable because she had a job and a good credit history. This rate was substantially lower than the one she was paying on her outstanding credit card debt.

Lenders (or investors) in social lending platforms obtain higher returns on their investments than in other types of fixed-income securities. They can choose to whom they wish to lend and in what amount. In order to minimize the default risk (the possibility that the borrower won't pay off the loan), lenders typically invest small amounts in many loans. It's customary for an investor with $1,000 in peer-to-peer loans to contribute $25 to 40 different borrowers. This diversification protects the lender from excessive losses should the borrower default on the loan.

Lenders can handpick the loans and choose preferred use and loan grades to fund. A conservative lender might choose to invest in only A- through C-grade loans. Henrik only invested in high-grade loans and never funded borrowers looking for money for a vacation or wedding. He preferred to fund smaller and shorter term loans.

Disadvantages of Social Lending Platforms

Lenders tie up their money for three to five years and may face loss of principal (that means they won't get all of their money back) if they need to sell a loan before it matures. This type of investing is less liquid than investing in the traditional financial markets. There are high default rates, and thus lenders need to diversify their investments among many individual loans.

Since this type of lending platform is so new, it hasn't been thoroughly tested during poor recessionary economic times. When the economy performs poorly, it is likely that loan default rates will rise. In fact, Prosper loans issued during the recession of 2007 lost money.

Lending Club states on page one of the SEC prospectus, "This offering is highly speculative and the Notes involve a high degree of risk. Investing in the Notes should be considered only by persons who can afford the loss of their entire investment." Since the loans are not secured by collateral as in a home mortgage or car loan, they are considered riskier. In other words, when the borrower does not make payments, their loan does not have any property attached that the lender can take in exchange for the missed payments.

Lending Club acknowledges that the borrower members may supply inaccurate information in order to obtain the loan. They state that the borrower-supplied information shouldn't be relied on.

Risks described in the Lending Club's SEC documents explain that they do not verify the borrower's time on the job, home ownership status, or use of the loan. Nor does Lending Club verify pay stubs, IRS forms, tax returns, bank and savings account balances, retirement account balances, home or car ownership records, or any records related to past legal proceedings. Thus borrowers may be submitting false information in order to receive the loan. In fact, during the last nine months of 2012, when borrower members' income and employment verifications were made, only approximately 60.1 percent of those individuals provided satisfactory responses to income or employment verification requests.

Additionally, not all states allow these companies to operate, and some states require that lenders demonstrate minimum income levels for participation. This information underscores the riskiness of the social lending platform for the investor.

Advantages of Peer-to-Peer Lending

In contrast with traditional lending, social lending streamlines the borrowing process. The middleman is the online platform. The lending platforms take approximately a 1 percent fee and the rest of the principal and interest repayments pass from borrowers to lenders. This affords lenders much higher returns on the amount of money loaned.

Borrowers who are unable to obtain a traditional loan may qualify through this platform at lower interest rates than credit card rates. This gives borrowers more financing possibilities.

The social lending platform gives investors greater investment opportunities and access to a market previously unavailable. Investors in these loans obtain higher returns than is otherwise available in the financial markets.

For example, Maria wants to fund a new business venture and cannot obtain a traditional loan. She borrows $5,000 from Prosper Marketplace. Due to her credit score and her financial and work background her interest rate is 11 percent. Duane invests $25 in Maria's loan as part of his loan portfolio. After the 1 percent fee to Prosper, Duane receives a prorated portion of all of Maria's loan repayments. If Maria defaults on her loan and after six months stops making payments on the loan, Duane does not receive any additional interest or principal payments on this particular loan. The advantage to Duane is that he has many other loans to offset the loss on this one. Further, most loans are repaid and he earns a higher interest rate than can be found in the financial marketplace.

In the peer-to-peer lending platform, borrowers get fixed-rate personal loans that may have lower interest rates than credit card debt, which may take many years to pay off. Peer-to-peer lending transforms the borrowing and lending activities from traditional financial institutions to individuals borrowing from and lending to other individuals.

Barbara Friedberg

See also: Banking; Bonds; Cash; Credit Card; Debt; Interest Rates; Liquidity; Loans; Risk; Year 2007–2009: Global Recession and Breakdown of Major Wall Street Institutions

Further Reading

Kaufman, Wendy. 2013. "Peers Find Less Pressure Borrowing from Each Other." May 10. http://www.npr.org/blogs/alltechconsidered/2013/05/10/182651552/peers-find-less -pressure-borrowing-from-each-other

Lending Club. 2014. Accessed January 11. https://www.lendingclub.com/

Prosper. 2014. Accessed January 11. http://www.prosper.com/

Social Security

Social Security, created in 1935, is a federal program of social insurance and benefits. This program is the foundation of financial security for retirees, disabled persons, and families of retired, disabled, or deceased workers. The program is funded though the Social Security tax (Federal Insurance Contributions Act or FICA) paid by U.S. workers and their employers. It is a pay-as-you-go program, which means that today's workers pay Social Security taxes and their payments form the Social Security benefits of current retirees.

Social Security differs from the traditional company pension, which is "pre-funded." Prefunded program funds are paid in advance, saved, and subsequently disbursed at a later date. Funded-in-advance programs protect employees from the possibility that a company goes bankrupt, out of business, or is unable to pay its pension obligation.

History of Social Security

The Social Security Administration (SSA), initially called the Social Security Board (SSB), was created in 1935 with the passage of the Social Security Act under President Roosevelt. The stock market crash and ensuing Great Depression prompted President Roosevelt to develop a social insurance system to protect against the major personal economic hazards such as unemployment and old age. The three-member board, created to administer the Social Security Act, targeted old-age insurance, unemployment compensation, and public assistance.

The SSA began as an independent agency whose chair of the board reported to the president. In 1939, the board became a sub-Cabinet member of the Federal Security Agency.

In 1995 the SSA returned to independent status. Throughout its history, the SSA has undergone much reorganization and may yet experience new changes as the Affordable Care Act of 2013 is implemented.

Social Security Retirement Benefits

The earliest a worker can receive Social Security retirement benefits is 62 years of age. If a worker elects to receive benefits before full retirement age, he or she will receive only a percentage of the full retirement benefit. The full retirement age is the age when a person may receive full or unreduced retirement benefits. If the retiree chooses to receive benefits after full retirement age, the monthly benefit may increase.

The full retirement age is based on birth year. Full retirement age is 65 for those born in 1937 or earlier. The full retirement age increases monthly until a birth year of 1943, when full retirement age becomes 66. Full retirement age remains at 66 for those born between 1943 and 1954. The full retirement age increases to 67 for those born in 1960 or later. In general, once a retiree begins taking Social Security, the benefit amount remains constant.

Who Receives Social Security Benefits?

Although most assume senior citizens are the only recipients of Social Security, a disabled 50-year-old factory worker might also receive Social Security benefits. The Social Security program helps the widows and orphans of both military and nonmilitary citizens as well. For example, children of an Army private killed in Iraq receive survivor Social Security payments.

Approximately 57 million people or one in six U.S. residents receive Social Security. One in four households has someone receiving Social Security. Retired workers receive approximately 65 percent of the total Social Security benefits paid or $36.9 million. Adults disabled since childhood are the smallest group of Social Security recipients at just $1 million or 1.76 percent of the total. Other disabled Americans receive 15.49 percent of the total or $8.8 million. Widows and widowers, spouses, and children make up the rest of the Social Security beneficiaries (Reno and Walker, 2013).

How Much Do Social Security Recipients Receive?

According to the National Academy of Social Insurance, in January 2013, the average monthly Social Security benefits were $1,264 for retired workers, $1,217 for widows or widowers over the age of 60, and $1,130 for disabled workers. For a worker retiring at age 66, full retirement age, the maximum monthly benefit is $2,533 per month. Benefits are indexed annually to keep pace with inflation.

Although higher paid workers receive greater amounts of Social Security benefits in retirement, a smaller percentage of their preretirement income is replaced. For example, a worker who was paid $110,100 per year receives $29,020 annual Social Security benefits or 26 percent of his or her preretirement income. The lowest paid worker who earned $19,670 before retirement receives 56 percent of his or her preretirement income or $11,070.

What Is Social Security Disability Insurance?

Initiated in 1957, Social Security Disability Insurance (DI) provides monthly payments to disabled workers who cannot work due to a major disability expected to last at least a year or result in death within a year. Workers who paid Social Security taxes in prior employment are covered. Benefits are determined by past earnings and are paid to the worker and his or her dependent family members. Two years after receiving DI, these individuals are eligible for Medicare.

Additional Social Security Facts

Through FICA Social Security payroll tax reduction, workers pay 6.2 percent of their earnings for Social Security and 1.45 percent of their earnings for Hospital Insurance (HI), earmarked for Medicare (Part A). Employers pay an equivalent amount into the Social Security system. If an employee earns more than $113,700 (in 2013), no additional Social Security FICA tax is owed.

Social Security payments are held in the Social Security trust funds. In 2012, the trust funds income included $840.2 billion from contributions and $785.8 billion benefit payments (1 percent of the outgoing funds include administrative costs). This resulted in a $54.4 billion surplus (Reno and Walker, 2013).The surplus is legally required to be invested in U.S. Treasury securities whose interest payments are returned to the trust funds.

Retirees need to provide for additional income during their nonworking years as Social Security does not contribute enough to cover all retirees' living expenses. In spite of the fact that Social Security is not designed to be the sole source of a worker's retirement income, 36 percent of Social Security recipients receive almost all of their income from Social Security, according to the National Academy of Social Insurance (Reno and Walker, 2013).

Social Security, Demographic Trends, and the Future

The full retirement benefit age was increased to accommodate both the growing number of future retirees and the expected increase in their lifespans. Additionally, out-of-pocket Medicare premiums and the share of benefits subject to income taxes also will rise. The effect of these changes is that earners' average income replacement percentage will decline from approximately 39 percent in 2002 to 31 percent in 2030.

In less than 10 years, Social Security revenues will not cover benefits owed. By 2021, Social Security projects revenues and interest income to the trust funds will not cover expenditures. At this point, reserves will be tapped to fund benefits. By 2033, trust fund reserves are expected to be spent. Social Security predicts income will cover only 77 percent of benefits due in 2033 (Reno and Walker, 2013).

This is not the definitive Social Security projection scenario. A positive view predicts trust fund reserves lasting until 2068. A more dire analysis posits trust fund reserves will be exhausted by 2027.

There are many options being considered to increase both Social Security funding and benefits for the underserved. For Social Security to continue in a semblance of its present form, changes are necessary in the Social Security program.

Barbara Friedberg

See also: Affordable Care Act; Estate Planning; Inflation; Medicare; Retirement; U.S. Federal Tax System Overview

Further Reading

Reno, Virginia P., and Elisa A. Walker. 2013. National Academy of Social Insurance. "Social Security Benefits, Finances, and Policy Options; A Primer." Accessed September 23, 2013. http://www.nasi.org/sites/default/files/research/2013_Social _Security_Primer_PDF.pdf

Social Security Web site. Accessed September 23, 2013. http://www.ssa.gov/

Stockbroker *(see Financial Advisor)*

Stock Market

A stock is a share of ownership of a company. Companies offer shares of their ownership in order to raise additional sources of capital. In the U.S. market, individuals invest in the stock market to save for retirement and other long-term financial goals.

The stock market, also called equity market, is the aggregation of buyers and sellers exchanging stocks. The stock market has grown to become a multitrillion-dollar market. The full spectrum of asset classes available to investors offers a variety of risk and return profiles, and the stock market remains relatively attractive. In 2013, the S&P 500, the stock market index composed of 500 large U.S. companies, soared by nearly 30 percent.

When buying or selling stocks, the transactions historically were made in a physical location such as the New York Stock Exchange. There market makers or representatives of investment brokerage companies physically bought and sold stocks for their firms. Today, most stock trades are executed electronically through a variety of trading networks.

The Stock Market as a Source of Funds for Companies

Before tackling the stock market from an investor's perspective, it is critical to understand the essence of the market and its function as an important economic agent. The stock market is an important place for companies to raise funds. The first time that a company decides to raise money through the stock market is called an initial public offering or IPO. This offering happens in a primary market and is orchestrated by investment bankers. Once the IPO is completed, the stocks continue to trade in the stock market (secondary market).

By listing their stock in the stock market, firms become public corporations. A public corporation's goal is to maximize the shareholders' wealth. As a result, an increasing value of the stock becomes the essential metric to assess the corporation's success.

Companies can raise funds by issuing equity or by borrowing money in the debt markets. While debt is usually considered cheaper than equity, because of the tax advantages of interest expenses being tax deductible (unlike dividends, for instance), increasing debt is not always optimal when it comes to managing the firm's capital mix. Managers will seek to find the right balance between debt and equity, and this balance can be found by issuing more money in the stock market.

The Stock Market as a Mirror of the Economy

The stock market is often considered a good proxy for the U.S. economy. A positive trend in the stock market often translates into a positive trend in GDP growth, a positive consumer sentiment, a strengthening housing market, and positive trends in most of the macroeconomic drivers. Investors reward stocks of companies with good growth prospects. As a result, the aggregation of all the stock should approximate an aggregation of growth prospects for all the companies. Also, stocks' performance, when divided into sectors, industries, or other categorizations, can offer intelligent insights on how a particular group is anticipated to behave.

How to Invest in the Stock Market

The U.S. stock market offers a diversified range of investment options. Investors can choose to buy stock in companies with different categories of market capitalization or size, different sectors' appurtenance, different positions in the business cycle (growth companies, mature companies), different exposure to the global marketplace, different risk profiles, and so on.

Before investing in or purchasing a stock, the investor needs to analyze the company. The investment analysis to conduct when investing in the stock market will depend on whether you are investing in many stocks or one security alone. When looking at one particular stock, it is very important to understand what causes stocks to appreciate or depreciate. When valuing stocks, investors always consider the ability of the firm to create future value. The ability of the firm to generate future cash flows will be rewarded by an appreciation of the value of the stock. The methods used to value a stock will differ depending on the company. The reader interested in stock valuation methodologies should consult literature about valuations. Professor Aswath Damodaran at NYU Stern has a Web site with all the stock valuation models.

When valuing a firm, it is important to keep in mind the key drivers of growth associated with the business model. For example, if the investor is looking at a pharmaceutical company, the competition around the drugs and the patents associated with the drugs are key drivers of the top line. When looking at a biotechnology firm, the value of its research pipeline and its ability to innovate as well as the regulation of the drug industry will be critical in making financial forecasts.

The equity analyst should be familiar with business analysis, accounting, and financial statements analysis as well as the ability to analyze intelligently special trends in the industry where the company is involved. Different investors in the stock market have different investment philosophies and value different signals and drivers. New trends in equity investments also involve high-frequency traders who use advanced technologies to make money by reacting very rapidly to small changes that happen at the stock level.

Equity Portfolios

When investing in many stocks at the same time, you are building an equity portfolio, and the relationship between the different stocks requires an additional overlay of analysis. For example, an investor who is trying to build a portfolio with an exposure to all the sectors will have to think about the allocation of money in every sector. Also, investing in a portfolio of stocks versus one stock alone is usually done by investors as a way to diversify their investments and reduce the risk of holding one very volatile security.

The principle of diversification is based on the fact that if an investor is able to find companies that are uncorrelated, when one of them is being hurt financially, the others will be able to offset the investment loss. When managing a portfolio of equities, the portfolio construction becomes as important as the selection of the stocks. Also, building a portfolio could be a way for the investor to incorporate his or her macroeconomic outlook in the investment process. For instance, an investor who thinks that oil prices are going to increase because of a shortage in the supply due to increasing turmoil in the Middle East might want to buy oil companies that generate their revenues by selling oil to companies that use oil as a raw material. Institutional investors who manage portfolios of equities will usually use an existing index as a benchmark for their stock picking skills. For example, an investor who focuses on large U.S. companies will compare his or her returns to the returns of the S&P 500 index.

Most consumers invest in the stock market by purchasing mutual funds, instead of individual stocks. As discussed in the Mutual Funds and Exchange-Traded Funds entry, these investment vehicles allow investors to pool their money with others and buy a basket of stocks managed by a professional. This gives consumers exposure to investing in the stock market without the responsibility or effort of researching and buying and selling individual stocks.

Yousra Acherqui

See also: Asset Allocation; Bonds; Capital Gains and Capital Losses; Capitalism; Compound Interest/Return; Investing; Mutual Funds and Exchange-Traded Funds; Stocks; Systematic Market Risk; Time Value of Money; Year 1987: Stock Market Crash

Further Reading

Damodaran, Aswath. Web site. Accessed April 10, 2014. http://pages.stern.nyu .edu/~adamodar/

Teweles, Richard J., and Edward S. Bradely. 1998. *The Stock Market,* 7th ed. New York: John Wiley.

Stocks

A stock, also called equity, is a financial security that represents an ownership stake in a publicly listed corporation's equity. A corporation can finance its operations by using debt or equity. Debt means borrowing money. Equity refers to the nondebt cash injected in the company by the owners and the investors.

The terms *stocks*, *shares*, and *equity* are often used interchangeably. There are two types of stock: common stock and preferred stock. Common stock refers to a stock that confers voting rights to the stockholder on top of receiving cash payments called dividends. Preferred stockholders do not have voting rights but have seniority over common stockholders. Seniority means that preferred stockholders receive dividend payments before common stockholders. It also means that in case of bankruptcy or liquidation, preferred stockholders are paid prior to common stockholders.

A public corporation's goal is to maximize shareholder wealth, and the value of the company's stock is a good proxy for shareholder value. Thus, every corporation will make financial decisions that will increase its stock price. When a consumer purchases stock in a corporation, she or he becomes a partial owner. When the corporation prospers, share price goes up, and the stockholder makes money.

Equity Financing

Corporations can use equity, debt, or both to finance their operations. The proportions of debt and equity define the capital structure of the corporation. Debt financing is generally cheaper than equity financing because debt expenses are tax deductible. However, debt is not always available to corporations, and using too much debt can alter a corporation's financial strength. If a corporation has too much debt and experiences a drop in sales, the interest payments may be too great to handle. That is why reasonable debt levels are important for corporations.

Public corporations are able to raise money by issuing new shares of equity. In order to issue new stock, corporations need to use investment bankers who orchestrate the new issue by underwriting the stocks and organizing the primary sale in the stock market. For example, Twitter and Facebook recently issued stock and began trading in the public stock markets. Investors can buy shares in these newly issued stocks and become part owners of these companies.

Investing in Equity

Most of the retail investors invest in the secondary market by buying or selling shares of stocks from equity retail brokers. Investors will buy a company's stock if they think that the value of the company will appreciate over time. The gains made by holding a stock and selling it at a higher price are called capital gains. Investors will also buy a stock if they think that they will receive dividend payments. The total gains or losses incurred by a stockholder are calculated as the sum of capital gains and dividend payments. For example, if an investor buys company ABC stock at $100, receives $10 in dividends, and sells it for $200, the total gains are $110, comprised of $100 capital gains and $10 from dividend gains. If we divide the total gains by the initial investment, we calculate a total return of 110 percent.

Equity Valuation

In order to make profitable investments, investors need to educate themselves on the stock they are choosing. An investor needs to value the company in order to derive the value of one share of the equity. Fundamental equity valuation has evolved to become a whole industry comprised of analysts who thoroughly follow a universe of stocks or a particular industry.

In order to value a stock, an analyst prepares financial projections for the company drawing on forecasts of the economy, the industry, and the revenue drivers. Once future cash flows are projected, they are discounted to the present to derive the equity value.

This equity value divided by the number of shares outstanding is equal to the intrinsic or true value of a stock. If this intrinsic value is higher than the market price, an investor should consider investing in the stock, and inversely.

Although equity or stock valuation sounds straightforward, it is based on assumptions and future projections. The intrinsic value is very sensitive to the assumptions made about the future; this is why the stock market is considered to be a barometer of investors' sentiment about the economy. Since future projections may or may not be accurate, it is difficult to definitively value a stock.

Another way to value a stock is to compare it to the stock of a comparable company. If a comparable stock trades at a certain multiple of its earnings, we can assume that our stock would trade at the same multiple of its earnings. For example, if company A trades at five times its earnings per share, and we know that comparable company B's earnings per share are $2, then we can price company B at $10 per share. We can also use multiples of revenues or any other fundamental measure. Most analysts will apply different valuation frameworks and take some weighted average of the results as the intrinsic value. As inferred earlier, knowledge of a stock and its industry is essential to conduct equity valuation. In addition to fundamental equity valuation, there are many other methods to value stocks such as quantitative analysis and technical analysis. Stock valuation is considered both an art and a science.

Risk

When investing in a stock, investors expose themselves to two kinds of risks. Systematic risk refers to how the stock moves when the market fluctuates. Systematic or market risk is common to all stocks. For example, a major disaster such as a tsunami in Japan will likely impact all stocks in Japan. This risk is captured by a measure called beta. Beta measures the co-movement of a stock with the market. Market risk is inherent in all stock investing and cannot be diversified away. In other words, no matter how many stocks are in an investment portfolio, systematic or market risk remains.

The second type of risk is related to the company's specific risk and is called nonsystematic or firm-specific risk. It is measured by the company's volatility, which is commonly calculated as the standard deviation of historical returns. Unlike systematic risk, stand-alone risk is diversifiable. This means that by investing in negatively correlated stocks, an investor can hold a portfolio that is overall less risky than investing in one stock alone, because the different holdings' stand-alone risks will cancel out. In popular terms, diversification is comparable to the old maxim "Don't put all your eggs in one basket."

For example, if we know that when company A is profitable, company B does not perform well, then we can say that these two companies are negatively correlated. Thus, company A and company B stock prices will tend to move in opposite directions. If we hold a portfolio comprised of company A and company B, we are offsetting movements in company A by movements in company B, which makes our position less volatile than holding a single stock. When investing in stocks, assessing risk is as important as the valuation. Investing in the stock market offers individuals an opportunity to participate in the growth of corporations and offers companies a ready source of funding.

Yousra Acherqui

See also: Asset Allocation; Behavioral Finance; Capital Gains and Capital Losses; Capitalism; Compound Interest/Return; Dividend Income; Index Mutual Funds; Investing; Mutual Funds and Exchange-Traded Funds; Risk; Stock Market; Systematic Market Risk

Further Reading

Brigham, Eugene F., and Joel F. Houston. 2012. *Fundamentals of Financial Management*, 13th ed. Southwestern.

Graham, Benjamin. 1949. *The Intelligent Investor*. New York: Harper & Brothers.

O'Neil, William J. 2003. *How to Make Money in Stocks*. New York, NY: McGraw-Hill.

Systematic Market Risk

Systematic market risk is those risks that impact the entire financial markets, not just a specific stock or industry. Other names for systematic risk include undiversifiable risk, nondiversifiable risk, or market risk.

Risk is an unavoidable by-product of investing in financial markets. Even a well-diversified investment portfolio cannot avoid systematic risk. There is a risk that the entire stock market as a whole might fall in value because of economic events such as changes in interest rates, a recession, or unforeseeable acts such as an act of terrorism or war.

Systematic risk influences all securities in the marketplace. When a source of systematic risk occurs, all stock prices move in the same downward direction. Systematic risk generally refers to types of risks that affect all securities in a similar manner, that is, the risk is not specific to a certain stock.

Systematic risk can be understood in contrast with nonsystematic or firm-specific risk. Nonsystematic risk describes an event particular to an individual firm. For example, the BP oil spill impacted the stock price of BP Oil, not the entire stock market. Firm-specific or nonsystematic risk can be eliminated with diversification. If an investor owns many stocks or diversified mutual funds, when one company's stock price declines, it's likely that another stock's price will rise, thus minimizing portfolio (a group of investments pooled together) volatility. Diversifying into many stocks eliminates the risk of a portfolio losing value due to the prospects of a few holdings.

Systematic Risk, Nonsystematic Risk, and Diversification

In an investment portfolio context, firm-specific or nonsystematic risk can be eliminated with diversification, whereas systematic risk cannot be eliminated by diversification. Diversification is the act of distributing one's funds into many different types of investments in a variety of industries and sectors rather than just focusing on one investment. Diversifying into many stocks reduces the risk of losing on an individual stock. By increasing the number of stocks in a portfolio, the individual risk of each stock declines. This individual risk is the diversifiable risk or the nonsystematic risk,

Systematic Risk Examples over the Years

The 9/11 World Trade Center bombings were an example of systematic risk. This horrific catastrophe impacted the population on many fronts with loss of life and grave fear. The terrorist attack caused a systematic decline across the entire economy, causing financial stock price declines in almost all industries. No amount of diversification could protect investors from this systematic risk.

The recent recession of 2008 hit the entire stock market as well. The economy reeled during the 2007–2008 subprime housing crisis and mortgage meltdown. The U.S. economy and stock market declined due to an overvalued housing market that subsequently returned to fair value. Other economic excesses (discussed further in the entry Year 2007–2008: Subprime Housing Crisis and Mortgage Meltdown) caused this recession, which led to the systematic decline of the overall stock market.

Another worldwide event, the Year 1997–1998: Asian Financial Crisis, caused a worldwide systematic market decline. Many systematic risks impact the world such as wars, weather events (tsunamis, floods, and earthquakes), and economic catastrophes.

and it is firm-specific, that is, it does not affect other stocks. Diversification can push down the level of risk of a portfolio but not to zero, because of the systematic risk, which will affect all stocks (though in different proportions).

It is important for consumers and investors to understand systematic risk and its relationship to diversification. Investors who hold many assets in their portfolio can never completely eliminate risk. Holding many securities in various industries eliminates the possibility that one stock's price movement will significantly impact the return of the entire portfolio, yet systematic risk is always present.

Asset Allocation and Systematic Risk

Creating an asset allocation that includes stocks, bonds, and cash will temper the impact of systematic risk. Should stock values fall due to a systematic market event, such as an unforeseen spike in inflation and interest rates or a global terrorist event, the cash portion of the portfolio will remain stable. It is also possible that a systematic market event may not influence bond prices in the same way as stock prices. Thus, although systematic risk cannot be diversified away, owning cash and bonds in addition to stocks in one's portfolio may lessen the impact of a systematic risk on the total portfolio value.

For example, if the investor holds 40 percent of the portfolio in stocks and 60 percent in cash, the value of cash will never decline. Thus, even if a systematic event causes stocks to fall 20 percent, the investor will only suffer a total portfolio decline of 8 percent (40 percent multiplied by 20 percent). That is the benefit of diversification and the only way to lessen the impact of systematic risk on a portfolio.

Modern money management requires consumers to understand the inherent risks and unpredictability in the investment markets. Systematic risk can never be eliminated or diversified away completely.

Yasmine H. Abdel Razek

See also: Asset Allocation; Bonds; Investing; Risk; Risk Premium; Stock Market; Stocks; Year 1997–1998: Asian Financial Crisis; Year 2007–2008: Subprime Housing Crisis and Mortgage Meltdown

Further Reading

Bodie, Zvi, Alex Kane, and Alan Marcus. 2011. *Essentials of Investments*, pp. 197–198. New York, NY: McGraw-Hill.

Tax Deferral

Tax deferral is a useful financial strategy for putting off payment of tax until a future date, ideally at time when the tax bill will be lower. There are two primary tax deferral methods. The first method postpones income into a future period, thus deferring when the tax will be due on that earned income.

In the second method, funds are transferred to a special type of account where access to the funds and the tax payment itself are deferred. Specifically, this method requires the individual to place the income in a special retirement account for many years.

In determining whether tax deferral is appropriate, one must take into account income and current budgetary requirements, current and future tax rates, and an assessment of future retirement goals and what the tax scenario might be in those coming years.

Deferring Income

When facing a potentially large tax bill a common approach is to defer some of the taxable income into the future. This can be done by delaying receipt of income or by accelerating tax-deductible expenses.

Most salaried employees have little control over when they receive their regular compensation. However, they may have workplace options that allow them to transfer receipt of income into a later period. Self-employed individuals have more control over when income is received by how they bill their customers.

Retirement Accounts for Tax Deferral

The most popular tax-deferral strategy is enrollment in a workplace retirement savings plan. The plans are known as defined contribution plans because workers put a specific amount of their pay into the accounts. In some cases, the employer matches a portion of the money workers contribute to these retirement accounts.

The most common type of defined contribution account is the 401(k) plan, named after the section of the tax code that created the retirement savings option. The primary benefit of a 401(k) plan is that one regularly saves for retirement. But there is a tax benefit, too.

The worker contributions are made with pretax dollars; that is, the 401(k) money is automatically deducted from the paycheck before federal and state income taxes are withheld. This reduces the worker's taxable take-home pay, lowering tax liability.

Take, for example, a single worker making $40,000 in 2012 who contributed 6 percent of his salary to a 401(k). That $2,400 annual contribution total lowered the worker's taxable salary to $37,600. Assuming all of the $40,000 income was taxable, the individual's tax bill in 2012 would have been $6,024. After contributing $2,400, the single taxpayer's federal tax bill on an income of $37,600 is $5,436. By saving in a tax-deferred retirement account, the worker reduced his tax bill by almost $600 and deferred paying taxes on that money until retirement. Many workers find that the tax savings of 401(k) contributions can help ease the blow of reduced take-home pay.

Compounded Earnings

Both the worker's contributions and any amount put into the account by the employer grow tax-deferred. In other words, no tax is due on the principal or earnings until the funds are withdrawn.

The combination of compounding earnings and no taxes being collected works to dramatically increase retirement savings. This principal also applies to a traditional individual retirement account (IRA) or to a Roth IRA, another type of tax-deferred retirement account.

In 2013, a worker younger than age 50 could put up to $5,000 (or as much as the worker earned if she made less than $5,000) into a traditional IRA. IRA contribution amounts are adjusted annually to reflect inflation.

If a worker invests $3,000 in a traditional IRA or 401(k) at the beginning of each tax year with a hypothetical 8 percent investment return, compounded annually with reinvestment of dividends and capital gains, in 30 years the investment will be worth $367,038. The end return value of this tax-deferred retirement account far surpasses the identical taxable investment account whose final value after 30 years is $173,181. Even after taxes are due, the tax-deferred account is worth $264,267 or $91,086 more than the retirement account.

Deferring Taxes

With a 401(k), traditional IRA, or any tax-deferred account it is important to remember that taxes eventually will be due. But by delaying the withdrawal of the retirement account money until the account owner is older, the taxes due on the distributions are usually taxed at a lower rate because the owner is receiving less taxable income.

The tax code calls for specific withdrawals, known as required minimum distributions or RMDs, from certain tax-deferred retirement accounts once the account holder turns 70½. These annual withdrawal amounts are calculated as a percentage of the total tax-deferred accounts based on the account owner's age. The RMD amount then is taxed at the owner's ordinary income tax rate.

If an account holder fails to take an RMD, he or she could face a penalty of 50 percent of the amount that was to have been withdrawn. And while the Internal Revenue Code demands that money eventually be withdrawn from tax-deferred accounts so that the federal government can finally begin collecting taxes on the funds, early distributions are penalized. Taking money from a tax-deferred retirement account before age 59½ could be subject to a penalty of 10 percent of the amount withdrawn.

Tax-Rate Crystal Ball

A lower future tax bill, however, is not necessarily a given. While a taxpayer might expect to be in a lower tax bracket in the future when the deferred tax amount is paid, that cannot be guaranteed.

An older owner of a tax-deferred retirement account might be working in retirement or have other investments that add to his or her overall taxable income amount, pushing the older taxpayer into a higher tax bracket. It also is possible that individual income tax rates could increase in coming years.

Because each person's tax situation is unique, tax-deferral strategies must be carefully evaluated based on individual tax and financial goals and needs. Before contributing to a tax-deferred account it is important to examine current budgetary requirements to determine how much one can afford to reduce daily living expense cash flow in order to contribute to a tax-deferred account. And always be aware of the possibility of future tax rate hikes.

Kay Bell

See also: Investing, Retirement; Retirement Accounts; Tax Return, Federal; U.S. Federal Tax System Overview

Further Reading

Brandon, Emily. 2013."How to Save for Retirement on a Small Salary: Don't Let a Low Income Prevent You from Building a Retirement Nest Egg," *U.S. News* (July 15). http://money.usnews.com/money/retirement/articles/2013/07/15/how-to-save-for-retirement-on-a-small-salary?s_cid=related-links:TOP

"Power of Tax Deferral: Putting the Power of Tax Deferral to Work for You." First Investors Corporation. Last modified April 2011. https://www.firstinvestors.com/docs/pdf/marketing/think-first-tax-deferral.pdf

Purcell, Patrick, and Topelski, John J. 2009. "401(k) Plans and Retirement Savings: Issues for Congress," *Congressional Research Services* (July 14). http://digital.library.unt.edu/ark:/67531/metadc26189/m1/1/high_res_d/R40707_2009Jul14.pdf

"Tax-Deferred and Tax-Free Accounts." FINRA, *Building Your Portfolio.* Accessed August 1, 2013. http://www.finra.org/Investors/SmartInvesting/GettingStarted/Building YourPortfolio/P117327

Tax Return, Federal

The federal tax return is calculated on Form 1040, the granddaddy of tax returns. It was created in 1913 when the current tax code was enacted. How much a taxpayer owes in taxes or is due as a refund is figured each year during tax filing season. An individual's ultimate tax bill or tax refund calculations are made on this tax return.

There are, however, three versions of the federal tax Form 1040 from which to choose. In addition to Form 1040, the Internal Revenue Service also offers taxpayers Form 1040A and Form 1040EZ. Each of the three individual tax return forms offers different filing options and ways to possibly reduce a tax bill. Each tax form also has its own set of requirements.

While it is tempting to file the tax return that is the easiest to complete for one's filing situation, that could be a costly move. The most complex of the returns offers the most tax breaks.

Form 1040EZ

As the name indicates, Form 1040EZ is the easiest of the three individual tax returns. This single-page tax return generally is used by taxpayers who have a relatively uncomplicated tax life, such as students or young workers.

However, 1040EZ filers must meet 10 specific requirements, listed in the form's instruction booklet, before they can file the simplest income tax return. Tax software will also guide taxpayers through the tests they must meet in order to use the 1040EZ.

Most younger taxpayers easily meet the filing status test. A Form 1040EZ filer must be either a single taxpayer or if married, file a joint return. In either filing situation, the taxpayers cannot claim any dependents.

The form's earnings limit is generally not a problem for younger taxpayers. A 1040EZ filer's income must be less than $100,000. But how that money was acquired must also be considered. It must come only from wages, salaries, tips, taxable scholarship or fellowship grants, unemployment compensation, or Alaska Permanent Fund dividends. And if tips were earned, that compensation must be shown in boxes 5 and 7 of Form W-2.

Some interest earnings are allowed for 1040EZ filers, but only if the amount is less than $1,500 for the tax year. If other types of investment income such as dividends or capital gains are received, the taxpayer cannot file Form 1040EZ.

For most young filers, Form 1040EZ is the correct tax filing choice. But it offers few opportunities for a taxpayer to reduce a tax bill. A standard deduction amount for single filers and another for married filers is listed on the form. Other than that, the only tax break on the 1040EZ is the Earned Income Tax Credit, or EITC.

This tax break is designed for workers who do not earn very much money. Because it is a credit, it reduces a tax bill dollar for dollar. If the tax bill for a single person with no dependents is $1,000 and that taxpayer qualifies for a $487 Earned Income Tax Credit claim (the maximum amount for 2013; amounts are adjusted annually for inflation), that taxpayer's bill is cut to $513. Even better, the EITC is a refundable credit, meaning it could produce a tax refund if the taxpayer does not owe any or little tax. If a single taxpayer owes $300 and qualifies for a $487 EITC claim, the filer would get a $187 refund.

Form 1040A

Many young taxpayers find that as they enter the workforce, their financial and tax situations become a bit more complicated. In these cases, they graduate to the next level of tax filing, Form 1040A.

More taxpayers can use Form 1040A because there are no income or filing status limitations. Taxpayers with dependents can use 1040A. This two-page tax return also offers several tax deductions and credits that are not found on the 1040EZ.

The first set of deductions is found on page one of the form. Technically, the deductions are adjustments to income. There are four adjustments on Form 1040A: out-of-pocket expenses incurred by educators, traditional individual retirement account (IRA) contributions, student loan interest paid, and higher education tuition and fees. These amounts are subtracted from the Form 1040A filer's gross, or total, income to arrive at adjusted gross income.

Additional tax breaks are found on page two of Form 1040A, including a variety of tax credits that reduce a tax bill dollar for dollar. Of particular interest to young taxpayers are the EITC; various education tax credits (the American Opportunity or Lifetime Learning credits); and the retirement savings contribution credit, which could produce a credit up to $1,000 when a taxpayer puts money into an IRA—Roth or traditional—or a workplace retirement account, such as a 401(k) plan.

A Form 1040A filer, however, does not have the option to itemize expenses; the standard deduction amount must be claimed. The standard deduction is a separate dollar figure for each filing status, adjusted annually for inflation, and is usually found directly on the 1040A. The deduction amount helps reduce the taxpayer income from the adjusted gross income level to a smaller taxable income amount.

Form 1040

Form 1040, the longest of the tax returns, allows the most deduction and tax credit options. The final section on page one of Form 1040 is labeled "Adjusted Gross Income." This section contains more than a dozen ways to reduce the taxpayer's total, or gross income. The tax breaks here are often referred to as above-the-line deductions because they are listed just before the last line, where adjusted gross income is entered, of the form's first page.

In addition to the four adjustments to income found on the 1040A, Form 1040's above-the-line deductions include the option to deduct moving costs. This could be of use to a new graduate taking a job that is a distance from his or her previous home. The job-related moving expenses are claimed directly on Form 1040. As for credits, the same ones that appear on Form 1040A also are found on Form 1040, as well as more specialized credits such as expenses for adopting a child and offsetting taxes paid to a foreign country.

The longest of the individual tax returns also offers filers a choice of claiming the standard deduction or itemizing expenses on Schedule A. Most taxpayers claim the standard deduction. The advantage is that it is easier as there are no receipts to collect or added forms to fill out. If, however, a filer has enough itemized expenses to exceed the standard deduction for his or her filing status, claiming itemized expenses on Schedule A is the wiser tax move.

Itemized deduction options include medical and dental expenses once they exceed 10 percent of adjusted gross income; charitable contributions; state and local income taxes paid; real estate taxes paid; mortgage interest paid; and a variety of miscellaneous expenses that exceed 2 percent of adjusted gross income. A Form 1040 taxpayer can choose each filing season whether to claim the standard deduction or itemize expenses.

Form Filing Deadline

All three individual income tax return forms have one thing in common. They are due on April 15. If that mid-April day falls on a federal holiday or weekend, the tax deadline is extended to the next business day.

Taxpayers who cannot finish returns by the April date can get an automatic six-month extension by submitting Form 4868 to the Internal Revenue Service. This will allow taxpayers until October 15 to complete tax paperwork. Any due tax, however, or a close approximation of the amount must be submitted with Form 4868 by April 15 or penalties and interest on the unpaid taxes will be assessed.

Kay Bell

See also: Capital Gains and Capital Losses; Inflation; Tax Deferral; U.S. Federal Tax System Overview

Further Reading

Bell, S. Kay. 2009. "The Truth About Paying Fewer Taxes: Truth #9—Why Credits Are Better." *The Truth About Paying Fewer Taxes.* FT Press. Accessed August 1, 2013. http://www.ftpress.com/articles/article.aspx?p=1327957

IRS.gov Web site. *RS Understanding Taxes*. Accessed August 6, 2013. http://www.irs.gov/pub/irs-pdf/p2181.pdf

Tax Policy Center, Urban Institute and Brookings Institution Web site. "Historical Standard Deduction." Accessed April 1, 2013. http://www.taxpolicycenter.org/taxfacts/displayafact.cfm?Docid=171

Zelenak, Lawrence A. March 31, 2013. "When We Loved Form 1040." *New York Times.* http://www.nytimes.com/2013/04/01/opinion/we-can-love-form-1040.html?_r=0

Time Value of Money

Time value of money refers to the famous notion that "a dollar today is worth more than a dollar tomorrow." The reason this statement is true is because of the interest or return earned by the money. There are two types of interest, simple interest and compound interest. Simple interest is earning interest on the original amount invested (e.g., money deposited in a bank). For example, if one deposits $100 in a bank savings account earning 5 percent per year, then the interest earned for the first year is $5 (100 × 0.05). Interest earned is the same amount each year. Given that the investor earns only interest on the original $100 invested, the deposit grows in the following manner: year 1 ($105), year 2 ($110), year 3 ($115), and so forth.

But that is a rather naïve method of calculation, because in reality one doesn't earn interest only on the original amount but rather on the original amount and on the interest earned. Earning interest on interest is referred to as compound interest. According to this method, the deposit in the previous example will grow at a slightly higher rate. In the first year, the deposit will grow to $105, but in the second year it will reach $110.25 ($105 × 0.05 = $5.25 interest + 105 = $110.25).

If we think of money as we would any other commodity, then it should have a price. And the price of money is the interest rate. When a company or individual needs to buy money (borrow), it will pay interest as the cost, and when a company or individual wants to sell money (save/invest), they receive interest from the buyer as a return on the investment. Inflation must be accounted for when investing or borrowing. An increase in inflation decreases the amount a dollar will purchase. With inflation, today's dollar buys more goods than that same dollar tomorrow.

Now, we know that a dollar today is worth more than a dollar tomorrow, but how much more? That question is answered with time value calculations. Time value calculations have two basic concepts, present value and future value. In order to determine present value and future value using time value calculations one must determine an expected rate of interest during the time period in question.

Present Value

The present value calculation determines today's value of a future amount of funds to be received at a certain date in the future. So if an investment pays $1,000 in one year, present value answers the question "What is the maximum amount an investor will be willing to pay now in order to receive this future sum?" To answer this question, we need to identify the interest rate (referred to as the discount rate) expected to prevail during that year and reduce the $1,000 by that rate. If the interest rate expected is 3 percent, then the maximum amount an investor will be willing to pay is equal to $\frac{1000}{(1+0.03)^1} = $970.90. This amount is referred to as the *present value* of the $1,000. The previous process is referred to as *discounting* and it simply means the act of removing the interest effect period by period from a future sum of money. As a general rule:

$$PV = \frac{FV}{(1+i)^n}$$

Where:
PV: Present value
FV: Future value

i: Interest or discount rate
n: number of time periods

The cash flow pattern may differ. Instead of receiving a future sum as a lump sum amount, we could receive it in equal installments. In this case, the cash flow pattern is referred to as an annuity. Calculating the present value of an annuity is a bit different and uses the following equation (the Internet offers many online present value calculators, which will complete the calculations):

$$PVA = PMT \times \left[\frac{1-(1+i)^{-n}}{i}\right]$$

Where:
PVA: Present value of the annuity
PMT: Cash flow per period
i: Interest rates
N: Number of periods

Future Value

Future value is the opposite of present value. Rather than calculating the present value of a future sum now, it is calculating the future value of a sum invested now after a period of time. For example, future value calculations can help estimate the future value of a sum of money deposited today in a savings account after a specified period of time. The interest rate is the key component in the calculation. Simply, future value calculation builds interest into a certain amount of money invested. The process is referred to as *compounding*. Following from the previous formula of present value is the future value formula:

$$FV = PV \times (1 + i)^n$$

In cases when the cash flow pattern is an annuity, we use this formula to obtain the future value:

$$FVA = PMT \times \left[\frac{(1+i)^n-1}{i}\right]$$

Sometimes, the cash flow is neither an annuity nor a lump sum amount. If an investment makes different payments every period, it is said to be following a mixed stream cash flow pattern. If that is the case, one can use lump sum amount calculations every period and sum them all at the end to obtain present or future value.

A perpetuity refers to cash flows that occur periodically but without a given maturity. Thus, a perpetuity is an annuity without an identified number of years. A good example of a perpetuity is retirement benefits. The beneficiary receives a monthly sum for an unknown amount of time into the future.

The key idea to understanding present value and future value calculations is to understand that one cannot compare different investments unless one places them all at one point in time; whether that point is the future or the present is irrelevant. That way one can compare investments with different life spans and cash flow patterns to choose the best-paying investment.

Importance of Time Value

Time value is important because it explains why one would give up consumption now in favor of investing for future returns. If there were no advantage to saving and investing, people would not give up consumption. People give up consumption now for a promise to consume more in the future, and that can only be possible if the amount saved or invested today will grow into a larger sum through compounding of returns (i.e., interest).

Consumers use time value calculations to decide between taking a lump sum payout or an annuity. For example, if you were offered $50,000 today or $5,500 per year for 10 years, which would you choose? A time value calculation would determine the potential present value of each of those sums. The one with the higher present value would be the optimal choice. The decision is not perfect as it seems. The consumer must choose an accurate discount (interest) rate by which to calculate the present value of the future cash flows, and there is no guarantee what a future interest rate will be. For example, calculate the present value of a $5,500 per year cash flow for 10 years with an interest rate of 3 percent and the result is $48,324. Use a discount rate of 7 percent and the present value falls to $41,334. The higher the discount rate employed, the riskier the present value calculation. It's more difficult to obtain higher rates of return than lower. In either case, the consumer is better served taking the $50,000 today than $5,500 each year for the next 10 years.

For a corporation, time value is very important for capital budgeting. Capital budgeting is the process by which a corporation decides among long-term investments such as expansion, research and development, or purchasing equipment. Given the nature of the decisions, cash flows may take years to materialize, and thus a corporation needs to estimate if the expected cash flows will be worth the initial investment or not. Time value calculations answer that question.

Yasmine H. Abdel Razek

See also: Annuity; Compound Interest/Return; Discount Rate; Inflation; Interest Income and Payments; Investing; Retirement; Risk

Further Reading

Kapoor, Jack, Les Dlabay, and Robert J. Hughes. 2007. *Personal Finance*. New York: McGraw-Hill. Accessed September 6, 2013, http://highered.mcgraw-hill.com/sites/0073106712/student_view0/ebook/chapter1/chbody1/opportunity_costs_and_the_time_value_of_money.html

Merrit, Cam. "Why Is the Time Value of Money So Important in Capital Budgeting Decisions?" *Houston Chronicle*. Accessed August 16, 2013. http://smallbusiness.chron.com/time-value-money-important-capital-budgeting-decisions-61898.html

TIPS—Treasury Inflation-Protected Securities (see *Inflation-Protected Investments*)

Treasury Securities

U.S. Treasury marketable securities are debt securities similar to bond investments. These debt instruments are issued by the U.S. government to raise funds needed to manage the federal government. Additionally, the funds raised by the sale of government Treasury securities pay off previously issued maturing government debt. These are widely accepted as the most secure debt instruments available worldwide due to the global confidence in the U.S. government. Investors seeking safe investments for the cash and fixed portions of their savings and investing portfolios frequently turn to Treasury securities investments.

There are several varieties of Treasury securities with varying characteristics: Treasury bills, notes, bonds, floating rate notes (FRNs), Treasury inflation-protected securities (TIPs), and savings bonds.

Treasury Bills, Notes, and Bonds

These are the staples of the Treasury security debt offerings. Treasury notes, bills, and bond securities are differentiated primarily by their term. Term indicates when the investor can redeem the bonds for full face value. Treasury bills are short-term securities and mature in one year or less. Treasury notes are intermediate-term debt instruments and mature from 1 to 10 years from the issue date. Treasury bonds are long-term and mature in 30 years.

Treasury bills, unlike notes and bonds, are sold at a discount to face value and at maturity can be redeemed at full value. The difference between the discounted purchase price and the face value determines the effective yield or interest rate. Treasury bills are sold in 4-, 13-, 26-, and 52-week terms.

Treasury notes have maturities of 2, 3, 5, 7, and 10 years and pay interest twice per year. The interest payment amount is stated as a percentage and called the *coupon rate* (a term common to most bond investments). The coupon rate is determined when the bond is created. For example, a $1,000 five-year Treasury note with a coupon of 2 percent pays 1 percent or $10 every six months.

Treasury bonds are issued with a term of 30 years and pay interest every six months, like Treasury notes. The interest payment or coupon rate is determined at issue, similar to the Treasury note, although Treasury bonds have higher coupon rates than Treasury notes due to the inherent riskiness of longer term debt instruments. When an investor buys longer term debt, there is more uncertainty regarding future interest rates, and consequently investors demand higher interest rates for longer term securities than for shorter term debt.

Treasury notes, bills, and bonds have several qualities in common. The minimum purchase amount is $100. They may be purchased at the Treasury auction (from the treasurydirect.gov Web site) or in the secondary market from a broker or financial institution. They may be held to maturity when they will be redeemed for face value or sold at market value prior to maturity.

When sold before maturity, a debt security's redemption price varies depending on the relationship between the security coupon rate, time to maturity, and market interest rate. If the market interest rate and consequently the yield to maturity is lower than the coupon rate, then the price of the bond will be higher than par (face value), if sold prior to maturity. For example, if a $1,000 Treasury bill has a coupon rate of 3 percent and the market interest rate is 2 percent, the bill will sell for more than $1,000 if redeemed prior to maturity.

Floating-Rate Notes

Initiated in July 2013, floating-rate notes (FRNs) are the newest addition to the government's portfolio of debt offerings. A FRN has a floating interest rate, or one that changes over time along with the market interest rates. Interest on FRNs is paid quarterly.

As market interest rates rise, so will the interest rate on the floating-rate note. Conversely, as interest rates fall, so will the rate on the floating-rate note. The interest rate will be tied to the highest rate of the most recent 13-week Treasury bill rate. This means that rates will adjust quite rapidly to changes in interest rates.

FRNs can be purchased at auction through the government Treasury securities Web site (treasurydirect.gov) in denominations as small as $100. Additionally, these securities may be obtained through a broker or financial institution. Like most other government securities, they may be held until maturity for face value or transferred to a financial institution where they can be redeemed at the going market rate.

Savings Bonds

Savings bonds are offered by the Treasury in several varieties: EE/E bonds, HH/H bonds, and I bonds (discussed in the Inflation-Protected Investments entry).

EE/E bonds purchased between May 1997 and April 2005 earn a variable market-based rate of return. The interest rate on these bonds changes every six months, each May 1 and November 1, for new EE bonds. Those issued after May 2005 earn a fixed rate of interest, determined at purchase. Interest payments are added to the value of the bond each month and paid out when the bond is cashed in.

The minimum purchase amount for EE bonds is $25. An individual is entitled to purchase up to $10,000 of EE bonds each year. These savings investments earn interest up to 30 years.

EE/E bonds may be redeemed for face value any time after the bond is one year old, although if the bond is redeemed before five years, the saver loses the last three months of interest. Regardless of when the bond is redeemed, the saver receives the face value of the bond plus any interest earned according to the previous stipulations.

HH/H savings bonds earn interest for up to 20 years. H bonds were last issued in December 1979 and HH bonds were issued from 1980 through August 2004. These bonds are no longer being issued, although existing HH bonds issued up to 2004 will earn interest until 2024.

Inflation-Protected Government Securities

Treasury inflation-protected securities (TIPs) along with inflation I bonds are discussed in the Inflation-Protected Investments entry.

Savings Bonds and College Planning

There are special tax benefits for savings bond holders if the proceeds of the bond are used to pay for qualified higher education expenses in their redemption year. The savings bond education tax exclusion enables holders of series EE and I bonds issued after 1989 to exclude from their income all of the interest received. Thus, the bond interest income is not only state and local tax exempt, but federal tax exempt as well. More information about using savings bonds for college planning is available from IRS Publication 550, "Investment Income and Expenses," and on the treasurydirect.gov Web site.

Tax Consequences

All Treasury securities are subject to federal tax but exempt from state and local taxes. Those E/EE and I bonds used for qualified education expenses may be exempt from federal taxes as well. This makes them excellent choices for investors and savers in high-tax locations.

The government's Treasury security offerings are not widely promoted by financial advisors, as advisors aren't financially compensated for their recommendation. Consequently, these excellent savings tools are frequently underpublicized or misunderstood. They are very safe investments for savers and investors.

Barbara Friedberg

See also: Bonds; Compound Interest/Return; Debt; Dividend Income; Inflation-Protected Investments; Interest Income and Payments; Interest Rates; Investing; Risk

Further Reading

Treasury Direct Web site. Accessed November 27, 2013. http://www.treasurydirect.gov/tdhome.htm

Umbrella Insurance

An umbrella insurance policy is the next personal finance asset protection a consumer may need after homeowner's (or renter's) and vehicle insurance coverage. This policy, as its name suggests, is a broad protection against the cost of losing a lawsuit over a

---

What Is a Bumbershoot Policy?

Most individuals haven't heard of a bumbershoot insurance policy and will get along fine without one. But if you work in or manage a shipyard, you need to investigate a bumbershoot liability policy.

This is a specialized form of umbrella liability insurance that protects shipyards. The bumbershoot policy covers marine and nonmarine risks. For example, it protects the shipyard from liabilities arising from collision and salvage legal actions.

Bumbershoot actually means "umbrella." This type of policy is designed to provide complete protection and indemnity coverage under the Longshoreman and Harbor Worker's Act.

---

vehicle accident or an accident on one's property. Umbrella insurance provides additional coverage, over that of the consumer's home and vehicle insurance protection.

The umbrella policy protects the consumer's existing assets as well as future potential assets (such as wages, future inheritance, or lottery winnings) against the cost of losing a lawsuit from a car accident or accident on one's property. Even if the consumer currently has few assets, umbrella insurance may be recommended to avoid the potential loss of future wages. If the consumer loses the lawsuit, he or she would be responsible for paying the winning party for medical expenses, lost wages, and other costs.

How Does Umbrella Insurance Work?

Since this is an additional insurance policy after homeowner's and vehicle insurance, there are certain minimum insurance coverage requirements for the vehicle and homeowner's policies. For example, let's assume that your vehicle insurance pays $300,000 per person per accident for medical expenses and you have a $1 million umbrella insurance policy. If you are in an accident and sued for $900,000 and lose the lawsuit, your auto insurance will pay $300,000 and the umbrella policy will cover the remaining $600,000 ($300,000 + $600,000 = $900,000).

The typical umbrella policy covers from $1 million to $5 million (or more if you have more assets to protect). As with all insurance, there will be a deductible or amount that the insured (or policyholder) pays before the insurance pays out.

What Level of Vehicle and Homeowner's Insurance Is Necessary with an Umbrella Policy?

Umbrella insurance requires the policyholder to purchase a baseline amount of both vehicle and homeowner's (if property is owned) insurance along with the umbrella policy. Although vehicle insurance is required by law in most states and homeowner's insurance is required by a mortgage company, the levels of coverage are specified by the umbrella insurance policy.

According to Amy Fontinelle (2012) in "It's Raining Lawsuits: Do You Need An Umbrella Policy?" typical umbrella insurance requires the vehicle policy to provide a minimum level of coverage; usually at least $250,000 per person bodily injury coverage and $500,000 per accident. Auto insurance property damage minimum coverage is usually at least $100,000 per accident, and homeowner's insurance personal liability coverage must be at least $500,000.

These minimum vehicle and homeowner's policy amounts may vary depending on the specific umbrella policy. The examples above provide an idea of how the three types of insurance policies interrelate. It's helpful to purchase home, vehicle, and umbrella insurance from the same vendor to coordinate the policies.

Additional Benefits of Umbrella Insurance Coverage

The umbrella policy may also cover the policyholder's dependent children. For example, when 16-year-old Amelia causes a car accident, the umbrella policy can protect her as well. Depending on the specific provisions of the policy, it may cover the holder and family from lawsuits arising from slander, libel, defamation of character, false arrest, detention or imprisonment, abuse of process, malicious prosecution, shock/mental anguish, and more, although the consumer's umbrella policy should not be considered insurance for "business-related" liability. Additionally, the umbrella policy can be written to cover accidents caused by the policyholder and family while driving a boat or accidents that happen on one's rental property.

Limitations of an Umbrella Insurance Policy

There are many exclusions to an umbrella policy and, as with any insurance policy, the consumer needs to understand the policy exclusions. As stated in the prior section, umbrella insurance is personal coverage and won't protect one from lawsuits related to a business the policyholder owns. For example, if you offer child care in your home, an umbrella policy is not the appropriate liability coverage.

Umbrella insurance isn't for risky activities such as drag racing or piloting an airplane. It may not cover all types of vehicles, such as recreational motor vehicles, tractor-trailer trucks, farm vehicles, or other vehicles that exceed a particular weight limit. Umbrella insurance does not cover damage to the policyholder's own car or property; that coverage is provided by standard vehicle and homeowner's coverage.

If you lose a liability suit after committing a crime, the umbrella insurance will not cover the damages. If Jamal is convicted of driving under the influence and required to pay restitution, an umbrella insurance policy will not pay. Other illegal acts such as sexual harassment, discrimination, intentional harm to another's person or property, or malicious acts aren't covered.

Umbrella insurance does not supplement health insurance nor pay health insurance–related claims. For additional health-related coverage, the consumer should purchase a policy designed to compensate for medical-related concerns.

Some umbrella insurance policies require the policyholder to use the same insurance carrier not only for the umbrella policy, but for the vehicle and homeowner policies as well. In general, premium rates are usually less expensive the more policies the consumer has with the same insurance company.

Who Needs an Umbrella Policy?

If you ride the bus and don't own a home, you probably don't need an umbrella liability policy. Consumers with a pool, a dog, and a long commute are more likely to encounter a scenario where they are sued. If one is at greater risk, purchasing an umbrella policy will provide peace of mind and additional protection.

In general, umbrella policies are reasonably priced due to the fact that they are supplemental to home and auto insurance. As the consumer acquires greater income and assets, this type of insurance may be an important addition to his or her insurance protection suite of products.

Barbara Friedberg

See also: Homeowner's and Renter's Insurance; Risk

Further Reading

Businessdictionary.com. "Bumbershoot Policy." Accessed April 1, 2014. http://www.businessdictionary.com/definition/bumbershoot-policy.html

Fontinelle, Amy. 2012. "It's Raining Lawsuits: Do You Need an Umbrella Policy?" March 12. Investopedia. http://www.investopedia.com/articles/insurance/09/do-you-need-an-umbrella-policy.asp

Unemployment

Unemployment happens when an out-of-work individual is seeking employment. The unemployment rate is frequently in the news and is often viewed as one measure of the health of the economy. The unemployment rate is calculated by dividing the number of unemployed people by those working in the labor force. As of this writing, the latest U.S. unemployment rate (December 2013) was 6.7 percent. When the country is in a recession (a slowdown in economic activity), there is usually a high unemployment rate. For example, during the recent recession, the unemployment rate rose from 4.7 percent in November 2007 to its peak of 10 percent in October 2009.

Unemployment is defined and measured by the U.S. Bureau of Labor Statistics. To be considered unemployed, a worker must have these three qualities: the individual (1) is not working—even part-time; (2) is available and wants to work; and (3) has actively looked for a job in the past four weeks.

The Bureau of Labor Statistics considers those with jobs as employed. The unemployed are jobless, are looking for jobs, and are available for work. Those who are neither employed nor unemployed are not in the labor force.

Types of Unemployment

Economists give various theories and reasons for unemployment. Following are some of these reasons.

Classical Unemployment

Classical unemployment happens when workers are paid more than the market wage. A market wage is determined by the interacting forces of supply and demand. When this happens, the company must pay more per worker, and thus, due to the overpayment of existing workers, the employer can't afford to hire additional workers. In this case, the employer may even have to lay off some workers.

Cyclical Unemployment

Cyclical unemployment happens when workers lose their jobs during downturns in the business cycle. This type of unemployment is usually the cause of high unemployment, when rates quickly grow to 8 or even 10 percent of the labor force. It is referred to as cyclical because, when the economy resumes growth, the unemployed are usually rehired. Cyclical unemployment is temporary but may last anywhere from 18 months (the typical time frame of a recession) to 10 years (during a depression).

The cause of cyclical unemployment is a large drop-off in demand. This usually begins with less personal consumption. When people buy less, the demand for products decreases. When this happens, business revenues go down and, as a result, companies have to lay off their employees to keep their profit margins at a positive rate. This type of unemployment occurred during the recent housing crisis. When the demand for homes decreased, many builders had to lay off their employees because of the reduced demand for new houses. Cyclical unemployment is impacted by the normal business cycle, the multiyear increases and decreases in economic productivity.

Natural Unemployment

There will always be a level of unemployment, even when the economy is doing well. In fact, the lowest level of unemployment was in 1952 when it was 3 percent. This is why some level of unemployment is actually a good sign. If the rate is too low, there is usually some sort of economic excess or bubble that will eventually burst and lead to a high rate of job loss.

Frictional Unemployment

There is always frictional unemployment in the economy. This type of unemployment is caused when workers leave a job but have not found another one yet. Frictional unemployment is usually short-term and can actually benefit the economy, since it allows workers to move to another job where they can be more productive.

There are several causes for frictional unemployment, such as failing firms, which force employees to look for another employer; poor job performance, which leads to an employee's termination; or obsolete skills, which force employees to retool their skills. Another example of frictional unemployment occurs when graduated students look for their first job or parents reenter the workforce after child rearing.

Structural Unemployment

Structural unemployment occurs when there is a mismatch between available workers and skills needed in the economy. Currently, there is structural unemployment in the manufacturing industry as the need for skilled factory workers decreases in the United States. The large number of unemployed factory workers facing a lack of jobs are struggling to retool for more "in demand" jobs.

Recent advances in technology are causing an employment shift in the economy. Demand is increasing for highly skilled engineers and technical workers, and decreasing in other areas. Another example of structural unemployment is when a grocery store installs automatic checkouts and no longer needs cashiers at every register. The cashiers need to learn how to manage the automated checkouts that replaced them. This shift to self-checkout also reduces the number of cashiers that are needed in each retail store.

A long recession (similar to the recent 2007–2009 recession) can create structural unemployment. If workers are unemployed for too long, their skills may become outdated. These workers may remain unemployed for a long while unless they are willing and able to take a lower-level, unskilled job. Thus, structural unemployment can lead to a higher rate of natural unemployment.

Seasonal Unemployment

Seasonal unemployment is caused by employment changes during the calendar year. For example, farmworkers face seasonal unemployment during the certain months. In Florida, when oranges and grapefruit are in season, there are many jobs for people needed to pick and process this fruit; however, during the summer months, many of these individuals are no longer needed. Other examples of these types of seasonal workers include workers at summer and ski resorts.

Underemployment

Underemployment refers to workers that have jobs but are not working to their full capability. The underemployed include workers that are working part-time but want full-time employment. This occurs during a recession as many people will take whatever job is available in order to provide for their needs.

Real Unemployment

The real unemployment rate is not calculated by the U.S. Bureau of Labor Statistics, but many feel this is the most accurate level of the true unemployment rate. If the U.S. Bureau of Labor Statistics did calculate the real unemployment rate, it would consider people who have not looked for a job in the past month but have looked for work during the past year; those who have given up entirely on looking for work; and part-time workers who want to work more. If these people were counted, the nation's unemployment rate would, obviously, be much higher. In fact, according to a

Forbes article (Diamond, 2013), "Why the 'Real' Unemployment Rate Is Higher Than You Think," if real unemployment were calculated, our country's unemployment rate would be close to 14.3 percent.

In summary, unemployment happens when people are out of work and are looking to land a job. A person is considered unemployed if he or she is not working (even part-time), is available, and wants to work, or has actively looked for a job in the past four weeks.

Danny Kofke

See also: Year 2007–2008: Subprime Housing Crisis and Mortgage Meltdown; Year 2007–2009: Global Recession and Breakdown of Major Wall Street Institutions

Further Reading

Diamond, Dan. 2013. "Why the 'Real' Unemployment Rate Is Higher Than You Think." July 5. http://www.forbes.com/sites/dandiamond/2013/07/05/why-the-real-unemployment-rate-is-higher-than-you-think/

Econport. "Types of Unemployment." Accessed March 16, 2014. http://www.econport.org/content/handbook/Unemployment/Types.html

U.S. Department of Labor, Bureau of Labor Statistics. "Labor Force Statistics from the Current Population Survey." Accessed March 16, 2014. http://www.bls.gov/cps/cps_htgm.htm

U.S. Federal Tax System Overview

U.S. Supreme Court justice Oliver Wendell Holmes summarized taxes in two sentences: "I like to pay taxes. With them I buy civilization."

Holmes's characterization of taxes is straightforward. A nation uses money collected primarily via taxes from its citizenry to provide services—schools, roads, the military, national parks, and more—for the overall good of the country and its residents. However, the tax structure used to collect the United States' necessary operating cash is not that simple.

The current federal tax system has four main elements. There is an income tax on individuals and corporations. Payroll taxes are collected by employers on workers' wages, and individuals who work as contractors or have their own businesses pay corresponding taxes on self-employment income. There are federal estate and gift taxes. Finally, excise taxes are imposed on selected goods and services. Although each citizen likely will encounter all of these tax components at some point, the most direct involvement most Americans have with taxes is through the income tax.

Income Tax's Civil War Origin

On August 5, 1861, President Abraham Lincoln signed the Revenue Act, creating the first federal income tax. The 3 percent tax on annual incomes of more than $800 and

5 percent on incomes above $10,000 was authorized as a way to pay Civil War costs. To put these taxes into perspective, according to a National Bureau of Economic Research publication (Long, 1960), in 1860 the U.S. census reported $289 average annual earnings. By 1880, the average annual income was $347.

The taxation of individual incomes was a new revenue-raising approach. Previously, the federal Treasury relied on excise taxes and customs duties. When the war ended and budget needs eased, Congress tweaked the income tax, reducing rates and increasing exemptions. The income tax was allowed to lapse in 1872.

A flat-rate income tax was tried in 1894, but the law was challenged. The U.S. Supreme Court ruled the following year that under the Constitution, Congress could impose direct taxes only if they were levied in proportion to each state's population.

To prevent another constitutional challenge, in 1909 Congress passed the Sixteenth Amendment, which established the federal income tax system used today. On February 3, 1913, Delaware became the 36th state to ratify the Sixteenth Amendment and Congress quickly passed the Revenue Act of 1913. The 1913 tax rates ranged from 1 percent for taxpayers making $20,000 to 7 percent for taxpayers with incomes of more than $500,000. Less than 1 percent of the population paid income tax in 1913.

The Bureau of Internal Revenue established a Personal Income Tax Division to collect the new tax. Form 1040, which is still filed today, was introduced as the standard tax reporting form.

Annual Taxes on Worldwide Income

Today's income taxes are collected by the Internal Revenue Service, a branch of the U.S. Treasury. The federal tax year is the same as the calendar year. Changes in one's life throughout the year could affect a citizen's tax filing and eventual tax bill. Common lifestyle changes that affect taxes include getting married, having a child, getting a pay raise, and getting divorced. In most instances, the tax responsibilities provide real financial value at an affordable cost based on one's situation on December 31, the end of the tax year.

Tax due each year applies to all one's income, regardless of where it is earned. This is known as a worldwide system of taxation, as opposed to a territorial tax system where taxes are collected only on money earned within a country's borders.

Progressive Tax Brackets and Rates

Today's tax brackets, that is, the income amounts taxed at certain rates, are progressive just as they were in 1913. That means that the tax rate is greater for higher incomes than for lower incomes. Currently, there are seven income tax rates: 10 percent, 15 percent, 25 percent, 28 percent, 33 percent, 35 percent, and 39.6 percent.

Progressivity also means that a higher income earner's money is not all taxed at his or her top rate. A person in the top 39.6 percent income bracket has a portion of income taxed at all the other rates, too. Only the amount in the top bracket is taxed at that highest rate. This is known as the effective tax rate.

The different tax brackets and their progressivity mean that while a single taxpayer who makes $100,000 is in the 28 percent tax bracket (based on 2013 tax rates and brackets; the brackets are adjusted annually for inflation), not all of that individual's income is taxed at 28 percent. The individual's first $8,925 is taxed at 10 percent. Earnings of $8,926 to $36,250 are taxed at 15 percent. The 25 percent tax bracket applies to earnings of $36,251 to $87,850. The final salary of $87,851 to $100,000 is taxed at 28 percent.

When this individual earns more, earnings between $87,851 up to $183,250 of the income will stay in the 28 percent bracket. Additional earnings will be taxed in the 35 percent and 39.6 percent tax brackets. Again, the amount of earnings in each tax bracket is adjusted annually for inflation. The tax rates can be changed only by Congress.

The tax code also imposes different tax rates on different types of income. Money paid for work done is considered ordinary income to which the current seven tax rates apply. Money made from investments is considered unearned income and in certain cases receives more favorable tax treatment. For example, the sale of an asset that has been owned for more than a year is taxed at a lower rate. This income is called a capital gain as opposed to earned income.

Pay-as-You-Earn Withholding

The U.S. tax system operates on a pay-as-you-earn system. This means that individuals pay income taxes incrementally throughout the tax year, typically through payroll withholding.

Employers, using tax tables formulated each year based on tax rates and income brackets, take out a portion of each worker's pay for taxes, both federal and, where applicable depending on the worker's residency and tax law there, state and local income tax amounts. In addition, Federal Insurance Contributions Act (FICA) taxes are taken out of a worker's pay and matched by the employer to go toward Social Security and Medicare.

The exact amount of payroll withholding is based on the Form W-4 each taxpayer completes and gives to his or her employer. The W-4 takes into account marital status and how many children or other dependents a taxpayer has. Whenever there is a life change that could affect an individual's taxes, such as buying a home for which deductions can be claimed or having a child, the worker should give the employer an updated W-4 so that the withholding amount will be accurate.

The self-employed must pay taxes throughout the year. But instead of remitting taxes when paid for each job, the self-employed individual files estimated tax payments using Form 1040ES four times a year.

When too much is withheld from wages or overpaid in estimated taxes, the taxpayer gets a refund. If withholding is too little, the individual owes taxes.

Exactly how much is owed Uncle Sam or is to be issued to the taxpayer as a refund is figured when the annual tax return, due each April 15 (or by October 15 if an extension request is completed), is filed. At this time, the information entered on the tax return will be used to reconcile how much the individual paid via withholding with the filer's actual final tax bill.

The Future of Taxes

The last major overhaul of the Internal Revenue Code was the Tax Reform Act of 1986, a bipartisan effort between Democratic members of Congress and Republican president Ronald Reagan. The law not only eliminated many tax shelters, but it also lowered the top tax rate while simultaneously raising the bottom tax rate, a rate-change first for the U.S. tax code.

In 2001 and 2003, under bills championed by Republican president George W. Bush, tax rates that had shifted upward in the 1990s were lowered and new tax breaks added. These changes, dubbed the Bush-era tax cuts, were scheduled to expire at the end of 2010, but after much congressional debate they were extended through 2012.

On January 2, 2013, the Taxpayer Relief Act of 2012 was signed into law by Democratic president Barack Obama. Also known as the fiscal cliff bill because it forestalled potential fiscal calamities posed by the eventual expiration of the Bush-era tax laws, the 2013 bill raised the top tax rate from 35 percent to 39.6 percent.

As the continual legislative revisions demonstrate, the U.S. tax system is not static. The U.S. tax code will continue to evolve as America's fiscal needs and the political landscape change.

Kay Bell

See also: Bush, George W., 43rd President of the United States; Capital Gains and Capital Losses; Obama, Barack, President of the United States; Tax Deferral; Tax Return, Federal

Further Reading

IRS. "IRS Understanding Taxes." IRS.gov Web site. Accessed August 6, 2013. http://www.irs.gov/pub/irs-pdf/p2181.pdf

Joint Committee on Taxation, Congress of the United States Web site. "Overview of the Federal Tax System as in Effect for 2012." Accessed August 6, 2013. https://www.jct.gov/publications.html?func=startdown&id=4400

Long, Clarence D. 1960. "Annual Earnings." Chapter 3 of *Wages and Earnings in the United States, 1860–1890*, pp. 39–49. Princeton University Press. http://www.nber.org/chapters/c2497.pdf

Piketty, Thomas, and Emmanuel Saez. 2007. "How Progressive Is the U.S. Federal Tax System? A Historical and International Perspective." *Journal of Economic Perspectives* (Winter), Vol. 21, No. 1, 3–24. http://elsa.berkeley.edu/~saez/piketty-saezJEP07tax-prog.pdf

Tax Analysts Web site. "Tax History Museum." Accessed August 6, 2013. http://www.tax-history.org/www/website.nsf/Web/TaxHistoryMuseum?OpenDocument

Tax Foundation Web site. "Federal Individual Income Tax Rates History." Accessed August 6, 2013. http://taxfoundation.org/sites/taxfoundation.org/files/docs/fed_rates_history_nominal_1913_2013_0.pdf

Wills and Trusts

A will is a legal document in which a person states who should receive their possessions after they die. A trust is a fiduciary (when one trusted individual is directed to act on behalf of another) relationship in which one person, known as a trustor, gives another person, the trustee, the right to hold title to property or assets for the benefit of another, who is known as the beneficiary. A trust can be in effect during the trustor's lifetime or created upon his or her death. Both wills and trusts are governed by state law.

History of Wills and Trust

During the Middle Ages the Christian Church exercised its authority over domestic matters, such as probate. Probate is the legal process by which a court validates a will. Under religious beliefs at this time, it was thought to be sinful not to have a will, and it was expected that some portion of the deceased's estate would go to the Church for the saying of masses. Therefore, the ecclesiastical (religious) courts would oversee the distribution of all personal property, and if an individual died without having made a will, the Church would then assume jurisdiction of the dead person's goods. In 1857, England passed legislation that transferred probate from the ecclesiastical courts to the Courts of Probate. Early American colonists brought English traditions with them and established the first probate court in the United States in Massachusetts.

The idea of trusts being created upon the death of the trustor can be traced back to Roman times, but it is not until the Middle Ages and the Crusades that we see the introduction of living trusts. When a knight fought in a foreign land, he conveyed ownership of his lands and income generated from those lands to another with the understanding that upon his return, the lands would be returned. The other party (the trustee) was holding the lands and income for the knight's benefit. However, when many of these knights returned, the trustees refused to reconvey the lands and rents. The knights then had to petition the king, who set up the Courts of Chancery to hear the cases. It quickly was established that the knights did not "give" their land away but in fact had established a trust relationship stating that the land was held for the benefit of the knights while they were away fighting for the king. It is from this circumstance that the modern-day inter vivos or living trust concept developed (Beyer, 2012).

Wills

The idea behind a last will and testament is that individuals have the ability to own property during their lifetime and should have a say as to the dispensation of their property upon death. A will gives one the ability to make one's wishes known regarding how one's personal belongings will be distributed, who should care for any minor children left behind, and how any final expenses should be paid for. Many people, however, die without their wishes being made known. It is estimated that upward of 70 percent of Americans currently do not have a will. Dying without a will is known as dying intestate.

When a person dies intestate the court does not have a document to follow, so it must look to the state law of intestacy to determine who will inherit the decedent's estate. Though this varies from state to state, typically the property goes first to a surviving spouse, then to children and their descendants. If there is no spouse or children, the law of intestacy looks to the decedent's parents, then siblings, the siblings' descendants, the grandparents, and so forth until a surviving relative can be found. If no surviving relative can be found, then the decedent's estate will be turned over to the state government. Today, many commercial legal publishers have created do-it-yourself will kits that allow individuals with no legal training to create basic last will and testament documents inexpensively.

Trusts

Trusts take two different forms. Those that are created by an individual's death for the benefit of another are known as testamentary trusts. Those created while an individual is still alive are known as either inter vivos trusts or living trusts.

A testamentary trust is created by the terms of a will and only goes into effect after the person's death. The person who creates this type of trust is known as the trustor or settlor. They may name an individual to act as the trustee, and that person oversees how the assets are managed in the trust and makes payouts to the beneficiary, who will receive funds from the trust. Often these types of trusts are used for the benefit of an individual, such as a minor child or incapacitated individual. Testamentary trusts are irrevocable because they only fund after an individual has died.

A living trust is created during the trustor's lifetime through the declaration of trust document and placing of property into the trust. This type of trust has a duration that is determined at its creation and can include distribution of assets to the beneficiary during or after the trustor's lifetime. Often this type of trust is used in estate planning to avoid the lengthy probate court process, which can be costly and expose a wealthy family's private financial matters to the public. Living trusts can be either revocable or irrevocable.

Revocable trusts allow trustors to retain control of all the assets in the trust, and they can revoke or change the terms of the trust at any time. Irrevocable trusts do not allow the trustors to revoke or make changes to the trust once it has been created.

Specialty Trusts

There are certain situations when families need trusts to assist them in managing more complex financial or medical circumstances. The following is a brief synopsis of some of these specialty trusts.

Credit Shelter Trust

A credit shelter trust allows a spouse to include in his or her will the amount up to but not exceeding the estate-tax exemption. This is a dollar amount that may be inherited federally tax exempt to the heir. The remaining assets fund a testamentary trust for the benefit of the heirs and avoid estate taxes. The amount equal to the estate-tax exemption passes tax-free to the surviving spouse.

Generation-Skipping Trust

A generation-skipping trust is used to transfer a substantial amount of money tax-free to beneficiaries who are at least two generations the junior, typically grandchildren, of the trustor.

Health and Education Exclusion Trust

A health and education exclusion trust is a trust that is created to pay for the education and medical care of grandchildren and more remote descendants without being subject to the generation-skipping tax.

Pet Trusts

A pet trust is used for the care and maintenance of a trustor's pets in the event of their owner's disability or death. In some states, the trust may continue for the rest of the animal's life or for 21 years, whichever comes first.

Special Needs Trust

A special needs trust is created for the care of beneficiaries who are disabled or mentally ill. These types of trust also may shelter beneficiaries from losing access to essential government benefits.

Qualified Terminable Interest Property Trust

Qualified terminable interest property trusts are often used when there are families in which there have been divorces, remarriages, and stepchildren. This type of trust allows a surviving spouse to either receive income from the trust or remain in a home during his or her lifetime, and the beneficiaries (e.g., children from a first marriage) will get the principal or home upon the surviving spouse's death.

Wills and trusts are part of the overall estate planning process. They are tools individuals can use to manage the effective disposal of their assets in accordance with their wishes. They are in effect the last personal financial activity in which one will engage.

John C. Linfield

See also: Estate Planning; Life Insurance; Probate; U.S. Federal Tax System Overview

Further Reading

American Bar Association Web site. "Family Law in the 50 States." Accessed October 16, 2013. http://www.americanbar.org/groups/family_law/resources/family_law_in_the_50_states.html

Beyer, Gerry W. 2012. *Examples & Explanations: Wills, Trusts, and Estates,* 5th ed. New York, NY: Aspen Publishers.

Haertle, Eugene M. 1962. "The History of Probate Court." *Marquette Law Review* (Vol. 45, No. 4): 546–554.

Weisbord, Reid K. 2012. "Wills for Everyone: Helping Individuals Opt Out of Intestacy." *Boston College Law Review* (Vol. 53, No. 5): 877–952.

Events

Year 1930s: The Great Depression

The Great Depression was the deepest and longest economic downturn in the modern industrialized world. It began in October 1929 and its impacts were felt up to 1939. It impacted the stock market, unemployment, incomes, and production.

By 1933 unemployment was at 25 percent and more than half of the banks had failed. From 1933 until 1939 the economy began a slow recovery, although it wasn't until World War II that factories and the economy started growing at a steady pace.

The Stock Market Crash

In October 1929, the stock market crashed, causing panic and the loss of billions of dollars. The market began its decline at the start of September. September was a wildly fluctuating month with dips, followed by stabilizing and increases. This continued until October 23, when it began its steady decline. The first major crash day was on October 24 and is referred to as Black Thursday. On Black Thursday the market opened in a free fall and ended up trading 12.9 million shares, which was the highest trade volume in history.

A short five days later on October 29, 1929, another major crash came, named Black Tuesday. On this day 16 million shares were traded, beating Black Thursday. By the end of the five days, the market had crashed 25 percent and had wiped out $30 billion in value. By November 13, the lowest day in 1929, the market had lost $100 billion.

Why did the stock market crash in October? The stock market in 1929 was in a bubble, meaning that prices were not validated by any measure and prices were unreasonably high. Stock prices could not be tied to corporate profits or any other measure. People believed that the stock market would just keep going up and that it would never stop, so they continued to pay higher and higher prices for stocks. However, the overall U.S. economy was not doing well. In the spring of 1929, steel production was down, construction was down, car sales were dropping, and many people were deeply in debt because it was so easy to borrow.

This crash was made even worse by the fact that many traders in 1929 were trading on margin. Margin is debt used to buy more shares of stock than you have money for. For example, you could put 10 percent down and borrow the rest of the money from the bank. If you had $1,000, you could buy up to $10,000 in stock.

As the price of the stocks dropped, the stock owners received margin calls, which is when the lender asks for more money to back the shares because of a decreased value in the stocks. Thus as the shares dropped, investors had to pay money to keep their margin accounts out of default. They were required to maintain the 10 percent. If they didn't have the money, or could not borrow it from somewhere else, they'd have to sell the stock. As the market continued to fall, many did not have the available cash and credit was disappearing, so instead they had to sell their shares to cover the loan. This caused even more shares to be sold, creating a downward spiral in the market.

Banking

In the 1930s, people pulled their money from the local banks and kept it at home. People didn't trust the banks to be there the next day, since so many had collapsed, and instead preferred to control the location of their money.

More than half of the banks had failed and banks were failing every single day. In an attempt to save the banking institutions, the Hoover administration began loaning money to banks to try to create some stability. However, this wasn't working. When Franklin Delano Roosevelt was elected president, he instituted a bank holiday.

The banks closed for four days so that Congress had time to put some laws into place to help reopen the banks on a sound footing. Part of this process included not reopening those that were not financially healthy. This was intended to calm the nerves of Americans and help the banks get a foundation to work from without worrying about a run on the money.

New Programs That Came from the Great Depression

Because of all the instability, unemployment, and issues such as the U.S. Treasury not having enough money to pay federal government workers, President Roosevelt created some programs to help improve confidence in the system. One of those programs was the Fireside Chat, a speech presented by Roosevelt over the radio that told the nation what was happening. Before these talks, it was hard to communicate accurately what the government was doing to help the economy turn around.

The government also created the Federal Deposit Insurance Corporation (FDIC) to insure bank deposits at qualified banks. This allowed depositors to be confident that their money would be there if the bank closed its doors.

The Securities and Exchange Commission (SEC) was created to help control the stock market, adding more regulations for investors. Their job is to monitor the companies and people who trade in the financial markets, ensuring that they provide accurate information to the public. Part of the great run-up in the stock market was due to investors working together to profit from the market. These were called pools. Investors would put their money together, start buying a particular company, and at the same time get positive press about that company. As everyone else began to buy because it was a hot stock, the original investors would sell at the top, then the stock would collapse. At the time this was legal and commonplace, yet it was one of the problems with the market's growth. The SEC would correct this and other issues.

During the Great Depression the New Deal programs were started. The New Deal put into place public works projects, such as the Tennessee Valley Authority, to get people back to work.

Social Security also came out of the Great Depression. At the start of the Great Depression, the United States did not have a social aid system. The original focus of the program was for unemployment insurance and assistance for families with children. While retirement income was included in the original concept, it was not implemented until after the Great Depression officially ended.

The Cause of the Great Depression

What caused the Great Depression and why did it last so long? The stock market bubble triggered it because of the great amount of wealth that was wiped out, but that was not the only factor that made it last as long as it did or be as bad as it was. Additionally, there were many years of declining consumer confidence and consumer spending. This created a domino effect, which made the factories produce less, causing unemployment and deflation. With no confidence and no one spending, it was hard to get any upward movement in the economy.

The End of the Great Depression

The Great Depression finally came to an end with the start of World War II. This ramped up factory production, pulling the country out of the Depression. In 1941, when Pearl Harbor was attacked and the United States officially entered the war, the factories not only went into full production but would go over capacity. By 1942, unemployment was lower than at prerecession levels and spending had recovered.

Comparison to the Great Recession

Many people argue that the Great Recession (2008–2009) was more intense than the Great Depression. However, by definition, a recession is two quarters of a declining economy. A depression does not have a specific number of quarters for a definition but is instead defined as a sustained downward trend in the economy.

The Great Recession started in December 2007 and ended in June 2009 with only two years of a decline in GDP, and so far no return to recession. In contrast, the Great Depression was four years of a decline in GDP with a turnaround for three years, followed by another decline. Even with the few years of growth during the Depression, the impacts of unemployment and deflation were still being felt across the United States, which did not fully recover during those positive years. Additionally, the unemployment rate for the Great Recession was 10.1 percent, while for the Great Depression it was 25 percent.

Andrea Travillian

See also: Banking; Debt; Deflation; Gross Domestic Product (GDP) and Gross National Product (GNP); Federal Reserve Bank; Investing; Margin; Social Security; Stock Market; Stocks; Unemployment

Further Reading

About.com U.S. Economy. "Black Tuesday." Accessed March 26, 2014. http://useconomy
.about.com/od/glossary/g/Black_Tuesday.htm

About.com U.S. Economy. "US GDP by Year." Accessed March 26, 2014. http://useconomy
.about.com/od/GDP-by-Year/a/US-GDP-History.htm

History.com. "The Great Depression." Accessed March 26, 2014. http://www.history.com/
topics/great-depression

PBS. "The Crash of 1929." Accessed March 26, 2014. http://www.pbs.org/wgbh/american
experience/films/crash/

U.S. Securities and Exchange Commission. "The Investor's Advocate." Accessed March
26, 2014. http://www.sec.gov/about/whatwedo.shtml#.UzHwcoWKKvg

Year 1944: Creation of the International Monetary Fund and the World Bank at the Bretton Woods International Conference

The Bretton Woods agreement was the major milestone in establishing a working international currency system after World War II. It lasted 25 years, promoted trade, ensured stability, and enabled world recovery.

Background

World War I left the world in a terrible mess. Most of Europe was devastated as the old order collapsed. The classical gold standard for currencies that had evolved in the 19th century was largely abandoned.

Inflation was rife—prices doubled in the United States and United Kingdom and tripled in France. Large balance of payment deficits and surpluses developed, which the world financial system could not accommodate. Damage was done by the war reparations demanded of Germany, and the country's government struggled to meet the payments. Germany issued enormous sums of currency to support workers on strike against the French occupation of the German Ruhr region and to buy foreign currency with which to pay its war reparations.

The United States tried to help by granting loans to the German government so that much of the German debt was ultimately owed to U.S. banks. President Hoover proposed suspending repayments in 1931, but this was crucially delayed by France, leading to the well-documented German hyperinflation. The reparations were repudiated when Hitler came to power in 1933, but restarted after World War II and have since been repaid in full.

Wall Street Crash—1929

Meanwhile, the hedonistic abandonment and unregulated investment practices of the Roaring Twenties led to overconfidence in the stock market. Novice investors tried to climb on the bandwagon, some borrowing money in order to invest in the explosive stock market. (Investing with borrowed money is also called buying on margin.)

The resulting Wall Street crash of 1929 sent stock prices plummeting. The U.S. economy suffered from commodity price volatility, speculation, fraud, and loss of confidence. Various attempts were made to stabilize the market, but these did not last. Bankruptcies were rampant. Banks malfunctioned and many people lost their savings. Unemployment and poverty spread throughout the United States and to every country in the world. Over the next two and a half years the Dow-Jones index lost a total of 89 percent of its value from its peak and did not return to that level until September 1954.

There were international repercussions as well. Various countries enacted competitive currency devaluations, isolationist barriers, and protectionist policies. To further harm global trade and expansion, trading blocs evolved. These policies were frequently inconsistent, both within a currency zone as well as between zones. Runs on European banks led to the failure of the German central bank, and Germany adopted exchange controls in 1931.

The crash also resulted in a demand for U.S. gold. The United States outlawed and confiscated private gold holdings completely in 1933 and set the price of gold as $35 per ounce in 1934.

The stage was set for the Bretton Woods initiatives near the end of World War II. As World War II was entering its final stages, the Allies began to plan ahead for the postwar economic future, and work began in the United States and Britain to chart a course for rebuilding the world economy. All parties were especially keen to avoid the economic problems that bedeviled the era following World War I.

Bretton Woods Conference

The Bretton Woods Conference, held July 1–22, 1944, in Bretton Woods, New Hampshire, was the result of several years of planning and affirmed the right of nations to equal access to trade and raw materials, and freedom of the seas. The 44 Allied nations at the conference aimed to provide what had been lacking in the period between the wars, a system of international payments and stable exchange rates as well as open markets. Furthermore, the conference strived to alleviate global economic problems such as currency manipulations and restrictive trade policies, which led to economic deflation and the economic depression of the 1930s.

The conference divided into two groups, one looking above all for price stability, promoted by the United States and represented by Harry Dexter White. The other camp was championing economic growth, led by Great Britain and represented by the famous economist John Maynard Keynes. The British plan advocated for a world currency and a world bank with full powers and recommended actions for creditor as well as debtor nations. The United States saw this as too grandiose and was more concerned about inflation. To the United States, the debt problem was a problem for the debtor nations alone, while the UK proposal considered it a problem for creditors as well because of the risk of recession in debtor nations. As the United States was the only Allied nation not to be completely destroyed by the war, and therefore the major creditor, the only option was to accept U.S. leadership. The International Monetary Fund and the International Bank for Reconstruction and Development were born from the Bretton Woods Conference.

International Monetary Fund

The International Monetary Fund (IMF) was created after World War II to prevent future economic crises like the Great Depression. The organization was one of the outcomes of the Bretton Woods Conference.

The IMF is a partner of the United Nations and is based in Washington, D.C., with voting on the basis of quotas. The size of each country's quota is calculated by how much each government can pay, which is weighted by the size of its economy. The voting rights are based on the quota size, giving larger economies more voting rights than smaller ones. By accord, the managing director of the IMF is a European. Since 2011, the managing director has been Christine Lagarde, a French citizen.

The IMF oversees international monetary policy and attempts to create a systematic method for international payments. By facilitating international payments, international trade and world economies can thrive and grow. The IMF is an agency of the United Nations and is run by its 186 member countries. Any country that conducts foreign policy and abides by the IMF policies may join.

Along with the World Bank, the IMF is the largest public lender of funds in the world. The ultimate goal of the IMF is to create a balanced global economic system.

There was chaos and turmoil after World War II. All Allied governments, apart from the United States, were bankrupt and experienced economic devastation. Rather than revert to a gold standard, it was decided that all other currencies' values would be pegged against the dollar. At that time the U.S. dollar was fixed against gold at the $35 per ounce prewar level.

In this way the dollar acted as a proxy for gold as far as all other currencies were concerned, and it was unnecessary for countries to hold reserves of gold themselves. European nations involved in World War II were all in debt, so they transferred substantial amounts of gold to the United States in return for the support. The U.S. dollar became the de facto world reserve currency. Having a convertible dollar was a great benefit.

International Bank for Reconstruction and Development

Normality was required to implement these changes, and to this end the International Bank for Reconstruction and Development (IBRD), one of five institutions that constitute the World Bank, was devised to enable reconstruction of war-torn Europe by loans and securities. It offers long-term loans and lines of credit of up to 30 years. The goal of the IBRD is to improve the financial strength of middle-income countries through financial assistance and economic advice.

The IBRD raises money by issuing bonds. Members, who must also be members of the IMF, are shareholders. The bank only finances sovereign governments or government-backed projects. A member country can be a borrowing member, but once it has sufficiently mature long-term systems in place it may not need the resources of the IBRD.

The IBRD is part of what is known as the World Bank and was joined by the International Development Association in 1960. The IBRD is also an important partner for the United Nations, and by accord the president is always an American citizen. Since 2012, the president has been Jim Yong Kim, an American of Korean origin.

Postwar Events

As the postwar events unraveled, two things became evident. The first was that the scale of devastation would take a lot longer and a lot more money to correct than had been anticipated. The large number of refugees and stateless people, and the wide-spread destruction of infrastructure and civic institutions meant that there would be mass starvation and worse unless something was done.

The second was that Europe had become divided by the Iron Curtain, as Churchill dubbed it. In some countries communists were elected, voters knowing that some of the most effective opposition to Nazi fascism had been from that quarter.

The facilities within the IMF were not sufficient to deal with these issues and the European Recovery Plan, known as the Marshall Plan, was initiated by the United States in 1947 to provide grants rather than loans. Assistance under the Marshall Plan was rejected by the Soviets, who recognized that one of the goals of the plan was to help prevent the spread of communism. Over the years, some $12.7 billion was granted and the extreme austerity of the late 1940s was relaxed to the benefit of all.

End of Bretton Woods

Ultimately, pegging gold to $35 per ounce proved too hard to maintain as the market price of gold floated upward. Some nations, France in particular, started to build up their own gold reserves, even demanding gold for their dollars. Europe, in the form of the European Economic Community, and Japan had begun to be substantial players and to close the income gap with the United States. The costs of the Vietnam War resulted in a deterioration of the U.S. balance of payments. The IMF created the Special Drawing Rights as an international reserve asset. This represents a group of currencies that members could call on if necessary.

President Nixon unilaterally revoked the convertibility of dollars to gold in 1971. Soon afterward, Japan and the EEC countries decided to allow their currencies to float. A floating currency means that its value, in comparison with the value of other countries' currencies, adjusts based on various economic factors. For example, if the Canadian dollar and U.S. dollar floated, at one point in time 1 U.S. dollar would be equal to 1.10 Canadian dollars, and then, based on many factors, the exchange rate might change or float and 1 U.S. dollar would be worth .97 Canadian dollar.

Today almost all currencies float with the dollar as the most important, although the euro is prominent on the world currency scene. The Bretton Woods Conference was the driving force behind the dismissal of the gold standard.

Maria Nedeva

See also: Banking; Currency; Deflation; Gross Domestic Product (GDP) and Gross National Product (GNP); Federal Reserve Bank; Inflation; Lagarde, Christine, Managing Director, International Monetary Fund; Year 1999: Introduction of the Euro to World Financial Markets; Yellen, Janet, 15th Chair of the U.S. Federal Reserve Board

Further Reading

Markwell, Donald John. 2006. *John Maynard Keynes and International Relations: Economic Paths to War and Peace.* Oxford: Oxford University Press.

"Proceedings and Documents of the United Nations Monetary and Financial Conference, Bretton Woods, New Hampshire, July 1–22, 1944." Fraser: Federal Reserve Archive. Accessed October 26, 2013. http://fraser.stlouisfed.org/publication?pid=430

Wiggin, Addison. November 29, 2006. "Bretton Woods Agreement," *The Daily Reckoning.* http://www.dailyreckoning.com.au/bretton-woods-agreement/2006/11/29/

Year 1970s to 1980s: Economic Problems and the United States

The U.S. economy experienced a rapid transformation in the late 1970s and early 1980s, with a shift away from manufacturing toward an information-based service economy, an increasing participation of women in the labor force, and the emergence of a trade deficit. Inflation proved to be a persistent problem that could not be ignored and economic policies adopted to address these problems had long-lasting social implications. An understanding of these periods will help individuals appreciate the nature of the contemporary American economy and society.

Economic Problems in the Late 1970s and Early 1980s

Many Americans enjoyed a period of unprecedented prosperity in the post–World War II years, characterized by high employment, stable prices, and rising income. This prosperity was interrupted by the food and energy shock in 1973–1974, resulting in a rapid rise of inflation. The Consumer Price Index, one of the key measures of inflation, rocketed from 3.4 percent in 1972 to 12.2 percent in 1974 (Blinder, p. 265) and stunned many Americans.

Inflation fell in intervening years but from 1977 it climbed steadily, before reaching a new height in 1980 at 13.5 percent. Unemployment also rose hand in hand with inflation, puzzling policymakers due to the widespread belief of a trade-off between inflation and unemployment (when inflation is high, unemployment is low, and when unemployment is high, inflation is low). With unemployment reaching 7.4 percent in 1980, the United States suffered from classic symptoms of stagflation characterized by both high unemployment and high inflation.

For generations growing up in the postwar years accustomed to low inflation rates (less than 2 percent in the first half of the 1960s and about 4 percent in the early 1970s), the rise of inflation to over 12 percent in 1979 and 1980 tainted their economic optimism. By 1980, opinion polls revealed that the American public saw inflation as the problem of greatest concern and many were willing to tolerate drastic measures to reduce it (Feldstein, p. 4; Wells, p. 111).

Factors Contributing to Inflation

One theory traces the rise of inflation in the late 1970s to the rising food prices, which rose 22 percent between 1977 and 1979. Much of the increase is attributed to "meat inflation." Meat prices as measured by the CPI rose extraordinarily high and were quite variable during 1978–1979, partly due to a sharp drop (over 16 percent) in the country's cattle population (Blinder, 1982).

The high oil prices and the energy shock in 1979 ensured a continued acceleration of inflation. The political turmoil in Iran and the downfall of the shah resulted in disruptions in supply and chaos in the world oil market, resulting in lines at gasoline stations in various locations in the spring and summer months of 1979 (Blinder, p. 270). Between December 1978 and March 1980, the average cost per barrel of imported crude oil to U.S. refiners rose from about $15 to over $33. As a result, the CPI energy component rose 56 percent (a 43 percent annual rate) between December 1978 and March 1980 (Blinder, p. 271).

In addition, the increase in mortgage rates also fueled inflation. Mortgage interest rates were about 6 percent in the 1960s, and throughout 1977 they stood at 9 percent before increasing dramatically to 10 percent by December 1978 and 12 percent by 1980.

Interest rates have a huge impact on monthly mortgage payments, and the rising costs of borrowing (in addition to the rapid rise in prices) inflicted economic hardship on many American families in the 1980s as their household budget was badly squeezed. This had a long-term social impact, forcing many women to enter the labor market to help the family with the rising costs of living. Additionally, women entered the workforce because of the women's liberation movement.

These factors above do not tell the whole story. Inflation was a persistent problem in the 1970s because, with the Great Depression fresh in people's minds, unemployment had been the government's economic priority. Inflation was tolerated because it was thought that this would keep unemployment low. The United States, unlike other countries such as Switzerland and West Germany, saw its inflation rates rise high in 1979 because it did not make a more determined effort to reduce inflation after the first oil shock in 1973 (Mussa, 1994). When the second oil shock came, inflation was already at more than 9 percent, which ensured that inflation would jump to new peaks during 1979 (Mussa, p. 93).

President Reagan's Government and Economic Policies

It is generally agreed that the major economic success of President Reagan's policies (along with those of the Federal Reserve chair, Paul Volcker) lay in its triumphant battle against inflation. The CPI fell from 13.5 percent in 1980 to 3.9 percent in 1982 and remained at around 4 percent for the rest of Reagan's presidency.

The battle against inflation was won because inflation became the government's number one priority. In dealing with inflation, the government's strategy was influenced by Milton Friedman's theory, which sees the control of the money supply as an essential weapon.

From November 1980 (when President Reagan was elected president) and for 21 months until 1982, the Federal Reserve pursued a very tight monetary policy to combat inflation, even at the expense of business activity (Mussa, 1994). As a result, the American economy was plunged into a recession in 1981–1982, with an estimated loss of output of more than $200–$300 billion (in 1982 dollars). Consequently, unemployment soared to new heights in January 1983 with more than 11.5 million people unemployed, or 10.4 percent.

Taming inflation was only half the battle; higher standards of living required higher productivity. To get the American economy moving again, President Reagan believed it was essential to give people incentives to work, save, and invest by reducing federal expenditure and personal taxes. Social Security spending was cut by $40 billion, top tax rates were reduced from 70 to 50 percent, and income tax rates were reduced by 25 percent over three years (Wells, p. 115). During the 1980s 18 million new jobs were created, the economy grew by about 3.5 percent per year, and real disposable per capita income rose by 18 percent (Sloan, p. 7). Unemployment, however, remained at 5 percent throughout the 1980s, reflecting structural shifts in the economy.

The sharp appreciation of the dollar from the mid-1980s through mid-1981 may have helped reduce the inflation rate. It also accelerated the decline of manufacturing.

The United States had low savings, and high interest rates were intended to encourage savings, but these led to the appreciation of the dollar. Between 1980 and 1985, the dollar appreciated by more than 60 percent against other industrial democratic currencies. This made U.S. exports expensive and uncompetitive, and exports fell from 8.1 percent to 5.1 percent of GDP in this period. For the first time, the United States became a net debtor. The trade deficit peaked in 1987 at $152.13 billion (Wells, 2003).

Social Consequences—Women in the Workforce and Growing Inequality

There is a general consensus that economic progress in the 1980s was accompanied by a growing inequality in American society. In 1980, there were 4,414 millionaires in America, rising rapidly to 34,944 by 1987 (Sloan, p. 252). The number of persons living below the official poverty line, on the other hand, increased from 26.1 million in 1979 to 32.5 million in 1987 (Sloan, p. 100).

The reasons for this are less clear. One theory believes that the enterprise culture of the 1980s, the philosophy of limited government intervention, and low taxes contributed to the growing inequality in U.S. society (Wilber and Jameson, 1990, p. 119), while other theories point to the significant social and economic changes (Wells, 2003). Between the 1970s and 1980s, for example, single-parent households became more common and at the same time the rising costs of living encouraged many women to enter the workforce, and therefore widened the gulf between single- and two-income families. The economy was increasingly shifting away from heavy industry toward the information technology sector, thus disadvantaging older workers in the declining industries while richly rewarding those in the growing sector. These changes led many to question U.S. economic power and its ability to maintain its global role.

From a personal finance standpoint, it is important to understand the economy in a historical context. Although early in the 21st century the United States is experiencing historically low interest rates and high unemployment, these conditions should be viewed in a broader context. By understanding the cyclical nature of the economy, with highs and lows in interest rates, inflation, and employment rates, one is better equipped to understand the changing nature of one's own economic life as well as that of the national economy.

Lien Luu

See also: Deficit; Gross Domestic Product (GDP) and Gross National Product (GNP); Inflation; Interest Rates; Unemployment; U.S. Federal Tax System Overview; Volcker, Paul A., 12th Chair of the U.S. Federal Reserve Board

Further Reading

Blinder, A. 1982. "The Anatomy of Double-Digit Inflation in the 1970s," in Robert E. Hall, ed., *Inflation: Causes and Effects* (pp. 261–282). University of Chicago Press. http://www.nber.org/chapters/c11462

Feldstein, Martin, ed. 1994. *American Economic Policy in the 1980s*. University of Chicago Press.

Mussa, Michael L., Paul A. Volcker, and James Tobin. 1994. "Monetary Policy," in Martin Feldstein, ed., *American Economic Policy in the 1980s* (pp. 81–164). University of Chicago Press. http://www.nber.org/chapters/c7753.pdf?new_window=1

Sloan, John. 1999. *The Reagan Effect: Economics and Presidential Leadership*. Lawrence: University Press of Kansas.

Wells, Wyatt. 2003. *American Capitalism 1945–2000: Continuity and Change from Mass Production to the Information Society*. Chicago: Ivan R. Dee.

Wilber, Charles K., and Kenneth P. Jameson. 1991. *Beyond Reaganomics: A Further Enquiry into the Poverty of Economics*. Notre Dame, IN: University of Notre Dame Press.

Year 1987: Stock Market Crash

The stock market crash on October 19, 1987, also known as Black Monday, was the first major financial catastrophe of the second half of the 20th century. In a matter of hours the U.S. Dow Jones Industrial Average (DJIA or DOW) declined 508 points or 22.6 percent, the largest single-day stock market drop in in history. The value of the market drop was $500 billion, which means $500 billion of value vanished. It was also the most extreme market decline in the United States since the Great Depression. This single-day crash followed a two-week period when the Dow had already fallen 15 percent.

Unlike the 1929 market crash and subsequent Great Depression, the stock market quickly rebounded and ended the year higher than at the beginning of 1987. This was unusual stock market behavior for such a great stock market plunge.

In personal finance and money management, it is important to understand major historical financial activities. This historical awareness allows the consumer to better understand the context of current economic and financial events.

What Caused the 1987 Stock Market Crash?

There are a few theories about the cause of the crash, according to an October 19, 2011, *New York Times* and Learning Network article. One camp believed that the overall stock market became overvalued and needed to come down and return to a fair valuation.

Andrew Beattie (1987) elaborated on the theory that investors, who finally returned to the stock market in the 1960s and 1970s after recovering from fears of another 1929 crash, ignored stock valuations. Beattie suggested that investors became enthralled with some of the glamorous and newer corporations and bid up their prices, without regard for the companies' underlying financial strengths and growth prospects.

Another contributing cause for the crash could have been an increase in Securities and Exchange Commission (SEC) investigations into insider trading allegations. The increase in these illegal activities may have frightened investors, causing an increase in stock sales, which led to falling prices.

Another theory states that the actual crash was worsened by computerized trading, which automatically sold stocks that dropped below a specific price. Thus, the falling prices triggered the automated computerized trading programs. When the computerized trading programs were activated, stock sell orders increased, pushing prices down even lower.

As is discussed in the Behavioral Finance entry, investors tend to "follow the herd." So, as investors sold their stocks, leading to falling stock prices, more investors got scared and sold their equities as well. This herdlike behavior contributed to the mass exodus from the markets on October 19, 1987.

Response to the Crash by the Federal Reserve Bank

Although the crash was extreme in severity, it did not last as long as many other drastic stock market declines. A simple action by the Federal Reserve (the Fed) helped put the brakes on the falling stock prices.

On Tuesday, October 20, 1997, the day following the crash, the Federal Reserve made a statement designed to provide confidence in the markets and curtail the fear and the herd selling behavior. The Fed publicly promised that they would provide liquidity to the financial system. Following the confidence-building statement on Tuesday, the Fed acted quickly and reduced the federal funds interest rate to 7.0 percent from over 7.5 percent on Monday. The reason for this action was to increase liquidity in the markets and prove that the government would help the economy.

After the Fed funds rate declined, other short-term interest rates also fell. These actions by the Fed served to curtail the crisis on a psychological as well as a practical level. Psychologically, the Fed counteracted the public's fear of a continuing fall and greater crisis with the increase in liquidity. Practically, lower interest rates are a signal to consumers and businesses that there is more funding available for lending to the stock market brokers and dealers.

The increase in liquidity gives securities firms the confidence that they have access to cash and credit to return to share sellers if the number of sellers continues to increase. The government also took precautions to ensure that the banks were sound and not at risk. The swift and decisive actions by the Fed helped to calm the markets and improve market conditions.

How the Fed Contained the Crisis

The stock market crash of 1987 was important not only because of the size of the decline but also because of the disruption in how the markets functioned. As sell orders multiplied, trading stopped on certain securities, and there were additional problems meeting margin requirements for investors who bought stocks with borrowed funds.

The Fed used three tools to control the worsening of the financial crisis. The first tool increased market sentiment by publicly announcing plans to inject liquidity into the market. This calmed the participants and rapidly attacked the problem head-on. The second set of tools upped market liquidity by lowering interest rates. Finally, the Fed encouraged all market participants to cooperate and remain flexible with their customers. Those rapid actions, beginning the day after the crash, began the support for the market to resume a more stable trajectory of growth.

Long-Term Effects of the Crash and Subsequent Response

Bernhardt and Eckblad (1987) posit that the Fed's rapid response to the crisis began an era of increasing investor confidence in the government's ability to handle severe market crises. The fact that Black Monday wasn't followed by an economic recession or banking crisis further aided the consumer's confidence in the Fed.

The stock market rebounded well. In just two days, the Dow gained back 288 points or 57 percent of the total Black Monday loss. Within two years, the U.S. stock markets passed their precrash highs.

Since that 1987 market crash, there have been many others. In 1997, there was the Asian financial crisis. In the early part of this century, the markets crashed after a run-up in technology stocks, and more recently the markets peaked in October 2007, only to fall about 54 percent by early March 2009.

These periodic market crashes remind us of the cyclical nature of the economy and financial markets. The consumer who understands market and economic history is better equipped to understand and cope with the current financial ups and downs.

Barbara Friedberg

See also: Behavioral Finance; Capital Gains and Capital Losses; Discount Rate; Federal Reserve Bank; Interest Rates; Investing; Liquidity; Margin; Risk; Stock Market; Stocks; Systematic Market Risk; Year 1970s to 1980s: Economic Problems and the United States; Year 1997–1998: Asian Financial Crisis; Year 2000: Bursting of the Dot-Com Technology Bubble; Year 2010: Dodd-Frank Wall Street Reform and Consumer Protection Act

Further Reading

Beattie, Andrew. 1987. "Market Crashes: The Crash of 1987." October 19. http://www.investopedia.com/features/crashes/crashes6.asp

Bernhardt, Donald, and Marshall Eckblad. 1987. "Black Monday: The Stock Market Crash of 1987." http://www.federalreservehistory.org/Events/DetailView/48

Carlson, Mark. 2006. "A Brief History of the 1987 Stock Market Crash; with a Discussion of the Federal Reserve Response." Federal Reserve Board, Washington, D.C. http://www.federalreserve.gov/pubs/feds/2007/200713/200713pap.pdf

The Learning Network, *The New York Times*. 2011. "Oct. 19, 1987; Stock Market Crashes on 'Black Monday.'" October 19. http://learning.blogs.nytimes.com/2011/10/19/oct-19-1987-stock-market-crashes-on-black-monday/?_php=true&_type=blogs&_r=0

Ogg, Jon C. 2013. "Lessons of the 1987 Stock Market Crash, on Its 26th Anniversary." October 19. http://finance.yahoo.com/news/lessons-1987-stock-market-crash-150113253.html

Year 1989–1991: U.S. Savings and Loan Crisis

The savings and loan crisis (S&L crisis) of the 1980s and early 1990s was a major event in modern money management that tested the entire financial system in a way not seen since the Great Depression (1929–1939). Born out of accommodating public policy, vaulting inflation, and pure greed, the S&L crisis peaked when savings and loan institutions (S&Ls), unable to attract short-term capital to cover long-term liabilities, compelled legislators to loosen rules concerning their ownership of risky investments. The S&L crisis ultimately resulted in over 1,000 failed S&Ls and costs to U.S. taxpayers totaling many billions of dollars.

Years later, the S&L crisis continues to be studied in the finance industry, in academia, and in the public sector. As capital markets intertwine with regulations, many look to the S&L crisis as a case study on the impact of deregulation, monetary policy, and corruption on both bank lending and investment.

The late 1970s in the United States were accentuated by one major economic trend, inflation. During this time, while unemployment dropped from previously higher levels, gross domestic product increased, and the stock market entered a period of indifference, inflation in the United States rose toward a 1980 annual change of 13.5 percent—a level seen only a few other times in the history of the world's largest economy. Recession soon hit, both in 1980 and again in 1981, lasting almost the entire first two years of the new era. The federal funds rate, a monetary policy tool used by the Federal Reserve to combat inflation, was adjusted several times all the way up to an unprecedented 20 percent. Consumers could not afford the rising costs of goods and services nor the ensuing remarkably high borrowing costs (interest rates). Eventually, in 1982, domestic unemployment reached double digits. It was a unique period in U.S. and economic history, one that produced three Federal Reserve chairs (Arthur Burns, G. William Miller, and Paul Volker) and tremendous financial difficulties for Americans and the entire economy. Some have labeled this time "The Great Inflation."

S&Ls are institutions that take in deposits and use this money to make loans. Interest is paid on deposits, and profit is made on loans. Deposits are short-term in nature, making them highly flexible toward changes in interest rates; loans are long-term fixed instruments, making them almost incapable of adjusting. S&Ls followed a policy of borrowing short to lend long, meaning short-term deposits were used to fund long-term fixed-rate loans. When interest rates rose, S&Ls were often forced to pay their depositors higher interest rates than the institutions made from their long-term loans. When the Federal Reserve, in response to extreme inflation that eventually reached high double digits, raised interest rates, S&Ls were left with a deep maturity mismatch—their long-term fixed-rate loans were overwhelmed by the amount needed to pay depositors. Furthermore, a governing statute known as Regulation Q capped the amount of interest an S&L could pay its depositors. Once interest rates ascended above a certain level, it became more and more difficult for S&Ls to pay competitive rates, and deposits become harder and harder to come by. It was, by all accounts, a disaster waiting to happen, with the spark provided by the inflation of the late 1970s and early 1980s.

In 1980, at the onset of the S&L crisis, there were nearly 4,000 S&Ls in the United States with assets totaling $604 billion. During the first three years of the 1980s, 118 S&Ls failed, taking $43 billion in assets with them. The cost to resolve these initial failures was close to $3.5 billion. In perspective, over the 45-year period that preceded the S&L crisis, just 143 S&Ls failed, costing $306 million—a small relative amount. Some called the S&L crisis the biggest disaster in public finance since the Great Depression (1929 to 1939).

In response to the maturity mismatch that impacted so many, politicians—heavily lobbied by S&L executives—deregulated these financial institutions, allowing them to invest in commercial real estate lending, junk bonds, and other assets having much more inherent risk. Further, though allowed to participate in many more risky ventures, S&Ls that took advantage were not charged more for deposit insurance. Thus, S&Ls could take more risk without having to pay for it—a combination that often spells disaster in finance. In the early 1980s, this recipe created an environment ripe for corruption, attracting not only investors looking for opportunity but those wanting to debase the weakening system. The new variety of S&Ls was one of risk taking, significant political influence, and corruption—and one that attracted great sums of money from unwitting investors through the offer of higher returns as well as other sales techniques including outright lies about internal practices.

The failure of American politicians to proactively mitigate inflation's influence on S&Ls was a large contributor toward the commencement of the crisis, and the deregulation of S&Ls during the crisis changed the dynamic from an institutional structure with inherent problems to a free-for-all in risk taking with no ramifications. It was a perfect storm of greed mixed into poor governing judgment, with plenty of blame to go around.

In total, over 1,000 S&Ls failed during the crisis that lasted until the early 1990s. The total cost to taxpayers was over $120 billion. And the impact on hometown depositors who innocently put their life savings into corrupt, newly unregulated S&Ls was even more costly. The S&L crisis stands as a fascinating study into the side effects of monetary policy, the ability of governing persons to succumb to outside influence, and the human propensity to act criminally. The S&L crisis is a necessary component of any discussion on modern money management, and it contains many important lessons for the future betterment of financial practices.

Jonathan D. Citrin

See also: Accountant; Bankruptcy; Federal Reserve Bank; Gross Domestic Product (GDP) and Gross National Product (GNP); Inflation; Interest rates; Investing; Money Market Account; Risk; Savings Account; Volcker, Paul A., 12th Chair of the U.S. Federal Reserve Board; Year 1970s to 1980s: Economic Problems and the United States

Further Reading

Federal Deposit Insurance Corporation. "The Savings and Loan Crisis and Its Relationship to Banking." https://www.fdic.gov/bank/historical/history/167_188.pdf

Library of Economics and Liberty. "Savings and Loan Crisis." http://www.econlib.org/library/Enc/SavingsandLoanCrisis.html

Reuters. "Chronology—S&L crisis of the 1980s." http://www.reuters.com/article/2007/03/15/us-usa-subprime-bush-idUSB38105220070315

Trading Economics. "United States." http://www.tradingeconomics.com/united-states/indicators

Year 1994: North American Free Trade Agreement between Mexico, Canada, and the United States (NAFTA)

The North American Free Trade Agreement (NAFTA) was created on January 1, 1994, between the United States, Canada, and Mexico. It was signed by President Bill Clinton, Mexican president Carlos Salinas, and Canadian prime minister Jean Chretien. NAFTA created the largest free trade area in the world and eliminated most tariffs on products traded among the three participating counties. It included 450 million people who produce $17 trillion worth of goods and services.

Free trade is defined as international trade without tariffs, quotas, or other restrictions. The benefit of free trade to all parties is greater trade opportunities with lower costs and greater access to markets.

Although signed into law in 1994, the treaty took effect over time. The tariffs were phased out gradually and the final implementation took effect on January 1, 2008. NAFTA eliminated import tariffs in agriculture, automobiles, and textiles, among others. There were intellectual property protections set up as well.

NAFTA in Action

Imagine a beautiful, pristine Bombardier airplane manufacturing plant in Queretaro, Mexico. This plant is only two and a half hours from Mexico City, where it is joined by several other large manufacturing plants.

The plant is a picture of modern efficiency and cleanliness with technicians in face masks working behind glass in a dust-free environment. Carbon fiber is cut by laser, molded, and baked in a huge oven, which creates the fuselage. No dirty, smelly metal fabrication in this room.

This plant, only possible due to NAFTA, represents a partnership between Canada's Bombardier and Mexico. This Bombardier Learjet 85 is manufactured completely in North America (with the exception of the wings, which are made in Northern Ireland). Mexico's sophisticated manufacturing plant is a testament to the benefits of NAFTA collaboration. By locating in Mexico, this Canadian company, the world's only manufacturer of planes and trains, takes advantage of lower cost wages and free trade created by NAFTA.

What Is Significant about Free Trade?

International trade is an important way to increase the economic productivity of a country and its population. Consumers benefit when they can buy a wider range of goods for lower prices. Businesses profit from international trade with greater access to worldwide consumers who purchase their products.

A potential problem with international trade is the tariffs and other barriers that make global commerce expensive. By expanding international free trade agreements, barriers are reduced.

Analysis of NAFTA—Pros and Cons

After 20 years in existence, NAFTA has its supporters and detractors. This entry explores the promise of NAFTA and how its initiatives progressed during the last two decades. The analysis of NAFTA is complex, as it's impossible to compare how the United States, Mexico, and Canada's trade relations would have fared without NAFTA.

Recently, the Council on Foreign Relations completed a major analysis on the economic impact of NAFTA. In general, the trade relationships between the three NAFTA participants has increased and enabled the United States to create supply chains that further global trade. Of the three countries, Canada's economic growth grew the most with Mexico's growth the slowest.

In 2003, the U.S. Congressional Budget Office (as reported in the Council on Foreign Relations' NAFTA report) found that U.S. trade with Mexico was increasing before NAFTA's implementation and probably would have continued its expansion without NAFTA, although there is no way to compare trade statistics had NAFTA not been implemented. This study found that NAFTA's impact on U.S.-Mexico trade was small as was the direct impact on the U.S. labor market. The report also stated that NAFTA's trade impact on the GDP between the United States and Canada was also minimal.

The U.S. imports grew more than the exports to the NAFTA trading partners. This led to an increasing deficit between the United States and both Canada and Mexico.

On a more positive note, supply chains were expanded, providing the United States with greater access to lower cost inputs for production. This aspect of NAFTA benefits U.S. auto, electronics, machinery, and appliance manufacturers. NAFTA enabled production lines across North America to reduce manufacturing costs and compete better in the international arena. It is believed that this increase in ability to compete internationally wouldn't have been possible without NAFTA.

Drilling down even further, economists estimate that within the U.S. imports from Canada, 25 percent of the content is originally from the United States, whereas 40 percent of the content of U.S. imports from Mexico originates from the United States. These benefits from NAFTA are less visible and can't be underestimated (Sergie, 2014).

NAFTA's Impact on the U.S. Labor Market

The NAFTA supporters see a net positive impact from this free trade agreement. These individuals and economists claim that the new "export-related" jobs in the United States pay 15 to 20 percent more than the jobs focused solely on domestic production.

There are also negative employment repercussions. Wages lag productivity and income inequality continues to rise. These adverse effects occur as pressure grows to keep manufacturing costs low in order to maintain a competitive edge in global trade markets.

It seems as if the international free trade agreements exacerbate the negative U.S. income losses. With easier access to global markets for a wider number of trading partners, there is greater competition. This increasing competition forces companies to cut production costs to the bone so that their products and services will be purchased. The push toward lower production costs hurts the workers, who have little room to request and receive higher wages.

Labor unions are exceptionally opposed to NAFTA and other free trade agreements. Thea M. Lee, the deputy chief of staff at the AFL-CIO, believes that NAFTA compelled "workers into more direct competition with each other, while assuring them fewer rights and protections" (Sergie, 2014). The Public Citizen, a politically liberal nonprofit consumer rights organization, claims that by 2004 one million U.S. jobs were lost due to NAFTA.

Most economists disagree with these harsh criticisms of NAFTA and suggest that U.S. manufacturing was in trouble many years prior to NAFTA. The country has been undergoing a change in the employment mix as heavy manufacturing declines and is replaced by light manufacturing and high-end services. Technological advances add to the shifting of the American economy and its workforce. It is unrealistic to blame NAFTA and free trade for all of the economic workforce woes.

Historical Impacts of Global Economic Change

Historically, as new technologies emerge causing an upset to the status quo, there are casualties. The Industrial Revolution, which occurred from the 18th to 19th centuries, was a period when rural farming economies transitioned to become industrial and urban. Before the Industrial Revolution, families manufactured their own tools in their homes. Families wove fabric and fabricated their own clothing.

With the advent of the iron and textile industries, along with the development of the steam engine, more manufactured goods were available at reduced expense to consumers. These massive economic shifts caused certain craft jobs to disappear as new factory jobs evolved. The labor and economic shifts influenced by NAFTA are not unlike historical labor and economic shifts from other periods in time.

Other U.S. Free Trade Partners

Although this entry focuses on the impact of NAFTA, it is important to understand that this is not the country's only free trade partnership. The United States also has free trade agreements with Australia, Bahrain, Dominican Republic and Central America (CAFTA), Chile, Colombia, Israel, Jordan, Korea, Morocco, Oman, Panama, Peru, Singapore, and others.

Consider the issues of free trade and NAFTA as they might apply to other countries as well. Thus, this conversation about trading between the United States, Canada, and Mexico is an example of broader trade discussions and actions with many other countries worldwide. In total, all of the U.S. trading partners and free trade agreements have a broad impact on commerce in the United States.

The Future of NAFTA

Trade is a conflict-ridden issue in the United States with a variety of proposals for change to NAFTA on the table. The overriding concern is a desire to keep trade barriers to a minimum while maintaining reasonable wages for workers and protecting the environment.

A 2013 Congressional Research Service report proposed fortifying worker protections, increasing environmental protections, and improving cooperation and regulation among trading partners. Further, this report recommended supporting and advancing research and development, which would help U.S. industries better compete in global markets.

As with all economic and government policy issues, there are no easy answers. In summary, free trade policies give consumers access to a wider range of goods and services at lower costs. For manufacturers, free trade expands the markets in which they can sell their products and services.

Barbara Friedberg

See also: Capitalism; Clinton, William, 42nd President of the United States; Gross Domestic Product (GDP) and Gross National Product (GNP)

Further Reading

The Economist. 2014. "Ready to Take Off Again?" January 4. http://www.economist.com/news/briefing/21592631-two-decades-ago-north-american-free-trade-agreement-got-flying-start-then-it

History Web site. "Industrial Revolution." Accessed April 28, 2014. http://www.history
.com/topics/industrial-revolution
Office of the United States Trade Representative; Executive Office of the President. "North
American Free Trade Agreement (NAFTA)." Accessed April 28, 2014. http://www.ustr
.gov/trade-agreements/free-trade-agreements/north-american-free-trade-agreement-nafta
Sergie, Mohammed Aly. 2014. "NAFTA's Economic Impact." Council on Foreign Relations.
Updated February 14. http://www.cfr.org/trade/naftas-economic-impact/p15790

Year 1997–1998: Asian Financial Crisis

In 1997 through 1998 the foundation of the global financial markets and economy
were upset by what became known as the Asian financial crisis. Also called the "Asian
Contagion," this economic crisis officially began in Thailand when the government
decided to stop pegging the local currency to the U.S. dollar. This crisis underscores
the connectivity between international financial markets and how a decision in Asia
can have major financial implications in the United States and worldwide.

This financial crisis was a disruption in the financial markets (Eichengreen & Portes
1987) that was evident in depreciating currencies and insolvency. This crisis, although
centered in Asia, had worldwide repercussions. Its aftermath led to bankruptcies among
debtors and intermediaries such as banks and related corporations, and of course falling
equity prices on the world stock exchanges. This disruption spread throughout the international financial system, resulting in the misallocation of capital in the financial markets.

How Did the 1997–1998 Asian Financial Crisis Begin?

There are scores of papers discussing the origins of this global crisis. This entry will
outline the many causes, outcome, and lessons of this event.

According to research by the New York Federal Reserve Bank (Corsetti et al., 1999),
the crisis began with several interrelated conditions. During the 1990s, before the crisis,
the southeastern and eastern parts of Asia were experiencing high capital inflows. During
this period of high growth, the currencies were pegged to the value of the U.S. dollar.

In Thailand there was pressure to maintain high growth levels and a historical
precedent for the government to guarantee or subsidize these corporate projects, which
may not have been financially viable on their own. This "government support" led
corporations to believe that their projects were in some way protected from failure by
the government. In reality, many of these "subsidized" private projects were unprofitable. Many companies borrowed from abroad to finance the exceptional growth.

The second cause of the crisis was that the international banks that lent to Asian
markets lacked regard for the solvency of the borrowing businesses. The international
lenders assumed that in the case of default(s), the borrowing countries would bail out
the unprofitable companies. Thus, the international lenders did not properly vet the
businesses to which they were lending.

There was a lack of disclosure rules and transparency about the banks' operations
and their solvency, especially with respect to capital adequacy requirements. Capital

adequacy is the minimum amount of capital a financial institution such as a bank must hold in reserve as a measure of proof of their financial strength and stability.

This corruption was also evident during the crisis and its aftermath. Connections between politicians in power, certain private enterprises, and banks led to banks' lending to these organizations whether their operations were sound or not.

In some cases there was direct political interference by politicians in the allocation of credit to help create monopolies in certain business activities. This resulted in excessive resources and the misallocation of resources to the investment.

Consequently the rate of return on capital declined, while the risks kept rising. This added to the loss of confidence in the banking sector, particularly with the onset of the currency crisis in Thailand. The impact on the perceptions of people in the international financial markets was devastating, resulting in large capital outflows and a slowdown in capital inflows into the Asian countries that had become reliant on the foreign funds to fuel their economic growth.

The crisis ignited when Thailand's Central Bank decided to float the baht on July 2, 1997. According to a July 2, 1999, CNN Money article, Thailand devalued the baht currency in an effort to jump-start the country's economy. By devaluing the baht, Thai goods and services would be less expensive to international consumers.

As a result of the devaluation, the baht became the target for speculators who saw an opportunity to make speculative gains on the foreign currency markets. Speculators are financial market participants who make risky investments in the hope of making large financial gains. With the speculation, the currency value became quite volatile.

Within two months Thailand's currency devalued (depreciated) between 15 to 20 percent. In other words, the exchange value of the country's currency (Thai baht) declined rapidly in relation to other foreign currencies.

This began a localized financial currency crisis that spread to other parts of the Asian region. The Philippine peso, Malaysian ringgit, Indonesian rupiah, Hong Kong dollar, Indonesian rupiah, South Korean won, Taiwanese new dollar, and Singaporean dollar all followed suit and depreciated.

The currency crisis led to a decline in foreign capital inflows into these Asian countries, which put further downward pressure on these currencies. When a currency devalues, there are both internal and international impacts.

Implications of a Devaluing Currency

According to the New York Federal Reserve bank, "A key effect of devaluation is that it makes the domestic currency cheaper relative to other currencies. There are two implications of a devaluation. First, devaluation makes the country's exports relatively less expensive for foreigners. Second, the devaluation makes foreign products relatively more expensive for domestic consumers, thus discouraging imports. This may help to increase the country's exports and decrease imports, and may therefore help to reduce the current account deficit."

When one country devalues its currency in relation to the currency of its trading partners, the international countries' goods and services become more expensive to the devalued currency country. Thus when Thailand devalued the baht, the goods and services from abroad were more expensive, causing imports to decline and subsequently hurting the other nations' exports.

In turn, economic growth slowed down to zero percent annually for Thailand, Indonesia, and the Republic of Korea. Likewise the slowdown in economic growth had a minor effect in Singapore, Malaysia, and the Philippines.

Currency Crisis Impacts Corporate and Banking Sectors

The mass currency devaluations began a global panic. As the currencies began to collapse, the Asian banking and corporate sectors went into deep and significant distress. The Asian banking sector was heavily exposed to unhedged (unprotected) short-term loans to finance long-term domestic projects. This placed these organizations at a significant risk of defaulting on their loan obligations.

Many of these loans were invested in high-risk projects, and together with this financial currency crisis a banking crisis ensued. Interest rates started rising, which restricted the availability of credit (liquidity) to the corporations to finance their day-to-day operations, causing a liquidity crisis. Many of these private companies with restricted or no access to short-term credit were being forced to the brink of insolvency.

The liquidity crisis was preceded by financial and asset price crises, which spread to other parts of the world fairly quickly. Hong Kong's stock market collapsed first, sending shock waves to the stock markets in other parts of Asia. The stock markets of Latin America (Brazil, Argentina, and Mexico) and the stock markets of the Western countries (the United States, Great Britain, and Germany) were also impacted. These financial and asset price crises set the stage for further currency depreciations. This undermined confidence in the Asian economies, as growth rates declined further, causing the real economy in the Asian region to become destabilized.

International Monetary Fund Bailouts

Many large, costly, and politically motivated International Monetary Fund–led bailouts were arranged for those countries that were affected the most (Radelet and Sachs, 2000). Furthermore, the crisis alerted world leaders that there were issues of international and national public policy that should concern the international community. The international community represented by the United States, Japan, China, and other G-7 countries started to consider the factors that caused this crisis. Next, they evaluated the lessons learned from the crisis in an effort to avert or reduce the likelihood of similar crises in the future (Garay; Lee 1998; Sharma 2003).

The 1997–1998 Asian financial crisis was an event that began with a currency crisis that led to a banking crisis, turning into a liquidity crisis, which was finally preceded by an international stock market (international financial and asset prices) crisis. The international markets reacted violently to the panic that ensued once the crises broke out. Gross domestic product growth rates contracted significantly and quickly in the affected Asian countries, causing companies that were overexposed to foreign currency to risk severe financial distress.

The crisis exposed the weaknesses in the international financial systems at that time, which in some manner remain today. Together with market sentiment, these weaknesses triggered a financial and economic collapse that quickly spread to other economies in the world. Its effects, and governments' subsequent responses to it, have defined much of the world's economic and financial services policies and direction during the past two decades.

Angelique N. S. McInnes

See also: Banking; Bankruptcy; Behavioral Finance; Capitalism; Currency; Debt; Gross Domestic Product (GDP) and Gross National Product (GNP); Liquidity; Risk; Year 1944: Creation of the International Monetary Fund and the World Bank at the Bretton Woods International Conference

Further Reading

CNN Money. 1997. "Thailand Floats the Baht." July 2. Accessed March 20, 2014. http://money.cnn.com/1997/07/02/markets/thai_baht/

Corsetti, Giancarlo, Paolo Pesenti, and Nouriel Roubini. 1999. "What Caused the Asian Currency and Financial Crisis?" Accessed March 20, 2014. http://www.newyorkfed.org/research/economists/pesenti/whatjapwor.pdf

Eichengreen, Barry, and Richard Portes. 1987. *The Anatomy of Financial Crises*. National Bureau of Economic Research. Accessed October 22, 2013. http://www.nber.org/papers/w2126.pdf?new_window=1

Garay, Urbi. *The Asian Financial Crisis of 1997–1998 and the Behavior of Asian Stock Markets*. University of West Georgia; B>Quest. Accessed October 21, 2013. http://www.westga.edu/~bquest/2003/asian.htm

Lee, E. 1998. "The Asian Financial Crisis: Origins and Social Outlook." *International Labour Review* (Vol. 137, No. 1): 81.

Radelet, Steven, and Jeffrey Sachs. 2000. *Currency Crises*, ed. Paul Krugman. University of Chicago Press. Accessed December 30, 2014. http://www.nber.org/books/krug00-1

Sharma, S. D. 2003. *The Asian Financial Crisis: New International Financial Architecture: Crisis, Reform and Recovery*. Manchester University Press.

Tobin, J. 1998, "Asian Financial Crisis." *Japan and World Economy* (Vol. 10, No. 3): 351–353.

Year 1999: Introduction of the Euro to World Financial Markets

The euro (€) is the currency used by the majority of the members of the European Union, the largest trading bloc in the world. On January 1, 1999, 11 member countries of the European Union started to use the euro common currency for banking transactions. Three years later in 2002, the old national notes and coins were withdrawn in favor of new euro notes and coins, which are uniform throughout the zone. The implementation of the euro common currency was the culmination of many years of collaboration across euro zone member countries.

At the beginning of 2015, there are 19 countries of the 28 EU members that use the Euro. Known as the Eurozone, the countries include: Austria, Belgium, Cypress, Estonia, Finland, France, Germany, Greece, Ireland, Italy, Latvia, Lithuania, Luxembourg, Malta, the Netherlands, Portugal, Slovakia, and Spain. Over 175 million people worldwide claim the Euro or a currency pegged to the Euro, as their money.

Euro notes and coins are valid in all countries and utilized in banking and commerce. Just as in the United States you can earn $100 in Maine and spend it in California or send dollars from Florida to Washington State without thinking about it, you can take a euro banknote from Portugal and spend it in Finland or use a euro coin from Ireland and spend it in Greece. It makes it very easy to move, compare prices, or send money between any of the euro zone countries. Some countries do not use the euro. Most of these are new entrants to the European Union and must adopt it at some time in the future; a few have decided to remain outside the zone.

History

In 1960, six European countries came together to form the European Economic Community, also known as the EEC or Common Market, following the 1957 Treaty of Rome. These founding nations were scarred by the ravages of two world wars over the previous 50 years and saw trade as a way of unifying the countries.

Three additional countries joined in 1973, one in 1981, and two more in 1986 to make a coherent bloc of 12 countries. The Maastricht Treaty of 1992 changed the EEC into the European Union. In 2015 there were 19 countries in the euro zone.

Long ago it was recognized that one of the biggest barriers to improving trade across the bloc was the high price of currency conversion. Prices of goods and services were not easy to compare, and money was expensive to move between members. In addition, large currency fluctuations represented a risk of social and economic instability, as Germany experienced after World War I.

After the fall of the Bretton Woods system in 1971, which tied all currencies to the U.S. dollar, the EEC created a currency "snake" in 1972 where all currencies were held within tight limits. This was done by the individual central banks buying and selling dollars, gold, and so on or by changing their interest rates. In 1979, a European Monetary System (EMS) was established that defined a European Currency Unit, the ECU. Nations tried to maintain their respective currencies to within a few percent of the ECU using an Exchange Rate Mechanism (ERM) and were able to devalue or revalue their currencies with respect to the ECU. The dominant currency within the EMS became the German deutsche mark. Following speculative attacks on various currencies, the ERM effectively failed in the early 1990s, and the only solution for closer integration was to move to a single currency, the euro.

Plans to Create a Monetary Union

Starting in 1988, detailed proposals were sought to create a full monetary union. The initial decision to proceed was taken at Maastricht in 1992 and the decision to create the single currency by 1999, although without the United Kingdom, Denmark, and

Sweden. Germany was cautious about this step and was persuaded to join the monetary union in return for French support on reunification, a long-held German wish. A stability and growth pact was agreed on at Amsterdam in 1997 to ensure budget discipline on all EU member nations, and a new Exchange Rate Mechanism was devised.

The design of the notes and coins was finalized and the European Central Bank was created in 1998 to oversee the introduction of the new currency. The banknotes are all identical, but one side of the coins has an image chosen by each country.

The changeover for retailers was a particularly complex task. All tills, ATMs, banknotes, and coin-operated machinery had to be changed. There was an extensive education campaign for the public so that approximately 300 million people could understand their new currency. The final conversion rate for each of the 11 currencies was established immediately before the changeover.

Implementation of the Euro

There were two stages of implementation. On January 1, 1999, all bank transfers and electronic payments were made in euros; bank accounts were technically in euros but displayed in the national currencies as well. The original currencies ceased to exist. Government debt and bonds were denominated in euros and many larger businesses started to work in euros from this time. Cash payments continued in the old currencies, which acted as proxies for the euro due to the fixed exchange rate. Dual pricing was common to help people become familiar with the new costs and values.

On January 1, 2002, euro notes and coins were introduced and old currency withdrawn completely. Old notes and coins continued in circulation for a while and payment could still be made in the legacy currencies, but change was given in euros. During an additional period, banks accepted old notes for conversion.

Various countries have joined the European Union since the adoption of the euro. It is now a condition of membership that the euro will be adopted as soon as possible.

Market Response

The implementation of the euro has been very successful from a technical point of view. No real problems occurred in what was an enormous operation between 11 countries with highly sophisticated but different financial systems.

The euro's value versus the U.S. dollar began at $1.16 to €1.00. The initial wariness of the markets saw the euro's value drop substantially against the dollar, almost reaching $0.80. Today, this wariness about the euro has eased and in late 2013 the euro was trading at a bit over $1.25 to €1.00. The euro rose briefly to $1.50 during the financial and economic shocks starting in 2008. Periodic economic uncertainty leads to fluctuations in the euro's value and occasional discussions about the euro's future.

Additional Usage of the Euro

Four European microstates and five dependent territories use the euro by agreement; two other countries have adopted it unilaterally. A number of countries pegged their currencies to the euro—apart from EU members or aspirant members, these are all African or small Pacific nations. Despite substantial upheavals in the world economy, the stability of the euro has also led it to become a second reserve currency after the dollar, mainly following the deutsche mark so that a substantial amount of trading is carried out in the currency.

The mark is still in existence because unlike other euro zone members, Germany never officially retired the deutsche mark currency. According to Vanessa Fuhrmans in a 2012 *Wall Street Journal* article, "Who Needs the Euro When You Can Pay with Deutsche Marks?", the deutsche mark is still in circulation and accepted by many shopowners. Although Germany officially accepted the euro on January 1, 2002, as Germany's legal currency, the country never set a deadline for exchanging old deutsche marks for euros. Thus, if retailers accept marks, they can still exchange them for euros at German central bank branches.

During the global economic struggles the euro has been challenged as a replacement for the U.S. dollar as the leading international currency. At present, this is unlikely to occur.

Future of the Euro

There are some problems with the euro that led to the debt crisis of 2011–2012. The underlying problem is that the European Central Bank does not enjoy the full powers of other central banks. That said, there is strong political will in the success of the euro. While some skeptics doubted the euro's continued viability on technical grounds, these doubts haven't been particularly influential in the currency and economic markets.

Maria Nedeva

See also: Banking; Federal Reserve Bank; Lagarde, Christine, Managing Director, International Monetary Fund; Year 1944: Creation of the International Monetary Fund and the World Bank at the Bretton Woods International Conference; Year 2011–2012: European Debt Crisis

Further Reading

Baldwin, Richard, and Charles Wyplosz. 2009. *The Economics of European Integration*. New York: McGraw-Hill.

"Economic and Financial Affairs—The Euro." European Commission Web site. Accessed October 29, 2013. http://ec.europa.eu/economy_finance/euro/index_en.htm

"EMU: A Historical Documentation." European Union Web site (europa.eu). Accessed October 29, 2013. http://ec.europa.eu/economy_finance/emu_history/index_en.htm

"The Euro." The European Union Web site. Accessed February 8, 2015. http://europa.eu/about-eu/basic-information/money/euro/index_en.htm

Fuhrmans, Vanessa. July 18, 2012. *The Wall Street Journal*. "Who Needs the Euro When You Can Pay with Deutsche Marks?" http://online.wsj.com/news/articles/SB10001424052702304373804577520930784840596

Year 2000: Bursting of the Dot-Com Technology Bubble

1990s—Factors Creating the Technology Stock Bubble

Throughout history, assets such as gold, stocks, bonds, and even tulips have become more expensive than their intrinsic value. Consumers and investors must recognize the causes and occurrences of asset bubbles in order to avoid participating in the herd mentality and underlying economic factors that lead to overvalued asset prices and inevitable corrections. The 2000 technology stock bubble and subsequent crash highlight the personal finance importance of understanding this event.

The technology stock bubble began as U.S. stock market prices accelerated from a 10.4 percent annual return between 1990 and 1995 to a 21.2 percent annual return between 1995 and 2000. The U.S. stock market capitalization (total number of shares outstanding multiplied by the share price for each corporation) tripled between 1995 and the stock market peak in 2000. International stock prices increased during this period as well, although not as rapidly as those in the United States, at an annualized rate of 7.9 percent (Kraay and Ventura, 2007).

Driving the run-up in stock prices were the real and perceived increases in productivity. With the advent of groundbreaking technological advances and the growth of an exploding technology sector, investors believed that the productivity advances would continue indefinitely. These beliefs persuaded investors to pay more and more for the miracle technology stocks.

A positive economic environment encouraged the asset price bubble. Low inflation and interest rates during the late 1990s aided the robust stock market advances. The budget deficit during the 1990s shrank to historically low levels, further propelling stock prices upward. Increased productivity in the late 1990s led the world to invest money in the highly efficient U.S. companies, further driving up the stock prices. The highly productive technology sector led the advances in stock market prices. For example, during the 1990s Intel (INTC), the stock market darling, exploded from a low split-adjusted price of $0.79 in August 1990 to its peak of $50.88 in March 2000. That level of growth represents an unrealistic and unsustainable 50 percent return per year.

Stock Market Psychology

Rational economic factors explain only part of the growing asset prices in this and most asset bubbles. Market psychology and behavioral finance factors explain another part of the excess run-up in stock prices, although market factors such as supply and demand imply that assets are fairly priced and for the short periods of time when a stock might be overvalued, demand will decline for that stock, causing its price to fall to fair value. This efficient market theory does not explain the whole story.

Behavioral finance helps to explain how bubbles such as the technology stock bubble of the late 1990s occur. Herding, similar to that in animals, is a well-documented human behavior as well. This behavior was observed in the context of economics as early as 1759 when Adam Smith (1723–1790), father of modern economics, described how individuals who imagine themselves in another's situation tend to mimic their behavior. John Maynard Keynes (1883–1946), another renowned economist, further popularized the idea that contagious animal spirits among investors can move the markets, another description of human herding behavior (Baddeley, 2010).

When markets are moving upward, investors, afraid of missing the run-up in prices, rush in. Frequently, as prices become more and more overvalued, the prior stock price appreciation prods investors to buy in at inflated prices. This herd mentality, in direct contrast to the concept that individuals behave rationally, causes asset prices to rise beyond their intrinsic value.

Hyman Minsky (1919–1996) described bubbles as a natural outgrowth of periods of economic stability (Bodie, Kane, and Marcus, 2011). Investors assume the stability will continue into the future and are willing to take on more risk. This viewpoint describes framing, another behavioral bias, which says decisions are impacted by the perception of the environment in which they are made. In other words, during the late 1990s the economy was strong, asset prices were rising, and investors believed this golden economic environment would continue.

Alan Greenspan, former head of the Federal Reserve Bank, described this herding behavior as "irrational exuberance" (Pollock, 2013). During the late 1990s when Greenspan pointed out the inflated asset prices, another problem with asset prices was implied. The markets were inflated, but when they would return to fair value was uncertain. That reality describes a fundamental problem with asset price bubbles: even when one identifies overvalued assets, it is impossible to predict when the bubble will burst and the asset prices will reverse course. Only hindsight correctly identifies the bursting of inflated asset prices.

2000 Reverses the Upward Stock Market Trend

In 2000, the euphoria dissolved as markets reversed direction. According to the National Bureau of Economic Research, U.S. productivity fell in 2000, which ignited the stock market decline. Thus began the 30 percent decline in equity prices that occurred during the first three years of the 21st century. Investors were unwilling to buy overvalued assets from other investors. Thus, as demand declined, market forces pushed stock prices lower and lower.

Fiscal budget deficits began to rise in 2001 when the Bush administration came into office. These deficits were in stark contrast to the low budget deficits and small surpluses of the 1990s. The Middle East military conflicts added to the budget deficits.

By 2004, the U.S. budget deficit reached 4.8 percent of the gross national product (GNP). U.S. public debt grew from 33 to 37 percent of GNP from 2001 to 2004 (Kraay and Ventura, 2007). The National Bureau of Economic Research draws a relationship between the stock market bubbles, budget deficits, and current accounts (the relationship between U.S. expenditures and income).

One theory states that as the bubble bursts, stock prices fall, and there are more sellers than buyers for the existing equity investments, the government offers more debt investments and gives investors an alternate place for their funds. Since stock values are declining, investors choose alternate opportunities, such as investing in government debt. This increase in government debt subsequently continues growing the budget deficit. Unfortunately, for investors who previously enjoyed large capital appreciation from investing in the rapidly increasing stock market of the 1990s, government debt does not offer the same level of returns.

Just as the exaggerated increase in stock prices late in the 1990s was difficult to explain solely with economic factors, so was the rapid turnaround in market prices. Additionally, the theory that budget deficits and increased government debt is the benevolent U.S. government's solution to replace the inefficient and overvalued equities of the late 1990s is an insufficient explanation.

Behavioral economics also describes individuals' activities in a declining market. As investors follow one another to the exits and begin selling their assets, stock prices decline and the herding behavior works in the opposite way to burst the investment bubble.

During the 1990s, the U.S. economy, and to a lesser degree international markets, experienced a confluence of positive business and economic circumstances along with optimistic psychological factors. Asset prices exploded during this golden period to unsustainable levels. The bursting of the dot-com technology bubble was inevitable. By understanding historical economic and personal finance bubbles and subsequent reversals, the consumer is wiser and more likely to avoid following the crowd into overvalued investment opportunities.

Barbara Friedberg

See also: Behavioral Finance; Bush, George W., 43rd President of the United States; Debt; Deficit; Federal Reserve Bank; Greenspan, Alan, 13th Chair of the U.S. Federal Reserve Board; Gross Domestic Product (GDP) and Gross National Product (GNP); Inflation; Interest Rates; Investing; Stocks

Further Reading

Baddeley, Michelle. 2010. "Herding, Social Influence and Economic Decision-Making: Socio-Psychological and Neuroscientific Analyses." *Philosophical Transactions of the Royal Biological Sciences Society.* http://rstb.royalsocietypublishing.org/content/365 /1538/281.full

Bodie, Zvi, Alex Kane, and Alan J. Marcus. 2011. *Investments*. New York: McGraw-Hill/ Irwin, 166–167.

Kraay, Aart, and Jaume Ventura. 2007. "The Dot-Com Bubble, the Bush Deficits, and the U.S. Current Account," in Richard H. Clarida, *G7 Current Account Imbalances: Sustainability and Adjustment.* University of Chicago Press. http://www.nber.org/ chapters/c0124.pdf

The New York Times. 2000. "The Dot-Com Bubble Bursts." December 24. http://www .nytimes.com/2000/12/24/opinion/the-dot-com-bubble-bursts.html

Pollock, Alex J. 2013. "Mugged by Uncertainty: What Can Alan Greenspan Still Teach Us?" American Enterprise Institute. December 29. http://www.aei.org/article/economics /financial-services/banking/mugged-by-uncertainty-what-can-alan-greenspan-still -teach-us/

Year 2001: Enron, the Failure of Corporate Finance and Governance

Enron was formed in 1985 following a merger between Houston Natural Gas and Omaha-based InterNorth. Kenneth Lay became Enron's CEO and chair, and he decided to rebrand Enron into an energy trader and supplier. Enron was poised to take advantage of the deregulation of the energy markets that allowed companies to place bets on future prices. Several years later, Kenneth Lay was succeeded by new CEO Jeffrey Skilling. Skilling developed a staff of executives who were able to hide billions of dollars in debt from failed deals and projects with the help of accounting loopholes, special-purpose entities, and poor financial reporting.

Sell-Off and Bankruptcy

Shortly after the company achieved $100 billion in revenues in August 2001, CEO Jeffrey Skilling unexpectedly resigned, prompting many to question the health of the company. Kenneth Lay once again became the CEO. Lay, Skilling, and other Enron executives started selling large amounts of Enron stock as prices continued to drop— from a high of about $90.00 per share earlier in the year, to less than $1.00. The U.S. Securities and Exchange Commission (SEC) opened an investigation.

Less than a week after a takeover bid from Dynegy was called off, Enron filed for bankruptcy protection. The company had more than $38 billion in outstanding debts. The U.S. Justice Department would initiate a criminal investigation into Enron's bankruptcy. Many executives at Enron were indicted for a variety of charges and were later sentenced to prison. Enron's auditor, Arthur Andersen, was found guilty in a U.S. District Court. Employees and shareholders received limited returns in lawsuits, despite losing billions in pensions and stock prices.

Mark-to-Market Accounting

In its natural gas business, Enron followed straightforward accounting standards. The company listed actual costs of supplying the gas and actual revenues received from selling it in each time period. However, when Jeffrey Skilling joined the company, he decided to change that practice and made sure that the trading business adopted mark-to-market accounting. Mark-to-market accounting requires that once a long-term contract is signed, income is estimated as the present value of net future cash flow. Often, the viability of these contracts and their related costs were difficult to estimate. Thus, investors were typically given false or misleading reports.

Special-Purpose Entities

Enron also used special-purpose entities to fund or manage risks associated with specific assets. Special-purpose entities were limited partnerships or companies created to fulfill a temporary or specific purpose. The company disclosed very few details on its use of special-purpose entities. Enron had used hundreds of special-purpose

Creative Accounting

Misleading accounting practices allowed Enron to appear more powerful on paper than it really was. Special-purpose entities were used to hide risky investment activities and financial losses. Special-purpose entities are subsidiaries that have a single purpose and that did not need to be included on Enron's balance sheet. Investigations revealed that many of Enron's recorded assets and profits were inflated and in some cases completely fraudulent and nonexistent. Some of the company's debts and losses were absent from Enron's financial statements because they were recorded in offshore entities.

During the late 1990s and into the early 2000s, more and more special-purpose vehicles were created that allowed the company to keep debts off the books and inflate assets. These entities, along with other accounting loopholes and poor financial reporting, would allow Enron to hide billions in debt from special deals and projects.

entities to hide its debt. As a result, Enron's balance sheet understated its liabilities and overstated its equity, and its earnings were overstated. Prominent examples of special-purpose entities that Enron employed were JEDI, Chewco, Whitewing, and LJM.

Corporate Governance and Risk Management

Enron seemed to have a model board of directors comprised predominantly of outsiders with significant ownership stakes and a talented audit committee. In its 2000 review of best corporate boards, *Chief Executive* magazine included Enron among its five best boards.

Before its scandal, Enron was also praised for its sophisticated financial risk management tools. Enron established long-term fixed commitments, which needed to be hedged to prepare for the invariable fluctuation of future energy prices. Many critics attribute Enron's bankruptcy downfall to its reckless use of derivatives and special-purpose entities. By hedging its risks with special-purpose entities that it owned, Enron retained the risks associated with the transactions.

The board of directors was aware of Enron's aggressive accounting practices. Although not all of Enron's widespread improper accounting practices were revealed to the board, the practices were dependent on board decisions. Even though Enron extensively relied on derivatives for its business, the company's finance committee and board did not have enough experience with derivatives to understand what they were being told.

Ethical, Political, and Other Accounting Issues

Many observers believe that executive greed and a lack of corporate social responsibility were the reasons behind Enron's fall. Others blame post-1970s deregulation, and inadequate staff and funding for regulatory oversight. Some others believe that Enron's collapse resulted from its reliance on political lobbying, rent seeking, and gaming regulations.

Enron regularly recorded costs of cancelled projects as assets, with the rationale that no official letter had stated that the project was cancelled. This method was known as "the snowball." It was initially decided that such practices would be used only for projects worth less than $90 million. However, that figure was later increased to $200 million.

Whenever analysts toured the Enron Energy Services office, Skilling would order employees from other departments to move to that office to create the appearance that the division was larger than it was. This trick was used several times to fool analysts about the progress of different areas of Enron to help improve the stock price.

Increased Regulation and Oversight

Enron's collapse was the biggest corporate bankruptcy ever to hit the financial world. The Enron scandal drew attention to accounting and corporate fraud, as its shareholders lost $74 billion in the four years leading up to its bankruptcy, and its employees lost billions in pension benefits.

Increased regulation and oversight have been enacted to help prevent or eliminate corporate scandals of Enron's magnitude. As a consequence of the scandal, new regulations and legislation were enacted to expand the accuracy of financial reporting for public companies. One piece of legislation, the Sarbanes-Oxley Act, increased penalties for destroying, altering, or fabricating records in federal investigations or for attempting to defraud shareholders. The act also increased the accountability of auditing firms to remain unbiased and independent of their clients.

Ramya Ghosh

See also: Accountant; Bankruptcy; Investing; Year 2002: Sarbanes-Oxley Act

Further Reading

Keller, Bill. 2002. "Enron for Dummies." *The New York Times.* January 26. http://www.nytimes.com/2002/01/26/opinion/enron-for-dummies.html

Lavelle, Louis. January 20, 2002. "How Governance Rules Failed at Enron." *Bloomberg Businessweek.* http://www.businessweek.com/stories/2002-01-20/commentary-how-governance-rules-failed-at-enron

O'Leary, Christopher. "Enron—What Happened?: Year in Review 2002." *Encyclopaedia Britannica.* Accessed June 11, 2014. http://www.britannica.com/EBchecked/topic/1517868/Enron-What-Happened-Year-In-Review-2002

Year 2002: Sarbanes-Oxley Act

The Sarbanes-Oxley Act (SOX) was passed by the U.S. Congress in 2002 and signed into law by President George W. Bush. At the time of its enactment, the United States was the largest economy in the world (as measured by gross domestic product) and entangled in a crisis surrounding the fraudulent reporting of corporate financial data by a number of publicly traded companies. Shortly following a recession (March 2001 to November 2001) triggered by the collapse of technology companies losing billions of dollars in stock market value (the dot-com bubble), the illegal accounting methods that precipitated SOX cost additional billions lost, and forever changed the practices of investors, the government, and corporate executive management.

This entry encompasses the legislation as it pertains to finance and modern money management. Although there continues to be debate around its implementation and effectiveness, the act itself was substantial in how it changed the practices of publicly traded companies across the entire United States.

The years 2000–2009 produced several significant financial market corrections, causing trillions of dollars of paper losses to investors. Very early in the decade, stock prices soared as technology companies and others benefited from an existing exuberance. Of the two emotions that dominate security selection, greed was rampant. Market participants pushed prices higher and higher as they clamored for every available share of booming technology and other corporations that continuously showed giant profits and increasing potential on their income statements, balance sheets, and other financial documents. Unknown to almost everyone, including regulators at the Securities and Exchange Commission (SEC), several significant companies were purposely reporting fraudulent financial data.

In 2001, the energy corporation Enron—one of the largest companies in the United States—began to come under scrutiny for its accounting practices. Investor questions grew more and more common, and the complex use of shell companies beneath Enron's seemingly shiny exterior increasingly confused and concerned almost everyone from stockholders to Wall Street analysts. As the lies unfolded and the game of hiding debt was discovered, Enron stock fell from over $90 per share to under $1 per share. At the time, it was unprecedented. Employees lost their jobs and retirement savings while equity owners saw any invested capital disappear, taking markets and overall investor confidence with it. The calamity was ubiquitous as greed quickly turned to intense fear.

In the following year, two other corporations embedded in the fabric of American investment markets were also discovered to have fraudulently altered their accounting and financial statements to make large losses magically disappear, giving the appearance of very profitably run organizations. WorldCom, one of the world's largest telecommunications firms, and Tyco, a sizeable manufacturing company, were discovered to have lied to investors in many ways, including the misrepresentation of expenses, smuggling of money, and the sale of unauthorized company stock. All of these occurrences, due to the structure of laws and reporting at the time, were done undercover, without shareholder knowledge. As the layers of fraud and deception unraveled, share prices lost almost all value, investors lost billions of dollars, and many thousands were left without jobs as their former employers crumbled under the lens of justice. Markets and the entire country were now fully rattled—trust in the financial system, particularly that of corporate bookkeeping, was completely lost.

On July 30, 2002, President George W. Bush responded to the accounting scandals and ensuing crisis of confidence by signing into law the Sarbanes-Oxley Act (named for its congressional sponsors Senator Paul Sarbanes and Representative Michael Oxley). The act passed with overwhelming support, obtaining 98 percent of the vote in the House of Representatives and 99 percent of that in the Senate.

The Sarbanes-Oxley Act contains 11 sections that include the establishment of a public company accountability board, requirements for auditor independence, details concerning corporate responsibility, enhanced conflict of interest provisions, and new criminal penalties for corporate fraud. The act boosted the reliability of corporate disclosures and changed the way securities analysts interact with corporate management. In the wake of such tremendous financial losses directly due to fraud, this sweeping legislation even required top management to personally certify corporate financial information.

Opponents of SOX contend that the legislation, particularly its requirement that public companies achieve an independent audit of internal controls, is costly for corporations to implement; it was initially feared that relatively small companies would face crippling expenses when trying to facilitate an independent audit. However, supporters of SOX cite sharp bolstering of shareholder confidence that, in turn, results in increased share prices in markets; if investors are more confident, they will be more willing to deploy their capital.

Years after its passing, SOX remains largely intact. Proponents of free markets continue to argue its existence as an impediment toward the long-term health of the financial system. But, as an attack on large-scale corporate fraud, SOX stands as one of the most major pieces of financial legislation in modern times. Throughout the history of the relationship between government and capitalism as an economic system, there has always been a fine line between policing free markets without tinkering in them. In 2002, there was overwhelming support for SOX as the metaphorical flame of fear had been lit. Time will tell if SOX did too much or too little to mitigate the opportunities for fraudulent corporate activities, while the debate concerning how involved governments should be in free markets—which includes regulatory oversight—continues in earnest.

Jonathan D. Citrin

See also: Accountant; Bankruptcy; Bush, George W., 43rd President of the United States; Gross Domestic Product (GDP) and Gross National Product (GNP); Investing; Stock Market; Year 2000: Bursting of the Dot-Com Technology Bubble; Year 2001: Enron, the Failure of Corporate Finance and Governance

Further Reading

Library of Congress. "Bill Text—107th Congress (2001–2002), H.R.3763.ENR." http://thomas.loc.gov/cgi-bin/query/z?c107:H.R.3763.ENR:%20

U.S. Government Printing Office. "107th Congress Public Law 204." http://www.gpo.gov/fdsys/pkg/PLAW-107publ204/html/PLAW-107publ204.htm

Year 2003–2011: Iraq War's Impact on the U.S. Economy

The Iraq war began in 2003 when President George Bush launched an invasion of Iraq. After the September 11, 2001, destruction of the World Trade Center, the United States was determined to retaliate. The war was initiated due to the belief (which was later disproved) that Iraq owned nuclear weapons of mass destruction. Iraqi leader Saddam Hussein killed many of his own people and was considered one of the worst dictators, further fueling the desire to remove him from power. The war officially ended in December 2011 although the country still suffers conflict and unrest. Further, the United States is still feeling the economic repercussions of the Iraq war.

This entry will focus less on the war itself and more on its economic impact. There is a widely held belief that fighting a war and increased military spending improve a country's economy. According to Dean Baker from the Center for Economic and Policy Research, military spending diverts resources from more fruitful uses and in the end decreases employment and slows economic growth.

Problems Calculating the Cost of the Iraq War

Many sources explain that it is difficult, if not impossible, to accurately tabulate the economic costs to the United States of the Iraq war. Fred Foldvary (2008) on Econ Journal Watch attempted to quantify the costs. As of 2008, $3 trillion was the estimated cost to the United States of spending on the war in Iraq. The dollar amount is just one input into the economic costs of the war to the nation. The additional economic costs are far reaching and include both tangible and intangible economic costs.

An exceptionally difficult cost to quantify is the returning military costs. The returning military experience tremendous reentry issues, and those costs are far reaching and impact the country through medical, psychiatric, and employment damages.

The government is also accused of poor accounting and reporting, making it difficult to calculate the cost of the war. Unlike prior wars, this war did not have a separate account and the war payments were mixed in with other types of spending. The war was funded through many emergency allotments, not factored into the government's budgets. There was no specified budget category for Iraq war spending so a complete accounting of all financial war costs is exceedingly difficult.

Opportunity Costs of War

Opportunity cost is an economic term that refers to the cost of the choice that was not made. Making one choice means foregoing other choices, and those are called the opportunity costs. Spending on the war consequently meant there were many other projects unfunded due to lack of resources. For example, had the United States not spent on the Iraq war, the money could have been directed to reduce the federal debt, cut taxes, and/or increase funding for domestic programs.

For 10 years, trillions of dollars went to fund the war. It is difficult to calculate how those dollars, had they been spent on other domestic programs, debt, tax relief, and so on, would have affected the economy of the country. This is an example of an intangible economic cost of the war.

Costs to U.S. Citizens

The military, military contractors, and their families have felt the war costs most directly. The federal budget deficit grew significantly due to the Iraq war. This reality excludes the fact that the budget was already in a deficit at the start of the war. When the budget deficit increases, all citizens will ultimately have to pay for those increases, usually through higher future taxes. Additionally, when foreigners buy U.S. Treasury bonds, they are in effect funding our government, putting us in debt to our international debt buyers.

Economically, war always diverts production from the production of domestic goods to those war-related products. More war guns mean less domestic production and investment into technologies and new corporate capital projects. This creates a chain reaction that diminishes the investment in our country now, leading to lower domestic growth, development, and living standards in the future.

The costs of war impact not only the current generation, but have long-term effects on future generations. Future generations will pay the bills incurred by the war today. Since money is borrowed for war through the issuance of Treasury securities, that money will be paid back by future workers' taxes.

Stiglitz and Bilmes, authors of *The Three Trillion Dollar War: The True Cost of the Iraq Conflict*, allege that the war in Iraq influenced higher oil prices. There is a direct correlation between the start of the war and increasing oil prices. During the war, Iraqi oil production was halted. Additionally, the military used substantial amounts of oil. This does not mean oil prices would have remained stable if we hadn't gone to war with Iraq, but only that the war furthered the increase in oil prices due to the curtailing of the supply that the war created.

Costs to the Military and Related Population

Finally, the costs to the military and their families are immeasurable. There is a military class of citizens returning to this country with severe physical and mental problems. These soldiers return to an economy with high unemployment, leading to underemployment or no employment for many returning veterans. These social costs of war cannot be measured in dollars and cents, yet have a tremendous impact on our financial and social economies. Those returning veterans without employment create financial expenses to our social service systems as well as immeasurable emotional costs to a valuable segment of the population.

It is reported that almost 4,500 U.S. troops were killed and more than 32,000 wounded. No dollar amount can be allocated to those losses.

Regardless of whether one believes the war was just or successful, there are both tangible and intangible economic costs from the 10-year-long war in Iraq. The costs to the U.S. economy for this war span the current and future generations. There are individual financial costs to the soldiers and their families as well as broad economic costs to the United States.

Barbara Friedberg

See also: Bush, George W., 43rd President of the United States; Human Capital; Obama, Barack, President of the United States; Opportunity Cost; Unemployment

Further Reading

Baker, Dean. 2007. "The Economic Impact of the Iraq War and Higher Military Spending." http://www.cepr.net/documents/publications/military_spending_2007_05.pdf

Foldvary, Fred E. 2008. "Uncovering the Costs of the Iraq War." Econjournalwatch.org. (Vol. 5, No. 3): 373–379. http://econjwatch.org/articles/uncovering-the-costs-of-the-iraq-war

National Public Radio. 2013. "The Iraq War: 10 Years Later, Where Do We Stand?" http://www.npr.org/2013/03/16/174510069/the-iraq-war-10-years-later-where-do-we-stand

Stiglitz, Joseph E., and Linda J. Bilmes. 2008. *The Three Trillion Dollar War: The True Cost of the Iraq Conflict.* New York: W. W. Norton.

Trotta, Daniel. 2008. "Iraq War Hits U.S. Economy: Nobel Winner," March 2. http://www.reuters.com/article/2008/03/02/us-usa-economy-iraq-idUSN2921527420080302

Year 2005: Growth of China and India as World Economic Powers

The year 2005 marked the rise of China and India as powerhouse emerging markets in the world economy. After years of economic reform, political challenges, and private enterprise growth, both countries achieved new economic heights. The International Monetary Fund (IMF) (2007) estimates that the economies of China and India grew 11.3 percent and 9.1 percent in 2005, respectively, as measured by GDP growth. In contrast, during the same time period the U.S. GDP grew 3.5 percent. The exceptional growth drew interest from businesses around the world that wanted to enter these dynamic markets with expanding consumer and government spending. The increased number of international firms entering these markets also increased job opportunities in these two countries, which further helped to increase the size of the middle class and their buying power, thus improving their standard of living.

China

In 2005, as China completed its 10th Five-Year Economic Program, its emergence as a world economic power solidified. The economy continued to grow with its GDP increasing 11.3 percent, a rate not seen in the previous 10 years. The reasons for China's economic growth stem from major changes in government policies such as the valuation change of China's currency and the removal of regulations on private firms.

Currency Policy Change

Until 2005, the Chinese currency, the renminbi (RMB), was pegged to the dollar. The government changed its valuation of the RMB to be compiled in reference to a floating basket of currencies. At that time, the currency was revalued about 2 percent against the U.S. dollar and allowed to fluctuate. The currency valuation change gave the government more power in fiscal policy, specifically, inflation control, interest rate instabilities, and market economics.

Private Firms

Although the government was practicing more control in the financial arena, it moved to reduce its intervention in some market activities. State-owned enterprises (SOEs) were favored by the government in China across almost all industries. In 2004, the government removed multiple regulations that in effect, had impeded non-SOEs from entry into industries such as infrastructure and financial services. Although the result was not uniform or perfect, the relaxation of the dominance by SEOs provided opportunities for non-SEOs to diversify into upstream and downstream industries. Also, these changes facilitated the efficiency of production, which could reduce prices for consumers and increase profit margins for firms. In total, private firms contributed more to the country's GDP than SOEs for the first time.

International Relationships

China's diplomatic and trading relationships with other countries improved during the early years of the 21st century. The country was admitted to the World Trade Organization (WTO) in 2001, which opened foreign direct investment (FDI) opportunities by allowing firms from other countries to wholly own enterprises in many industries. At the end of 2004, China entered into the Agreement on Trade in Goods of the Framework Agreement on Comprehensive Economic Co-operation between the Association of Southeast Asian Nations and the People's Republic of China (China–ASEAN Agreement on Trade in Goods) with 10 member nations of the Association of Southeast Asian Nations: Indonesia, Malaysia, the Philippines, Singapore, Thailand, Brunei, Cambodia, Laos, Myanmar, and Vietnam.

The Agreement on Trade in Goods reduced tariffs on over 500 products and took effect in July 2005. In an unprecedented move, the leader of Taiwan's National Party, Lien Chan, visited China in April. This was the first time leaders from the Republic of China's Nationalists (in Taiwan) and the Communist Party of China met since the end of their civil war in 1950. In total, exports from China increased over 25 percent and imports increased almost 20 percent. China's Ministry of Commerce reported that FDI into China grew almost 20 percent from 2004 to $72.4 billion with an additional $11.8 billion FDI in banking, insurance, and securities.

India

In 2005, the Indian economy grew faster than ever before with the GDP increasing 9.1 percent (IMF). The increase in India's economic growth was due to a combination of many factors including government fiscal changes, foreign direct investment reform, and infrastructure industries investment. These changes were facilitated by the 2004 election of Manmohan Singh from the Indian National Congress political party as prime minister. This election marked a substantial change in political power from the incumbent National Democratic Alliance party. Confirmation of India's economic rise was provided when the U.S. secretary of state, Condoleezza Rice, visited in March 2005. In April, the Open Skies Agreement was signed between the United States and India, which eliminated restrictions between the countries. This was followed by Singh's visit to the United States in July, which initiated the 123 Agreement, also known as the U.S.–India Civil Nuclear Agreement.

Fiscal Reform

The Indian government passed the Fiscal Responsibility and Budgetary Management (FRBM) Act in 2003 and the FRBM Rules in 2004. The FRBM aimed to increase transparency in the Indian financial system, decrease the fiscal deficit, and balance the budget. The FRBM took effect at the beginning of 2004 and by 2005 had made an impact. The Organization for Economic Co-operation and Development (OECD) found that the FRBM reduced the governmental prevention of national savings and substantially reduced the fiscal deficit. India replaced the sales tax with a value-added tax (VAT) to simplify tax collection and improve efficiency.

FDI and Infrastructure Industries

In 2005, India enacted policy reform to improve the ability of foreign firms to invest in the country. For one, India changed its FDI policy to allow foreign firms to own up to 100 percent of ventures in some industries including textiles, construction, telecommunications, and domestic civil aviation. New regulations reduced the licensing requirements for firms and improved access to foreign technology. The federal government also lowered tariffs, which motivated the increase of market entry by foreign firms from multiple countries. As a result, those living in India enjoyed lower prices. Additionally, firms found it easier to import machinery into their new manufacturing facilities, thus supporting further economic growth. Overall, the changes in industrial policies increased the level of FDI in the country.

Employment Reform

Changes in the Indian government were also indicated in the employment reform. The Mahatma Gandhi National Rural Employment Guarantee Act (MGNREGA) was enacted in 2005 to provide jobs to semiskilled and unskilled adults in rural areas of the country for at least 100 days each year. The act was launched in 2006.

Summary

The year 2005 was an early signal of the growth ahead. Over the next few years, the growth in the economies of China and India continued to escalate until the global economic downturn in 2009. However, according to the International Monetary Fund (2007), both countries remained strong through 2012 with annual GDP growth over 5 percent, even in the face of GDP contraction in the United States and the European Union. Likewise, the two governments seek new ways to maintain economic growth and prosperity as the world becomes more interconnected.

Jennifer L. Woolley

See also: Capitalism; Gross Domestic Product (GDP) and Gross National Product (GNP); Year 1944: Creation of the International Monetary Fund and the World Bank at the Bretton Woods International Conference

Further Reading

Herd, Richard. "Policy Brief: Economic Survey of China, 2005." Accessed May 15, 2013. http://www.oecd.org/china/economicsurveyofchina2005.htm

International Monetary Fund. 2007. *World Economic Outlook, 2006.* Accessed May 15, 2013. http://www.imf.org/external/pubs/ft/weo/2006/02/

Morrison, Wayne M. 2006. "China's Economic Conditions." Accessed May 15, 2013. http://www.fas.org/sgp/crs/row/IB98014.pdf

OECD. 2008. "Policy Brief: Economic Survey of India, 2007." Accessed May 15, 2013. http://www.oecd.org/eco/surveys/39452196.pdf

Yuann, James K., and Jason Inch. 2008. *Supertrends of Future China: Billion Dollar Business Opportunities for China's Olympic Decade.* Hackensack, NJ: World Scientific Publishing.

Zhang, Marina Yue. 2010. *China 2.0: The Transformation of an Emerging Superpower and the New Opportunities.* Hoboken, NJ: John Wiley & Sons.

Year 2007–2008: Subprime Housing Crisis and Mortgage Meltdown

In 2007–2008, the United States faced a serious housing crisis. There was a combination of several factors that caused this crisis, which resulted in many mortgage defaults and falling home values.

After the dot-com bust early in this century, interest rates declined to low single digits. This cheap or low-interest money was widely available. The low-interest rates made mortgages very cheap. The availability of low-interest-rate loans, coupled with the desire to achieve the American dream, caused a spike in home ownership. This growing demand for homes rapidly drove up existing home prices.

All of the preceding factors caused lenders to improperly qualify loan borrowers. Many lenders granted loans to families and individuals who could not afford to repay the loans.

Many of these loans made to unqualified borrowers were subprime mortgages. This type of mortgage is made to borrowers that have a low credit rating—usually below 600. Since the borrower has a low credit rating, the lending institution views the consumer as a high-risk borrower with a higher than normal possibility of defaulting on the loan. Additionally, the interest rate on a subprime loan is higher than that on a conventional mortgage loan because of the risk the lender assumes.

The Causes of the Crisis

This crisis was due to a series of events. Historically, the borrower repaid the loan directly to the lending institution. The lender kept the loan and did not sell it. Therefore the lender still had a vested interest in the loan quality. The lender who kept the loan wanted the loan repaid. Because of this, lenders were concerned with the borrowers' credit history and job situation, and verified the information the prospective borrowers provided to ensure they were taking on a good risk.

As banking legislation was relaxed with the passage of the Glass-Steagall legislation in 1998 (which allowed banks to engage in risky activities), mortgage lenders began "selling" their loans to investment banks who packaged the mortgages and sold them to investors. The fact that a lender could sell a loan to another party gave that lender less of an incentive to properly qualify the repayment ability of the prospective borrowers. The lenders no longer cared if the borrowers could pay back the loans because they packaged these risky loans into securities and sold them to investors.

The bundled mortgages were securitized or converted into marketable securities and sold to investors hungry for higher yield investments. These packages of mortgages are referred to as mortgage-backed securities. With exceeding low market interest rates, there was high demand for securities that paid higher interest rates.

At first, these mortgage-backed securities offered very attractive rates of return to the investors due to the higher interest rates on these mortgages. However, starting in 2007, these "investments" started to show signs of distress. This was in large part due to the rise of subprime mortgages.

From 2004 to 2006, the percentage of subprime mortgages increased from the historical 8 percent or lower to approximately 20 percent of loans granted, according to "Subprime Mortgage Crisis." Some parts of the country granted an even higher percentage of subprime loans. To make matters worse, many of these subprime loans were adjustable-rate mortgages. In fact, in 2006, over 90 percent of subprime loans were adjustable-rate. Adjustable-rate mortgages were another contributor to the housing crisis.

Adjustable-Rate Mortgages

In the past, most mortgages were fixed-rate loans. In this type of loan, the rate stays the same for the duration of the loan, regardless of what occurs in the economy. If a buyer obtains a 15-year loan with a 4 percent fixed-interest rate, the interest rate remains at 4 percent for the entire 15 years.

In an adjustable-rate mortgage (also known as an ARM) the loan's interest rate can adjust. This rate varies according to a specific benchmark—the index and the margin. The index is a rate established by the forces of the market, and the margin is the number of percentage points that is added to the index to determine the rate. The margin is agreed to by the borrower. The initial interest rate is commonly fixed for a period of time and then adjusts periodically—sometimes every month. An example of this would be a 3/27 ARM—the interest rate is fixed for the first three years of the loan and then resets to a floating rate for the remaining 27 years. Many people bought homes they truly could not afford using an ARM. During the first few years, the interest rate was low and the borrowers were able to afford their monthly mortgage payments. However, after the initial fixed-rate period ended and the interest rate began to float, some borrowers faced monthly payment increases of hundreds of dollars. These borrowers were unable to pay the newly adjusted and higher loan payments.

The Crash

The confluence of these three factors contributed to the crash. The first contributor was low loan quality due to the opportunity to sell newly granted mortgages. Next, the rise of ARMs caused an onslaught of mortgage defaults and later foreclosures. Finally, with the advent of lower interest rates, consumers increased borrowing to unsustainable levels.

"Subprime Mortgage Crisis" from the University of North Carolina reported that household debt grew from $705 billion in December 1974 or 60 percent of disposable income to $7.4 trillion at year-end 2000, and finally to $14.5 trillion in mid-2008. By 2008, citizens held 134 percent debt when compared with their disposable income. Home mortgage debt as a percent of gross domestic product (total value of goods and services produced within the country in one year) grew from an average of 46 percent during the 1990s to 73 percent in 2008.

Toward the end of 2006 and in 2007, the prices of homes in the United States began to decrease in value—often by a large amount. Because of this decrease in value, many homeowners with adjustable-rate mortgages were unable to refinance (get a new mortgage loan) their mortgages at a lower interest rate. With the decline in home prices many homeowners owed more on their loans than their house was worth. This is referred to as being underwater on a mortgage. In combination with this, many ARMs began to adjust upward, which led to a perfect storm.

The homeowners who could not afford the newly adjusted higher payments began to default on their payments. They could not afford to pay the loans back and after a period of time, the lenders began to foreclose on these homes. That means the banks took possession of the mortgaged property because the borrowers could not keep up with the mortgage loan payments.

The increased number of foreclosures put downward pressure on home prices. The supply of available homes increased, which caused home prices to fall. As the mortgage holders defaulted, there was a ripple effect as payments into the packaged mortgage securities began to taper off.

Mortgage-backed securities lost much of their value and investors stopped purchasing these investments. In addition, many investors were worried about the security of America's credit and financial markets, which led to tightening credit and slowed the economic growth not only in the United States but also around the world, especially in Europe.

The major rating agencies, Fitch, Moody's, and Standard & Poor's (S&P), were also implicated in the financial crisis. Their job is to rate the safety of financial instruments. Investors rely on the agencies' ratings to understand the riskiness of their bond investments. Initially, these mortgage-backed securities were rated higher than their underlying assets warranted. This gave buyers of these mortgage-backed securities a false sense of comfort. The rampant defaults of the underlying mortgages that the securities packaged in fact was out of line with these financial instruments' higher ratings. The rating agencies are considered contributors to the financial crisis due to their inaccurate ratings on the mortgage debt securities.

The Consequences

This mortgage meltdown had grave consequences for the United States. The country went through a big recession and almost 9 million jobs were lost between 2008 and 2009. This represented almost 6 percent of the entire workforce. The average home value in the United States dropped almost 30 percent and the stock market pretty much lost half of its value. By the end of 2013, the stock market had recovered and was actually at record highs, but housing prices remained lower in most parts of the country than they were during the housing boom and unemployment remained above historical averages.

In summary, the United States faced a mortgage meltdown in 2007–2008 due in large part to risky loans made by mortgage lenders. This meltdown led the Great Recession that began in 2008 and was the catalyst that sparked our country's unemployment problems.

Danny Kofke

See also: Banking; Bankruptcy; Bonds; Credit (or Bond) Rating Agency; Debt; Delinquency; Derivatives; Loans; Mortgage; Year 2000: Bursting of the Dot-Com Technology Bubble; Year 2007–2009: Global Recession and Breakdown of Major Wall Street Institutions; Year 2010: Dodd-Frank Wall Street Reform and Consumer Protection Act; Year 2011–2012: European Debt Crisis

Further Reading

Department of Statistics and Operations, University of North Carolina. "Subprime Mortgage Crisis." Accessed March 11, 2014. http://www.stat.unc.edu/faculty/cji/fys/2012/Subprime%20mortgage%20crisis.pdf

Forbes.com. "Lest We Forget: Why We Had a Financial Crisis." http://www.forbes.com/sites/stevedenning/2011/11/22/5086/

White, Lawrence J. "Credit Rating Agencies and the Financial Crisis: Less Regulation of CRAs Is a Better Response." Accessed March 11, 2014. http://web-docs.stern.nyu.edu/old_web/economics/docs/workingpapers/2010/White_Credit%20Rating%20Agencies%20for%20JIBLR.pdf

Year 2007–2009: Global Recession and Breakdown of Major Wall Street Institutions

During the 2007–2008 global economic decline, the United States experienced the worst recession since the Great Depression of the 1930s. The United States fell into a major recession during 2007 and led the world in a multiyear economic crisis.

The United States suffered a number of bank failures, increased unemployment, rampant home foreclosures, and a stock market decline. This contagion eventually spread worldwide, impacting global trading partners and yielding an international economic crisis. Reckless mortgage financing initiated this economic downward spiral.

A mortgage is a debt instrument by which a loan is made to a borrower who pledges interest in property (usually real estate) to the lender as collateral to secure the repayment of the loan. Once the loan has been repaid in full, the lender no longer has a claim on the property.

If the borrower does not make the monthly mortgage payments to repay the loan, after a period of time, the mortgage goes into default. This means that the borrower has reneged on the responsibility to repay the loan. If the borrow does not pay the required monthly mortgage payments, the bank (lender) can foreclose on the property. Foreclosure means the bank has the right to sell the property and keep the proceeds from the sale due to the fact that the property was pledged as collateral for the loan.

If this happens to a bank once, there is not much of a problem. Preceding the global recession, many loans were made to individuals who did not have the means to repay. Thus, thousands of loans went into default, causing not only hardship for the borrowers but financial problems for the lenders as well.

Causes of the Foreclosures

Interest rates were very low during the mid-2000s decade. The low interest rates, accompanied with the belief that it's important to own a home, spurred an excess of home buying.

Many lenders did not properly vet or investigate the borrowers' ability to repay the loans. Additionally, subprime loans were made with higher interest rates to riskier borrowers, or borrowers with poor credit histories. Finally, many loans had adjustable rates, which meant that the interest rate on the loan could rise. When these loan payments increased, many borrowers could not afford to make their mortgage payments, feeding into the increase in defaults and foreclosures.

In sum, the inappropriate mortgage financing that spurred the crisis included falsifying documents by the lenders, qualifying buyers to purchase who were financially unworthy, loaning too much money on individual properties, and encouraging borrowers to borrow more money than they could reasonably pay back.

The Economic Climate Preceding the Crisis

During 2006, housing prices reached a peak and interest rates were at record lows. These two facts combined led banks to extend credit to borrowers without enough investigation into their repayment ability. The rationale was that if the borrowers could not repay, the increasing real estate prices would cover the loan value ratio (the percentage of the assessed value of the property that is debt; lower is better and more conservative) in addition to accrued interest (Dodd and Mills, 2008).

Many banks sold their loans to third parties, and the loans were then repackaged as mortgage-backed securities (MBS) and sold to investors to distribute the risk in a process referred to as securitization. Securitization refers to the procedure of distributing risk by aggregating debt instruments into one group and issuing other securities backed by that pool (Downes and Goodman, 2003). The issued securities are backed by mortgages, and this is where they get their name (mortgage-backed securities).

This enabled lenders to take the loans off their books. Special-purpose vehicles (SPVs) were used to keep these loans off the balance sheet, which allowed financial institutions to increase their debt levels even further. SPVs are entities established as separate legal entities with an asset and liability structure that makes their obligations separate from the parent company.

Typically, when loans are securitized, they combine similar types of loans bearing equivalent risk levels. During this period, low- and high-risk loans were combined with the borrowers and issuers frequently unsure of the actual risk of the newly packaged securities. These packages of home mortgages were securitized into a financial product called mortgage-backed securities (MBS). Investors liked to purchase these "bond-like" investments because the low-interest-rate environment made it difficult to find high-interest-rate investments for their funds. The MBSs had higher dividend payments than many other investments such as bank certificates of deposit and corporate bonds. With the inclusion of the lower rated subprime mortgage debt, the securities interest payments were driven higher than many other types of fixed-income investment opportunities.

The MBSs might not have been so popular had not the public believed that these securities were safe. Many of the MBSs received A, AA, and AAA ratings from the agencies, implying a "seal of approval" for these investments.

The rating agencies also contributed to the crisis because the MBSs were rated inaccurately by rating agencies such as Standard & Poor's and Moody's. These rating agencies are created to independently rank an investment's potential riskiness. During this time period the rating process lacked regulatory oversight and improper understanding of the mortgage-backed securities. Thus, the ratings issued for these securities did not reflect the true risk exposure of the underlying assets. In other words, riskier securities that should have received low ratings were mistakenly ranked highly. Investors bought an MBS rated AA thinking they had a safe investment. That investment, had it been properly ranked, should have been ranked C.

Impact on Real Estate and Banks

When real estate prices began to drop in 2007, two effects occurred. On the household level, Americans lost one-quarter of their net worth in a year and a half. Total home equity in the United States, valued at $13 trillion at its peak in 2006, dropped to $8.8 trillion by mid-2008. Total retirement assets dropped by 22 percent, from $10.3 trillion in 2006 to $8 trillion in mid-2008. During the same period, savings and investment assets lost $1.2 trillion and pension assets lost $1.3 trillion. All losses combined totaled $8.3 trillion (Altman, 2009).

The second effect was on banks that suffered huge losses because they were heavily invested in mortgages. This troubled position of the banks raised worries about their solvency, especially as major investment banks Bear Stearns and Lehman Brothers failed in 2008. The U.S. government stepped in to bail out Wall Street institutions for the first time since the Great Depression.

Since banks suffered great financial losses due to their poor lending tactics, they reversed their prior practices. Instead of loaning money freely and barely checking the buyer's ability to repay the debt, they reversed their practices. By the latter part of the decade, banks drastically cut back their lending to everyone. For fear of a repeat of the debt foreclosures, even the most qualified of borrowers had difficulty obtaining a loan. This pullback led to a "credit crunch" and a hesitation by banks to lend. This severely limited the borrowing ability and available credit for qualified businesses and individuals.

In April 2008, the International Monetary Fund (IMF) in its *Global Financial Stability Report* estimated that global losses could reach $945 billion. This forced the U.S. government to take action in an attempt to curtail the losses (Dodd and Mills, 2008). Thus, a bill was developed and finalized in October 2008 to authorize the U.S. Treasury to spend $700 billion to purchase troubled assets domestically and internationally through the Troubled Assets Relief Program (TARP). The intervention by government was criticized as many citizens believed the bill offered a bailout to Wall Street bankers who, according to critics, should have been held responsible for the amount of risk they incurred.

Government Intervention

Many major institutions failed, were acquired by other institutions, or were subject to government takeover. These included Merrill Lynch, which was acquired by Bank of America; Washington Mutual, which was acquired by JP Morgan Chase; Wachovia, which was acquired by Wells Fargo; Citigroup, which was bailed out, receiving $45 billion from TARP funds; and AIG, which was also bailed out by receiving $67.8 billion from TARP funds (Pro Publica, 2013).

In November 2008, the U.S. government began a program entitled Quantitative Easing. Simply, the government began a monthly program of buying the poorly ranked debt (sometimes called toxic) from the banks and government-sponsored entities called Fannie, Freddie, and Ginnie Mae. (These agencies bought many of the bad loans from the initiating banks.)

The government's motivation was to help the U.S. economy. The quantitative easing was designed to encourage banks to lend again by removing the bad debt from their books.

The government intervention prevented the collapse of the banking system but could not restore economic growth to precrisis levels. Thus, the U.S. economy entered a deep recession in December 2007 and is estimated to have shrunk by 2.7 percent in 2009 (Verick and Islam, 2010). Despite the announcement by the National Bureau of

Economic Research that the recession ended in June 2009, recovery has been slow, with the U.S. economy experiencing both low growth and high unemployment rates, which puts pressure on the budget deficit. Another factor contributing to the recession was increasing crude oil prices, which doubled from June 2007 to June 2008 (Goodman and Mance, 2011).

The Crisis Becomes International

Many developing economies were affected by the recession in the United States. Among countries that were hit hard were Armenia, Mexico, South Africa, Turkey, the Baltic states, and Ukraine. Other countries were able to escape the recession and managed to get their economies to continue growing through huge government stimulus packages, as in China and India.

When U.S. economic growth stalls, imports also slow, thereby hurting our international trading partners' economies. Financial and economic markets are more intertwined than ever before with many international buyers of the inappropriately rated MBSs. This also caused losses worldwide. Furthermore, there were weak banking and lending practices with minimal oversight internationally, which caused global economic crises similar to that in the United States.

In general, as the global financial crisis began to spread, governments all over the world felt the severity of the problem and intervened through one or all of the following measures. Most countries followed the lead of the United States by issuing bailouts and injecting money into the financial system. Interest rates were reduced to help stimulate borrowing and investment. Fiscal spending was increased to boost aggregate demand. These measures helped to stop further economic slowdown and ultimately maintain employment levels at precrisis levels, but the effects have been very diverse across different countries.

It is worth noting that even countries that were not integrated in the global financial system were eventually hurt by the recession. Even the countries that were not exposed to the mortgage-backed securities markets were still affected through the slowdown of global trade.

The global financial crisis raised questions about capitalism as a valid economic system. Following the government intervention that occurred during the crisis, the credibility of developed countries' preaching capitalist values and the rule of market forces has come under greater scrutiny.

Yasmine H. Abdel Razek

See also: Bonds; Capitalism; Mortgage; Real Estate; Year 2007–2008: Subprime Housing Crisis and Mortgage Meltdown; Year 2010: Dodd-Frank Wall Street Reform and Consumer Protection Act; Year 2011–2012: European Debt Crisis

Further Reading

Altman, Roger C. 2009. "The Great Crash, 2008: A Geopolitical Setback for the West." *Foreign Affairs* (January) 88 (1): 2–14.

Dodd, Randall, and Paul Mills. 2008. "Outbreak: U.S. Subprime Contagion." *Finance and Development* (June): 45 (2), 14–18. Accessed August 20, 2013. http://www.imf.org/external/pubs/ft/fandd/2008/06/dodd.htm

Downes, John, and Jordan E. Goodman. 2003. *Dictionary of Finance and Investment Terms,* p. 626. New York: Barron's Educational Series.

The Economist Web site. 2013. "Crash Course." Accessed April 4, 2014. http://www.economist.com/news/schoolsbrief/21584534-effects-financial-crisis-are-still-being-felt-five-years-article

Goodman, Christopher J., and Steven M. Mance. 2011. "Employment Loss and the 2007–2009 Recession: An Overview." *Monthly Labor Review* (April).

Pro Publica Web site. 2013. "Bailout Recipients." Last modified August 27, 2013. http://projects.propublica.org/bailout/list

Verick, Sher, and Iyanatul Islam. 2010. "The Great Recession of 2008–2009: Causes, Consequences and Policy Responses." Forschungsinstitut zur Zukunft der Arbeit [Institute for the Study of Labor] (May). http://ftp.iza.org/dp4934.pdf

Year 2010: Dodd-Frank Wall Street Reform and Consumer Protection Act

The Dodd-Frank Wall Street Reform and Consumer Protection Act was enacted in 2010 in response to the financial crisis that began in 2007. It addresses shortcomings in the financial regulatory system and was signed into law by President Obama on July 21, 2010. Commonly called "Dodd-Frank," the act affected almost every aspect of the U.S. financial system and was the most significant reform of financial regulations since those that followed in the wake of the Great Depression.

Some critics allege that Dodd-Frank did not go far enough and failed to address the root causes of the financial crisis. Others claim that Dodd-Frank is overly intrusive and will eventually strangle the financial services industry in bureaucracy. Regardless, Dodd-Frank is complex and far reaching, consisting of provisions that impact almost every aspect of the U.S. financial system. Its various components expand regulatory monitoring of financial institutions' corporate activities, create and eliminate multiple government agencies, expand the types of financial professionals subject to registration and licensing, establish governmental oversight of how financial institutions communicate and do business with consumers, and make a host of other changes.

Sixteen Titles of the Dodd-Frank Act

Dodd-Frank contains 16 titles, some of which constitute acts in their own right, as discussed below. The breadth of this law is extensive and touches most aspects of consumer and professional finance. Title I, Financial Stability, is also known as the Financial Stability Act of 2010. Title I establishes two new agencies attached to the Treasury Department, the Financial Stability Oversight Council and the Office of Financial Research.

The Financial Stability Oversight Council, chaired by the Treasury secretary, has three purposes: to identify risks to the financial stability of the United States arising from large, interconnected financial and nonfinancial companies; to promote market discipline by eliminating expectations that such companies will be shielded from losses by the government in the event of failure; and to respond to emerging threats to the stability of the U.S. financial system. This council is charged with foreseeing and avoiding massive financial breakdowns. The Office of Financial Research is established within the Treasury Department for the purpose of supporting the council in the fulfillment of its duties.

The second title, the Orderly Liquidation Authority, oversees the sale of the assets of a business, with the proceeds used to pay creditors and any leftovers distributed to shareholders. Title II provides authority for the liquidation of covered financial companies, including insurance and nonbank financial companies whose liquidation is not provided for under other statutes. It also makes changes to the procedures for liquidating banks, establishes methods for the government to appoint receivers to take over failing financial companies, and directs the research and reporting on the effectiveness of the bankruptcy process with regard to financial companies.

Title III has a major impact on consumers. It permanently increases the deposit insurance offered by the Federal Deposit Insurance Corporation (FDIC) from $100,000 to $250,000 per depositor per financial institution and makes a number of technical changes to the operation of the FDIC and OCC. This change gives consumers additional security and protection for their bank deposits. Other provisions of this title, also known as the Enhancing Financial Institution Safety and Soundness Act of 2010, eliminates the Office of Thrift Supervision, which previously had regulatory oversight of savings and loan holding companies, federal savings associations, and state savings associations. Oversight of these entities is transferred to the Board of Governors of the Federal Reserve System, the FDIC, and the Office of the Comptroller of the Currency.

For a long time, there has been interest in regulating hedge funds, which have been one of the few financial vehicles without much oversight. Title IV, Regulation of Advisers to Hedge Funds and Others, is also known as the Private Fund Investment Advisers Registration Act of 2010. This section establishes a new requirement that certain hedge fund managers and private equity fund managers register as financial advisers, as was required of other types of advisers prior to this. It also changes the reporting requirements for all registered financial advisers to provide more data to the government.

The Federal Insurance Office Act of 2010, Title V, establishes the Federal Insurance Office within the Department of Treasury. The Federal Insurance Office monitors all aspects of the insurance industry with a focus on preventing a financial crisis.

Title VI, known as the Bank Savings Association Holding Company and Depository Institution Regulatory Improvement Act of 2010, aims to improve and expand the regulatory oversight of banking entities by reducing the amount of risk they are allowed to expose themselves to through their investment portfolios. The most well-known provision of this title is the "Volcker Rule," which amends the Bank Holding Act of 1956 and applies only to banking entities. The Volcker Rule requires a bank's capital to increase during times of economic expansion and decrease in times of economic contraction. This "countercyclical" capital requirement is intended to improve the safety and soundness of the individual banks and the financial system as a whole.

Title VII, the Wall Street Transparency and Accountability Act of 2010, addresses the regulation of credit default swaps and credit derivatives, which are financial instruments used by large financial services companies to shift their exposure to risk from credit-related products in their portfolios to other companies. These derivative financial instruments are widely seen as a catalyst of the financial crisis that started in 2007 and are responsible for the failure of several prominent banks. This title tightly regulates these securities by both the Commodity Futures Trading Commission and the Securities and Exchange Commission.

Title VIII is known as the Payment, Clearing and Settlement Supervision Act of 2010. It is designed to reduce risk to the financial system and promote stability by promoting uniform standards governing payment, clearing, and settlement activities between financial institutions, as well as the systems used to conduct those activities (also known as financial market utilities).

In an ongoing effort to protect investors, Title IX, formally known as the Investor Protection and Securities Reform Act of 2010, amends the Securities and Exchange Act of 1934, which was enacted in response to the 1929 stock market crash and ensuing financial problems. This act creates a new infrastructure within the Securities and Exchange Commission specifically tasked with advocating for investors, and gives the SEC broader regulatory authority and enforcement powers, addressing a wide variety of regulatory areas such as credit rating agencies, asset-backed securities, whistleblowers, executive compensation, corporate governance, municipal securities, and even the management and funding of the SEC itself.

Title X creates the Bureau of Consumer Financial Protection and is known as the Consumer Financial Protection Act of 2010. Title X has perhaps the most substantial impact on consumer financial issues and regulations of any aspect of Dodd-Frank through its creation of the bureau, an independent federal bureau within the Federal Reserve System. The bureau is provided with far-reaching regulatory authority over how financial products and services are marketed, sold, and provided to consumers.

The bureau's Web site offers extensive personal finance resources. Its purpose is to ensure, through the consistent implementation and enforcement of federal consumer financial law, that all consumers have access to fair, transparent, and competitive markets for consumer financial products and services.

Title XI, Federal Reserve System Provisions, makes changes to the Federal Reserve Act regarding the governance, oversight, and responsibilities of the Federal Reserve System. These changes include the establishment of the position of vice chair for supervision on the board, audits of the Federal Reserve System by the GAO, and requirements for establishing additional financial standards for the institutions supervised by the Fed.

Title XII helps low- and moderate-income individuals gain greater access to financial services. Known as the Improving Access to Mainstream Financial Institutions Act of 2010, Title XII authorizes financial incentives to a variety of financial institutions and nonprofit organizations to encourage participation in the "financial mainstream" by formerly marginalized lower income individuals through bank accounts, small-dollar-value loans, and financial counseling and education.

Designed to help with the budget deficit, Title XIII, the "Pay It Back Act," amends the Emergency Economic Stabilization Act of 2008 to recover unused funds from the Troubled Asset Relief Program (TARP) and related programs, as well as proceeds from the sale of assets purchased as part of those programs. The proceeds can be used for deficit reduction.

During the financial crisis and mortgage meltdown in the mid-2000s there was extensive malfeasance in the mortgage industry. In an attempt to rectify those wrongs, Title XIV, known as the Mortgage Reform and Anti-Predatory Lending Act, was created. Title XIV addresses residential mortgage loan origination standards, practices, and liability, with a particular focus on borrowers' ability to repay. It also establishes minimum acceptable standards for mortgage products, addresses high-cost mortgages, establishes the Office of Housing Counseling in the Department of Housing and Urban Development, amends requirements for mortgage servicing and appraisal activities, and addresses mortgage resolution and modification issues unique to at-risk multifamily properties.

Titles XV and XVI clean up other financial areas not previously covered by the first 14 acts. The massive Dodd-Frank law renovates most aspects of the financial laws promising to protect consumers and improve access to financial products, along with many other advantages.

Leslie E. Linfield

See also: Banking; Bernanke, Ben S., 14th Chair of the U.S. Federal Reserve Board; Derivatives; Federal Reserve Bank; Financial Advisor; Mortgage; Volcker, Paul A., 12th Chair of the U.S. Federal Reserve Board; Year 1987: Stock Market Crash; Year 2007–2008: Subprime Housing Crisis and Mortgage Meltdown

Further Reading

Consumer Financial Protection Bureau Web site. Accessed February 28, 2014. http://www
.consumerfinance.gov/
The White House Web site. "Wall Street Reform: The Dodd-Frank Act." Accessed October 9,
2013. http://www.whitehouse.gov/economy/middle-class/dodd-frank-wall-street-reform

Year 2011–2012: European Debt Crisis

The effects of the 2007–2008 world financial crisis initiated by writing and trading subprime U.S. mortgages are still being felt more than five years later. The resulting liquidity crisis made banks hesitant to lend. By 2010–2011, the euro zone was engulfed in its own crisis. Although the 2007–2008 U.S. subprime mortgage crisis and subsequent recession could be said to have been the initiator, there were two factors peculiar to the euro zone without which the euro zone might have weathered the storm.

At the time of the 2007–2008 events, many euro zone politicians considered it to be an "Anglo-Saxon" problem, caused by unhealthy speculation, hedge funds, and derivatives. However, their schadenfreude was short-lived because the two euro zone problems had created their own potential perfect storm.

Precursor to the European Debt Crisis

The formation of the European Economic Community began with the Maastricht Treaty of 1992. Also known as the Treaty on European Union (TEU), which set the foundation for what was to become the European Union, this treaty included the launch of the economic and monetary union (EMU). There was a lack of true convergence between the initial members of the European Community. Since there were five requirements laid down in the Maastricht Treaty, it was crucial for the criteria to be met by all nations. They weren't.

Two critical criteria required by the community members were an annual government deficit of no more than 3 percent of gross domestic product (GDP) and a total debt of no more than 60 percent of GDP. At least three and possibly up to eight of the countries failed to meet these criteria.

Greece, Italy, and Belgium had debt to GDP ratios exceeding 100 percent. Spain and the Netherlands were just above 60 percent, although decreasing. A strict interpretation would have excluded Austria and Germany as these countries had public debt increasing to just over 60 percent in 1998. Belgium, France, and Italy massaged their deficits by claiming state company pension funds as current expenditure while not including liabilities. Italy hadn't been a member of the Exchange Rate Mechanism for long enough, and Greece had a deficit over 4 percent in 1998. In addition, it was widely suspected that Greece had been "fiddling the books" for a long time. These statistics disclose significant debt problems across the European Community.

Crisis

In 2009, Greece, Spain, Ireland, and France were all told to reduce their budget deficits. Greece had ineffective tax collection and high public-sector wages and pensions. Ratings agencies downgraded Greek government bonds so that their renewal would be much more expensive. Irregularities found in Greece's 2009 budget led to increasing the deficit from 5 to 13.6 percent of GDP, and Greek debt was over €300 billion, 113 percent of GDP.

Bailout followed bailout, austerity measure followed austerity measure, €110 billion was followed by €130 billion, and there was the possibility that the government would be replaced by one looking to leave the euro. Ultimately a pro-austerity administration was returned at the Greek ballot box. The price was extreme austerity and a "haircut," which meant that some depositors in some banks lost as much as half their money. Military expenditure was part of the cause with debt held by French and German banks in particular.

Other problems emerged elsewhere. In 2010, some of Ireland's banks were rescued by the government because of a collapsed property bubble. An €85 billion bailout package was agreed on and a very tough budget passed. Portugal followed in early 2011, asking for help, and a €78 billion package was delivered. But these were the small countries and the world could support them.

The big worry was Spain, Italy, and even France. Spain's problems were property-based like Ireland's, but there is a big difference between a country of 4 million and one of 40 million. Something had to be done. All these countries ended up passing austerity budgets, which resulted in high unemployment, particularly of the young, with increasing poverty and public dissent.

The next issue became Cyprus, a tiny member of the euro zone. Exposure to the Greek haircut, an explosion at a naval base, and the effect of the global crisis on its large financial services sector meant that the Cypriot economy struggled. Cypriot debt was downgraded to junk status and borrowing costs skyrocketed to 12 percent. Negotiations with the European Union (EU), International Monetary fund (IMF), and European Central Bank (ECB) went on through 2012.

The upshot was that capital controls were introduced, taxes increased, expenditures slashed. One bank closed with share capital forfeited, smaller accounts transferred, and larger deposits frozen pending sequestration in return for a €10 billion bailout. This was an unprecedented raid on bank deposits and affected many innocent people and businesses. The capital controls broke a fundamental condition of the European Union, let alone the euro zone itself.

European Central Bank Problems

Euro zone countries cannot devalue their currency, so other remedies followed. Austerity budgets were created, but the central bank, the ECB, was also handcuffed. It is essential to understand the difference between the ECB and other central banks such as the U.S. Federal Reserve Bank.

Unlike the U.S. Federal Reserve Bank, the ECB operated under different rules. The ECB tools were designed to handle short-term problems and maintain price stability assuming converged economies. It was unable to support the widespread economic problems and maintain the currency properly.

A central bank can create an unlimited amount of money and distribute it as required, but this would be a cross-country subsidy, so this approach was not undertaken. There was strong resistance from creditor nations who blamed the problems on debtors' profligacy. Bank refinancing was largely left to national governments with increased taxes along with cuts in public services, salaries, and jobs. Unlike the U.S. and UK central banks, the ECB could not and did not buy substantial quantities of government debt.

Resolution

The European financial stabilization mechanism set up systems to safeguard the euro zone members' financial stability and provide financial assistance to euro area members. They issued bonds whose proceeds could be lent to member nations. In 2012, this program evolved into a permanent European Stability Mechanism (ESM) to assist members with broad financial and economic problems.

The crisis both highlighted formation problems and questioned the sovereign status of the euro. The actions taken have ensured continued viability, but better control is needed. There are proposals for banking union and/or fiscal authority. Euro bonds have been suggested, but they would only provide short-term relief and are strongly opposed by some countries. Germany in particular is against the issuance of euro bonds. As the strongest euro zone country with the lowest borrowing costs, in the case of default, Germany would potentially experience the responsibility of underwriting or bailing out the weaker European Union member states.

The euro zone continues to struggle with economic and financial pressures into mid-2014.

Maria Nedeva

See also: Banking; Bonds; Debt; Deflation; Inflation; Interest Rates; Liabilities; Loans; Year 1944: Creation of the International Monetary Fund and the World Bank at the Bretton Woods International Conference; Year 1999: Introduction of the Euro to World Financial Markets; Year 2007–2009: Global Recession and Breakdown of Major Wall Street Institutions

Further Reading

De Grauwe, Paul. April 15, 2009. "The Politics of the Maastricht Convergence Criteria." VOW Web site. http://www.voxeu.org/article/politics-maastricht-convergence-criteria

"The EU Crisis Pocket Guide—2012 Edition." *Democratising Europe*. Transnational Institute Web site. Last modified November 6, 2012. http://www.tni.org/briefing/eu-crisis-pocket-guide

Stanislav Eminescu, Iulia. "Structure of Government Debt." European Commission Eurostat Web site. Last modified July 25, 2013. http://epp.eurostat.ec.europa.eu/statistics_explained/index.php/Structure_of_government_debt

"Taking Europe's Pulse." The Economist.com Web site. July 18, 2013. http://www.economist.com/blogs/dailychart/2011/02/europes_economies

People

Bernanke, Ben S., 14th Chair of the U.S. Federal Reserve Board

Ben S. Bernanke (born 1953) was the 14th chair of the board of governors of the Federal Reserve System. He served from February 1, 2006, to January 31, 2014. During his tenure the U.S. economy experienced the worst financial crisis since the Great Depression.

Bernanke is a 1975 graduate of Harvard University (summa cum laude) with a BA in economics; in 1979 he was awarded a PhD in economics from the Massachusetts Institute of Technology. Bernanke had been involved with the Federal Reserve System (the Fed) since 1987. The Federal Reserve Board (Fed) was established by Congress under the Federal Reserve Act with three objectives for monetary policy: maximum employment, stable prices, and moderate long-term interest rates.

Bernanke served as chair of President George W. Bush's Council of Economic Advisers from 2005 to 2006. On February 1, 2006, President Bush appointed him as chair of the Federal Reserve to replace the retiring chair, Alan Greenspan. Bernanke was confirmed to serve a second four-year term as chair on January 28, 2010, during the administration of President Barack Obama.

Bernanke's public service experience spans many years and is expected to continue into the future. He served as chair of the Federal Open Market Committee, the Federal Reserve System's principal monetary policymaking body. He originally took office as chair on February 1, 2006, when he also began a 14-year term as a member of the board. His second term as chair ended January 31, 2014, and his term as a board member will end January 31, 2020.

Before his work with the Fed and appointment as chair, Bernanke was a respected academic and taught at several prestigious institutions. From 1985 to 2002, Bernanke was a professor of economics and public affairs at Princeton and served as the chair of the Economics Department from 1996 to 2002. He also taught at Stanford from 1979 to 1985, at New York University (1993), and at the Massachusetts Institute of Technology (1989–1990).

Bernanke is well published with many scholarly articles on economic issues, including monetary policy, deflation, macroeconomics, and the area in which he is considered a foremost expert, the Great Depression. In July 2001, he was appointed editor of the *American Economic Review*. He has also authored several scholarly books, including two economics textbooks.

During his tenure as chair of the Federal Reserve, the U.S. economy experienced the worst financial crisis since the Great Depression. It began in 2007 with the bursting of the U.S. housing bubble and high rates of defaults on subprime mortgages. This led to a breakdown of major Wall Street institutions holding mortgage-backed securities, and this rippled into a global recession that by 2008 nearly collapsed the banking system, drove stock markets to record lows, and led to high unemployment.

Bernanke has been criticized for failing to foresee the financial crisis, for bailing out Wall Street, and for the policy known as quantitative easing—where the Fed has purchased $2.6 trillion in government bonds and mortgage-backed securities in order to encourage banks to lend and further economic growth. Bernanke did, however, use the tools afforded him as chair during the worst days of the crisis. Between September 2007 and December 2008 he lowered the Fed funds interest rate, the rate charged by banks overnight to each other, from 5.25 percent to 0 percent. When this wasn't enough to restore liquidity to the banking system, Bernanke went on to lower the Fed discount rate—the rate charged by the Fed on overnight loans to banks—and eventually the Fed began providing credit directly to the banks themselves through the Term Auction Facility and allowed the banks to put up bad debt as collateral. Lowering these interest rates was part of Bernanke's attempts to encourage banks to lend, which in turn would stimulate and grow the economy.

By the end of his term his governance saw a recovery of the stock markets as well as improving growth in the U.S. housing market. In fact, the housing market in some locations had returned to precrash levels. Although unemployment still remained above normal levels, it was declining.

In February 2012, Bernanke popularized the term *fiscal cliff* while testifying before Congress on the impact of sequestration—the fiscal policy that automatically reduced the federal budget across most departments—and forever entered popular culture. He also introduced a Twitter channel, @federalreserve, and thereby achieved one of his goals, accessibility and availability of the Fed to the general public.

A respected American economist and public servant for decades, in 2013 Bernanke left the Federal Reserve to continue in the private sector. His successor is Janet Yellen.

The Fed and its chair directly impact the personal finances of consumers through its monetary policy. Interest rate and employment policy directly impact the banking industry, which in turn provides financial products for consumers such as home and auto loans and savings and checking accounts.

Leslie E. Linfield

See also: Federal Reserve Bank; Greenspan, Alan, 13th Chair of the U.S. Federal Reserve Board; Interest Rates; Obama, Barack, President of the United States; Treasury Securities; Year 2007–2008: Subprime Housing Crisis and Mortgage Meltdown; Year 2007–2009: Global Recession and Breakdown of Major Wall Street Institutions

Further Reading

Bernanke, Ben S. 2013. *The Federal Reserve and the Financial Crisis.* Princeton University Press.

Board of Governors of the Federal Reserve System Web site. "Board Members: Chairman Ben S. Bernanke." Accessed September 9, 2013. http://www.federalreserve.gov/about thefed/bios/board/bernanke.htm

Board of Governors of the Federal Reserve System Web site. "The Federal Reserve System: Purpose & Functions." Accessed October 4, 2013. http://www.federalreserve.gov/pf/pdf/pf_1.pdf#page=4

Bloomberg, Michael R., American Politician and Businessperson

Michael R. Bloomberg, born February 14, 1942, is an influential American politician and businessperson. His contributions to both New York City, where he served as the 108th mayor from 2001 to 2014, and the American economy, where he founded Bloomberg LP, a large global financial news and information service, solidified his place in modern personal finance.

Bloomberg was born and raised in Medford, Massachusetts, to a middle-class family. He attended Johns Hopkins University and paid his way through college with loans and a job as a parking lot attendant. He continued his education at Harvard Business School where he obtained an MBA.

After his education, he began work at Salomon Brothers, an investment bank, in an entry-level job. He was promoted to oversee equity trading and sales. In his final position with the firm he served as head of information systems. In 1981, when Salomon merged with Philipp Brothers (Phibro), a metals trading firm, Bloomberg was fired and given a $10 million severance package.

In 1982, Bloomberg used this severance pay to start Bloomberg LP, an information company that exploited emerging technology to provide financial information and news. Bloomberg's initial objective was to aid transparency in an opaque investment and business information world. By 1992, Bloomberg Professional service transformed the financial information industry with over 10,000 customers for the firm's private

---

Four Bloomberg Controversies

1. In 2006, the New York City Board of Health voted to post all calorie content on menus at New York restaurants. This initiative is consistent with Bloomberg's desire to fight the growing obesity epidemic.
2. In 2007, Bloomberg's commissioner of the Department of Health and Mental Hygiene, Dr. Thomas R. Frieden, attempted to enact a plan to cut sodium levels in processed and prepackaged foods by 25 percent. Current data suggest this plan never came to fruition.
3. Also in 2007, Bloomberg initiated a plan to convert the city's 13,000-strong taxi fleet into hybrid models. By 2008, approximately 1,100 were hybrids. By 2012, this initiative was defeated by the New York City taxi lobby.
4. In a nod to his banking roots, in 2009, in the aftermath of the financial crisis, Bloomberg devised a plan to invest $45 million to retrain laid-off bankers and traders. His thinking on this initiative was to prevent many professionals from leaving New York City.

financial network of information, data, and analytics. During the 1990s the company continued to expand, opened international offices, and began Bloomberg News.

Today, Bloomberg employs its data, news, and technology in the fields of government, law, energy, and sports. Currently, Michael Bloomberg's company employs over 15,000 employees in 192 locations where the company disseminates business and financial news and information. Bloomberg LP is an important contributor to the global business world.

Bloomberg's tenure as mayor of New York is important to the financial and economic community. In his unlikely run for mayor, he switched political parties from Democrat to Republican and won. As chief financial officer of the largest metropolitan area in the United States, his policies and legislation initiated in New York City influence the entire country. He has been characterized as brash and irritated by small talk, as reported in a recent interview in the *Atlantic*. The sum of his style is more of a man who is razor focused on getting things done for the benefit of his constituents.

His failed controversial attempt to tackle the growing obesity epidemic by limiting the size of soft drinks integrates the strategy of helping the poor by improving their health. Although the soda size ban never reached fruition, his administration was successful at banning trans fat, another contribution to obesity and poor health. Bloomberg's attention to obesity is not only an attempt to raise the life expectancy of the poor, but also to help the economic system by lessening obesity-related health care costs. His two-pronged approach works to improve individuals' health, which subsequently reduces excess medical community health care costs. Bloomberg initiated the idea of improving health and finances in 2003 when New York banned smoking throughout the city.

In November, 2013, Michael Bloomberg was replaced as New York mayor by Bill de Blasio. This was the first new mayor since 2001. At that point Bloomberg returned to work at his namesake company and resumed a life in the private sector.

Michael Bloomberg's mayoral platform was more like a global pulpit in which he became an outspoken leader on immigration, climate change, and gun control. His success at reducing crime and improving the New York economy served as a model for the rest of the country. Since 2001, under Bloomberg's leadership in New York City, crime is down 35 percent, welfare rolls dropped 25 percent, and high school graduation rates increased 27 percent

Bloomberg uses his massive wealth to improve the economic plight of others through Bloomberg Philanthropies. His service mindset began early in life when his parents instilled in him the principles of public service and giving back. His charitable work focuses on public health, the environment, government innovation, the arts, and education.

Michael Bloomberg's reported (2013) $31 billion net worth earned him the 29th place on *Forbes'* list of most powerful people. Bloomberg's influence touched New York City, the United States, and internationally. His company globally impacts how financial news and information is transmitted and consumed.

Barbara Friedberg

See also: Capitalism; Year 2007–2009: Global Recession and Breakdown of Major Wall Street Institutions; Year 2010: Dodd-Frank Wall Street Reform and Consumer Protection Act

Further Reading

Bennet, James. October 24, 2012. "The Bloomberg Way." *The Atlantic*. http://www.theatlantic.com/magazine/archive/2012/11/the-bloomberg-way/309136/

Bloomberg Company Web site. Accessed December 22, 2013. http://www.bloomberg.com/company/

Lemire, Jonathan. December 14, 2013. "Michael Bloomberg Reshaped New York City, but Leaves Behind a Debated Legacy." *The Huffington Post*. http://www.huffingtonpost.com/2013/12/14/michael-bloomberg_n_4445281.html

Melby, Caleb. 2012. "Before the Ban on Sugary Drinks: 7 Other Controversial Mayor Bloomberg Initiatives." May 31. *Forbes.com*. http://www.forbes.com/sites/calebmelby/2012/05/31/before-the-ban-on-sugary-drinks-7-other-controversial-mayor-bloomberg-initiatives/

Mike Bloomberg Web site. 2013. Accessed December 22, 2013. http://www.mikebloomberg.com/?gclid=CLSl1675ursCFQh1QgodQ3oAAQ

Bogle, John, Founder of The Vanguard Group

John "Jack" Bogle (born 1929) is the creator of the first index mutual fund and the founder of The Vanguard Group, one of the world's largest investment management companies. He was born in New Jersey and currently lives in Pennsylvania with his wife, Eve. They have 6 children and 12 grandchildren.

Bogle attended Blair Academy and graduated cum laude in 1947. He then attended Princeton University where he majored in economics and graduated magna cum laude in 1951. In 1959, he graduated from the University of Pennsylvania's Evening School of Business and Finance.

John Bogle first became interested in the mutual fund industry when he wrote his Princeton thesis on the topic. He wanted to write a unique thesis on a topic that had never been covered by a Princeton graduate. After he completed his thesis, he sent it to Walter Morgan, the founder of Wellington Management Company, and Morgan hired him. Bogle quickly moved through the ranks at Welllington, from his start as an assistant all the way to president of the company and chair of the Wellington and associated funds.

However, at that time, Bogle experienced a career-altering moment. After Wellington went through a merger, Bogle gained four new partners. Everything went well at first, but eventually, his new partners fired him on January 26, 1974. Although it was a challenging point in his career, Bogle has credited this moment as the reason he started the first index fund. Without being fired, he might never have created The Vanguard Group, which was founded on September 24, 1974.

Today, Vanguard is among the world's largest and most successful investment management companies. According to the Vanguard Web site, their total assets are approximately $2 trillion and they employ approximately 13,500 employees. Vanguard is best known for their commitment to cost efficiency and their many firsts, including creating the first index mutual fund for individual investors, creating the first international stock

John Bogle's 10 Rules of Investing from *The Clash of the Cultures*

1. "Remember reversion to the mean." Don't follow the crowd because ultimately, investment values return to their averages over time.
2. "Time is your friend, impulse is your enemy." Be patient and give compound interest time to work. Don't be seduced by the markets to buy high and sell low.
3. "Buy right and hold tight." After you set your asset allocation, sit tight and don't do anything.
4. "Have realistic expectations." Building wealth through investing takes time. A 7.5 percent future stock return and 3.5 percent future bond return are reasonable.
5. "Forget the needle, just buy the haystack." Don't worry about looking for the perfect stock; your odds are low. It's best to buy the market with low-cost index funds.
6. "Minimize the 'croupier's' take." Before costs, the casino and stock picking are zero-sum (the total of all gains and losses is zero) games.
7. "There's no escaping risk." Every investment including cash in a savings account has risk. Inflation risk may be the greatest risk of all.
8. "Beware of fighting the last war." Don't copy the last strategy that worked. It will likely fail the next time.
9. "Hedgehog beats the fox." The fox represents the financial industry, which charges high fees and offers complicated advice. The hedgehog is akin to the index fund investor who curls up in a ball with its index fund holdings in a desired asset allocation.
10. "Stay the course." The investing secret is that there is no secret. Own the entire stock and bond markets with diversified index funds, keep disciplined, and stay the course.

index funds, and introducing the industry's first series of tax-managed funds. Ultimately, the company has experienced tremendous growth since its inception and has only employed three CEOs in its history. Bill McNabb is the current CEO who was appointed in 2008. The company remains true to its original intentions, which is to keep costs low so that the investors themselves can benefit more.

Bogle has received numerous honors and awards throughout his career, including being named one of the four "Giants of the 20th Century" by *Fortune* and one of the world's most powerful and influential people by *TIME*. He has also written several best-selling books, including *Bogle on Mutual Funds: New Perspectives for the Intelligent Investor, John Bogle on Investing: The First 50 Years*, and many more. His most recent publication and 10th book is called *Clash of the Cultures: Investment vs. Speculation*. Bogle has also served on numerous boards including being chair of the board of governors of the Investment Company Institute. He has received several honorary doctorate degrees from top universities like Princeton University, the University of Rochester, Georgetown University, and many more.

Although Bogle is now in his 80s, he is still deeply committed to his life's work and continues to encourage financial literacy among others, consistently claiming that investing is simple. He also encourages people to invest for the long term, not to look at their earnings until they are ready to retire, and to understand the simple math of compounding interest. Bogle's creation of the first index fund radically changed the mutual fund and investing world for the better. This investment product slashes investors' costs and provides a vehicle for investors to buy a proxy for the entire stock market. He transformed the financial industry during his long and successful career and has enabled and inspired millions of people to invest their money wisely.

Catherine Alford

See also: Bonds; Index Mutual Funds; Investing; Stock Market; Stocks

Further Reading

Bogle, John C. 1994. *Bogle on Mutual Funds: New Perspectives for the Intelligent Investor.* Dell (reprint edition).

Bogle, John C. 2002. *John Bogle on Investing: The First 50 Years.* New York, NY: McGraw-Hill.

Bogle, John C., and Arthur Levitt. 2012. *The Clash of the Cultures: Investment vs. Speculation.* New Jersey: John Wiley & Sons.

John C. Bogle Web site. Accessed August 14, 2013. http://johncbogle.com/

Vanguard Web site. Accessed August 14, 2013. https://vanguard.com/

Buffett, Warren, Owner of Berkshire Hathaway Inc.

Warren Buffett (born 1930) is one of the wealthiest people in the world, a legendary investor, and the owner of Berkshire Hathaway. He is the son of Leila Buffett and Howard Buffett, who was a stockbroker and U.S. congressman. Warren Buffett was born in Omaha, Nebraska, and is the middle of three children and the only boy. It was evident that Buffett had an aptitude for investment at an early age, likely influenced by visiting his father's office. Buffett demonstrated his business acumen as a child and frequently resold items for a profit.

Buffett purchased his first shares at only 11 years old. The stock he purchased, Cities Service Preferred, dropped after he purchased it. Buffett waited patiently for the stock to rebound, and when it did, he sold it. However, he immediately regretted the decision, since the share price of Cities Service increased even more in the time following the sale. That buy and hold lesson is still the crux of Buffett's financial philosophy.

Buffett did not want to go to college since he already had made considerable money as a paperboy, a business that he started at age 13. He also purchased pinball machines with a friend, resold them, and within a few months, reaped quite a profit. He eventually sold that business, and at his father's insistence, he attended the Wharton School of Business at the University of Pennsylvania. Unimpressed with his education, Buffett eventually transferred to the University of Nebraska–Lincoln where he finished his education. For graduate school, Buffett attended Columbia in 1956 after being rejected by Harvard. At Columbia, he met Ben Graham, who became his mentor and teacher.

After graduation, Buffett wanted to work for Graham, but Graham did not hire him, so Buffett returned home to work for his father. Shortly thereafter, he met a woman named Susie Thompson and married her in 1952. The young couple did not make a large income, so they lived modestly, even using a drawer as a crib for their first child. Eventually, Buffett was able to fulfill his dream of working for Graham after Graham hired him and invited him to work at his firm in New York.

Buffett was extremely successful and hardworking and learned much about the investment industry under Graham's tutelage. He eventually formed his own investment partnership, which proved immensely successful. Just before he liquidated the partnership, Buffett became a major stakeholder in Berkshire Hathaway, which at the time was a textile company. It eventually morphed into a holding company, and Buffett began accumulating more stock and other companies like See's Candy, GEICO, Nebraska Furniture Mart, Scott & Fetzer, and Executive Jet. He also invested in *The Washington Post*, and perhaps his most well-known acquisition was purchasing a large percentage of the Coca-Cola Company.

Buffett's investment strategy has certainly changed over time, but overall his investment style can best be described as having patience in the market, studying the habits of business owners, learning from mistakes, and investing only in businesses that he truly understands. Buffett is also well known for going against popular opinion and for being frugal, even living in the same modest house that he has owned for many years.

Buffett has demonstrated a strong commitment to charitable giving over the past few decades. He has donated to many charities, and in 2006, he announced that he would give his entire wealth to charity ($62 billion). Buffett has not written any books, but many people have written books about him, with the most well-known being *The Snowball: Warren Buffett and the Business of Life* by Alice Schroeder.

Buffett's personal life was tumultuous. He and his wife separated, and in an unusual move, his wife Susie gave her blessing for Buffett to see other people. Buffett and his wife remained incredibly close, even traveling and spending Christmas together. With Susie's knowledge and approval, a waitress named Astrid Menks moved in with Buffett.

Buffett's wife has since passed away, and Buffett eventually married Menks in 2006 in a modest ceremony. He has three children, Susie, Howard, and Peter, who all work in different fields and own their own foundations. Buffett has donated heavily to each of their foundations, and recently donated $2 billion to the Bill and Melinda Gates Foundation. Although he is famous for not giving overwhelming amounts of money to his children individually, he has pledged to donate more to their foundations in the future so that they can continue their charitable work around the world.

Warren Buffett has had an extraordinary career thus far and is a prime example of someone succeeding in their pursuit of the American dream. He remains one of the most famous and most successful investors in history, inspiring millions of people along the way.

Catherine Alford

See also: Bonds; Investing; Stock Market; Stocks

Further Reading

Biography Web site. "Warren Buffet Biography." Accessed August 15, 2013. http://www .biography.com/people/warren-buffett-9230729?page=1

Business Insider Web site. "Here Are 18 Brilliant Quotes from the Greatest Investor of All Time." Accessed February 24, 2014. http://www.businessinsider.com/warren-buffett-quotes-2012-8#this-is-the-most-important-thing-1

"The Experts: What Lessons Can Investors Learn from Warren Buffet?" 2013. Amended April 7, 2013. *The Wall Street Journal* Web site. Accessed August 15, 2013. http://online.wsj.com/article/SB10001424127887323646604578403021463980536.html

Schroeder, Alice. 2009. *The Snowball: Warren Buffett and the Business of Life.* New York, NY: Bantam.

Bush, George W., 43rd President of the United States

George W. Bush (1946–), America's 43rd president, served the United States from 2001 to 2009. He presided during a time of great economic and financial upheaval, punctuated by the September 11, 2001 (9/11) terrorist attacks on the World Trade Center. This, along with the terrorist attacks on the Pentagon in Washington, D.C., and the thwarted airplane attack in Pennsylvania, launched a massive war on terrorism. The 9/11 attacks motivated Bush to authorize the wars in Iraq and Afghanistan, leading to major economic consequences in the United States.

This entry will focus predominantly on the president's financial and economic policies and their impact on personal finance and modern money management. The terrorist attacks and ensuing policies developed to fight future terrorism had worldwide repercussions and concurrent economic implications for the United States.

George W. Bush is the eldest son (of six children) of George H. W. Bush, the 41st U.S. president. He was born in New Haven, Connecticut, when his father was a student at Yale University. The senior Bush moved the family to Texas while he worked as an oil industry executive.

Like his father and grandfather, the younger Bush graduated from Yale University in 1968 where he earned a degree in history. He continued his education at Harvard Business School and received a master's degree in business administration in 1975. In 1977 he married Laura Welch, a librarian and schoolteacher. They have twin daughters, Jenna and Barbara (1981).

After completing his education, Bush returned to Texas where he followed his father into the oil industry. Additionally, Bush was an owner of the Texas Rangers baseball team.

In 1978, Bush continued the family political legacy. He ran for a spot in Congress. Bush lost his campaign for the U.S. House of Representatives, but was undeterred from a political career. Continuing his desire for public service, in 1994, he defeated incumbent Ann Richards and became governor of Texas where he served for two terms. In 2000, after a closely contested election, Bush beat Al Gore to become president of the United States.

Bush was lauded for his economic policies during his first term. With congressional approval he implemented several tax cut bills in 2001 (Economic Growth and Tax Relief Reconciliation Act) and 2003 (Jobs and Growth Tax Relief Reconciliation Act). The $1.7 trillion tax cuts were initiated to reverse the downward economic trend during the 2001 recession and bursting of the technology bubble.

The massive tax reduction legislation cut federal income tax rates for everyone, reduced the marriage penalty tax, lowered capital gains taxes, lowered the tax rate on dividend income, increased the child tax credit from $500 to $1,000 per child, and eliminated the phase-out on personal exemptions for higher-income taxpayers. In this sweeping legislation estate taxes were completely eliminated as was the phase-out on itemized deductions. These tax policies were time limited and set to expire in 2010.

As their 2010 expiration dates approached, there was resistance to letting the tax cuts, initiated as a temporary measure, expire. Both taxpayers and legislatures resisted the lifting of these financially beneficial measures.

There was conflict between those who wished to extend and possibly make some of the cuts permanent and those who wanted to let the tax cuts expire. The camp that wanted to let the tax cuts expire stated that the government needed the tax revenue to offset the massive U.S. budget deficits.

With the added expenses of fighting two wars and the reduced revenue from the tax cuts, the U.S. budget deficit expanded. A budget deficit in the simplest terms means the U.S. government was spending more money than it was taking in. The growing budget deficit is also considered a tax on citizens' future income. When there are insufficient tax revenues to pay the country's bills, the government must borrow money by issuing Treasury debt such as Treasury notes, bills, and bonds and use the proceeds to fund the government.

The parties in favor of extending or making permanent the consumer-centric tax cuts argued for the economic benefit of reduced taxes. This group claimed that higher taxes curb economic growth, entrepreneurship, and the desire to work. In other words, the negative impact of increasing taxes during a recession would further hurt consumers during an already fragile economic time.

Tax policy decisions are central to the understanding of modern money management. Simply, when citizens have more money in their pockets, due to lower tax rates, they are likely to spend more. This additional consumer spending helps the economy grow by increasing demand for the goods and services produced by businesses. When there is demand for consumer products, companies may hire additional workers or at least keep the workers already employed, maintaining stable employment. Bush's tax cuts were designed to pull the United States out of the 2001 recession and return the country to an improved economy with stronger growth (as measured by the gross domestic product or GDP).

The hoped-for results of the tax cuts were not rapidly realized. During President Bush's second term (2005–2009), the economy continued to struggle, particularly due to the expenses associated with the Iran and Afghanistan wars. The tax cuts led to large budget deficits, beginning in 2002. The United States was increasing spending and reducing income, and the difference was the deficit.

In 2008, another recession occurred as a result of the subprime housing crisis and mortgage meltdown. During the final year of his presidency Congress passed several Bush-sponsored plans to bail out the financial industry using hundreds of billions of government funds. By the end of Bush's presidency, the country was in an economic morass with a huge budget deficit and recession. The wars in Iraq and Afghanistan continued to pull on the country's resources as well.

In 2010, when the tax cuts were set to expire, President Obama and Congress extended all but the death tax phase-out for an additional two years. Subsequently, many of Bush's initial tax cuts have become permanent. Because the U.S. tax policy is continually being revised, it is better to state that some of Bush's tax cuts are permanent, for now.

President Bush will be remembered for his economic policies as well as his anti-terrorist initiatives. Americans continue to enjoy many tax benefits including lower capital gains and dividend taxes along with the increased earned income tax credit (EITC) and increased dependent care tax credit. The family-friendly policies further help American consumers. Through their policies and laws the president and Congress, along with other governmental agencies, influence citizens' personal finances.

Barbara Friedberg

See also: Bonds; Budget; Capitalism; Debt; Deficit; Federal Reserve Bank; Tax Return, Federal; Treasury Securities; U.S. Federal Tax System Overview; Year 2000: Bursting of the Dot-Com Technology Bubble; Year 2003–2011: Iraq War's Impact on the U.S. Economy; Year 2007–2008: Subprime Housing Crisis and Mortgage Meltdown; Year 2007–2009: Global Recession and Breakdown of Major Wall Street Institutions; Year 2010: Dodd-Frank Wall Street Reform and Consumer Protection Act

Further Reading

Dubay, Curtis S. 2013. "The Bush Tax Cuts Explained: Where Are They Now?" The Heritage Foundation. February 20. http://www.heritage.org/research/reports/2013/02/bush-tax-cuts-explained-facts-costs-tax-rates-charts

History.com Web site. "George W. Bush." Accessed April 22, 2014. http://www.history.com/topics/us-presidents/george-w-bush

The White House; President George W. Bush. "President Bush's Tax Relief." Accessed April 22, 2014. http://georgewbush-whitehouse.archives.gov/infocus/taxes/

Clinton, William, 42nd President of the United States

William Jefferson Clinton (1946–) was the 42nd president of the United States, serving from 1993 to 2001. His time in office produced consistently increasing gross domestic product, reduced unemployment, moderate inflation, and a budget surplus for the first time in the United States since the 1950s. Domestic stock markets, including the Standard & Poor's 500 index, rose during much of his two terms as president. Clinton's legacy is often linked to the greatest peacetime economic expansion in modern-day America, though he left office (January 20, 2001) just prior to a colossal shift in finance and modern money management including a recession (March 2001–November 2001), the bursting of dot-com bubble, and the September 11, 2001, terror attacks.

While a study of Clinton's two terms in the White House could include a myriad of topics ranging from foreign policy to a failed attempt at health care reform, this entry focuses on the president's policies and approaches to finance and economics. To this day, the impact of Clinton's financial policies remains a highly debated subject, with some continuously touting the unprecedented growth of the American economy during his tenure while others link his decisions and leadership to the many economic crises that followed his time in office.

William Jefferson Clinton was born in Hope, Arkansas, three months after his father died in a traffic accident. Clinton attended Georgetown University, graduating in 1968 and winning an esteemed Rhodes scholarship to Oxford University. In 1973, he received his law degree from Yale University, returning to Arkansas to teach law at the University of Arkansas and begin a career in politics.

In 1974, Clinton ran for a seat in the U.S. Congress, losing the bid but remaining focused on a career in public service. Two years after his defeat, he was elected attorney general of Arkansas (1976), and then governor of Arkansas (1978), where he served from 1978 to 1980 and again from 1982 to 1992.

Clinton entered the 1992 race for the Democratic nomination for president, defeating his challengers while earning the opportunity to face Republican incumbent George Bush and independent Ross Perot. On November 3, 1992, candidate Clinton was elected president of the United States—winning 43 percent of the popular vote and almost 69 percent of the electoral vote.

Unlike the terms of many successive presidents before and the two that would follow him in office, Clinton spent two terms in the White House with no American recession. He presided over an economy that, for the most part, grew steadily from beginning to end. The stock market (Dow Jones Industrial Average) rose over 223 percent during his eight years in office; the NASDAQ index—which included many quickly growing technology companies—grew almost 288 percent. Moreover, the Clinton years saw more initial public offerings (IPOs) than under any other president in modern times. It was a time of economic increase, with stock prices at the forefront.

Two significant pieces of legislation are remembered from Clinton's time in office. The first, the Omnibus Budget Reconciliation Act of 1993, created higher tax rates for both individuals and corporations in the top income brackets. The legacy of this act is found in the present day, as the legislative and executive branches continue to quarrel over the proper level of tax rates. Higher taxes enable the government to reduce debt and spend on infrastructure and oversight but burden the public and theoretically make America a less competitive domain for businesses. Economic stability of government versus free market competitiveness have plagued both academia and politics throughout modern times, with Clinton's tax hikes only adding to the debate.

Additionally, Clinton was heavily involved in the North American Free Trade Agreement (NAFTA). Commencing on January 1, 1994, NAFTA eliminated tariffs and other barriers to trade between the United States, Canada, and Mexico. Through its implementation, NAFTA created the largest free trade area in the entire world, totaling $17 trillion of goods and services and 450 million people. Like many economic policies, the debate on NAFTA's effectiveness to the U.S. economy continues many years later. Some argue that removing barriers to trade enables the outsourcing of low-wage jobs and importing of cost-effective goods, while others claim access to affordable goods and services helps the American taxpayer, as does a shift in domestic demand toward high-wage occupations. As the argument continues, NAFTA has become a lasting economic policy of Clinton and part of his enduring legacy.

While a president who presides over the longest period of economic expansion in modern times may appear, at first glance, to necessitate a hero's welcome, finance is not so simple. Like markets themselves, economies are recurrent in nature—often the policy consequences of one president are not encountered until years later. President Clinton's governance of the American financial system preceded the dot-com bubble, the recession of 2001, and the eventual stalemate clash in politics over individual and corporate tax rates. His time in office was financially unique while standing as an important case study in the cyclical nature of the American economy.

Jonathan D. Citrin

See also: Budget; Bush, George W., 43rd President of the United States; Capitalism; Deficit; Greenspan, Alan, 13th Chair of the U.S. Federal Reserve Board; Gross Domestic Product (GDP) and Gross National Product (GNP); Inflation; Stock Market; Systematic Market Risk; Unemployment; U.S. Federal Tax System Overview; Year 1994: North American Free Trade Agreement between Mexico, Canada, and the United States (NAFTA); Year 1997–1998: Asian Financial Crisis; Year 2000: Bursting of the Dot-Com Technology Bubble

Further Reading

ClintonLibrary.gov Web site. "William J. Clinton." http://clintonlibrary.gov/william-j .-clinton-bio.html

Office of the United States Trade Representative. "North American Free Trade Agreement (NAFTA)." http://www.ustr.gov/trade-agreements/free-trade-agreements/north-amer ican-free-trade-agreement-nafta

SEC.gov Web site. "Where Have All the IPOs Gone?" http://www.sec.gov/info/smallbus /acsec/acsec-090712-ritter-slides.pdf

TradingEconomics.com Web site. "United States." http://www.tradingeconomics.com /united-states/indicators

WhiteHouse.gov Web site. "William J. Clinton." http://www.whitehouse.gov/about /presidents/williamjclinton

Geithner, Timothy F., 75th Secretary of the U.S. Treasury

Timothy F. Geithner (born 1961) was the 75th U.S. secretary of the Treasury. He served from January 26, 2009, to January 25, 2013. During his tenure he navigated the U.S. economy through the recession, housing crisis, and recovery.

The Treasury and its secretary directly impact the personal finances of consumers. They are the executive agency responsible for economic and financial activity. Their responsibilities include producing the nation's coin and currency, assessing and collecting taxes, and disbursing payments to the American public including tax refunds and Social Security checks. The Treasury department also advises the president on economic matters and financial policy.

Geithner is a 1983 graduate of Dartmouth College with an AB in government and Asian studies and in 1985 earned an MA in international economics and East Asian studies from Johns Hopkins School of Advanced International Studies. Geithner had been involved with the U.S. Treasury Department, established by Congress in 1789 to manage government revenue, since 1988 and served as undersecretary of the Treasury for international affairs under both secretaries Robert E. Rubin and Lawrence H. Summers (1999–2001). Geithner was the president of the Federal Reserve Bank (Fed) of New York (2003–2009) before President Obama nominated him to become secretary of the Treasury, which is a Cabinet-level position. His predecessor was Henry Paulson, who served in the prior administration. Geithner was confirmed as Treasury secretary by the U.S. Senate and sworn in on January 26, 2009, by Vice President Joe Biden.

Geithner, as president of the New York Fed, also served as vice chair of the Federal Open Market Committee, the system's principal monetary policymaking body. It was during his time at the New York Fed that the country first entered into the worst financial crisis since the Great Depression. Geithner, collaborating with Federal Reserve chair Ben Bernanke and Secretary of the Treasury Henry Paulson, worked to rescue Wall Street through a combination of coordinated bank mergers (Bear Stearns into JPMorgan Chase), bank failures (Lehman Bros.), and government bailouts (AIG). Geithner became a strong proponent for stronger regulation of Wall Street and better governmental strategies to deal with financial crises.

Geithner spent a total of six years dealing with the global financial crisis and aftermath of the housing bubble, first as president of the Federal Reserve Bank of New York and then as Treasury secretary. Upon arriving at the Treasury in 2009 he faced an economy well entrenched in a recession, rising unemployment, and increasing national home foreclosure rates. Geithner has been criticized for not putting more effort into the foreclosure crisis, and he is often associated with the bank bailouts of 2008–2009. However, by the end of his tenure he had helped to oversee the passage of the Dodd-Frank Wall Street Reform and Consumer Protection Act as well the enactment of comprehensive financial regulation of Wall Street. The Dodd-Frank Wall Street Reform and Consumer Protection Act, passed in 2010 in response to the 2008 financial crisis, is a compilation of federal regulations related to financial institutions and their customers. Additionally, Geithner worked closely with his international counterparts to help stem the European financial crisis.

Secretary Geithner resigned on January 25, 2013, after serving four years. He was succeeded by Jack Lew. In 2013, he joined the Council of Foreign Relations as a Distinguished Fellow, a position he had previously held, and began writing a book detailing his experiences at the Federal Reserve during the global financial crisis in 2008.

After leaving the public sector, Geithner transitioned to work on Wall Street as president of Warburg Pincus LLC, a buyout firm. In his new role he is responsible for helping to manage the company, invest the company's assets, and communicate with investors, according to a company statement.

John C. Linfield

See also: Bernanke, Ben S., 14th Chair of the U.S. Federal Reserve Board; Federal Reserve Bank; Interest Rates; Obama, Barack, President of the United States; Paulson Jr., Henry M., 74th U.S. Secretary of the Treasury; Year 2007–2008: Subprime Housing Crisis and Mortgage Meltdown; Year 2007–2009: Global Recession and Breakdown of Major Wall Street Institutions; Year 2010: Dodd-Frank Wall Street Reform and Consumer Protection Act

Further Reading

Banergee, Devin, and Ian Katz. 2013. "Geithner Joins Warburg in Shift to Buyouts from Bailouts." November 18. Bloomberg Personal Finance. http://www.bloomberg.com/news/2013-11-18/geithner-joins-warburg-in-shift-to-buyouts-from-bailouts.html

Bio.True Story Web site. "Timothy Geithner. Biography." Accessed October 9, 2013. http://www.biography.com/people/timothy-geithner-391494

Blinder, Alan S. 2013. *After the Music Stopped: The Financial Crisis, the Response, and the Work Ahead*. Penguin Press.

U.S. Department of the Treasury Web site. "Tim Geithner." Accessed October 8, 2013. http://www.treasury.gov/about/history/Pages/tgeithner.aspx

Greenspan, Alan, 13th Chair of the U.S. Federal Reserve Board

Alan Greenspan (born 1926) was the 13th chair of the board of governors of the Federal Reserve System and was the second longest person to serve in this role. He served from August 11, 1987, to January 31, 2006. During his tenure the U.S. economy experienced one of its most prosperous periods.

Greenspan is a 1948 graduate of New York University (summa cum laude) with a BS in economics and in 1977 was awarded a PhD in economics from New York University. Greenspan partnered with a colleague to form an economic consulting firm, Townsend-Greenspan & Co., where he served as the chair and president until his appointment to the board of governors of the Federal Reserve System (the Fed). The Fed was established by Congress under the Federal Reserve Act in 1913 with three objectives for monetary policy: maximum employment, stable prices, and moderate long-term interest rates.

Fun Facts about Alan Greenspan

Before transferring to New York University, Greenspan studied clarinet and saxophone at the prestigious Juilliard School in New York City. He played professionally with a touring jazz band.

Due to a 1971 back injury, Greenspan does most of his writing in the bathtub.

Greenspan's two nicknames are The Oracle and Mr. Bubble.

His wife is well-respected newswoman Andrea Mitchell of NBC News.

Greenspan served several presidential administrations in various capacities. He served as director of domestic policy for Richard Nixon's campaign in 1967 and as chair of President Gerald Ford's Council of Economic Advisers (1974–1977). On August 11, 1987, President Ronald Reagan appointed him chair of the Federal Reserve to replace the retiring chair, Paul Volcker. Greenspan served under both Republican and Democratic presidents, providing trusted advice to presidents Ronald Reagan, George H. W. Bush, Bill Clinton, and George W. Bush.

Greenspan was barely on the job when "Black Monday" occurred on October 19, 1987, and the U.S. stock market plummeted more than 500 points. This would not be the only economic shock of Greenspan's long tenure at the Fed. He navigated the economy through the 1990s, an unprecedented era of expanding stock market valuations. During that heady time he coined the phrase "irrational exuberance," describing the enthusiasm with which the public embraced highly priced equities. Greenspan was front and center beginning in 2000, when the dot-com bubble burst, sending stock prices sharply downward. The NASDAQ, the stock exchange where most of the dot-com technology stocks traded, fell 78 percent from a high of 5,046 to 1,114 on Greenspan's watch.

While he is widely respected for his economic knowledge and political savvy, Greenspan's critics have accused him of contributing to both the 2000 bursting of the dot-com bubble as well as the subprime housing mortgage crisis during mid-2000 because of his monetary policies. Economists from across the ideological spectrum have been more critical since the beginning of the global recession about the Fed policies under Greenspan. Specifically, his critics accuse Greenspan of letting the nation's real estate market rapidly expand due to inexpensive credit, created with low interest rates, lack of regulation on derivatives, and the Fed's failure to discipline banks for their indiscriminate mortgage lending. On a positive note, during Greenspan's tenure, unemployment in 1998 reached a 24-year low, inflation hit an 11-year low, and consumer confidence was the highest it had been in the prior 30-year period.

Greenspan is known for what he didn't say as much for what he did say. With each subsequent term Greenspan served he mastered the art of Fedspeak—a language of cautious, wordy, and ambiguous statements made by Fed chairs to prevent markets from reacting. Because financial markets can overreact when the Fed chair speaks, particularly before Congress, they have a tendency to make deliberately confusing, carefully cryptic, and cautious statements. Greenspan was notorious for saying much without saying anything, and in the rare cases when he did in fact make clear statements, the markets often reacted. He would note that his comments could move the markets 10 basis points in either direction.

A respected American economist, in 2006 he left the Federal Reserve after five terms; his successor was Ben Bernanke. Greenspan is the second-longest serving chair at the Fed. Since leaving the Fed he founded a private economic consulting firm and in 2007 published a memoir of his life.

The Fed and its chair directly impact the personal finances of consumers, specifically through interest rate and banking policies. The banking industry provides financial products useful for consumers such as home and auto loans and savings and checking accounts.

Leslie E. Linfield

See also: Bernanke, Ben S., 14th Chair of the U.S. Federal Reserve Board; Federal Reserve Bank; Inflation; Interest Rates; Investing; Stock Market; Treasury Securities; Year 1987: Stock Market Crash; Year 2000: Bursting of the Dot-Com Technology Bubble; Year 2007–2008: Subprime Housing Crisis and Mortgage Meltdown; Volcker, Paul A., 12th Chair of the U.S. Federal Reserve Board

Further Reading

Bio.True Story Web site. "Alan Greenspan.biography." Accessed October 7, 2013. http://www.biography.com/people/alan-greenspan-9319769?page=2

The Federal Reserve Bank of New York Web site. "Historical Echoes: Fedspeak as a Second Language." Accessed October 7, 2013. http://libertystreeteconomics.newyorkfed.org/2013/04/historical-echoes-fedspeak-as-a-second-language.html

Greenspan, Alan. 2007. *The Age of Turbulence: Adventures in a New World.* New York, NY: Penguin Press.

Lagarde, Christine, Managing Director, International Monetary Fund

Christine Lagarde is a French lawyer and managing director of the International Monetary Fund (IMF). Christine Madeleine Odette Lallouette was born on New Year's Day, 1956. Her father was a professor of English and her mother taught Latin. She has three younger brothers. The family lived in Le Havre, the major port on the northern French coast.

She was a member of the French synchronized swimming team, winning a bronze medal in the national championships when she was 15, and has retained a keen interest in sport, including cycling and scuba diving. She also sang backup in a ska (a blend of reggae and punk) band called Les Messages Mixé. Her father died when she was 16 and her mother brought up the four children alone. She regards her mother as her inspiration.

After high school in France, she won an AFS scholarship to spend a year in the United States, working as Representative William Cohen's congressional assistant during the Watergate hearings. She is fluent in English and Spanish. Her unusual understanding of the Anglo-Saxon world has been a hallmark of her career.

Lagarde has been married twice and has two sons from her first marriage, born in 1986 and 1988. She enjoys cooking and gardening and is a vegetarian who rarely drinks.

She holds two master's degrees—in law (business and English law) from Université Paris West Nanterre La Defénse and in political science from Aix-en-Provence Institute of Political Studies. She is considered an outsider in France in that not only does she not reject the Anglo-Saxon world, but she is also not a graduate of the École nationale d'administration—the elite graduate school established after World War II and attended by most French administrators. She applied twice but was refused.

She qualified as a lawyer at the Paris bar and joined the Paris office of the American global law firm Baker & McKenzie in 1981. Over the years she rose to become a partner and head the firm in Western Europe. In 1995, she joined the Executive Committee and became the first woman chair in 1999.

From 1995 to 2002 she served as a member of the Center for Strategic and International Studies think tank, a group focusing on liberalizing trade with Poland, co-chairing with Zbigniew Brzezinski, formerly national security advisor to President Jimmy Carter. She was awarded the highest honor in France when she was made a Chevalier de la Legion d'honneur in 2000.

Although she has always been political, she is not strictly a politician as she has never been elected to a public office. She was appointed to a number of posts in the French government. Her first post in 2005 was as trade minister in the government of Prime Minister Dominique de Villepin (President Chirac) where she concentrated on the technology sector. In 2007, she moved to agriculture and fisheries under Prime Minister Francois Fillon (President Sarkozy), and shortly afterward was appointed as finance minister—the first woman in that position. She was interviewed in Charles Ferguson's documentary *Inside Job* about the 2008 crisis.

In 2011, following the resignation of managing director of the IMF Dominique Strauss-Kahn, she was elected as the next managing director, the first woman to hold this office. Her experience, reputation for hard work, and ability to bridge divides with wit and warmth earned her the acceptance of many senior politicians. So, despite her being known as "l'Americaine" in France, it is not said with any hostility.

She has been described as the "woman with no enemies"—an admirable qualification for one of the top jobs in the world. And given the problems in the euro zone, having a head of the IMF with a pedigree as a euro zone finance minister possessing detailed knowledge of the problems and personalities in the zone is advantageous.

In late 2012, in "The Future Global Economy," Lagarde wrote: "History offers two clear lessons: reducing public debt is incredibly difficult without growth, and increasing growth is incredibly difficult with a huge burden of public debt. So we face a twofold imperative—securing growth while reducing debt. The key now is not only to move from deliberation to action on the policies that we know are needed, but to move together and on all fronts." Whether history will judge her time at the IMF a success will depend largely on whether the state of the world economy, and in particular the world financial system, is more stable than when she took office. Her tenure expires in 2016.

Lagarde appears to be admired by male and female colleagues alike for her abilities and capacity for work; she is, however, also well known for her gaffes. At one point in her career, she became known as Madame La Gaffe for her tendency to speak bluntly and plainly. Her best-known gaffe came at the height of the Greek euro crisis when she alluded to the widely held belief that tax evasion was endemic in Greece. As referenced in Helena Smith's 2012 *Guardian* article, her initial statement was that she was more concerned about poverty-stricken children in sub-Saharan Africa than the Greeks hit by the economic crisis. It was pointed out that, as managing director of the IMF, she, like many international figures, actually doesn't pay tax at all.

In 2010, while Lagarde was serving as French finance minister, French intelligence obtained a copy of a spreadsheet (allegedly stolen by a bank employee) containing some 130,000 names of wealthy HSBC customers from the bank's Geneva branch who were identified as possible tax evaders. Lagarde discreetly passed the list of names on to various EU governments as part of a tax crackdown. A list of 2,000 names was given directly to Greek authorities, but given the changes in the national government in Athens, these individuals were never properly investigated. Two years later, according to another Helena Smith *Guardian* article (2013), the identities of the 2,000 individuals from the list of names delivered to the Greek authorities were published (by Kostas Vaxevanis in *Hot Doc Investigative Magazine*) with Lagarde named as the source; henceforth the list has been known as the Lagarde list.

Maria Nedeva

See also: U.S. Federal Tax System Overview; Year 1944: Creation of the International Monetary Fund and the World Bank at the Bretton Woods International Conference; Year 1999: Introduction of the Euro to World Financial Markets; Year 2011–2012: European Debt Crisis; Yellen, Janet, 15th Chair of the U.S. Federal Reserve Board

Further Reading

"Christine Lagarde, Managing Director, IMF." International Monetary Fund Web site, July 5, 2011. http://www.imf.org/external/np/omd/bios/cl.htm

Ferguson, Charles, Chad Beck, et al. 2010. *Inside Job.* Documentary Movie. Directed by Charles Ferguson. Belgium: Sony Pictures Classics.

Lagarde, Christine. Commentaries. Project Syndicate Web site. Accessed October 26, 2013. http://www.project-syndicate.org/contributor/christine-lagarde

Lagarde, Christine. 2012. "The Future Global Economy." December 31. https://www.project-syndicate.org/commentary/sustainable-growth-means-equitable-growth-by-christine-lagarde

Smith, Helena. May 28, 2012. "Christine Lagarde's Greek Comments Provoke Fury," *The Guardian.* http://www.theguardian.com/world/2012/may/28/christine-lagarde-greek-comments-fury

Smith, Helena. November 27, 2013. "Greek Court Acquits Editor Who Leaked 'Lagarde List' of Suspected Tax Evaders," *The Guardian.* https://www.project-syndicate.org/commentary/sustainable-growth-means-equitable-growth-by-christine-lagarde

Markowitz, Harry M., Father of Modern Investment Portfolio Theory

Harry M. Markowitz, born in Chicago, Illinois on August 24, 1927, is considered the founder of modern investment portfolio theory. In 1990 he was awarded the Nobel Prize for Economics for his work with stock market risk and reward and asset valuation. His research drives the diversification and asset allocation emphasis in the investing community.

Markowitz was the only child of grocery store owners Mildred and Morris Markowitz. His early life was filled with ordinary pursuits of baseball, touch football, and playing the violin in the high school orchestra. He was a fervent reader, transitioning from comic books and adventure magazines when young to physics and astronomy in high school.

One of his early inspirations was the theory by Scottish philosopher David Hume who stated that although a ball is released a thousand times and although each time it falls to the ground, we lack sufficient proof that on the thousandth and first time the ball will also fall. Hume questioned common "cause–effect" relationships and attributed these relationships to habits of thinking instead of empirically proven facts.

Markowitz pursued his interest in philosophy at the University of Chicago. As an early student, he did not choose to pursue economics. Yet after the first two years at university he landed in the field of economics where his strongest interest was in the economics of uncertainty.

Markowitz had many mentors and influences in his work. He was interested in the Friedman-Savage utility function as well as L. J. Savage's defense of personal probability. He was fortunate to have all of the former professors (Friedman, Marschak, and Savage) as his mentors at the University of Chicago. An important inspiration for his later work on the efficient portfolio concept was Koopman, who taught the efficiency concept along with efficient sets. Markowitz continued his education as he pursued a PhD at the University of Chicago.

Markowitz's landmark dissertation research was inspired by a chance conversation, which considered integrating applying mathematical methods to the stock market. His basic concepts of portfolio theory, now well known and implemented across the investment community, were born while reading John Burr William's *Theory of Investment Value*. This stock valuation premise states that the value of a stock should equal the mathematical present value of future dividends, discounted back to today. Quite simply, this calculation adds up the future cash flow from dividend payments and calculates what those payments would be worth today. That amount should equal the price of the stock, and if not, the stock price might be over- or undervalued. The dividend discount stock valuation method is still practiced today. In fact, Morningstar, one of today's most important stock valuation and information services, uses this discount cash flow model in its stock valuation metrics.

In 1952, Markowitz joined the RAND Corporation. There he continued work, with George Dantzig, on the optimization techniques that became the Markowitz Efficient Frontier. He derived the "efficient frontier" concept of investment portfolios, which creates a graph of many stocks, optimized with the lowest risk and highest return for each possible combination. His famous article on "Portfolio Selection" was published in the *Journal of Finance* in 1952. In 1955, he received his PhD from the University of Chicago.

In practice, the Markowitz theory works like this. Assume Exxon and General Motors both have a high risk (or volatility in share price) and a high expected return. But, when the share price of Exxon goes up, the share price of General Motors goes down. The reason for this relationship is because when oil prices increase, Exxon makes more profit. In contrast, an automaker's shares might decline as the population will buy fewer new cars with higher gas prices. By combining these two companies in a portfolio, Markowitz found that the portfolio returns would be greater with a lower risk than holding either share individually.

In 1955 and 1956 James Tobin invited Markowitz to work at the Cowles Economic Research Foundation at Yale University. During that time he published a book, *Portfolio Selection: Efficient Diversification of Investments*, expanding on his landmark efficient frontier concepts.

Markowitz's contributions transcended economics with major discoveries in the computer science field as well. Markowitz, along with Bernard Hausner and Herb Karr, is responsible for developing Simscript. Simscript is a computer programming general-purpose simulation language. In the 1960s, Herb Karr and Markowitz began the California Analysis Center, Inc. (CACI). This company initially ran seminars to train users and further research and use of Simscript. One of the company's early contracts was with the U.S. Navy. This initial contract led to rapid growth. In 1968, six years after inception, the company went public and continues today as a $3.5 billion company supporting the U.S. defense missions.

In subsequent years, the theme of Markowitz's work was the application of mathematical or computer techniques to practical problems, specifically decisions under conditions of uncertainty. Markowitz's work history includes time at IBM, Baruch College, the City University of New York, and the University of California, San Diego Rady School of Management.

In 1989, Markowitz was awarded the Von Neumann Prize in Operations Research Theory by the Operations Research Society of America and the Institute of Management Sciences. In 1990, Harry M. Markowitz was awarded the Nobel Prize in economics along with Merton H. Miller and William F. Sharpe. He came to believe that simulation techniques were needed to solve many business problems, and analytic solutions did not work.

Markowitz holds a grand place in personal finance and modern money management. Many investment companies and individual investors use a diversified approach to investing with various types of securities and asset classes and are influenced by Markowitz's research. Markowitz continues working and consults and speaks on portfolio theory worldwide.

Barbara Friedberg

See also: Asset Allocation; Bonds; Buffett, Warren, Owner of Berkshire Hathaway Inc.; Discount Rate; Index Mutual Funds; Investing; Risk; Risk Premium; Shiller, Robert J., 2013 Nobel Laureate in Economics; Stock Market; Stocks

Further Reading

CACI Website. "A Look Back in Time: The CACI Story." Accessed January 29, 2014. http://www.caci.com/special/story.shtml

Internet Encyclopedia of Philosophy. "David Hume (1711–1776)." Accessed January 27, 2014. http://www.iep.utm.edu/hume/

Markowitz, Harry M. 1952. "Portfolio Selection." *Journal of Finance* (Vol. 7, No. 1): 77–91. http://www.math.ust.hk/~maykwok/courses/ma362/07F/markowitz_JF.pdf

Markowitz, Harry M. 1959. *Portfolio Selection: Efficient Diversification of Investments.* New York: John Wiley & Sons.

Nobelprize.org. "Harry M. Markowitz—Biographical." Accessed January 27, 2014. http:// www.nobelprize.org/nobel_prizes/economic-sciences/laureates/1990/markowitz-bio .html
Rady UC San Diego School of Management. "Harry Markowitz." Accessed January 27, 2014. http://rady.ucsd.edu/faculty/directory/markowitz/

Obama, Barack, President of the United States

Barack Hussein Obama II (1961–) is the 44th president of the United States, serving from 2009 to 2017. Elected just following the commencement of the Great Recession (2007–2009), Obama took office during the worst economic downturn in American history since the Great Depression (1929–1939). Soaring sovereign debt, deflation, and a double-digit (10.0 percent) unemployment rate rarely seen in a present-day developed economy meshed with trillions of dollars lost in investment markets and a sharply declining gross domestic product (GDP), causing Obama and the U.S. government to take unprecedented financial measures. The economic downturn, Obama's policy responses, and the aftermath of the Great Recession changed the course of modern money management forever.

This entry examines Obama's policies toward finance and economics. Outside factors such as trade and foreign policy impacted markets and investments during Obama's tenure, but lasting are his immediate reactions to the recession and his attempts thereafter to shape the future of the country through financial reform.

Obama was born in Hawaii to a mother from Kansas and a father from Kenya, Africa. After earning a degree in political science from Columbia University in New York City, he eventually attended Harvard Law School where he was president of the prestigious Harvard Law Review and graduated magna cum laude (1991). On finishing his juris doctorate, he moved to Chicago to pursue a career in law, teach at the University of Chicago Law School, and involve himself in politics.

Like many before him, Obama's political career included both wins and losses. In 1996, he won election as a Democrat to the Illinois State Senate. After serving for four years, Obama lost a bid in the Democratic primary of 2000 for the U.S. House of Representatives. In 2004, the determined state senator Obama reentered national politics and won a seat in the U.S. Senate. In 2008, building on negative public opinion toward both the Iraq war and the beginnings of the Great Recession, Barack Obama was elected president of the United States—winning almost 53 percent of the popular vote and nearly 68 percent of the electoral vote.

Not historically known for his role in economic policy, on taking the oath of office Obama was immediately thrown into the heart of a deep American recession. Many financial institutions, such as Goldman Sachs, JP Morgan Chase, Citigroup, Bank of America, American International Group, Wells Fargo, and Morgan Stanley had already received bailout funds from the 2008 Troubled Asset Relief Program (TARP). And, under Obama's guidance, additional bailout money would go to corporations in other industries such as General Motors and Chrysler. The decision to provide financial aid to the automotive industry was particularly controversial, with many arguing that the government's ownership of private-sector companies was too far reaching and jeopardized the system of capitalism as we know it. It was a time of intense financial stress and certainly debate over the role of government in backstopping the economy. The phrase "too big to fail" was heard often, referring to banks and other institutions that had been allowed to grow excessively large and therefore become fundamental to the stability of the economy itself.

The American Recovery and Reinvestment Act (ARRA) of 2009 was an immediate Obama response toward the severely ailing country. The United States was in a downward economic spiral, with a declining GDP and rapidly falling employment rate. This dramatic economic downturn continued amid the cries that TARP did not do enough to help individual taxpayers. As markets plunged and investors lost trillions of dollars, companies were forced to implement systematic downsizings. Hundreds of thousands of jobs were lost monthly, with the final total from the Great Recession reaching almost nine million.

ARRA attempted to create new jobs and increase demand for long-term investment through tax cuts, unemployment benefits, and government spending. In total, over $290 billion in tax benefits, $261 billion in contracts, grants, and loans, and $264 billion in entitlements were distributed. Years later, with debate on government involvement still ongoing, the American economy had returned to growth. The country recovered the total amount of jobs lost, witnessed financial markets reaching new all-time highs, and saw bailout funds returned by most corporations, from banks to automotives.

Another significant piece of legislation enacted by Obama is the Dodd-Frank Wall Street Reform and Consumer Protection Act (Dodd-Frank) of 2010. Named for its sponsors, Representative Barney Frank and Senator Chris Dodd, the act was intended to clamp down via stricter regulatory actions. With lax oversight and subsequent excessive risk taking seen as the major contributor to the environment that allowed for the Great Recession, Dodd-Frank sought to ensure taxpayers that future economic downturns would not result from a lack of accountability and transparency. "Too big to fail" and the previously blurred line between traditional banks and investment banking were its targets when signed into law on July 10, 2010.

After the noise of the recession quieted, Obama's work in economic policy was far from over. During his tenure, Congress undertook multiple standoffs with the executive branch, culminating in a shutdown of the government from October 1 through 16, 2013. The continuing disagreement concerns the most effective way to stimulate an economy. Those on the left, traditionally Democrats, argue that the government must be directly involved in healing the economy in times of need, while the right, mostly Republicans, hold the belief that a smaller government that allows an economy to heal itself is ultimately more healthy. It is a debate that has existed for hundreds of years, has threatened to derail even the largest economy in the world, and shows no signs of resolution any time soon. For his part, Obama has presided over a country that has slowly recovered from the worst financial downturn since the Great Recession and a government that has fought with itself over the best methods of assisting such regrowth.

Like most before him, President Obama has been involved in many transformative policies and decisions during his time in office. Universal health care (the Patient

Protection and Affordable Care Act of 2010), uprisings in the Middle East, and the ending of the Iraq and Afghanistan wars are just a few. However, this president's legacy in finance will impact markets and money management for many years to come.

Jonathan D. Citrin

See also: Affordable Care Act; Banking; Bernanke, Ben S., 14th Chair of the U.S. Federal Reserve Board; Budget; Bush, George W., 43rd President of the United States; Capitalism; Debt; Deficit; Geithner, Timothy F., 75th Secretary of the U.S. Treasury; Gross Domestic Product (GDP) and Gross National Product (GNP); Inflation; Interest Rates; Stock Market; Systematic Market Risk; Unemployment; U.S. Federal Tax System Overview; Warren, Elizabeth, Former Special Advisor for the Consumer Financial Protection Bureau; Year 1930s: The Great Depression; Year 2007–2008: Subprime Housing Crisis and Mortgage Meltdown; Year 2007–2009: Global Recession and Breakdown of Major Wall Street Institutions; Year 2010: Dodd-Frank Wall Street Reform and Consumer Protection Act

Further Reading

Recovery.gov Web site. "American Recovery and Reinvestment Act." http://www.recovery .gov/arra/Pages/default.aspx

TradingEconomics.com Web site. "United States." http://www.tradingeconomics.com/ united-states/indicators

WhiteHouse.gov Web site. "President Barack Obama." http://www.whitehouse.gov /administration/president-obama

Paulson Jr., Henry M., 74th U.S. Secretary of the Treasury

Henry M. "Hank" Paulson Jr. (born 1946) was the 74th U.S. secretary of the Treasury. He served from July 10, 2006, to January 20, 2009. During his tenure the U.S. economy experienced the worst financial crisis since the Great Depression.

Paulson is a 1968 graduate of Dartmouth College with an AB in English and in 1970 was awarded an MBA from Harvard Business School. After completing his master's program Paulson became the staff assistant to the assistant secretary of defense at the Pentagon (1970–1972). He then worked for President Richard Nixon, serving as a member of the White House Domestic Council (1972–1973).

In 1974 Paulson joined Goldman Sachs, a large investment banking firm, where during his 32-year career he rose through the ranks to become the firm's chair and CEO. On July 10, 2006, he left Goldman Sachs to serve as Treasury secretary under President George W. Bush, where he succeeded John Snow.

Secretary Paulson was a stark contrast to the previous Treasury secretary and other appointees of the Bush administration. Paulson is a vocal environmentalist (a position that was often at odds with the Bush administration) and insisted on being a fully invested, involved, and policymaking secretary, as opposed to his predecessor. Little did he or the administration know that within a year of his appointment the

U.S. economy would experience the worst financial crisis since the Great Depression.

As the country entered a recession in 2007, amid the bursting of the U.S. housing bubble and high default rates on subprime mortgages, Secretary Paulson spearheaded the creation of the Hope Now Alliance. This cooperative of government, housing counselors, and lenders assists struggling homeowners to avoid foreclosure. In September 2008, Secretary Paulson engineered the rescue of the government-backed private mortgage agencies Fannie Mae and Freddie Mac. Yet the damage was already done and these efforts could not prevent a breakdown of major Wall Street financial institutions holding mortgage-backed securities.

By the fall of 2008 the banking system nearly collapsed. Secretary Paulson, collaborating with Federal Reserve chair Ben Bernanke and Federal Reserve Bank of New York president Tim Geithner, worked to rescue Wall Street through a combination of coordinated bank mergers (Merrill Lynch into Bank of America), bank failures (Lehman Bros.), and government bailouts (AIG). What had begun as a subprime mortgage problem in the United States evolved into a global financial crisis and drove stock markets to record lows and unemployment to record highs.

Public sentiment about the Treasury secretary's actions during this critical economic period has been equivocal. Paulson was criticized for how he handled the financial crisis and questioned on the decision to let Lehman Brothers fail. *Time* magazine named him a runner-up for Person of the Year in 2008 but then later listed him as one of the "25 People to Blame for the Financial Crisis." His decisiveness and invocative thinking during the worst days of the crisis, such as crafting the Troubled Asset Relief Program (TARP), which Congress subsequently passed, most likely kept the United States from experiencing another Great Depression.

Secretary Paulson completed his tenure with the end of the Bush presidency in 2009 and was succeeded by Timothy Geithner. In 2010, he published a book with Barney Frank entitled *On the Brink: Inside the Race to Stop the Collapse of the Global Financial System*, detailing his experiences as Treasury secretary during the global financial crisis. Since leaving public service he founded the Paulson Institute at the University of Chicago and serves as its chair. This innovative think tank works to promote economic growth and environmental preservation in the United States and China.

The Treasury and its secretary directly impact the personal finances of consumers. They are the executive agency responsible for economic and financial activity. Their responsibilities include producing the nation's coin and currency, assessing and collecting taxes, and disbursing payments to the American public, including tax refunds and Social Security checks. Treasury also advises the president on economic matters and financial policy.

Leslie E. Linfield

See also: Bernanke, Ben S., 14th Chair of the U.S. Federal Reserve Board; Bush, George W., 43rd President of the United States; Federal Reserve Bank; Geithner, Timothy F., 75th Secretary of the U.S. Treasury; Year 2007–2008: Subprime Housing Crisis and Mortgage Meltdown; Year 2007–2009 Global Recession and Breakdown of Major Wall Street Institutions

Further Reading

Paulson, Henry. 2010. *On the Brink: Inside the Race to Stop the Collapse of the Global Financial System*. New York, NY: Grand Central Publishing.

The Paulson Institute at the University of Chicago Web site. "Henry M. Paulson, Jr., Chairman." Accessed October 7, 2013. http://www.paulsoninstitute.org/about-us/institute-staff/henry-m-paulson,-jr/

Time Lists. "25 People to Blame for the Financial Crisis." Accessed March 3, 2014. http://content.time.com/time/specials/packages/article/0,28804,1877351_1877350_1877341,00.html

Time Person of the Year. December 17, 2008. "Henry Paulson." http://content.time.com/time/specials/packages/article/0,28804,1861543_1865103_1865105,00.html

U.S. Department of the Treasury Web site. "Henry M. Paulson, Jr. (2006–2009)." Accessed October 7, 2013. http://www.treasury.gov/about/history/pages/hmpaulson.aspx

Rubin, Robert E., 70th U.S. Secretary of the Treasury

Robert Edward Rubin (born August 29, 1938) served as the 70th U.S. secretary of the Treasury under President Clinton. He is a founder of the Hamilton Project and is currently actively involved in its work. The Hamilton Project is an economic policy think tank that produces research and proposals on how to create a growing economy that benefits more Americans.

Rubin's Role in the Repeal of the Glass-Steagall Act

Journalist Robert Scheer, in his book *The Great American Stickup*, claims the repeal of the Glass-Steagall Act was a key factor in the 2008 financial crisis. Enacted just after the 1930s Great Depression, the Glass-Steagall Act separated commercial and investment banking. The law was repealed by Congress in 1999 during the Clinton presidency, while Rubin was Treasury secretary. It allowed the banks to develop and sell the mortgage-backed instruments that played a critical role in the financial collapse.

Many critics accuse Secretary Rubin of sharply opposing any regulation of collateralized debt obligations, credit default swaps, and other so-called "derivative" financial instruments, as they were becoming the chief instrument of profitability for Rubin's former employer Goldman Sachs and other Wall Street firms.

Rubin left the Treasury immediately after the Glass-Steagall Act was repealed by Congress. Three months later, he was hired at Citigroup, a bank that greatly benefited from his policies and would benefit even more from his connections. Rubin was brought to Citigroup as a board member and chair of the executive committee of Citigroup's board. Although he was paid a salary of $15 million a year by Citigroup, Rubin's position had no clear responsibilities. He received more than $126 million in cash and stock during his tenure at Citigroup. Citigroup was among the eight large U.S. banks that were bailed out by the Treasury Department during the global financial crisis in 2008.

Robert Rubin graduated summa cum laude from Harvard College in 1960 with an AB in economics. He received his LLB from Yale Law School in 1964 and attended the London School of Economics.

Before his government service, he spent 26 years at Goldman Sachs, including his stint as co-chair from 1990 to 1992. After his time at the government, Rubin served as director and senior counselor of Citigroup, where he performed advisory and representational roles for the firm.

He is author of *In an Uncertain World: Tough Choices from Wall Street to Washington*. The book was a *New York Times* best seller and one of *BusinessWeek*'s 10 best business books of the year.

National Economic Council

Robert Rubin served in the White House as assistant to the president for economic policy and director of the National Economic Council (NEC) from January 25, 1993, to January 10, 1995. The National Economic Council helped the White House to coordinate the works of the Cabinet departments and agencies on policies ranging from budget and tax to international trade and poverty alleviation. As director of the NEC, Rubin oversaw the administration's domestic and international economic policymaking process, coordinated economic policy recommendations to the president, and monitored the implementation of the president's economic policy goals.

Secretary of the Treasury

Rubin was sworn in as secretary of the Treasury in January 1995. As secretary of the Treasury, Rubin played a leading role in many of the nation's most important policy debates. He was involved in balancing the federal budget; opening trade policy to further globalization; helping to resolve the impasse between Congress and the executive branch over the public debt limit; safeguarding the nation's currency against counterfeiting; introducing inflation-indexed securities; strongly responding to issues at Treasury's law enforcement agencies; and guiding sensible reforms at the Internal Revenue Service.

Immediately after Rubin was sworn in as secretary of the Treasury, Mexico went through a financial crisis that almost caused it to default on its foreign obligations. President Bill Clinton, with the advice of Secretary Rubin and Federal Reserve Board chair Alan Greenspan, provided $20 billion in U.S. loan guarantees to the Mexican government through the Exchange Stabilization Fund (ESF).

In 1997 and 1998, Secretary Rubin also played an important role in combating financial crises in Russian, Asian, and Latin American financial markets. Along with Deputy Secretary Lawrence Summers and Federal Reserve Board chair Alan Greenspan, he worked with the International Monetary Fund (IMF) and others to effectively manage the crises. Rubin was succeeded on July 1, 1999, as Treasury secretary by his deputy, Lawrence H. Summers.

Postgovernment Career

Rubin was hired by Citigroup on October 26, 1999. He became a board member and chair of the executive committee of Citigroup's board. On November 4, 2007, he became the chair of Citigroup, and on January 9, 2009, he resigned from the position of senior counselor at Citigroup and announced he would not stand for reelection to the board. Rubin had drawn criticism for his role in the bank's problems that drove it to seek bailout by the U.S. government. Many critics argue that he did a very poor job at Citigroup even though he received significant personal compensation.

Other Positions Held

Besides working in the government, Rubin spent a number of years in the private sector. He has served on the board of directors of the New York Stock Exchange, Ford Motor Company, Citigroup, the Harvard Corporation, the New York Futures Exchange, the New York City Partnership, and the Center for National Policy. He has also served on the board of trustees of the Carnegie Corporation of New York, Mt. Sinai Hospital and Medical School, the President's Advisory Committee for Trade Negotiations, the U.S. Securities and Exchange Commission Market Oversight and Financial Services Advisory Committee, the Mayor of New York's Council of Economic Advisors, and the Governor's Council on Fiscal and Economic Priorities for the State of New York. He has been co-chair of the board of directors of the Council on Foreign Relations since June 2007. In 2010, Rubin joined Centerview Partners as a counselor of the firm.

Controversy in 2001

During the Enron scandal in 2001, Rubin sparked controversy when he contacted an acquaintance (Peter Fisher, undersecretary of the Treasury for domestic finance) at the U.S. Treasury Department and asked if the department could convince bond-rating agencies not to downgrade the corporate debt of Enron, a debtor of Citigroup. Mr. Fisher, the Treasury official, refused to oblige. A subsequent congressional staff investigation cleared Rubin of having done anything illegal. Later, Rubin said he had placed the call as both a bank executive protecting a financial position and a concerned former Treasury official. However, it must be noted that Citigroup faced huge losses. The bank ultimately paid $3.66 billion to settle legal claims against it and lost billions more when Enron collapsed.

Ramya Ghosh

See also: Banking; Clinton, William, 42nd President of the United States; Derivatives; Federal Reserve Bank; Hedge Funds; Year 2010: Dodd-Frank Wall Street Reform and Consumer Protection Act

Further Reading

Cohan, William D. September 30, 2012. "Rethinking Robert Rubin." *Bloomberg Businessweek.* http://www.businessweek.com/articles/2012-09-19/rethinking-robert-rubin#p1

Council on Foreign Relations. "Robert E. Rubin: Co-Chairman, Former Secretary of the U.S. Treasury." A June 10, 2014. http://www.cfr.org/experts/world/robert-e-rubin/b292
Rubin, Robert, and Jacob Weisberg. 2004. *In an Uncertain World: Tough Choices from Wall Street to Washington.* New York: Random House.

Schapiro, Mary, 29th Chair of the U.S. Securities and Exchange Commission

Mary Schapiro (born 1955) was the 29th chair of the U.S. Securities and Exchange Commission (SEC) and the first woman in this role. She served from January 2009 to April 2013. Although appointed as the first woman chair, Schapiro's contributions are noteworthy in and of themselves.

Mary Schapiro is a 1977 graduate of Franklin and Marshall College in Lancaster, Pennsylvania, and a 1980 juris doctor (with honors) from George Washington University. In 1996 Schapiro joined the Financial Industry Regulatory Authority (FINRA), the largest nongovernmental agency charged with oversight of securities firms in the United States. In 2007 she led the integration of NASD and NYSE Member Regulation to form FINRA and advanced to FINRA CEO in 2002. In 2006, she was named National Association of Securities Dealers (NASD) chair and CEO.

From 1988 to 1994, before becoming chair of the SEC, Schapiro was appointed by presidents Reagan, Bush, and Clinton to serve as a commissioner of the Securities and Exchange Commission (SEC). This institution is the governing board of the securities and investment industry, and as such provides the rules and regulations that ensure that

Additional Financial Regulatory Contributions

- Required investment advisers to provide specific information to clients such as fees, conflicts of interest, backgrounds of advisers, disciplinary actions, and business practices.
- Oversaw largest ever number of enforcement actions (in 2011 and 2012) against investment advisers and companies.
- Instituted standards to improve money market mutual funds including strengthening underlying holdings and providing information about actual net asset value of holdings.
- Detected and prosecuted the largest insider trading scheme ever, resulting in a $92.8 million fine against Raj Rajaratnam, Calleon Hedge Fund CEO.
- Set up hedge and private fund registration requirements. Four thousand funds subsequently registered and became subject to SEC rules.
- Initiated regulation of the derivatives market, which was largely unregulated before her tenure.
- Impacted shareholder accountability and required companies to involve shareholders in executive pay decisions.
- Penalized an exchange that gave certain investors a trading advantage.

corporations are properly funded through the issuance of securities, that the markets run efficiently, and that investors are protected.

During this period she also served as acting chair of the SEC. Prior to her nomination as permanent chair of the SEC, President Clinton appointed her chair of the Commodity Futures Trading Commission (CFTC). She is the first individual to chair both the CFTC and the SEC.

In 2009, Schapiro was appointed by President Obama and unanimously confirmed by the U.S. Senate as the chairperson of the Securities and Exchange Commission. In April 2013, she left her role as SEC chair and now serves as a managing director and chair at Promontory Financial Group, a private firm that assists financial firms with interpreting government regulations.

During her tenure, Schapiro oversaw tremendous improvement in enforcement and regulation, creating an improved capital markets environment. Her impact included SEC investor protection reforms, inspections, and enforcements. These initiatives fundamentally improved market efficiency by minimizing the chance of market flash crashes and technology errors. The entirety of Schapiro's accomplishments during her tenure as SEC chair are far-reaching and impact investors and investment advisors, as well as the public.

Under her tenure, billions of dollars were returned to investors from fraudulent investment schemes. The 2007–2008 financial crisis and mortgage meltdown spurred the SEC to revamp the entire regulatory environment in order to better protect consumers while more closely monitoring the financial industry. Her work will serve investors for years to come.

Schapiro significantly impacted the direction and oversight of the SEC. It is a footnote that she happens to be the first woman in that position. Additionally, Schapiro is an active member of the International Organization of Securities Commissions (IOSCO) and was chair of the IOSCO SRO (Self-Regulatory Organization) Consultative Committee from 2002 until 2006. She is a member of the board of trustees of Franklin and Marshall College as well as a member of the boards of directors of Duke Energy and Kraft Foods. Schapiro was named the Financial Women's Association Public Sector Woman of the Year in 2000 and serves on the RAND Corporation's LRN-RAND Center of Corporate Ethics, Law and Governance Advisory Board. A prominent figure in the public sector regulatory environment for decades, in 2013 she left government work to continue in the private sector.

The SEC and its chair directly impact the personal finance and money management of consumers. The investment industry provides investing markets and products in which investors can save for retirement and future goals. Proper oversight and regulation by the SEC maintains orderly markets in which consumers are assured of a fair industry for their investment dollars.

Barbara Friedberg

See also: Bonds; Commodities; Financial Advisor; Hedge Funds; Investing; Stocks; Year 2007–2008: Subprime Housing Crisis and Mortgage Meltdown; Year 2010: Dodd-Frank Wall Street Reform and Consumer Protection Act

Further Reading

"SEC Biography: Chairman Mary L. Schapiro." The U.S. Securities and Exchange Web site. Accessed May 1, 2013. http://www.sec.gov/about/commissioner/schapiro.htm

Stock, Kyle. April 2, 2013. "Mary Schapiro: Out of the SEC and into the Shadows." *BloombergBusinessweek*. http://www.businessweek.com/articles/2013-04-02/mary-schapiro -out-of-the-sec-and-into-the-shadows

"What Is the SEC?" The U.S. Securities and Exchange Web site. Accessed May 1, 2013. http://www.sec.gov/about/whatwedo.shtml

Shiller, Robert J., 2013 Nobel Laureate in Economics

Robert J. Shiller was born March 29, 1946, in Detroit, Michigan. He is a world-renowned and controversial economist. His work covers the fields of finance, behavioral economics, real estate, and more. Shiller is well known for predicting two financial bubbles, the technology bubble at the end of the last century and the more recent housing bubble that peaked in 2006. Widely recognized throughout his career, in 2013 he was awarded the Nobel Prize in Economic Sciences "for his empirical analysis of asset prices" in the field of financial economics.

Robert Shiller comes from an immigrant background. His father and grandfather were Lithuanian farmers from the region adjacent to Poland. The turmoil fostered by Russia and the possibility of being drafted into the Russian army drove Shiller's father, George, to emigrate to America.

Shiller received his BA from the University of Michigan in 1967 and his PhD in economics from MIT in 1972. Before joining the Yale faculty in 1982, Shiller held academic appointments at the University of Minnesota, MIT, and the University of Pennsylvania. His work traverses financial markets, financial innovation, behavioral economics, macroeconomics, real estate, and statistical methods, as well as views on public attitudes, opinions, and moral judgments regarding markets.

At present, Shiller is the Sterling Professor of Economics, Department of Economics and Cowles Foundation for Research in Economics at Yale University. He is also a professor of finance and fellow at the International Center for Finance, Yale School of Management.

Shiller's distinguished career goes beyond academia and includes major roles at several private and government entities. He cofounded Case Shiller Weiss, Inc., an economics research and information firm. Shiller also cofounded Macro Securities Research, LLC, a securities firm. In the public sector, Shiller serves on the Academic Advisory Panel of the Federal Reserve Bank of New York.

Shiller's additional contributions to the financial economics field include work as a research associate at the National Bureau of Economic Research (NBER), where he's worked since 1980. Since 1991, he further served the NBER by co-organizing their workshops. He was vice president of the American Economic Association in 2005 and president of the Eastern Economic Association in 2006.

The following paragraphs touch on the depth and breadth of Shiller's research. Examples from real estate, behavioral economics, investment asset pricing, and more demonstrate the scope of his contributions.

Shiller seamlessly integrates finance, economics, statistics, and psychology into his work to improve our knowledge of how our financial markets function. He was catapulted into the economic forefront with an article in the June 1981 edition of the *American Economic Review*, where he questioned the popular "efficient market hypothesis." This theory states that asset prices (the prices of stocks, bonds, and other financial securities) reflect the true underlying value of the securities, and historical information is baked into the asset price. The efficient market hypothesis alleges that it is difficult to obtain returns greater than those of the overall market, and thus investors should not try to outperform the market. According to the efficient market hypothesis, investors are "unable to beat the market" on a risk-adjusted basis. Shiller posited that the efficient market hypothesis was flawed.

Shiller became interested in behavioral finance through several paths. He was influenced by his wife, Virginia M. Shiller, a clinical psychologist. He also believed there were gaps in the widely adopted efficient market hypothesis. Shiller refers to asset bubbles as refuting the efficient market hypothesis and indicates that psychology plays a part in asset pricing as well.

Shiller, along with Nobel Prize–winning Richard Thaler, considered the importance of emotions on investing and posited that investors are not rational. These behavioral market anomalies that cast doubt on the efficient market hypothesis have grown into the popular and well-respected field of behavioral economics or behavioral finance.

Questioning the efficient market hypothesis was a bold move. Taking on the efficient market hypothesis was an indirect swipe at the index fund. The index fund movement, one of the most popular investment strategies, was originally based on the idea that it is extremely difficult, if not impossible to beat the investment returns of the overall market. Thus, an investor would be best served to invest in low-cost index funds and strive to match the returns of the market.

Shiller further challenged the academic community with his revision of the price earnings ratio, a widely accepted asset valuation tool. Shiller augmented the popular price earnings ratio (price divided by earnings per share) stock valuation metric. His iteration of the price earnings ratio (PE ratio), called the cyclically adjusted price-earnings (CAPE) ratio, takes the S&P 500 and divides it by the prior 10 years' average earnings. The CAPE PE is also called the PE 10. The CAPE PE uses smoothed or averaged earnings to minimize normal business cycle profit margin variations. The resulting figure indicates a relative valuation of the current stock market. In other words, a higher CAPE PE ratio means the stock market may be overvalued and likely to deliver lower returns in the next few years. A lower CAPE PE ratio suggests the market may be undervalued and will offer a higher average annual return in the near term.

Shiller's contributions to the real estate field are embedded in his namesake indices. Shiller, along with Karl E. Case, created the repeat-sales home price indices. These metrics, which have been widely adopted as a leading measure of U.S. residential real estate prices, track changes in the value of residential real estate. Currently known as the S&P/Case-Shiller Home Price Indices, these indicators have grown to include not only national data but region-specific information for 20 of the largest U.S. markets. This information offers important economic data about home buying trends in the United States and informs the public, as well as government policymakers.

Shiller is a prolific writer. His books include *Animal Spirits: How Human Psychology Drives the Economy and Why It Matters for Global Capitalism* (with G. Akerloff), *Macro Markets: Creating Institutions for Managing Society's Largest Economic Risks, Irrational Exuberance, The New Financial Order: Risk in the 21st Century,* and most recently, *Finance and the Good Society.* In addition to books, he writes papers and articles for both the scholarly community and the general public.

Shiller's prizes and awards are numerous in addition to his Nobel Prize. He served as an American Academy of Arts and Sciences fellow, an Econometric Society fellow, and a Guggenheim fellow in 1991. In 2009, Shiller received the Deutsche Bank Prize in Financial Economics for his groundbreaking research in financial economics with relation to fixed income, equities, and real estate asset prices.

Many of Shiller's books also received recognition. In 1996 TIAA-CREF awarded him the Paul A. Samuelson Award for *Macro Markets.* In 2000, *Irrational Exuberance* received the Common Fund Prize. In 2003, *The New Financial Order* received the *Financial Times* getAbstract Business Book Award.

He is widely recognized as one of the most influential economists of our times. In fact, in 2011 *Bloomberg Businessweek* magazine named him one of the "50 Most Influential People with the Power in Global Finance." In 2010, *Foreign Policy* magazine named him to its list of top global thinkers. His international reach was further highlighted when the German newspaper *Die Zeit* cited Shiller as one of 21 thinkers for the 21st century.

In a recent interview for the *Yale News* feed (October 14, 2013) Shiller described his work: "Many of the problems that beset financial markets—and that are behind the financial crisis of the last five years—can be fixed with the application of our improved understanding of asset pricing. Despite problems, our financial markets do serve people and can serve them better in the future."

Students today have direct access to Shiller. He offers a free online Financial Markets course on the Open Yale Courses Web site. His newest Financial Markets online course is offered to the general public on Coursera. According to Shiller in a recent *New York Times* interview, there are 50,000 students signed up to take this course.

Barbara Friedberg

See also: Asset Allocation; Behavioral Finance; Index Mutual Funds; Investing; Markowitz, Harry M., Father of Modern Investment Portfolio Theory; Online Personal Finance; Real Estate; Risk; Stock Market; Year 2000: Bursting of the Dot-Com Technology Bubble; Year 2007–2008: Subprime Housing Crisis and Mortgage Meltdown

Further Reading

Read, Colin. 2012. *The Efficient Market Hypothesists: Bachelier, Samuelson, Fama, Ross, Tobin and Shiller.* New York, NY: Palgrave Macmillan. http://www.palgraveconnect .com/pc/doifinder/10.1057/9781137292216.0036

Sommer, Jeff. 2013. "Robert Shiller: A Skeptic and a Nobel Winner." October 15. http://www.nytimes.com/2013/10/20/business/robert-shiller-a-skeptic-and-a-nobel-winner.html?_r=0

Yale News. 2013. "Another Yale Nobel: Robert Shiller." October 14. http://news.yale.edu/2013/10/14/another-yale-nobel-robert-shiller

Yale Web site. "Robert Shiller: Sterling Professor of Economics, Yale University." Accessed February 12, 2014. http://som.yale.edu/robert-shiller

Siebert, Muriel, First Woman to Own a Seat on the New York Stock Exchange

Muriel Siebert (1928–2013) was the first woman to buy a seat on the New York Stock Exchange, the first woman superintendent of banking in New York, and one of the first people to found a discount brokerage firm in the United States. Born in Cleveland, Ohio, Siebert attended Case Western Reserve University and studied accounting, but she did not graduate. Her father's death after a long fight with cancer necessitated more income for her family, so she dropped out of school to work and help contribute to the family income.

In 1954, after visiting her sister in New York and taking a tour of the U.S. Stock Exchange, Siebert decided to move to New York to find work with only $500 to her name. She applied to and was rejected for several jobs in New York, including positions at the UN (rejected because she didn't speak two languages) and Merrill Lynch (rejected because she did not have a college degree). Eventually, she got her first job as a research trainee at Bache & Company for $65 a week and slept on her sister's couch. She worked at numerous financial firms and was made a partner at two firms during the 1960s: Fickle & Company from 1962 to 1963 and Brimberg and Company from 1965 to 1967.

Yet, despite the fact that Siebert was a talented, hard worker and quickly built a name for herself in New York financial circles, she still made less money than her male counterparts and wanted to become an equal. Ready to take the next career step, she set out to purchase a seat on the New York Stock Exchange, which was not an easy process.

Owning a seat on the New York Stock Exchange (NYSE) grants a person the opportunity to trade stocks and financial assets on the floor of the NYSE. Owners can trade for their own account or as an agent for others' accounts. Prices for a seat are set by supply and demand.

First, she went home and studied the constitution of the Stock Exchange and found that there was no law against a woman buying a seat. Then, she had to find two sponsors. It took her 10 tries to get her sponsors. Ultimately, James O'Brien, a partner at Solomon Brothers and Hutzler, and Kenneth Ward, a partner at Hayden Stone and

Readers will find a discrepancy in Muriel Siebert's birth year. During her working life she typically listed her birth year as 1932, although she was actually born on September 12, 1928.

Company, supported her, and then the New York Stock Exchange required her to get a $300,000 loan to secure her position. She struggled to secure the loan but after paying $445,000 on December 28, 1967, for one of NYSE's coveted 1,366 memberships, she became the first woman to own a seat on the New York Stock Exchange.

She also founded her own brokerage firm, Muriel Siebert & Co., Inc., which became very successful. Siebert transitioned her company into a discount brokerage house in 1975. In 1977, she took some time off from her own brokerage company because she was offered the position of superintendent of banking for the State of New York. She was the first woman to have this position, and since then several other women have held the same role. Siebert served in that position from 1977 to 1982. As superintendent, her primary responsibility was overseeing the banks throughout the state. Although she received some criticism during her tenure as superintendent, no banks failed during her time in that position, despite the fact that many banks failed nationwide at that time. When she resigned from her superintendent post in 1982, she ran for the U.S. Senate in the Republican primary but lost. In 1996, she took her firm public.

In addition to her noteworthy career, Siebert has devoted considerable time and money to philanthropic organizations. In 1990, she introduced the Siebert Entrepreneurial Philanthropic Plan, which gives half of her firm's profits to charity. She also developed a program to help increase financial literacy among women, and her biggest passion is teaching financial literacy to youth. She developed a program in 1999 to educate children in New York City about personal finance, investing over a million dollars of her own money. Now her course, the Siebert Personal Finance Program, is in use in New York City as well as other districts across the country. It has since been adapted for adults. Siebert has also been on numerous boards of philanthropies in New York and founded the New York Women's Forum.

Over the duration of her career, Siebert has received multiple honorary doctorate degrees and numerous awards. In 1994, she was inducted into the Women's Hall of Fame, and in 2002, her autobiography, *Changing the Rules—Adventures of a Wall Street Maverick*, was published.

Until her death on August 24, 2013, Siebert continued to work as the head of her firm and routinely gave media interviews to discuss financial trends. She is called "The First Woman of Finance" because of her impressive career, which is full of firsts. She will continue to be known as someone who champions financial education and isn't afraid to take risks in order to see progress, like her lifetime of work to ensure that men and women are treated equally in the workplace. Ultimately, she is a role model to women and will be remembered as a leader in the women's movement and someone who improved financial literacy in the United States.

Catherine Alford

See also: Banking; Financial Advisor; Investing; Stock Market

Further Reading

Makers Web site. "First Lady of Wall Street." Accessed August 13, 2013. http://www.makers.com/muriel-siebert

National Women's Hall of Fame Web site. "Muriel Siebert." Accessed August 13, 2013. http://www.greatwomen.org/women-of-the-hall/search-the-hall/details/2/142-Siebert

Nemy, Enid. 2013. "Muriel Siebert a Determined Trailblazer for Women on Wall Street, Dies at 84." *The New York Times*. August 25. http://www.nytimes.com/2013/08/26/business/muriel-siebert-first-woman-to-own-a-seat-on-wall-st-dies-at-80.html

Think Advisor Web site. "Weekend Interview: Muriel Siebert on Financial Reform and Financial Literacy." Accessed August 13, 2013. http://www.thinkadvisor.com/2010/07/09/weekend-interview-muriel-siebert-on-financial-refo

Volcker, Paul A., 12th Chair of the U.S. Federal Reserve Board

Paul A. Volcker (1927–), an American economist, is best known for his work as chair of the board of governors of the Federal Reserve System (1979–1987). He was in office during a time of excessively high inflation and served as the catalyst for reducing inflation and interest rates and stabilizing the economy during the 1980s.

Volcker was born in Cape May, New Jersey, and received a bachelor's degree from Princeton University in 1949 and a master's degree from the Graduate School of Public Administration at Harvard University in 1951. From 1951 to 1952 Volcker was a Rotary Foundation fellow at the London School of Economics.

His career included work in banking in both the private and the public sectors. He served as an economist for the Federal Reserve Bank of New York from 1953 to 1957. This was his first introduction to the Federal Reserve Banking System. From 1957 to 1961, he transitioned into the private sector as an economist for Chase Manhattan Bank. Next, moving back into the public sector, Volcker worked as a deputy undersecretary in the Department of the Treasury (1963–1965). Next, he returned to Chase Manhattan Bank to serve as vice president.

From 1975 to 1979 he served as president of the powerful New York Federal Reserve Bank. In 1979, U.S. President Jimmy L. Carter appointed him to serve as the leader of the Federal Reserve System.

Volcker's work began in the U.S. Federal Reserve (Fed) system during a period marked by historically high interest rates, high unemployment, and high inflation. During the time of Volcker's appointment to the chairmanship of the Federal Reserve, the United States' desperate economic state included inflation running about 9 percent annually. He was committed to end the ongoing high inflation. In order to stabilize the U.S. economy and high inflation levels, the Federal Reserve slowed the supply of the money supply and allowed interest rates to rise.

Volcker's economic policies of raising interest rates led to a snowball effect with interest rates topping out in the low double digits. Due to the Federal Reserve's policies and restrictive monetary policy parameters, the federal funds interest rate reached a high of 20 percent in late 1980. Inflation had topped out at 11.6 percent in March 1980 and unemployment was skyrocketing. In contrast with the low interest rates of the 21st century, by 1982, the economic policies and high interest rates pushed the United States into the worst recession since the Great Depression (Britannica, 2013).

During this unstable economic period, Volcker faced tremendous criticism. After President Reagan defeated Jimmy Carter in the 1980 presidential election, the Treasury secretary, Donald Regan, publicly criticized the Fed's actions in a *New York Times* article. There were even calls for Volcker's resignation (Medley, 1979).

By summer 1982, the recession began to reverse course, and inflation began to fall (reaching 6.1 percent in early 1982 and down to 3.7 percent in 1983). Unemployment, after peaking at 10.8 percent in 1982, also began a steady decline in 1983. The animus toward Volcker subsided with the improving economy.

In 1983, Volcker was reappointed to a second term as chair of the board of governors of the Federal Reserve System, and to a third term after that, which terminated in 1987. Ultimately, his work was widely praised in taming inflation and interest rates and moving the United States out of the 1980–1982 recession.

After leaving the Federal Reserve he taught economics at Princeton and several other universities and worked as an investment banker. In 1988, Volcker once again transitioned into the private sector as chair and part owner of the James D. Wolfensohn international financial services firm. From 1996 to 1999 Volcker was head of a committee investigating dormant Swiss bank accounts in search of assets of the victims of Nazi persecution.

In 2000, he was appointed as the chair of the trustees for the international Accounting Standards Board. Subsequently, in 2002, Arthur Andersen tapped Volcker to chair an independent oversight board focused on the company's auditing practices. This appointment was in direct response to allegations that Arthur Andersen played a part in the collapse of Enron, the energy conglomerate.

In 2003, Volcker headed another private Commission on the Public Service, which recommended a broad overhaul of the U.S. federal government organization and personnel practices, according to the Whitehouse.gov Web site. Volcker also served in an investigative role as leader of a team looking into alleged corruption in the UN Oil for Food Program. This program gave Iraq permission to sell oil worldwide to finance infrastructure expenses such as food and medicine. (The program was discontinued in 2003 at the start of the Iraq war.)

Continuing his public service, Volcker was appointed chair of the board of trustees of the Group of Thirty (G-30), a private nonprofit group of academics and financial professionals attempting to improve international, financial, economic, and policy issues. More recently, in 2008, U.S. president-elect Barack Obama asked Volcker to chair the Economic Recovery Advisory Board. This was a White House panel charged with responding to the global financial crisis that began in that period. Consistent with his historical work, the board was designed to counsel the president about methods to stabilize financial markets and create jobs.

In 2009, when Volcker officially accepted the position as chair of the Economic Recovery Advisory Board, he spearheaded a drive for stricter financial regulations in order to avoid future financial crises. These changes, which became known as the Volcker Rule, limited banks from trading on their own accounts and constrained the banks' private equity and hedge fund investments. This rule was important in that it prevented banks from making speculative or risky investments (with customers' money), a practice that had contributed to the 2008 financial crisis. Although not immediately accepted, the Volcker Rule ultimately passed in 2010.

In January 2011, Volcker left the position as head of the Economic Recovery Advisory Board. The Volcker Rule was incorporated into the expansive regulatory legislation of the Dodd-Frank Wall Street Reform and Consumer Protection Act, which went into effect on April 1, 2014.

Volcker's public-sector work includes contributions to the Japan Society, the Institute of International Economics, and the American Assembly, along with many other organizations. Paul Volcker has made significant contributions to the U.S. and global financial communities.

Barbara Friedberg

See also: Federal Reserve Bank; Greenspan, Alan, 13th Chair of the U.S. Federal Reserve Board; Inflation; Interest Rates; Year 1970s to 1980s: Economic Problems and the United States; Year 2001: Enron, the Failure of Corporate Finance and Governance; Year 2010: Dodd-Frank Wall Street Reform and Consumer Protection Act

Further Reading

Federal Reserve Bank of New York. "Paul Volcker." Accessed April 18, 2014. http://www.newyorkfed.org/aboutthefed/PVolckerbio.html

Federal Reserve History Web site. "Paul A. Volcker." Accessed April 18, 2014. http://www.federalreservehistory.org/People/DetailView/82

Medley, Bill. 1979. "Volcker's Announcement of Anti-Inflation Measures." October. Accessed April 17, 2014. http://www.federalreservehistory.org/events/DetailView/41

The White House Web site. "President's Economic Recovery Advisory Board: Chairman Paul A. Volcker." Accessed April 18, 2014 http://www.whitehouse.gov/administration/eop/perab/members/volcker

Warren, Elizabeth, Former Special Advisor for the Consumer Financial Protection Bureau

Elizabeth Warren (born 1949) is the first female U.S. senator from Massachusetts. She received her law degree from Rutgers University and is a tenured professor at Harvard Law School. She is best known for helping create the Consumer Financial Protection Bureau, a consumer financial protection agency and is a champion for middle-class families in America.

Warren was born in Oklahoma City to a middle-class family and is the youngest of four children. When she was in junior high, her father suffered a heart attack, which caused financial hardships for her family and led her mother to work at Sears to help pay the bills. Warren's three older brothers and Warren all worked as well. Warren secured her first job at age 9 as a babysitter, and by the time she was 13, she was a waitress at a restaurant. All three of her brothers served in the military.

Warren was a state debate champion in high school and earned a scholarship to George Washington University, where she attended college for two years. At age 19, she married her first husband, moved to Texas, and earned her speech pathology and audiology degree at the University of Houston, where she graduated in 1970.

After graduating from college, Warren worked with children with disabilities for one year. She then moved to New Jersey where she gave birth to her first child, Amelia, and became a stay-at-home mom. Warren admitted feeling restless and wanted to pursue a career. Her old debate school friends encouraged her to attend law school, so she took all of the necessary tests and applied. When her daughter turned two, she began law school at Rutgers University. In 1976, Warren graduated with her JD and three weeks later had her second child, Alexander. In order to both care for her children and utilize her new degree, she hung a sign outside her house and practiced law from home.

Shortly thereafter, a faculty member at Rutgers called her and asked her if she wanted to teach a law school course. She accepted, and when her husband's job required a move to Houston, Warren secured a position teaching at the University of Houston. After divorcing her first husband and remarrying, she taught at several top universities and eventually became the Leo Gottlieb Professor of Law at Harvard Law School.

One of her first research projects as an academic was to do an empirical study on families who filed for bankruptcy, and Warren was surprised at the results. Instead of finding families who were abusing the system, she discovered a hard-working middle class who had no other options. So, when Congress had a commission on bankruptcy in 1995, Warren was asked to share her thoughts and her research. Initially reluctant, she eventually agreed and found herself in the political realm. She unsuccessfully tried to oppose legislation that made it more difficult for consumers to file for bankruptcy, and in 2005, Congress passed the Bankruptcy Abuse Prevention and Consumer Protection Act. Warren was also on the FDIC Advisory Committee on Economic Inclusion from 2006 to 2010.

Another notable position that Warren held was being the chair of the Congressional Oversight Panel, a position that she took over in late 2008. Her responsibilities in that role were to keep banks accountable while they utilized the Troubled Asset Relief Program, also known as the $800 billion bank bailout. Her work in this area helped secure her role as a leader in Washington, and the following year she was named Bostonian of the Year for her efforts. Furthermore, on November 6, 2012, she was elected to the U.S. Senate.

Warren is best known for helping create the Consumer Financial Protection Bureau, which was founded with the sole purpose of protecting consumers from taking out bad loans. The Consumer Financial Protection Bureau acts as both watchdogs and educators, enforcing financial laws, educating consumers about the financial decisions they make for themselves and their families, and ensuring all potential financial risks are apparent to consumers as well.

A prolific author, Warren has authored nine books. Two of them, *The Two-Income Trap* and *All Your Worth*, were best sellers. Warren co-wrote both books with her daughter, Amelia Warren Tyagi. *The Two-Income Trap* highlights the financial hardships faced by the middle class including declaring bankruptcy and credit card debt. It also argues that having children is one of the best predictors for bankruptcy and that many families are not going bankrupt due to purchasing luxury goods. Instead, their financial hardships are due to their mortgages, as more and more people in the middle class seek better neighborhoods and better education for their children. *All Your Worth* is a comprehensive guide to managing finances and creating a budget. Their innovative approach is based on years of research and helps middle-class families take control of their finances and learn how to save, even when money is tight.

In addition to her promising political career, Elizabeth Warren has received numerous awards including the Sacks-Freund Award for being an excellent teacher at Harvard Law School. She was also named one of the Most Influential Lawyers of the Decade by the *National Law Journal* and received the Lelia J. Robinson Award from the Massachusetts Women's Bar Association. As previously mentioned, she was also named Bostonian of the Year in 2009.

Ultimately, Elizabeth Warren continues to be a champion for the middle class. She is known for being highly passionate about her quest to bring financial literacy and financial regulation to America. She is perhaps most successful because she is unafraid of her critics. She mentioned in an interview that because she has a lifetime tenure as a Harvard law professor, she has no reason to be afraid of political backlash and is determined to focus her energies on making a difference and helping the middle class as a true public servant.

Warren introduced her first U. S. Senate bill in May 2013, the Bank on Student Loans Fairness Act. This important bill was proposed to prevent the doubling of the interest rate for federal subsidized student loans for the 2013–2014 academic year. The bill would make more money available for student loans through the Federal Reserve System in an attempt to keep interest rates affordable for students. At present (March 2014), the bill is in committee.

Elizabeth Warren currently lives in Cambridge, Massachusetts, with her husband of 32 years, Bruce Mann. She has three grandchildren.

Catherine Alford

See also: Bankruptcy; Consumer Credit/Debt; Debt; Delinquency; Loans; Risk; Year 2007–2008: Subprime Housing Crisis and Mortgage Meltdown

Further Reading

Consumer Financial Protection Bureau Web site. Accessed August 12, 2013. http://www.consumerfinance.gov/the-bureau/

"Elizabeth Warren Interview: Conversations with History." Institute of International Studies, UC Berkeley Web site. Accessed August 12, 2013. http://globetrotter.berkeley.edu/people7/Warren/warren-con1.html

Elizabeth Warren US Senator for Massachusetts Web site. Accessed August 12, 2013. http://www.warren.senate.gov/?p=about_senator

Yellen, Janet, 15th Chair of the U.S. Federal Reserve Board

Janet Yellen was born in Brooklyn, New York, in 1946 to Julius and Anna Yellen. She grew up in the Bay Ridge area of Brooklyn and went to Fort Hamilton High School. She attended Brown University where she earned a bachelor's degree in economics and graduated summa cum laude. She then went on to Yale University where she earned her PhD in economics. She was a highly talented and motivated student. Yellen's classmates at Yale noticed early on that she had an aptitude for writing notes, and many benefited from her ability to explain intricate concepts in a simplified manner. This skill would help her immensely later in her career.

She married George A. Akerlof, a fellow economist and recent Nobel Prize winner. The couple has published numerous economic papers together and have a son named Robert.

Early in her career, Yellen taught at Harvard and worked as an economist with the Federal Reserve board of governors. She is now a professor emeritus at the University of California, Berkeley and was most recently vice chair of the board of governors of the Federal Reserve System (Fed), which is the governing body of the Federal Reserve.

Yellen worked with several presidents of the United States. In 1994 Yellen took a leave from Berkeley. From 1994 to 1997 she was appointed by President Bill Clinton to serve as a member of the board of governors of the Federal Reserve System. In 1997, she left the Fed and was appointed by President Bill Clinton to chair the Council of Economic Advisers (through 1999). Additionally, Yellen chaired the Economic Policy Committee of the Organization for Economic Cooperation and development from 1997 to 1999.

In 2004, Yellen received another prestigious appointment from President Bill Clinton. From 2004 to 2010, Yellen served as president and chief executive officer of the Federal Reserve Bank of San Francisco. In 2010, President Barack Obama appointed her to the position of vice chair of the board of governors of the Federal Reserve System.

Who Is Janet Yellen?

According to Kolhatkar and Philips in the *Bloomberg Businessweek* article, "Who Is Janet Yellen?" her friends at Fort Hamilton High in Brooklyn, New York, called Yellen an overachiever. In her school yearbook, Yellen's accomplishments included class scholar, member of the honor roll, member of the boosters club, the psychology club, and the history club, and editor-in-chief of the *Pilot*, the school newspaper.

At Yellen's 1963 high school graduation, she won the Phi Beta Kappa award, the Mayor's Committee Scholastic Award, the math award, the science award, and the overall English department prize. And Yellen was also the class valedictorian.

A former classmate, Charles Saydah, stated in the above *Businessweek* article, "She was obviously the smartest person in the class—it wasn't even close."

Current friends consider her a "brilliant thinker" who looks at the human elements of economics. She thinks about how policies impact individuals.

Yellen has received numerous awards in her career including the Wilbur Cross Medal from Yale and honorary doctorate degrees from top universities like Brown University. She also won the Adam Smith Award and has been named one of the most influential people in America.

Yellen is the author of a book entitled *The Fabulous Decade: Macroeconomic Lessons from the 1990s* and has published numerous scholarly articles. She writes frequently about macroeconomic issues, most specifically on the topic of unemployment and its causes and effects. Her recent focus is on international economics and the trade balance.

She can remain as governor of the Federal Reserve Board until 2024. These 14-year terms ensure that members span numerous presidencies. Members can only be removed from their positions by the president.

In 2013, she was nominated by President Obama to be the first woman chair of the Federal Reserve. At the end of 2013, she was confirmed by Congress to serve as the head of the Federal Reserve Banking system. In this role, she will be able to drastically influence modern money management and serve as an inspiration to women who have an interest in finance, public policy, and economics.

Yellen's economic policies are summarized in a *Christian Science Monitor* article by Schuyler Velasco (2013) and include using monetary policy to reduce the length and depth of inevitable recessions. She is concerned about the human side of economics and has studied unemployment and its implications and causes. A main priority of Yellen is to grow jobs and reduce long-term unemployment. She is less concerned about inflation rates than some of her predecessors. Thus far, she is showing a hesitancy to raise interest rates and is expected to keep interest rates low.

Yellen's regard for the less fortunate is shown in her interest in assisting low- and moderate-income households. She would like to develop home ownership opportunities for the underserved.

Presently, Yellen's story is still being written. Her work as the head of the Fed is yet to be determined. The future will uncover her ultimate contribution to the U.S. economy.

Catherine Alford

See also: Banking; Federal Reserve Bank; Inflation; Interest Rates; Obama, Barack, President of the United States

Further Reading

Board of Governors of the Federal Reserve Web site. "Janet L. Yellen." Accessed August 15, 2013. http://www.federalreserve.gov/aboutthefed/bios/board/yellen.htm

Federal Reserve Bank of San Francisco Web site. "Janet L. Yellen's Speeches." Accessed August 15, 2013. http://www.frbsf.org/our-district/press/presidents-speeches/yellen-speeches/

Kolhatkar, Sheelah, and Matthew Phillips. 2013. "Who Is Janet Yellen? A Look at the Front-Runner for the Next Fed Chairman." *Bloomberg Businessweek*. September 19.

http://www.businessweek.com/articles/2013-09-19/who-is-janet-yellen-a-look-at-the
-front-runner-for-the-next-fed-chairman

Velasco, Schuyler. 2013. "Janet Yellen: Where She Stands on Five Key Economic Policy Issues." *The Christian Science Monitor*. October 9. http://www.csmonitor.com /Business/2013/1009/Janet-Yellen-Where-she-stands-on-five-key-economic-policy -issues/Tapering

The White House—Council of Economic Advisors. "Dr. Janet L. Yellen, Chair Council of Economic Advisers." Accessed August 15, 2013. http://clinton4.nara.gov/WH/EOP /CEA/html/yellen.html

Glossary

Account—An account is a financial record of activities for an individual or organization at a business, bank, credit card company, or investment brokerage firm. An account is also used in accounting as the organizational system for recording debits, credits, and financial transactions in a business.

Accounts Payable—This term is used in accounting and business and describes the money owed by a company to its creditors and vendors for the products and services the company has purchased. For example, when a company purchases office supplies on credit, the amount due to the supply company is in the accounts payable category.

Adjustable-Rate Mortgage (ARM)—A type of mortgage or real estate loan that has an interest rate that changes. This changing interest rate is usually tied to an easily accessible and public interest rate. The rate usually starts out low and then adjusts at regular and predetermined time periods.

Adjusted Gross Income (AGI)—The AGI, also referred to as net income, is calculated after completing one's income tax return. It refers to the amount of earned income that is taxable. The Internal Revenue Service defines adjusted gross income as gross income minus adjustments to income. The adjustments might include the standard deduction, personal exemptions, IRA deduction, and many more.

Advance—A payment that is made ahead of schedule. An employee who is due a paycheck on Friday might ask for an advance on her paycheck on Wednesday. Sellers sometimes ask for a partial payment in advance as protection against nonpayment.

Amortization—A predetermined repayment schedule of a debt. Consumers are given an amortization schedule when repaying a mortgage or car loan. The schedule includes what part of the payment is apportioned to repaying the principal debt and which portion of the payment repays the interest part of the loan.

Annual Percentage Rate (APR)—When borrowing money, the interest rate, stated as a percentage, explains the cost of borrowing money. The APR takes into account the interest rate plus any additional fees and charges when taking out a loan. These additional charges may include broker fees, points, and other charges. Also expressed as a percentage, the APR is usually higher than the interest rate.

Annual Percentage Yield (APY)—A yield is comparable to a return on savings or an investment. The APY is a method of standardizing that yield in order to make an apples-to-apples comparison of various investment products. This APY is the investment return, which takes into account the frequency of compounding the return. The APY is calculated with this formula:

$$APY = (1 + \text{periodic rate})^{\# \text{Periods}} - 1$$

Annuity—An annuity is created by contract between the buyer of the annuity and the issuer (or seller). After the purchaser buys the annuity product with a lump sum or regular payments, the benefit pays a fixed sum of money to someone for life or for specified period of time. An annuity is an insurance/investment product designed to provide an income stream over time.

Appraise—In financial terms, to appraise means to assess the value. This term is frequently used in real estate to determine a home's value for the purchaser and the lender, in order to determine how much to lend to the home buyer. The term *appraisal* (a form of the word *appraise*) is also used when determining the value of fine art, heirlooms, and jewelry.

Assets—In general terms, an asset is a valuable quality, person, or thing, similar to a benefit. In accounting and business, an asset is anything owned with value that can be converted into cash such as a building, machinery, or financial investments such as stocks and bonds. On a balance sheet, an accounting document, an asset lists everything that a company owns.

Attorney—This profession describes an individual who has gone through law school and passed the bar exam. An attorney is hired to act on behalf of another in business and/or legal matters. This individual also gives counsel to others on legal matters. Sometimes *attorney* is used interchangeably with *lawyer*, although a lawyer is specifically one who has gone through law school and may or may not have passed the bar.

Audit—The process of examining an individual's or company's accounting records by an independent individual. An audit may be conducted by an accountant. An audit is done to verify that the accounts are correct and to search for errors or discrepancies in the recordkeeping.

Automated Bill Payment—An automatic system set up by the consumer through a bank or brokerage account to pay bills. The individual usually authorizes regular payments such as credit card and utility bills to be paid automatically with funds drawn on the consumer's bank account. These automatic payments may be halted at any time.

Automated Clearing House (ACH)—An electronic network that facilitates electronic funds transfer. The payment system is run by the National Automated Clearing House Association and deals with various types of financial payments such as payroll, direct deposit, tax refunds, consumer bills, tax payments, and others.

Automated Teller Machine (ATM)—An ATM dispenses cash from a machine after the user inputs a special card and personal identification number (PIN). The cash is withdrawn from the user's bank account. ATMs can also perform many of the services bank tellers provide such as printing out a record of the bank balance, or even accepting deposits. ATMs are owned either by the bank or by a private company. Fees may or may not be charged for use of an ATM.

Balance Sheet—One of the most widely used accounting statements, also called a statement of financial position, a balance sheet lists a current snapshot of the assets, liabilities, and capital (shareholders' equity or net worth) of a business or organization. The balance sheet is used to understand what a company owns and owes and is compared on a regular basis, usually quarterly, as one measure of the financial worth of a company.

Basis—Also called cost or tax basis, it is a security's (such as a stock or bond) price after commissions and expenses are subtracted. This number is used when an investor sells a security to determine the profit or loss.

Beneficiary—This is the recipient of the proceeds of a trust, will, life insurance policy, or other type of payment. The individual (or individuals) is named in advance by the creator or owner of the trust, will, etc. There may be one or more beneficiaries.

Bequeath—This term is frequently associated with a will and refers to the action of giving. For example, as stated in a last will and testament, the deceased bequeathed her home to her daughter.

Bill—A bill is the abbreviated name for a bill of exchange, a document that explains what one party owes another. In modern America, there are bills from the electric company, the credit card company, and the restaurant at the end of dinner. Another type of bill is issued by the U.S. government. This short-term government bond refers to a Treasury bill. (See Treasury Securities entry.)

Bill of Lading—This document is issued by a transportation company to the shipper of goods. It also serves as a receipt or proof the cargo being transported is received. The bill of lading must be presented when the goods are delivered. The bill of lading includes the names of the shipping company, the buyer, the seller, the name of the transport, dates of departure and arrival, along with an itemized list of goods transported and more.

Broker—A broker is someone who buys and sells on behalf of another. In real estate, a broker is licensed to manage a real estate office, as well as to assist buyers and sellers with real estate transactions. In the investment business a stockbroker is a licensed individual who buys and sells stocks and other investments on behalf of clients in exchange for a commission.

Brokerage Account—This is a type of account located at an investment company. The brokerage account is used by investors to buy and sell investments such as mutual funds, individual stocks, and bonds.

Budget Deficit—A financial state where spending is greater than income. The term *deficit* is frequently used when describing the U.S. government budget. The condition occurs when income from taxes is less than government spending. The opposite of the deficit is a budget surplus, a condition when revenues are greater than spending. A balanced budget means income is equal to expenses.

Cash Advance Fee—Credit cards are ordinarily used to buy goods and services with credit, to be paid back later. Another use of credit cards is to obtain cash, or a loan with a credit card. When the consumer uses a credit card to obtain cash, the credit card company charges a fee, called a cash advance fee. This fee is on top of the interest charges, which begin accruing on the date the cash is received. The cash advance fee might be a set amount or a percentage of the amount borrowed.

Cashier's Check—In contrast with a personal check, a cashier's check is written by a financial institution, such as a bank, on its own funds. The consumer pays a fee to the financial institution, as well as the full value of the check, in order to use a cashier's check. This check is more secure than a personal check and is frequently required by a car dealership when an individual is buying a car. A cashier's check is also customarily required as a down payment on a home. The use of a cashier's check is more reliable for the recipient than a personal check.

Check—A check is a written document that is used to pay a specific amount of money to another. The check represents an amount of money drawn on the check owner's bank account. Written checks are rapidly being replaced by electronic bill payment, which allows consumers and merchants to transfer funds electronically through the Internet.

Check Card or Debit Card—A card, similar to a credit card, issued to a bank account holder and used as payment for goods and services. This card is linked to an individual's bank account and when used for purchase, transfers the money from the purchaser's account to the merchant. Those without a bank account may use a check or debit card in place of cash after loading cash onto the card. Many vendors sell debit or check cards and will load the purchaser's cash onto the card for use at a later time.

Check Hold—A period of time in which a bank "holds on to" a depositor's funds before they can be used by the depositor. There is a legal amount of time during which a bank can hold the money deposited from a check. This policy is used to ensure that the bank can collect the funds from the check issuer.

Closed-End Credit—This is a type of loan in which the total amount of borrowed money is dispensed at one time (when the loan closes). Additionally, there is a prespecified date when all payments and interest must be repaid. A mortgage and vehicle loan are usually closed-end credit. In contrast, credit cards are considered open-end (or revolving) credit.

Closing or Settlement—This term is frequently used in business to represent the meeting when all documents of a transaction are signed and the obligation of the agreement is put into effect. A settlement or closing is frequently used when referring to a real estate transaction when the buyers and sellers get together with other related parties to sign all legal documents, after which the ownership of the property is transferred.

Collateral—When taking out a loan, the lender wants to be certain the loan is repaid, along with interest. To facilitate loan repayment, in many cases, a physical security (or collateral) is required to secure the loan, should the borrower fail to repay the loan. A mortgage is an example of a collateral loan. The real estate is the collateral, and should the borrower fail to pay back the loan, the real estate reverts to the lender.

Commission—A fee or charge levied by a broker or agent in exchange for facilitating some type of business transaction. Real estate agents receive a percentage of the sale price of a real estate transaction for handling all the details that accompany the sale. Investment brokers receive a commission for handling stock, bond, and other financial asset purchases and sales.

Conglomerate—A large company that consists of many separate businesses. In some cases, the businesses are not related other than by ownership. Corporations implement a growth strategy of purchasing other companies in order to diversify their holdings and improve growth prospects.

Cooperative (Co-Op) Housing—A method of home ownership similar to that of condominium ownership. The co-op housing property, usually a multifamily unit, is owned by an organization. The organization then sells "shares" to the buyers of the co-op. The "shares" correspond to a particular housing unit, which is similar to an apartment or condominium home. The share owners pay to maintain the property and pay for amenities and common areas. The share owners also participate in governing the community and normally have certain rules, regulations, or even a particular lifestyle philosophy for the members. Purchasers of a cooperative share should understand the articles of incorporation, bylaws, rules, and any other documentation.

Co-payment—Most frequently, a co-payment is a small payment made by an individual with health insurance as a partial amount of the total cost of medical services or a medial prescription. The co-payment amount is specified by the health insurance policy and offsets the total cost of treatment.

Credit Crunch—An economic environment during which it is difficult for consumers and business to obtain loans. During a credit crunch, banks and lenders are hesitant to lend funds. This scenario may occur at the end of a recession because lenders are afraid companies and individuals won't have funds to repay the loans.

Credit Insurance—This is a specific type of life insurance policy. This insurance pays off the debts of the policy owner in the event of the insured's death or disability and infrequently, unemployment.

Creditor—This accounting term refers to a business, bank, individual, or service provider who lends money to another. A personal creditor might lend money to a friend. A business creditor, such as a department store, might lend money to a customer so that she can purchase a mattress. A creditor is owed money from another.

Crowdfunding—A burgeoning strategy for individuals, companies, and other entities to raise money for specific projects or endeavors. The funds are raised through an intermediary or crowdfunding Web site where those seeking capital post their project and solicit funds from friends, contacts, and other interested parties for a predetermined package of benefits. For example, an independent movie producer might solicit money through a crowdfunding Web site to finance a new movie project.

Debit—In accounting double-entry bookkeeping, the debit refers to the left-hand side of an accounting record. A debit records an increase in assets (what is owned) or a decrease in liabilities (what is owed). In accounting, a debit must be accompanied by a corresponding credit in order to maintain a balanced account.

Debt Limit—This term, also called a debt ceiling, refers to the total amount of money the United States, a state, or a municipality is authorized by law to borrow. The borrowed funds are used to pay liabilities such as Social Security payments, military salaries, tax refunds, and any government financial obligations.

Debt Service—The amount of money needed to make debt payments for a particular period of time. The debt payments include both repayment of the principal amount borrowed along with interest. For an individual, the debt service might include repayment of credit card and student loan debt. For a company, debt service includes payment of bond interest and other loan repayments. The debt-service coverage ratio is a calculation that compares net operating income with debt payments. A higher ratio denotes greater financial solvency.

Debtor—A company or individual who owes money to another person, corporation, or entity. When a loan is granted, a debtor may also be considered a borrower. If a corporation issues bonds for sale, the debtor corporation is also considered an issuer.

Deed—A legal document that when signed and delivered, grants ownership rights. A deed is commonly used when transferring the ownership rights of a vehicle or real estate. There are several varieties of deeds including quitclaim, grant, and warranty. Each type implies certain information about the underlying property.

Default—In financial terms, a default is a failure to repay a debt or to complete a previously agreed upon obligation. Default also means a predetermined setting or option used by a computer program or other type of scenario where choices are involved. For example, a company may have a default option of enrolling every new employee in the corporate retirement program.

Depreciation—A decline in value. Depreciation is an accounting term that reduces the value of an asset, resulting from age or wear and tear, by a certain amount every year by deducting a certain dollar amount from the company's earnings. When referring to currency, depreciation of one currency versus another denotes reduction in value. A new vehicle depreciates, or becomes worth less, after a very short period of ownership.

Depression—An economic condition of severe and long-lasting drop in economic activity. A depression is measured by negative economic activity as measured by the gross domestic product. It is also considered a more severe form of recession lasting two years or more. A depression manifests with long-term unemployment, credit defaults, declines in income and production, with longer term negative economic events. Depressions occur less frequently than recessions.

Digital Wallet—See E-Wallet.

Discount Investment Brokerage—Frequently called a discount broker, this is a firm that offers lower commission charges for buying and selling financial securities (such as stocks and bonds) than a traditional full-service brokerage firm. The discount broker may provide less research, advice, and other services than a full-service investment brokerage company.

Dow Jones Averages—The oldest tool to measure the composite changes in price of the shares of U.S. blue chip (large, established, and well-regarded company) stocks. The Dow Jones Averages include four specific market capitalization (price multiplied by number of shares) weighted stock indexes: Dow Jones Industrial Average (DJIA), Dow Jones Transportation Average (DJTA), Dow Jones Utility Average (DJUA), and Dow Jones Composite Average (DJCA). The value of these four indexes is computed at the end of each trading day and is widely used as a representation of the overall U.S. stock market.

Early Withdrawal Penalty—A financial charge or loss of promised interest payment imposed on depositors who withdraw money from a particular financial account before a maturity date. A five-year certificate of deposit (CD) might charge a penalty of three months' interest if the funds are withdrawn from the CD before the five years are up. Most retirement accounts impose a 10 percent early withdrawal penalty when money is removed before the specified minimum date.

Earned Income—Money that is gained from employment. These funds include income from selling goods, providing services, earning commissions, tips, pension, and annuities from income previously earned. According to the Internal Revenue Service (IRS), earned income also includes union strike benefits and long-term disability benefits (received before retirement).

Economics—A social science that examines how consumers, companies, governments, and sovereign countries decide how to allocate limited resources. Economics is divided into two major categories: microeconomics, which examines the individual consumer's behavior, and macroeconomics, which focuses on the larger economy as a whole.

Economist—A job title that describes one who examines and interprets data and information regarding supply and demand, related to inflation, unemployment, and other economic factors. Economists may study the smallest local economies or national and global resources and production. Economists work in both the public and private sectors.

Effective Annual Return—Also called effective annual yield, it refers to the total return earned when all interest is compounded during the specified time period. For example, an account that pays 5 percent interest, compounded semiannually, has an effective annual yield of 5.062 percent $[1 + (.05/2)^2] - 1$.

Effective Tax Rate—The average tax rate for an individual or corporation. This rate takes into account all taxes paid. The effective annual tax rate is calculated by adding all taxes paid, less any offsets or credits, and dividing the sum by the total taxable income. The effective tax rate is typically lower than the marginal tax rate, which is the percentage of tax paid on the last dollar of taxable income. For example, if total taxes paid are $7,500 and total taxable income is $50,000, then the effective tax rate is 15 percent.

Endorse—To sign a legal document such as a check. When a check is deposited into the financial institution account, it must be endorsed by the payee. A second definition of endorse is to support an idea, plan, or individual. Political candidates appreciate an endorsement from an important citizen.

Equity—Refers to the value of ownership; usually denotes ownership of a financial asset or real estate after debt is deducted. For example, the owner of a $200,000 home with a $150,000 mortgage loan has $50,000 equity ($200,000 – $150,000).

Escrow—An arrangement, financial instrument, or account that safeguards money or documents for a third party. The escrow agent is a neutral third party and is engaged to hold a potential homeowner's deposit check, which accompanies an offer to purchase a property. A mortgage company also collects anticipated tax and insurance payments from a homeowner and safeguards the funds in an escrow account, to be dispersed to the insurance company and taxing authority when due.

E-Wallet—Also called a digital wallet, this is an encrypted electronic storage account that holds financial and credit card information. A digital wallet may also be loaded with cash (similar to a prepaid account) to be used for future payments. It is used to complete online transactions without reentering confidential account information as well as to pay for goods and services with affiliated merchants.

Face Value—When referring to bonds, the face value or par value is the full amount of the bond paid at maturity. This amount is ordinarily $1,000. This term also identifies the value printed on a banknote, postage stamp, ticket, or coin. The face value may or may not be the actual value of the item.

Fair Market Value (FMV)—The price agreed upon between a buyer and a seller. FMV is also assessed by a tax authority when calculating property tax amounts.

Federal Deposit Insurance Corporation (FDIC)—An independent U.S. government agency, created in 1933 after the bank failures of the 1920s, to insure consumers' bank deposits. Presently, each bank depositor's funds are insured up to $250,000.

Federal Funds Rate—The interest rate that member banks of the U.S. Federal Reserve System levy when they lend to one another. This is an important economic signal of the Federal Reserve Bank's monetary policy.

Fiduciary—This legal term refers to a person or other entity, such as a bank or credit union, who acts as an agent-in-trust (carries out financial or legal duties on behalf of another) for another. A fiduciary might manage a financial trust for a minor. The fiduciary has the responsibility to behave in a trustworthy manner.

Finance Charge—A broad term that has several meanings. It may mean the total cost of borrowing including interest charges and any fees associated with borrowing money. A finance charge may also be a flat fee or percentage of the amount borrowed.

Financial Account—The record of an individual's bank, brokerage, credit card, or retail store financial transactions. A financial account is also a record of a nation's total payments to foreign countries, including cash and gold and the corresponding receipts from abroad.

Financial Aid—Monetary or in-kind assistance to students in need. Financial aid is frequently given to post–high school or private school students. The term may also refer to contributions given to a variety of people and businesses in need of assistance paying expenses.

Financial Asset—Money, stocks, bonds, cash in accounts, accounts receivable, especially marketable securities. Financial assets are considered in contrast with real assets such as tangible items of worth such as real estate, antiques, land, machinery, commodities, stamp collections, and others. For example, Joe's investment brokerage account holds the following financial assets: stock mutual funds, cash, and individual bonds.

Financial Plan—A written program to help an individual or family to outline their financial goals that usually includes steps to reach their goals. Financial plans examine income, investments, expenses, and future lifestyle scenarios. A financial plan is frequently used for retirement planning. A financial professional may assist the consumer in creating the project.

First Mortgage—The primary real estate loan with a claim on the property. Should the borrower fail to make the debt payments, the institution with the first mortgage has priority over all others with claims on the property. The first mortgage is viewed in the scope of other loans on the property such as a construction loan or home equity line of credit, which are considered secondary (or additional) creditors.

Fiscal—Applies to government finances, expenditures, revenues, and debt. Usually referred to as fiscal policy and specifically applies to one method a government uses to adjust spending and tax policy in order to influence the country's economy. The other strategy the government uses to control the economy is called monetary policy, which controls a nation's money supply.

Fixed Cost—A business term that describes production costs that remain the same, regardless of the number of units of a good produced. The company must pay these costs whether manufacturing one or one million units. An example might be the salary of a human resources employee or the rent on a factory. (See also Variable Cost.)

Fixed-Rate Mortgage—A real estate loan with an interest rate that remains the same throughout the term of the loan. This is in contrast with a variable-rate mortgage, in which the interest rate changes during the life of the loan.

Foreclosure—A legal process where a bank or mortgage holder cancels a borrower's loan and takes possession of the collateral property. In effect, the borrower's right to the property is cancelled. This occurs after the mortgage holder defaults or fails to make the mortgage payments on a loan. The property is frequently auctioned off to the public and the proceeds of the auction are applied to the remaining mortgage debt.

Forfeiture—The loss of money, property, or other right because of the failure to uphold a legal responsibility. For example, if a tenant in a rental apartment fails to pay rent, the renter is subject to forfeiture of the unit and must move out.

Franchise—A license purchased by an individual that gives the purchaser the right to use the franchisor's (seller of the license) proprietary knowledge. Franchise is frequently used to represent a type of business, such as a Subway Restaurant, where a person pays a fee to use the expertise, guidance, and name of the company for his or her own Subway Restaurant.

Free Market—An economic concept that describes an economy based on supply and demand without governmental control. In reality, the term applies to an economy such as that of the United States, which ideally has minimal government interference in trade. Since taxes and governmental regulation are a reality, a pure free market may not exist.

Free Trade—An agreement between trading partners of countries or geographic regions that allows trade without taxes, tariffs, duties, quotas, or other constraints. Free trade helps the participating countries sell more, gain access to international goods, and improve their individual economies. (See the entry Year 1994: North American Free Trade Agreement between Mexico, Canada, and the United States.)

Garnish—The legal right of an entity to withhold salary or property because an individual failed to make debt or tax payments. A parent who fails to make child support payments may have a portion of his or her salary withheld or garnished.

Gross Income—An individual's total income before any withdrawals for taxes, insurance, or deductions. This is the stated amount of one's salary, not the actual amount of money an employee can spend. For example, an individual's gross income might be $1,000 per week. After $300 of taxes and other deductions are withdrawn, the individual receives $700 (net income).

Guarantee—A promise, usually in writing, that a product, service, or legal arrangement will be fulfilled. For example, a vendor might promise a product will function for one year, or be replaced free of charge. A bank may provide a guarantee that a borrower will pay certain debts (or the bank will cover the obligation).

Health Maintenance Organization (HMO)—An organization that contracts with employers and individuals to provide health care coverage to its members. The member fees are generally capped as the participants are restricted to obtain care only from providers within the HMO network. (See Health Insurance entry.)

Home Equity—The true ownership amount in one's home. Home equity is the difference between the mortgage loan value and the market value of the home. For example, if a home is worth $375,000 and the mortgage loan value is $200,000, then the home equity is $175,000.

Home Equity Line of Credit (HELOC)—A type of loan (line of credit signifies a type of loan). Under normal circumstances a homeowner borrows money to purchase a home or condominium with a mortgage loan, using the property as collateral. If the homeowner defaults or doesn't pay the mortgage payment for a period of time, the lender has a right to foreclose or take back the property. A HELOC is another type of loan homeowners use to borrow money using the underlying property as collateral. This loan has a maximum amount and allows the borrower to withdraw any sum up to and including the full amount of the loan. Borrowing from the homeowner's line of credit is called drawing on the loan. The interest rate on the loan is decided at the time of issue and is usually a variable rate determined by market interest rates. To repay, the borrower is required to make minimum payments monthly, although more than the minimum can be paid at the borrower's discretion. The length or term of the loan ranges from less than 5 to up to 20 years. At the term's end, all outstanding balances must be paid in full.

HUD—U.S. Department of Housing and Urban Development, a U.S. government agency founded in 1965 to increase opportunities for home ownership. HUD offers programs for affordable homeownership and rental options. HUD also works to reduce housing discrimination and lend a voice to the underserved.

Illiquid—Describes the condition of an asset that is difficult to sell or exchange for cash quickly and expeditiously. For example, real estate is considered illiquid as it ordinarily takes several months to complete a real estate sale. In contrast, stocks are liquid and may be sold within minutes on a stock market exchange.

Import—A product or service brought into another country. Ordinarily, imports are transported from one country to sell in another. Imports (and exports) facilitate global trade. Countries typically import goods that are unique to another country or can be manufactured abroad at a lower cost.

Impound—There are several meanings for this term. In a broad sense, impound means to take possession of an item or funds, frequently with the idea that if certain conditions are met, the item or funds will be returned. For example, an illegally parked car may be impounded and taken to a secure parking lot, to be returned after a fee is paid. Impound is also a type of account, similar to an escrow account, which holds funds allocated to mortgage-related expenses such as future insurance and property tax payments.

Income—Cash payments made in exchange for work performed, investment in financial assets, apartment rental, or other commercial activity. Income for a business refers to the difference between sales and expenses.

Income Tax—A legal tax imposed by governments on individuals and businesses on earned income. Income taxes are the primary source of government funds used to provide public goods and services for its citizens.

Indemnify—To compensate someone for harm or loss. For example, homeowner's insurance compensates and indemnifies the homeowner for financial losses.

Index Fund—Refers to a type of investment mutual fund that attempts to copy the investments held in a publicly available market index. These market indexes track a basket of individual financial assets. For example, the Standard & Poor's 500 market index tracks the stock price (multiplied by number of shares outstanding) of 500 of the most important U.S. companies. This particular index is widely considered a proxy for the complete U.S. stock market.

Insider Trading—The illegal buying and selling of stock investments by individuals or corporations who act on information that is not readily available to the public. Normally, this information is garnered by individuals with direct access to the corporation. For example, it is illegal for a corporate officer to buy and sell stock based on nonpublic information such as in advance of the release of a new product. When corporate officers buy and sell stock in their own company, they are legally required to report the information to the Securities and Exchange Commission (SEC), although not all purchases and sales of company stock are illegal.

Insolvent—Referring to either a company or individual unable to pay their financial obligations. Specifically, the liabilities are greater than the entity's assets. The Internal Revenue Service (IRS) has special provisions to deal with insolvent taxpayers. Legal methods may be taken to repay the debts owed.

Insurance—A contract, called an insurance policy, which gives an individual or policy owner financial compensation in the event of loss. Life insurance pays a sum of money to the beneficiary of the policy when the insured dies. Vehicle insurance compensates for losses due to a vehicle accident or theft.

Insurance Policy—A contract between the policy owner and the policy issuer. The contract details the perils the policy covers and the terms and conditions under which the beneficiary receives the payment.

Interest—A sum of money paid in exchange for the use of another's funds. Normally interest is expressed as a percentage of the amount borrowed. For example, a bank lends a business $10,000 for one year at an interest rate of 8 percent. The borrower owes $800 in interest payments to the bank. Interest may be repaid, along with a portion of the principal repayment, one time per month.

Internal Rate of Return (IRR)—This is a calculation used in capital budgeting to compare the profitability of various investments. It may also be called the rate of return or effective interest rate. Specifically, the IRR is the interest rate that incorporates all future cash flows of an investment. A higher IRR is better and means a greater return on the investment.

Intrinsic Worth—Sometimes called intrinsic value, intrinsic worth has a variety of meanings. In general, intrinsic worth is the essential underlying value. In economics intrinsic worth is determined between supply and demand, or the market price agreed upon between a buyer and seller. Another example is the value of a company, which includes all assets of the entity, both financial and intangible, such as patents, brands, and goodwill.

Investment Banking—A specific banking function that deals with highly complex banking activities. For example, investment bankers help companies obtain funds and issue stock shares in order to transition from a private entity to a public company. Many investment banks also have retail banking departments.

Joint Account—A bank or brokerage account used by more than one individual. These accounts are frequently used by spouses or family members. Anyone named on the account has access to the funds. Upon the death of one owner, the account ownership reverts solely to the remaining account holder.

Joint Tenancy—A legal type of property ownership or rental. Two or more individuals own or rent a property together (called joint tenants) with equal rights and responsibilities. When one party dies, that individual's interest in the property passes on to the other joint tenants without the real estate going through probate. For example, if Dean and his mother own a home in joint tenancy, when his mother dies, Dean becomes the sole owner and the property avoids the probate process.

Junior Claim—Junior or subordinate claim is a right that follows the primary claim. For example, when a home is sold, a second mortgage loan is a junior claim and is repaid after the first mortgage is settled.

Junk Bond—A low-rated bond. Standard & Poor's considers bonds rated BB or lower non–investment grade, or junk. Moody's rating service considers bonds rated Ba higher risk. These bonds are considered junk because of their higher default risk. Investors who seek higher returns and are willing to accept higher risk may invest in junk bonds or junk bond mutual funds.

Landlord—A landlord or landlady is the real estate owner who rents out the property. The landlord may own apartments or commercial real estate and, in exchange for receiving rent, is obligated to maintain the property in a livable condition and make necessary repairs and maintenance.

Late Charge—A fee imposed on an account for a delinquent payment or one made after its due date. The fee is set by the financial institution and disclosed in advance.

Lease—A lease is a legal contract. The lessor agrees to lend property to the lessee (renter) for a designated period of time at a specific price. The contract describes the details of the arrangement. Leases are commonly used when renting an apartment to an individual for a specific rent payment and particular period of time. Normally, the rental amount is constant during the length of the lease. Today, cars are frequently leased as well. For example, Jeremy likes driving a newer car, but doesn't have the money to buy a new car every two years. In this case, he decides to lease a car for a monthly amount and when the lease period (or term) is up, he can turn around and lease another new vehicle.

Leverage—The degree to which an individual or company uses borrowed money to fund their lifestyle or business. A company is said to be highly leveraged when a large percentage of their business operates with borrowed money. A certain amount of borrowing is beneficial, both to a company and an individual. Too much leverage can lead to bankruptcy or financial difficulty if the entity is unable to make debt payments.

Lien—A legal notice placed on real estate or a creditor, which states money is owed to the company or individual (who placed the lien). For example, if a contractor replaces a roof on a home and isn't paid in full, he may place a lien on the home. When the property is sold, the roofer or lien holder is paid the amount owed, before the property title can be transferred to the new owner.

Liquid—In finance or investing liquid refers to an asset that can be immediately converted into cash. For example, most public stocks are highly liquid, can be sold on a public stock exchange, and rapidly converted into cash. In contrast, real estate is considered illiquid because it takes a while to sell real estate and receive the cash from the sale.

Liquidity—The ease with which an asset can be converted into cash, without a price discount.

Loan—An agreement between two people in which someone (or a business) gives money to another with the expectation of repayment in the future. There are many types of loans with various terms. A mortgage or car loan requires repayment within a predetermined time period with interest repayment owed in addition to the original principal payment. A loan between family members may not require interest payments.

Long-Term Care Insurance (LTC)—An insurance policy that benefits policy owners who are chronically ill or disabled over a long-term period, frequently purchased as an additional income source above Medicare and other health insurance in the case of disability. LTC coverage includes nursing home care, home health care, and personal or adult day care for the elderly with health conditions. Long-term care, such as nursing home costs, is quite expensive, and long-term care insurance offsets those expenses.

Loss—In business and investing, loss refers to a decline in the value of an asset or investment. A corporate loss occurs when a company's expenses are greater than its income. For example, Jose buys 100 shares of stock for $10 per share or $1,000. The stock later declines in price to $9 per share, at which time he sells his shares for $900. He realizes a loss of $100 ($1,000 – $900).

Market Rate—The prevailing interest rate or price in a particular marketplace or economic system. For example, in central Ohio, the average market rate for a 30-year fixed-rate mortgage loan is 4 percent. In another case, the market rate for apples in the summer in Michigan is $1.50 per pound.

Merger—The joining of two or more business entities into one. After a merger, the individual organizations combine their businesses and become a new business. Businesses merge to increase market share, gain access to new technologies, to diversify their business, and for many other reasons.

Middleman—The intermediary between two business entities. For example, one company manufactures paper boxes, and another company uses the boxes to ship their product. The intermediary or middleman sells the boxes from the manufacturer to the end user.

Minimum Wage—A legal wage set by the federal and/or state government. This payment is the lowest hourly wage allowed by law to be paid to a worker. There is tremendous controversy surrounding this wage in the United States. One side believes that if the minimum wage is increased, the extra costs will force businesses to close. The other side claims that the minimum wage is not a livable wage for an individual or family.

Motor Vehicle Bodily Injury Coverage—Included with motor vehicle insurance, this pays for injuries caused to others after a motor vehicle accident. The insurance notation is "a/b," where "a" is the maximum dollar amount of coverage per person per accident and "b" is the maximum total coverage per accident.

Motor Vehicle Property Damage—This insurance coverage pays in the event that one's motor vehicle damages (a negligent act or act of omission) another's property. If the insured's vehicle crashes into a neighbor's fence, the motor vehicle property damage coverage will pay the repair costs (after the insured's deductible is satisfied or paid).

Net—In business, finance, and accounting, net means the amount remaining after deductions from or adjustment to a gross (usually larger) amount have been made.

Net Income—Sometimes called net pay, the amount that remains after the employer subtracts tax payments, retirement account contributions, and any other deductions. Net income is usually less than the individual's stated pay rate. For example, a worker might have a stated wage (gross income) of $18 per hour, and after taxes and other deductions are made, may have net income or pay of $14 per hour. (For a corporation, see Net Profit.)

Net Profit—The difference between a company's revenue and the total expenses. The net profit, also called net income or net earnings, is the dollar amount a company has earned (or lost) during a specific time period.

Net Worth—This concept applies both to individuals and businesses. Regarding businesses, net worth may also be called net equity or shareholders' equity. The phrase is the difference between assets, or what is owned, and liabilities, what is owed. For example, if Sophia has $50,000 in a retirement account, $20,000 in a savings account, and owns a home worth $175,000, then her assets total $245,000. If her only debt is a home mortgage loan valued at $110,000, then her net worth is $245,000 less $110,000 or $135,000.

Note—In general, a loan or debt security. When referring to Treasury securities (or bonds), a Treasury note has a term between 1 and 10 years and a fixed-interest rate. A promissory note is a written promise by one party to another detailing the terms of a loan. There are many types of notes including mortgage-backed notes, unsecured notes, municipal notes, bank notes, euro notes, demand notes, and structured notes.

Offset—In simplest terms, offset means to counterbalance. When a borrower fails to pay an agreed-upon sum, then the lender can take possession of other asset(s) to obtain the agreed-upon amount. More specifically, in banking or other types of lending, the lender has the right to offset a debt owed by seizing the delinquent debtor's account balance or other assets.

On Demand—This phrase applies to a variety of circumstances and means as soon as requested. For example, a bank checking account is sometimes called a demand account, as the funds are available immediately upon the request of the depositor.

Open-End Credit—A type of credit, also called a line of credit or revolving line of credit. An ongoing loan that is pre-approved by a financial institution. The loan has a maximum limit, and the borrower is entitled to borrow frequently, any amount up to the maximum limit. The repayment terms are set out in advance with a minimum repayment percent or amount predetermined. The borrower may repay any amount above the minimum at his or her discretion. Types of open-end credit include credit card debt and home equity lines of credit.

Overdraft—An overdraft occurs when a depositor attempts to withdraw more from an account than is available. For example, if June has an account balance of $150 and writes a check for $175, she triggers an overdraft. In some cases, a bank will pay a check that is overdrawn and subsequently charge a fee to the consumer. In other cases, the bank will return the check to the payee with a notice that there are "insufficient funds" in the account to cover the amount. Banks offer a service for a small fee to automatically pay overdrawn checks or payments.

Par Value—The true or nominal worth of a financial asset. For example, most bonds have a par value of $1,000, payable to the bond holder on maturity. The par value of a $20 bill is 20 dollars. The market price may or may not be equal to the par value.

Payables—In business, payables may also be called account payables and means money owed to others. The money could be owed to creditors, lenders, employees, the government (taxes), or others. In accounting, payables are shown on a financial statement balance sheet as a short-term liability (amount owed).

Per Diem—This Latin phrase is in common use today and means per day or daily. If you are paid per diem, it means you are paid at the end of each day.

Perpetuity—This term means lasting forever. It is commonly used when referring to the cash flow or income from a particular type of investment. In reality nothing lasts forever, but the mathematical calculations involved in valuing perpetuities assumes payments go on indefinitely.

Portfolio—In business and investing, a portfolio is a group of investments owned by an individual, corporation, or business entity. The investments might include stocks, bonds, real estate, and/or any combination of financial assets.

Preferred Provider Organization (PPO)—Similar to an HMO, a PPO is a health care group with physicians, hospitals, and/or other health care providers, which offer services at a reduced fee. In contrast with an HMO, a PPO requires care to be paid for as it is received rather than in advance, according to a standard rate. PPOs may be more flexible than HMOs and allow visits to non-network providers (for an additional fee). In-network visits are at low cost. The member schedules all care through a primary in-network physician. (See Health Insurance entry.)

Premium—In insurance, a premium is the dollar amount of the bill or payment due (insurance premium). When referring to investments, a premium refers to the additional amount charged above the asset's intrinsic value. For example, a bond might have an intrinsic or par value of $1,000 and sell for $1,1000, a premium of $100.

Prepayment—The repayment of a debt in advance. A prepayment may consist of the entire amount owed or a partial payment. Some mortgage loans charge a penalty (prepayment penalty) if a loan is repaid within a prespecified time period.

Pretax—Before taxes are deducted. In effect, any items paid for from pretax income reduce one's income tax payments. The U.S. tax law permits certain payments to be made pretax with the effect of lowering one's taxable income. These items may be health benefit payments, vision care premiums, dental care premiums, and more.

Prime Lending Rate—Also called prime interest rate. This is the interest rate charged by commercial banks when lending to the most creditworthy corporations. This interest rate is important as many other market interest rates follow the direction of the prime interest rate.

Principal—Refers to both an individual and a concept. The individual might be an owner or executive in a company or an investment broker/dealer who trades securities for his or her own account. The principal concept is the original amount of an investment, or the amount of a loan that is unpaid at a particular point in time. When Tran makes his mortgage payment, part of the payment goes to repay the interest on the loan and part of the payment reduces the total amount owed and is applied to the principal of the loan.

Pro Forma—This Latin term means "for the sake of form." Practically, the term is used in accounting to describe an "as if" situation. The pro forma data include assumed, forecasted, or informal information that is used to create a "what if" or "as if" scenario. For example, if a company had a large legal payment due in a quarter, which significantly reduced its earnings, it might create two sets of the financial income statement. One is the actual statement and includes the legal costs that show a decline in net income. The company may create a pro forma income statement without charges for the legal settlement to give investors an idea of the company's profits under normal circumstances.

Pro Rata—A Latin term that means proportional. A pro rata share is the percent share attributed to one entity. In a group of four, where each individual owns 25 percent of a business, the pro rata share of expenses and income is 25 percent.

Profit—The amount of money remaining from a sale or investment after expenses are deducted from revenue or income. Profit is the opposite of loss. If the Granola Company made $1 million in sales and had $900,000 in expenses, their profit would be $100,000.

Rate Lock—Also called a lock-in. An interest rate guaranteed by a lender for a particular period of time. For example, if Kris is buying a home and secures financing in advance, the lender might "lock in" for two months the interest rate of 4.5 percent for a home mortgage.

Rate of Return—One of the most important finance, investing, and business concepts. This is the percentage one earns on the total amount of an investment. It is used to evaluate various investments as well as to measure one's investment performance. For example, if one invests $1,000 in an investment and at the end of the year that investment is worth $1,100, one earned a 10 percent rate of return ($100/$1,000).

Ratio—A ratio explains one value in terms of another. For example, the ratio of employees to managers in the Vista Bleu Corporation is 50 to 1.

Real Asset—In contrast with a financial asset, a real asset is a physical or tangible resource. Examples of real assets are precious metals, commodities, real estate, agricultural land, and oil. Land and buildings are also considered real assets.

Real Estate Agent—A member of a profession who is licensed and charged with assisting buyers and sellers to purchase residential and/or commercial property. Real estate agents are paid by commission, or a percentage of the sale price of the real estate property. They work for a real estate brokerage company.

Real Estate Broker—In contrast with an agent, a broker is licensed to manage his or her own real estate business. A real estate agent must work with a licensed real estate broker.

Receipt—A written record of a business purchase or transaction. When one purchases goods or services, the seller provides a written record of the items purchased and the price to the buyer. Receipt may also refer to goods received. For example, Horace is in receipt of a truckload of inventory.

Recession—An economic state represented by a decline in a country's productivity. The technical definition is two consecutive quarters of negative economic growth as measured by the country's gross domestic product (GDP). In most cases a recession is called so after the fact. Recessions are a normal part of the business cycle and are represented by increased unemployment and declining corporate profits.

Redeem—In marketing, redeem means to exchange a token or reward for a promised compensation. For example, the Grande Bicycle Company offers to redeem a coupon in exchange for a 10 percent discount. In finance, redeem means to buy back a security such as a bond on or before the maturity date. It also means to undo a prior mistake. She redeemed her former poor employee evaluation by working extra hard.

Refund—Return of consumer's original payment. Refers to compensation repaid to the consumer upon return of defective or unneeded merchandise. A return by taxing authorities of overpayment of income taxes is also called a tax refund.

Repossess—When a lender or seller takes back property from a buyer or borrower. This is usually a legal process, permitted when the buyer or borrower fails to make agreed-upon payments. For example, Julian purchases a Ford with a loan. If Julian fails to make the agreed-upon payments, the lender has the right to take back or repossess the vehicle.

Revenue—The business term for income derived from sales of goods and/or services during a particular time period. For example, Duke's Home Appliance Store earned $1 million in revenue last year. Revenue is also called sales.

Revolving Account—Another word for a credit card account. It is called revolving because the account owner does not need to pay back the total amount borrowed at the end of the month. After a minimum payment, the remaining borrowed amount carries over to subsequent months. (See Open-End Credit.)

Rule of 72—When investing, it's important to know the expected rate of return. The rule of 72 is a simple way to figure out how long it will take for the investment to double, given a particular fixed rate of interest. To get a rough estimate of how many years it takes for an investment to double in value, divide 72 by the investment's annual rate of return. For example, with a 10 percent interest rate, an investment will double in approximately 7.2 years (72/10).

Secured—Also called secured debt. A type of loan that promises the lender access to collateral or physical property in the event that the seller fails to repay the loan. A mortgage loan is secured by the real estate. If the borrower defaults on the loan, the lender has the right to take possession of the property.

Securities—The name of investment products bought and sold in financial markets. For example, another name for stocks and bonds are securities. Other types of securities include debentures, notes, options, shares, and warrants.

Securities and Exchange Commission (SEC)—A government agency created to protect investors. With the increasing number of new investors and the variety of investment products, the SEC is an important agency that helps keep the investment markets stable. There are a variety of laws and regulations that govern the investment markets. The SEC is charged with making sure those laws are followed. This allows the U.S. financial markets to operate efficiently. The Securities Exchange Act of 1934 and the recent Sarbanes-Oxley Act are examples of two of the laws the SEC enforces.

Shareholder—Also called a stockholder. An individual or corporation who owns a percent of a corporation. The shareholder receives a certificate (paper or digital record) stating the ownership amount or number of shares.

Short Sale—A type of financial transaction that may apply to both financial securities and real estate. With respect to financial securities, a short sale is a strategy used by sophisticated investors to benefit financially when a stock price falls. The investor (with the help of an investment broker) borrows securities and sells them at the current price. If the price declines, as the investor anticipates, she buys the securities and returns them to the lender while keeping the profit, less fees and commissions. If the stock price goes up, the short seller loses money. For example, Sharon sells 100 shares short at $25 per share and $2,500 is transferred into her account. If the share price drops to $20, Sharon buys 100 shares at $20 each ($2,000) and profits from the difference between the sale at $2,500 and buy at $2,000, or $500 (less fees and expenses). In real estate, a short sale is selling a home for less than the value of the mortgage on the home. This type of transaction happens when prices are falling in a real estate market and the homeowner can't afford to make the mortgage payments. In that situation, the bank may allow the seller to sell the house for less than the mortgage amount. The bank realizes a loss in this circumstance. The benefit to the bank is removing the loan from its inventory when the borrower isn't making the mortgage payments.

Speculate—Speculate has several meanings. In general, it means to guess or assume without any firm evidence. In investing, it means to invest in risky financial assets with the hope of a gain and also the possibility of a loss. For example, investing in a new company without a proven track record is a speculative investment.

Spread—In investing, the spread is the difference between the amount paid by a buyer and seller of a financial security. For example, the ask (buyer) price of JKL stock might be $25.38 and the bid (sell) price might be $25.36. Thus, the spread is $0.02.

Stagflation—An economic scenario that occurs when there is slow economic growth and relatively high unemployment, along with a rise in prices, or inflation. This is a negative economic scenario and happens when an economy isn't growing but prices are rising.

Standard & Poor's Composite Index—Also called the S&P Composite 1500®. This is an unmanaged index or group of stocks designed to represent approximately 90 percent of the U.S. stock market. It combines three leading indexes, the S&P 500®, the S&P MidCap 400®, and the S&P SmallCap 600®. Each of these separate indexes represents companies with various market capitalizations or sizes. (See Index Mutual Funds entry.)

Start-up—The name for a new company in the beginning stage of operations. Frequently, these companies are financed by the company founders or specific venture capital firms that specialize in funding brand-new companies.

Stockbroker—An agent that charges a commission to buy and sell stocks for an investor. This individual may also offer investment-related advice. A stockbroker works for an investment company and is required to pass certain licensing examinations in order to obtain certification.

Stock Exchange—Also called stock market, a stock exchange was originally set up as a physical location or marketplace for traders to buy and sell securities on behalf of their clients. The prices of the securities (bonds, stock shares, and other financial instruments) are determined by supply and demand. The three largest stock exchanges are the New York Stock Exchange (NYSE), the London Stock Exchange (LSE), and the Tokyo Stock Exchange (TSE). Today there are also electronic stock exchanges such as the National Association of Securities Dealers (NASDAQ).

Student Loan—Loans offered to students to help pay for education and related expenses. There are a variety of loans sponsored by the government as well as other banks and lenders. Some of the loans offer students lower interest rates and special provisions regarding the loan repayment terms. Repayment is usually not required until after a grace period (normally six months) following graduation.

Sublease—A rental agreement that is instituted when an original renter cannot fulfill the terms of a lease and finds another to continue renting the property under the original terms of the lease. For example, Kevin leases an apartment for one year. After six months Kevin gets transferred to another state. Kevin subleases his apartment to Juan, who continues paying the rent and fulfilling the terms of the original lease. A sublease must be approved by the landlord. (See Lease.)

Subprime—This term applies to both a type of borrower as well as a type of loan. A subprime borrower has a short or damaged credit history. Lenders use a borrower's credit score to determine the likelihood that the borrower will repay a loan. Lower credit scores equate to riskier borrowers. Riskier borrowers are classified as subprime and pay higher interest rates due to their weaker credit rating. A subprime borrower may be awarded a subprime loan. (See Prime Lending Rate.)

Trust—A legal document in which one entity (the trustor) gives another party (the trustee) financial assets that benefit a third party (the beneficiary). The living trust is in effect during the trustor's lifetime. The testamentary trust is created through the will of a deceased individual. For example, Sean's (beneficiary) grandparents (trustor) set up a trust with money for his college expenses. Sean's mother serves as the trustee of the trust and manages the money in the trust.

U.S. Savings Bonds—The U.S. government issues bonds (debt securities) available for purchase with a fixed rate of interest. These bonds are considered the safest investment because they are issued by the U.S. government, a secure country. The bonds offer an interest payment and are not subject to state or local income taxes.

Usury—A term that refers to lending money at unreasonably high interest rates. There are laws that govern interest rates in order to prevent usury.

VA Loan—Abbreviation for Veterans Affairs Loan. A mortgage loan available to veterans of the U.S. armed forces to help the ex–military members purchase real estate. The VA loan is issued by a traditional lender with backing by the government. In the event of a default, the government will repay a portion of the loan. A VA loan does not require a down payment by the borrower.

Variable Cost—Used in business finance, a variable cost increases or decreases depending on production levels. For example, raw material costs are variable. The more product a company sells, the greater the cost of the raw material inputs. (See Fixed Cost.)

Variable Interest Rate—An interest rate on a loan that varies or goes up or down. The conditions under which the interest rate varies are outlined in advance, and the rate moves depending on changes in an index. For example, a variable rate mortgage pegged to the LIBOR (London Interbank Offered Rate) will go up, according to the terms of the mortgage, when the LIBOR interest rate increases. (See Fixed-Rate Mortgage.)

Venture Capital—Funds provided by private investors (also called venture capitalists) to help new companies grow. Also called risk capital. (See Start-up.)

Wall Street—Also called "The Street," it is an actual street in New York City located in the financial district. This region of New York City is home to the New York Stock Exchange (NYSE) and the American Stock Exchange (AMEX), as well as many major banks and financial institutions. The term is used to mean the financial and investing sector.

Warranty—A promise or legal guarantee supporting a product or service. The warranty has specific stipulations such as replacement of parts during the first year of operation.

Wire Transfer—An electronic transfer of funds through cable, wireless, or other networks. These networks connect banking and financial systems. A wire transfer is also called a cable transfer or bank wire.

Withholding Tax—Tax on earned income, withheld by an employer and paid throughout the year to the Internal Revenue Service (IRS), state, and local taxing authorities on behalf of the taxpayer. The tax may also be withheld from a pension, gambling winnings, bonuses, or commissions. These taxes, paid in advance, are allocated to the taxpayer's IRS account and used to offset annual income taxes owed by the taxpayer to the government.

Write-Off—An accounting procedure that removes an asset from the financial accounting records of a company when it is determined to be uncollectible. For example, Sam stopped paying his phone bill several months ago. After several attempts to collect the amount due, the phone company writes off the debt and assumes it will never be collected. The write-off is considered a financial loss to the creditor company and hurts the credit rating of the individual or corporation whose debt is written off.

Yield—Similar to a rate of return, a yield is the annual income earned from an investment, stated as a percentage. For example, a $1,000 bond that pays $50 interest per year has a yield of 5 percent [(50/1,000) x 100].

Bibliography

Baker, Dean. 2007. "The Economic Impact of the Iraq War and Higher Military Spending." http://www.cepr.net/documents/publications/military_spending_2007_05.pdf

Bernstein, Peter, and Paul A. Volker. 2008. *A Primer on Money, Banking and Gold,* 3rd ed. Hoboken, NJ: Wiley.

Beyer, Gerry W. 2012. *Examples & Explanations: Wills, Trusts, and Estates,* 5th ed. Aspen Publishers.

Bodie, Zvi, Alex Kane, and Alan Marcus. 2013. *Investments.* New York: McGraw-Hill Irwin.

Bogle, John C. 1994. *Bogle on Mutual Funds: New Perspectives for the Intelligent Investor.* Dell (reprint edition).

Bogle, John C., and Arthur Levitt. 2012. *The Clash of the Cultures: Investment vs. Speculation.* New Jersey: John Wiley & Sons.

Brue, S. L., C. R. McConnell, and S. M. Flynn. 2010. *Essentials of Economics,* 2nd ed. New York: McGraw-Hill Irwin.

Bureau of Labor Statistics. Consumer Price Index. http://www.bls.gov/cpi/y

Consumer Financial Protection Bureau Web site. Accessed February 28, 2014. http://www.consumerfinance.gov/

Cox, James, Robert W. Hillman, and Donald C. Langvoot, 2013. *Securities Regulations,* 7th ed. New York: Aspen Publishers.

Damodaran, Aswarth. "Risk Premiums: Looking Backwards and Forwards." Accessed August 16, 2013. http://people.stern.nyu.edu/adamodar/pdfiles/country/riskpremiums.pdf

Davis, Joseph, Roger Aliaga-Diaz, and Charles J. Thomas. October 2012. "Forecasting Stock Returns: What Signals Matter and What Do They Say Now?" *Vanguard Research.* https://personal.vanguard.com/pdf/s338.pdf

Downes, John, and Jordan E Goodman. 2003. *Dictionary of Finance and Investment Terms,* p. 626. New York: Barron's Educational Series.

Drake, Pamela Peterson, and Frank J. Fabozzi. 2010. *The Basics of Finance: An Introduction to Financial Markets, Business Finance, and Portfolio Management.* New York: John Wiley & Sons.

Droms, William G., and Jay O. Wright. 2009. *Finance and Accounting for Nonfinancial Managers: All the Basics You Need to Know,* 6th ed. New York: Basic Books.

The Economist. 2013. "The Bitcoin Bubble." November 30. http://www.economist .com/news/leaders/21590901-it-looks-overvalued-even-if-digital-currency-crashes-others-will-follow-bitcoin

"The Experts: What Lessons Can Investors Learn from Warren Buffet?" 2013. Amended April 7, 2013. *The Wall Street Journal* Web site. Accessed August 15, 2013. http:// online.wsj.com/article/SB10001424127887323646604578403021463980536.html

Fabozzi, Frank J. 2007. *Fixed Income Analysis (CFA Institute Investment Series),* pp. 1–92. John Wiley & Sons.

Federal Reserve Bank of New York. "Discount Window." Accessed May 27, 2014. http://www.newyorkfed.org/banking/discountwindow.html

Federal Reserve Bank of New York Web site. "Historical Echoes: Fedspeak as a Second Language." Accessed October 7, 2013. http://libertystreeteconomics.newyorkfed .org/2013/04/historical-echoes-fedspeak-as-a-second-language.html

Federal Reserve Bank of San Francisco. "What Is Deflation and How Is It Different from Disinflation?" Accessed March 25, 2014. http://www.frbsf.org/education /publications/doctor-econ/1999/september/deflation-disinflation-causes

Federal Trade Commission. "Choosing a Credit Counselor." Last modified November 2012. http://www.consumer.ftc.gov/articles/0153-choosing-credit-counselor

Feldstein, Martin. 1994. *American Economic Policy in the 1980s.* Chicago, IL: The University of Chicago Press.

Frasca, Ralph R. 2009. *Personal Finance: An Integrated Planning Approach,* 8th ed. New Jersey: Prentice Hall.

Garman, E. Thomas, and Raymond Forgue. 2009. *Personal Finance,* 10th ed. Cincinnati, OH: South-Western Educational Publishing.

Graham, Benjamin. 2005. *The Intelligent Investor: The Classic Text on Value Investing.* New York: Harper Business.

Greenspan, Alan. 2007. *The Age of Turbulence: Adventures in a New World.* New York, NY: Penguin Press.

Harvard Business School Press. 2007. *Understanding Finance: Expert Solutions to Everyday Challenges (Pocket Mentor).* Boston, MA: Harvard Business Review Press.

International Monetary Fund. 2013. Accessed May 16. http://www.imf.org

IRS.gov Web site. "Tax Information for Retirement Plans." Accessed March 13, 2014. http://www.irs.gov/Retirement-Plans/

Kapoor, Jack R., Less R. Dlabay, and Robert J. Hughes. 2009. *Personal Finance,* 9th ed. New York: McGraw-Hill Irwin.

Kemp-Robertson, Paul. July 2013. "Bitcoin. Sweat. Tide. Meet the Future of Branded Currency." TED Global YouTube video. http://www.ted.com/talks/paul_kemp _robertson_bitcoin_sweat_tide_meet_the_future_of_branded_currency.html

Langelett, G. (2002). "Human Capital: A Summary of the 20th Century Research." *Journal of Education Finance* 28(1), 1–23.

Levinson, Mark. "Guide to Financial Markets." *The Economist—Guide to the Financial Markets.pdf.* Accessed October 24, 2013, https://docs.google.com/file/d/0B_ Qxj5U7eaJTZTJkODYzN2ItZjE3Yy00Y2M0LTk2ZmUtZGU0NzA3NGI4Y2Y5/ edit?usp=drive_web&urp=https://www.google.com/&pli=1&hl=en#

Lusardi, Annamaria. 2010. "Americans' Financial Capability." Financial Crisis Inquiry Commission. Accessed January 22, 2014. http://www.astrid-online.it/Dossier-d1/United-Sta/FINANCIAL-1/Forum-to-E/Lusardi_Forum_02_10.pdf

Lusardi, Annamaria, and Olivia S. Mitchell, 2006. "Baby Boomer Retirement Security: The Roles of Planning, Financial Literacy, and Housing Wealth." National Bureau of Economic Research. October. http://www.nber.org/papers/w12585

Madura, Jeff. 2013. *Personal Finance*, 5th ed. New Jersey: Prentice Hall.

Malkiel, Burton G. 2011. *A Random Walk down Wall Street,* 10th ed. New York: W. W. Norton.

Markowitz, Harry M. 1952. "Portfolio Selection." *Journal of Finance* (Vol. 7, No.1): 77–91. http://www.math.ust.hk/~maykwok/courses/ma362/07F/markowitz_JF.pdf

Markowitz, Harry M. 1959. *Portfolio Selection: Efficient Diversification of Investments.* New York: John Wiley & Sons.

Medicare.gov Web site. "The Affordable Care Act & Medicare." Accessed March 4, 2014. http://www.medicare.gov/about-us/affordable-care-act/affordable-care-act.html

Murray, Gordon, and Daniel C. Goldie. 2011. *The Investment Answer: Learn to Manage Your Money and Protect Your Financial Future.* New York: Business Plus–Hatchette Book Group.

Nakamoto, Satoshi, 2009. "Bitcoin: A Peer-to-Peer Electronic Cash System." https://bitcoin.org/bitcoin.pdf

National Public Radio. 2013. "The Iraq War: 10 Years Later, Where Do We Stand?" http://www.npr.org/2013/03/16/174510069/the-iraq-war-10-years-later-where-do-we-stand

New York Times. 2000. "The Dot-Com Bubble Bursts." December 24, 2000. http://www.nytimes.com/2000/12/24/opinion/the-dot-com-bubble-bursts.html

New York Times. "Why Is Deflation Bad." Accessed March 25, 2014. http://krugman.blogs.nytimes.com/2010/08/02/why-is-deflation-bad/?_php=true&_type=blogs&_r=0

Nissen, W. G., and M. K. Buckingham. 2011. "New Investment Adviser Requirements of the Dodd-Frank Act: What CPAs Should Know." *Journal of Accountancy 211*(1): 34–41.

Nofsinger, John, Troy Adair, and Marcia Cornett. 2012. *Finance: Applications and Theory,* 2nd ed. (McGraw-Hill/Irwin Series in Finance, Insurance and Real Estate). New York: McGraw-Hill Irwin.

Opdyke, Jeff D. 2006. *The Wall Street Journal Complete Personal Finance Guidebook.* New York: Three Rivers Press.

Organisation for Economic Cooperation and Development. 2013. Accessed May 16. http://www.oecd.org

Patient Protection and Affordable Care Act. Accessed February 1, 2014. http://www.dpc.senate.gov/healthreformbill/healthbill04.pdf

PBS. *The Crash of 1929.* Accessed March 26, 2014. http://www.pbs.org/wgbh/americanexperience/films/crash/

Ross, Stephen A., Randolpf W. Westerfield, and Jeffrey Jaffee. 2007. *Modern Financial Management.* New York: McGraw-Hill Irwin.

Rubin, Robert, and Jacob Weisberg. 2004. *In an Uncertain World: Tough Choices from Wall Street to Washington.* New York: Random House.

Schroeder, Alice. 2009. *The Snowball: Warren Buffett and the Business of Life.* New York, NY: Bantam.

Seburn, Patrick W. 1991. "Evolution of Employer-Provided Defined Benefit Pensions." *Monthly Labor Review.* December. http://www.bls.gov/opub/mlr/1991/12/art3full.pdf

Sergie, Mohammed Aly. 2014. "NAFTA's Economic Impact." Council on Foreign Relations. Updated February 14. http://www.cfr.org/trade/naftas-economic-impact/p15790

Sharpe, William F. 1964. "Capital Asset Prices: A Theory of Market Equilibrium under Conditions of Risk." *Journal of Finance* (Vol. 19): 425–442.

Shiller, Robert J. 2012. *Finance and the Good Society.* New Jersey: Princeton University Press.

Shiller, Robert J. 2006. *Irrational Exuberance,* 2nd ed. New York: Crown Business.

Shiller, Robert. 2008. *Subprime Solution: How Today's Global Financial Crisis Happened and What to Do About It.* Princeton, NJ: Princeton University Press.

Shiller, Robert J. Web site. "Workshop in Behavioral Finance." Accessed August 13, 2013. http://www.econ.yale.edu/~shiller/behfin/

Smart, Scott, Lawrence Gitman, and Michael Jehnk. 2013. *Fundamentals of Investing,* 12th ed. New Jersey: Prentice Hall.

Smith, Adam. 1933. *The Wealth of Nations 1776.* New York: E. P. Dutton.

Soros, George, and Paul A. Volcker. 2003. *The Alchemy of Finance.* New Jersey: John Wiley & Sons.

Stanley, Thomas J. 2010. *The Millionaire Next Door.* New York: RosettaBooks.

Stern, Gary H., Ron J. Feldman, and Paul A. Volcker. 2009. *Too Big to Fail: The Hazards of Bank Bailouts.* Washington, DC: Brookings Institution Press.

Stiglitz, Joseph E., and Linda J. Bilmes. 2008. *The Three Trillion Dollar War: The True Cost of the Iraq Conflict.* New York: W. W. Norton.

Swanenberg, August. 2005. *Macroeconomics Demystified.* New York: McGraw-Hill.

Titman, Sheridan, Arthur J. Keown, and John D. Martin. 2011. *Financial Management: Principles and Applications,* 11th ed., pp. 88–90. Pearson.

Treasury Direct Web site. Accessed November 27, 2013. http://www.treasurydirect.gov/tdhome.htm

U.S. Department of Justice. "Identity Theft and Identity Fraud." Accessed November 5, 2013. http://www.justice.gov/criminal/fraud/websites/idtheft.html

U.S. Department of Justice. "List of Credit Counseling Agencies Approved Pursuant to 11 U.S.C. 111." Accessed July 7, 2013. http://www.justice.gov/ust/eo/bapcpa/ccde/cc_approved.htm

U.S. Securities and Exchange Commission. 2008. "Financial Planners." Last modified August 20, 2008. http://www.sec.gov/answers/finplan.htm

U.S. Securities and Exchange Commission. "Index Funds." Last modified May 14, 2007. http://www.sec.gov/answers/indexf.htm

U.S. Securities and Exchange Commission Web site. Accessed May 15, 2014. http://www.sec.gov/

USA.gov. "Credit Counseling Services." Last modified June 27, 2013. http://www.usa.gov/topics/money/credit/debt/out-of-control.shtml.

The White House Web site. "Wall Street Reform: The Dodd-Frank Act." Accessed October 9, 2013. http://www.whitehouse.gov/economy/middle-class/dodd-frank-wall-street-reform

The World Bank. 2013. Accessed May 16. http://www.worldbank.org

Yuann, James K., and Jason Inch. 2008. *Supertrends of Future China: Billion Dollar Business Opportunities for China's Olympic Decade.* New Jersey: World Scientific Publishing.

Zhang, Marina Yue. 2010. *China 2.0: The Transformation of an Emerging Superpower and the New Opportunities.* New Jersey: John Wiley & Sons.

About the Editor and Contributors

Editor

Barbara Friedberg, MBA, MS, holds a BS in economics, an MBA in finance, and an MS in counseling and personnel services. She has taught undergraduate and graduate university students in corporate finance and investments. Friedberg has several decades of experience as a professional portfolio manager for a diversified real estate holding company. Her other published works include *How to Get Rich; Without Winning the Lottery* and *Invest and Beat the Pros—Create and Manage a Successful Investment Portfolio*. She is also the editor of the internationally recognized Web site, Barbara Friedberg Personal Finance.com.

Contributors

Yousra Acherqui, MS, is an equity research analyst working at Delphin Investments LLC in Stamford, Connecticut. Prior to her role at Delphin, she held various positions in the investment management and financial services industries. She holds an MS in finance from Northeastern University as well as a bachelor's degree in business administration from CEFAM, International School of Business and Management.

Catherine Alford is a former demonstrator and course director at St. George's University in Grenada, West Indies. She received her master's degree from Virginia Tech and her bachelor's degree from the College of William and Mary. She is currently a professional finance writer who maintains a portfolio at www.BudgetBlonde.com.

Kay Bell has been a journalist her entire professional life. She started her writing career as a West Texas daily newspaper reporter, detoured into constituent communications for a member of Congress and the U.S. House Ways and Means Committee, then segued into corporate communications and government relations for two Fortune 500 companies in Washington, DC. She returned to her writing roots in 1999 as a tax specialist for the personal finance Web site Bankrate.com and has operated SKB Editorial Services since 2005. A former Internal Revenue Service Taxpayer Advocacy Panel member, she writes the award-winning *Don't Mess with Taxes* blog. She is the author of *The Truth About Paying Fewer Taxes* (FT Press, 2009) and contributor to three other financial books. The Texas Tech University alumna and her husband live in Austin, Texas.

Leo H. Chan is an associate professor of finance at Utah Valley University. He received his PhD in economics from the University of Kansas in 2001. He has published over 20 scholarly articles in referred academic journals in a wide variety of subjects, ranging from futures and options to financial market efficiency. An expert in value investing, he has been teaching investments, corporate finance, and international finance at the Woodbury School of Business at Utah Valley University since 2008.

Jonathan D. Citrin is founder of investment counselor CitrinGroup and an international speaker on markets and financial theory; in his current role, he oversees the firm's investment portfolios and serves as chief compliance officer. From 2007 through 2013, he was Adjunct Faculty of Finance at Wayne State University's School of Business, where his classes included security analysis, investment policies, advanced corporate finance, and international finance. Prior to forming CitrinGroup, he managed investment accounts at Morgan Stanley and Morgan Stanley Dean Witter. He received his BA from Tulane University and his MA from New York University, and he has worked as an educator in both New York and Texas.

Ramya Ghosh, PhD, is an assistant clinical professor in the School of Economics at LeBow College of Business, Drexel University. He received his master's in economics from the University of San Francisco and his PhD in economics from Claremont Graduate University. His area of expertise is in international finance, and his current research interests are in international capital flows, capital controls, exchange rates, and monetary policies. He has published research articles in the *Journal of Financial Economic Policy*, *Macroeconomics and Finance in Emerging Market Economies*, and the *International Journal of Economic Policy in Emerging Economies*. He was also a consultant for the World Bank and the evaluation office of the International Monetary Fund (IMF) in Washington, DC.

Scott Glenn has a BA in history and government, a Pennsylvania Social Studies Certificate (Private School), an MBA in business administration and marketing, and is a doctor of education. Besides being employed as an instructor of business and economics at Pennsylvania State University, he also serves on the board of Empowering Women's Engagement Foundation, Inc., in Orlando, Florida; is the CEO of marketing for the Thai Princess Enterprise (San Antonio, Texas); and provides The Ruddy Group with invaluable insight into the dynamics of cultural and intellectual diversity in marketing. Before teaching at Penn State University, he was a professor in principles of marketing, principles of e-commerce, and fundamentals of selling at Camden County College in Blackwood, New Jersey.

Danny Kofke is currently a retirement consultant in Georgia (he was an elementary schoolteacher for 14 years before recently getting out of the classroom). He is also the author of three other personal finance books: *A Bright Financial Future: Teaching Kids About Money Pre-K through College for Life-Long Success* (September 2014), *A Simple Book of Financial Wisdom: Teach Yourself (and Your Kids) How to Live Wealthy* *with Little Money* (September 2011), and *How to Survive (and Perhaps Thrive) on a Teacher's Salary* (October 2007). He has appeared on numerous television shows.

Joseph Krupka, PhD, CPA/PFS, CGMA, is the founder of Krupka Financial Group. For over 25 years, he has been highly successful in providing clients with exceptional tax, retirement, and estate planning services coupled with sound financial advice. He speaks to numerous associations on topics including tax law changes, retirement, and estate planning. Currently, he is an assistant professor of accounting at Texas A&M University–Commerce.

John C. Linfield is the executive director of the Institute for Financial Literacy, a nonprofit organization promoting effective financial education and counseling. The institute's financial certification and accreditation activities have been recognized by state and federal regulatory authorities and were highlighted in a June 2011 GAO Report on financial literacy. A graduate of Norwich University and New England Law, he has been a nonprofit executive, university fundraising professional, adjunct professor, and practicing attorney.

Leslie E. Linfield, Esq., is the executive director emeritus and founder of the Institute for Financial Literacy™. An authority on adult financial literacy education and consumer finance issues, she has been a banker, stockbroker, housing counselor, financial counselor, attorney, speaker, and author. Her work has been covered in *The New York Times, Newsweek, Time Magazine, The Wall Street Journal, Washington Post, Los Angeles Times, Boston Globe, Kiplinger's,* and *SmartMoney*.

Lien Luu, PhD, CFP, is currently teaching personal finance and financial services at the University of Northampton (United Kingdom). As a certified financial planner, she is also responsible for training students to become financial planners. She is passionate about teaching young people basic money skills so that they can live fulfilling lives free from money worries and is working on a book on personal finance.

Angelique N. S. McInnes received her qualifications from Nelson Mandela Metropolitan University (South Africa), Canterbury University (New Zealand), and Lincoln University (New Zealand), and is currently working on a PhD at Flinders University (Australia). She is a senior lecturer and tutor of finance and financial planning at Central Queensland University as well as author of an academic publication, *Working Capital Management: Theory and Evidence.*

Maria Nedeva is a professor of science and innovation dynamics and policy at the University of Manchester, Manchester, United Kingdom. She publishes on important issues of science policy in high-reputation scientific journals, including *Science*, and teaches sociology and philosophy of science, innovation, and creativity. When she is not busy with her students, she studies finance and writes for her blog, *The Money Principle.*

Surya Mrunalini Pisapati, MBA, MS, CFA, is focused on alternative investments, performing manager due diligence, and sourcing investment ideas across mutual fund and hedge fund strategies. Her experience includes working at a publicly traded REIT at Macquire Group in Australia as well as on research and writing assignments. She has an undergraduate degree in mechanical engineering from Jawaharlal Nehru Technological University (India), an MBA (finance) from the Indian Institute of Management (India), and a master's in finance degree from Villanova University.

Yasmine H. Abdel Razek, PhD, MBA, holds a BA in business administration, an MBA with concentration in international business, and a PhD in business administration with concentration in financial management. She has taught undergraduate university students in managerial finance, international finance, corporate finance, and investment analysis. She has over 10 years of experience in international debt capital markets. Her research interests are focused on the fields of behavioral finance, market efficiency, and asset pricing.

Andrea Travillian, MBA, is a financial coach, author, and speaker. She has her MBA from Creighton University and her undergraduate degree in finance from the University of Iowa. She has worked in banking, corporate finance with budgets and forecasts, taxes, and retirement investing both in the United States and in Australia. She currently helps business owners manage their personal finances and business.

Jennifer L. Woolley is an associate professor of management at Santa Clara University. Her research, which focuses on the emergence of firms, industries, and technologies around the world, has been published in several leading management journals including *Organization Science, Strategic Entrepreneurship Journal*, and *Entrepreneurship Theory and Practice*. She teaches a range of classes on entrepreneurship and international business, and she works with entrepreneurs across industries to grow ideas to market.

Index

Please note the **boldface** locators indicated a complete discussion of the topic.

accountant, **1–4**; accounting certifications, 3; bookkeeper and, 4; Certified Management Accountant (CMA) designation, 3; Certified Public Accountant (CPA) designation, 3; definition of, 1; generally accepted accounting principles (GAAP), 3; professional certifications and types of accountants, 3–4; skills and job tasks of, 1–2; tax practitioners, 3

accounting scandals: Bernie Madoff, 2; Enron, 2; Lehman Brothers, 2; Waste Management, 2

Acherqui, Yousra, 377

adjustable-rate mortgage (ARM), 138, 290

Affordable Care Act (ACA), **4–8**; background of, 4; Congressional Budget Office (CBO) on, 7; controversies concerning, 7; deficiencies of, 7; evaluation of, 8; Health Care and Education Reconciliation Act, 7; overview of, 4; Patient Protection and Affordable Care Act, 7; sections of, 7; as a work in progress, 6. *See also* health insurance; U. S. health care history

AIG, 294

Akerlof, George A., 343

Akers, Douglas, et al., 54, 55

Alford, Catherine, 377

alimony, **8–11**; alternative name for, 8; definition of, 8; fun alimony settlement facts, 9; gender and, 9–10; history of, 9; palimony, 10; payment of, 8–9; permanent alimony, 10; as a punitive device, 10; purpose of, 8–9; reform of, 10; rehabilitative alimony, 10; relationships, evolving, 10; Uniform Marriage and Divorce Act (UMDA) and, 8

The American (Becker and Murphy), 123, 124

American Campus Communities Inc., 193

American Capital Agency Corp., 194

American Express, 60

American Institute of Certified Public Accountants, 3

American Recovery and Reinvestment Act (ARRA), 325

American society, inequality in, xxi, 258–259

Anderson, M. H., and Jackson, R., 197

annuity, **11–14**; complexity of, 13; considerations in, 13–14; definition of, 11; discount brokerages, 13; drawback of, 11; equity index annuities, 13; fees and commissions, 13; Ferro, Gustavo, on, 13, 14; Fidelity and, 13; fixed, veritable, and equity index annuities, 12–13; funding of, 11–12; Hube, Karen. on, 13, 14; immediate or deferred annuity, 12; importance of, 14; inflation and, 13–14; joint-life with last survivor annuity, 12; number of annuity products, 13; origin of, 11; purpose of, 11; risk aversion, 13; security of, 13; single life annuity, 12; Social Security and, 11; types of, 12; Vanguard and, 13; variable annuities, 13

Apple Pay, 70

Arthur Andersen, 278

"Asian Contagion". *See* Year 1997–1998: Asian financial crisis